This photo is of a scene (?) from the *Nura: Rise of the Yokai Clan* Millennium Demon Capital Banquet held on December 25, 2011. They've held this event two years in a row, so I'm all smiles! And it was on Christmas! One of the voice actors is too scared to watch the DVDs (*laugh*), but I've watched the one from two years ago several times. Of course, last year's will come out too! (Was that a plug?)

—HIROSHI SHIIBASHI,
2012

HIROSHI SHIIBASHI debuted in BUSINESS JUMP magazine with *Aratama*. NURA: RISE OF THE YOKAI CLAN is his breakout hit. He was an assistant to manga artist Hirohiko Araki, the creator of *Jojo's Bizarre Adventure*. *Steel Ball Run* by Araki is one of his favorite manga.

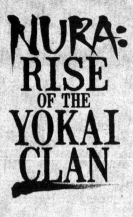

NURA: RISE OF THE YOKAI CLAN

NURA: RISE OF THE YOKAI CLAN
VOLUME 20
SHONEN JUMP Manga Edition

Story and Art by HIROSHI SHIIBASHI

Translation – John Werry
Touch-up Art and Lettering – Annaliese Christman
Graphics and Cover Design – Fawn Lau
Editors – Megan Bates, Joel Enos

Printed in Canada

Published by VIZ Media, LLC
P.O. Box 77010
San Francisco, CA 94107

10 9 8 7 6 5 4 3 2 1
First printing, April 2014

www.viz.com www.shonenjump.com

TABLE OF CONTENTS | NURA:RISE OF THE YOKAI CLAN

YANAGIDA

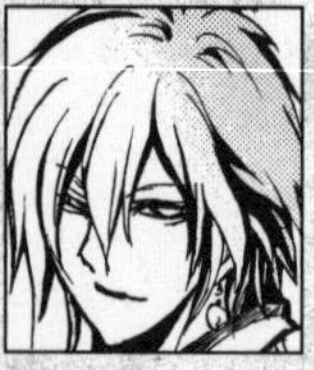

The ayakashi known as Sanmoto's "ears" and one of the Hundred Stories clan's seven leaders. He's held a grudge against the Nura clan since Rihan defeated Sanmoto.

GOROZAEMON SANMOTO

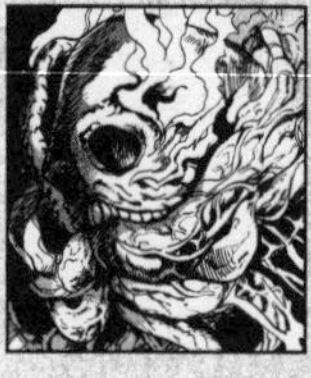

He has a history with Rikuo's father, Rihan, and holds a grudge against the Nura clan. He was originally human but transformed into an ayakashi and separated into seven different body parts. Leader of the Hundred Stories clan.

RAIDEN

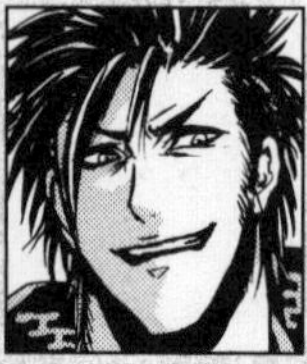

The ayakashi known as Sanmoto's "bones" and one of the Hundred Stories clan's seven leaders. He has a large and powerful body able to release monstrous strength.

ENCHO

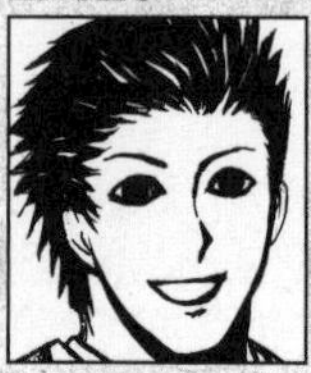

The ayakashi known as Sanmoto's "mouth" and one of the Hundred Stories clan's seven leaders. He has plotted a game of tag in Tokyo for the Nura clan.

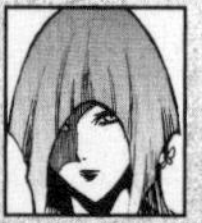

TAMASABURO

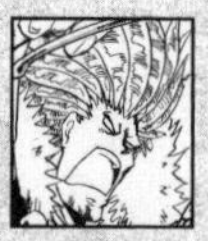

AOTABO

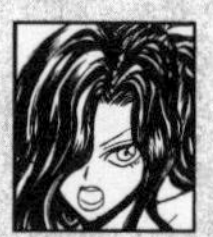

KEJORO

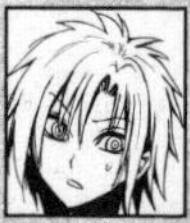

KUBINASHI

STORY SO FAR

Rikuo Nura is a seventh-grader at Ukiyoe Middle School. At a glance, he appears to be just another average, normal boy. But he's actually the grandson of the yokai Overlord Nurarihyon. He's also the Third Heir of the powerful Nura clan. He spends his days in hopes that he will someday become a great clan boss who leads a Hundred Demons.

Half a year after Yanagida's plot, when Rikuo and Tsurara begin investigating the Hundred Stories clan, average everyday citizens suddenly attack them because of a prophecy by Kudan that Rikuo is evil and is out to harm humanity!

Those citizens who believe the prophecy attack Rikuo, while Nokaze from the Hundred Stories clan emerges to try to force Nura into his yokai form by attacking Kana. Left with no choice, Rikuo changes into his ayakashi form right before their eyes and defeats Nokaze.

Rikuo finally meets the elusive Encho and Yanagida. They set the conditions for a game of tag in Tokyo. With the people of the city hostage, Rikuo must find and defeat all seven leaders of the Hundred Stories clan before dawn. Rikuo and others in the Nura clan devote their full strength to finding the Hundred Stories clan's leaders as they protect the Tokyoites!!

Rikuo encounters the leader known as Raiden for the first time, as danger approaches Kubinashi.

CHARACTERS

NURARIHYON

Rikuo's grandfather and the Lord of Pandemonium. To prepare for all-out war with Nue, he intends to pass leadership of the Nura clan—a powerful yokai consortium—to Rikuo. He's a mischievous sort.

RIKUO NURA

Though he appears to be a human boy, he's actually the grandson of Nurarihyon, a yokai. His grandfather's blood makes him one-quarter yokai, and he transforms into a yokai at times.

KIYOTSUGU

Rikuo's classmate. He has adored yokai ever since he was saved by Rikuo in his yokai form, leading him to form the Kiyojuji Paranormal Patrol.

KANA IENAGA

Rikuo's classmate and a childhood friend. Even though she hates scary things, she's a member of the Kiyojuji Paranormal Patrol for some reason.

KUROTABO

A Nura clan yokai, also known as the Father of Destruction. One of the clan's best warriors, he hides a healthy arsenal of lethal weapons under his priest's robe. He teaches Rikuo an Equip technique called Meld.

YUKI-ONNA

A yokai of the Nura clan who is in charge of looking after Rikuo. She disguises herself as a human and attends the same school as Rikuo to protect him from danger. When in human form, she goes by the name Tsurara Oikawa. Her mother is Setsura.

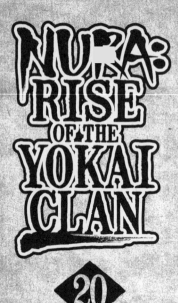

NURA: RISE OF THE YOKAI CLAN

20

KUSOZU

STORY AND ART BY
HIROSHI SHIIBASHI

Act 166: Tamasaburo

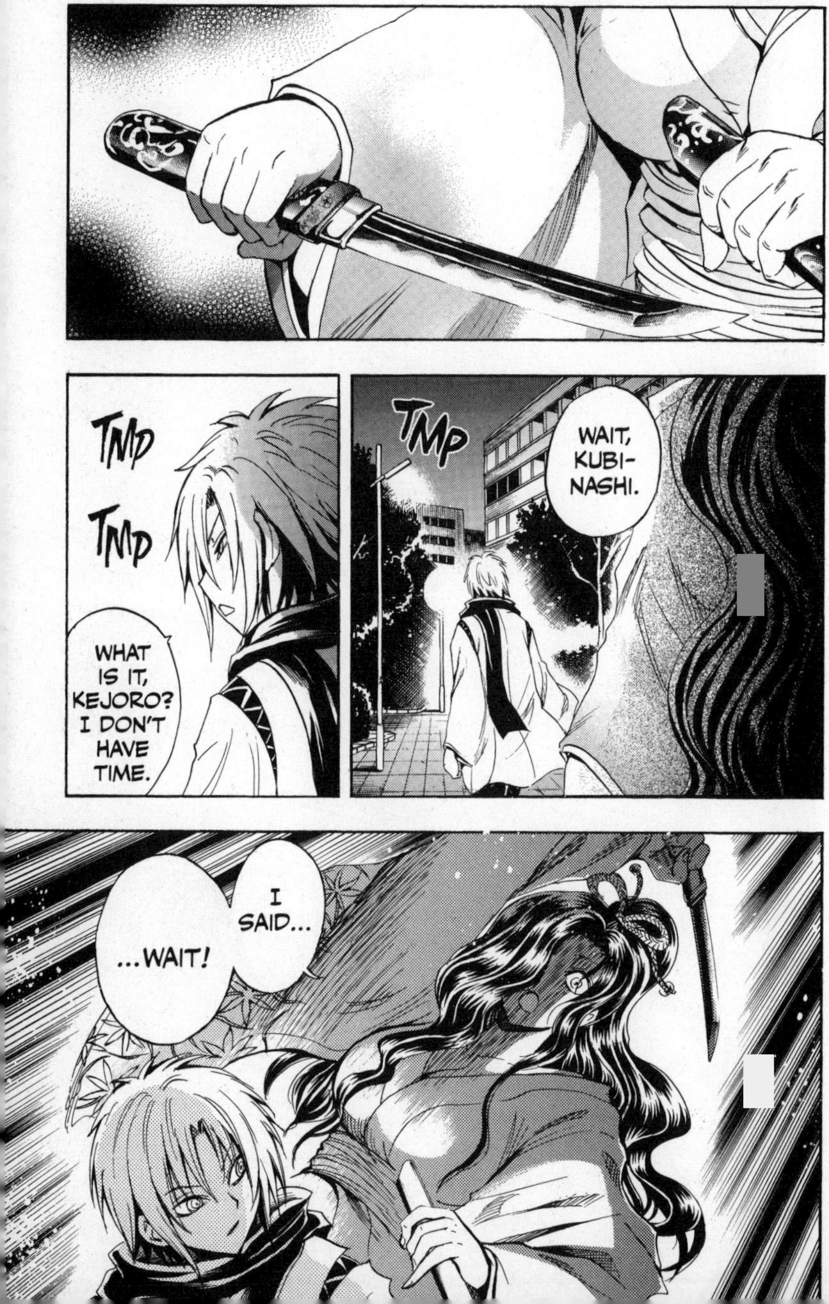
TMP
WAIT, KUBI-NASHI.
TMP
TMP
WHAT IS IT, KEJORO? I DON'T HAVE TIME.
I SAID...
...WAIT!

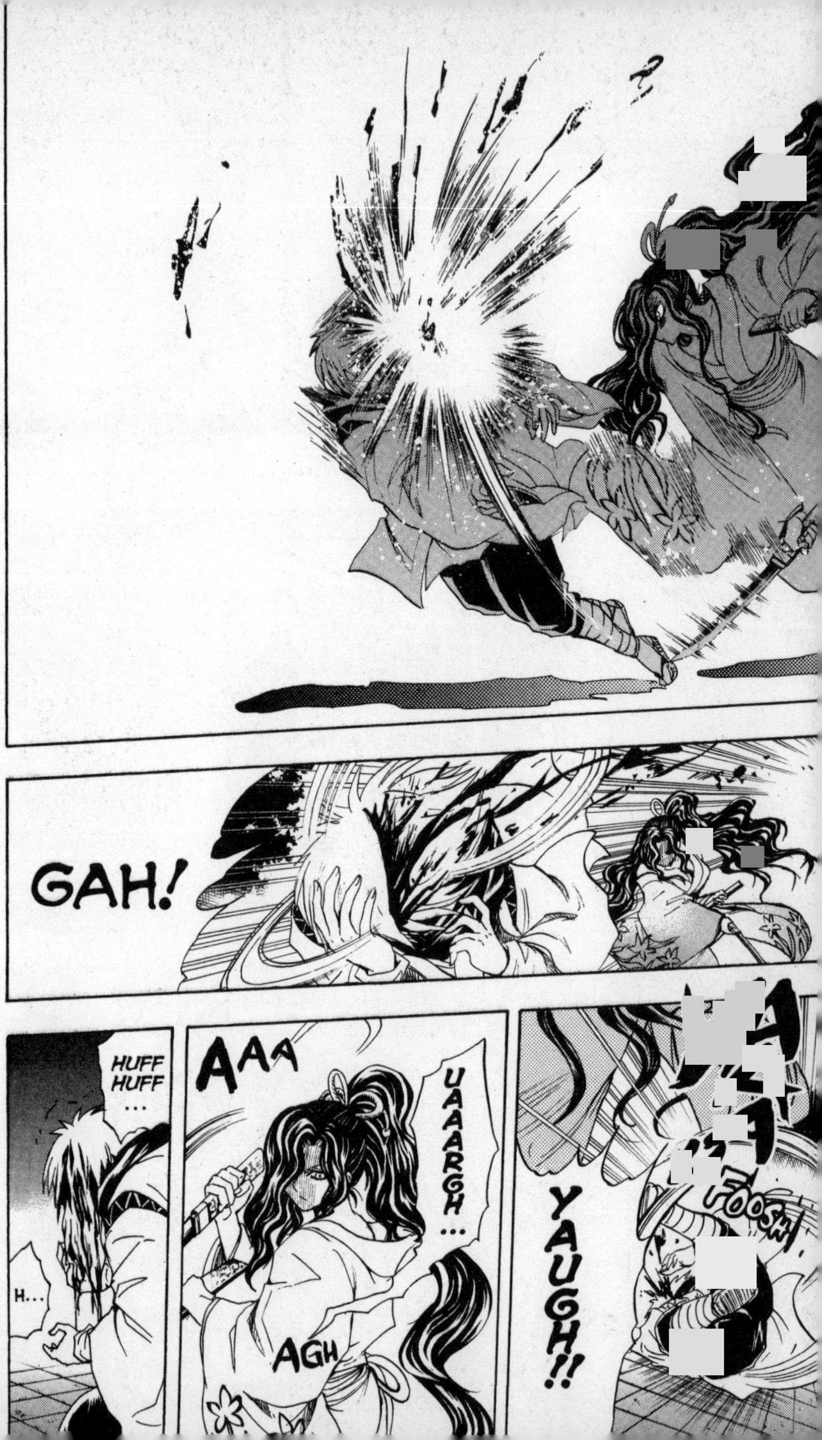
GAH!
FOOSH
YAUGH!!
AAA
UAAARGH...
AGH
HUFF HUFF ...
H...

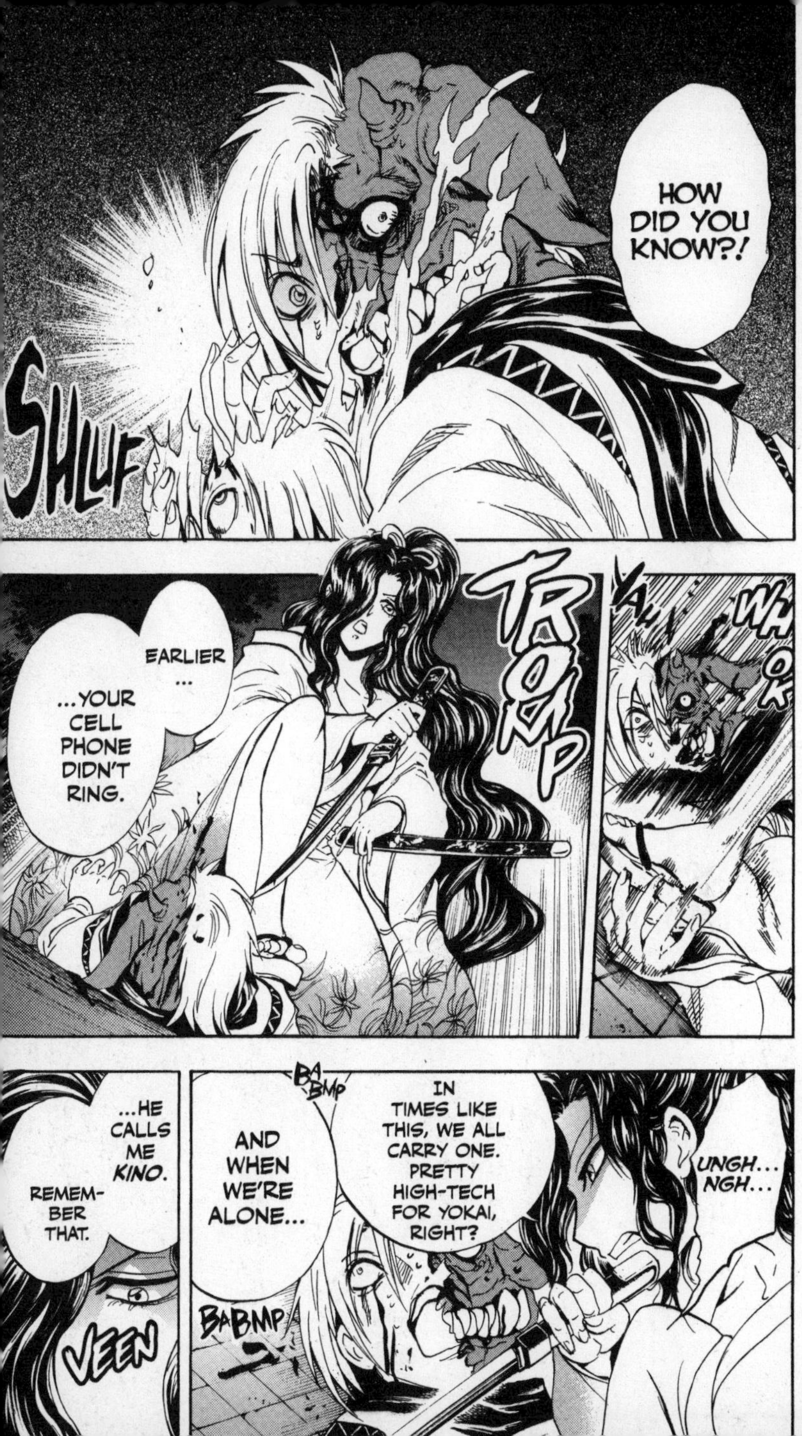
HOW DID YOU KNOW?!
SHLUF
WHOK
TROMP
EARLIER...
...YOUR CELL PHONE DIDN'T RING.
UNGH... NGH...
IN TIMES LIKE THIS, WE ALL CARRY ONE. PRETTY HIGH-TECH FOR YOKAI, RIGHT?
BA-BMP
AND WHEN WE'RE ALONE...
BABMP
...HE CALLS ME *KINO*.
REMEMBER THAT.
VEEN

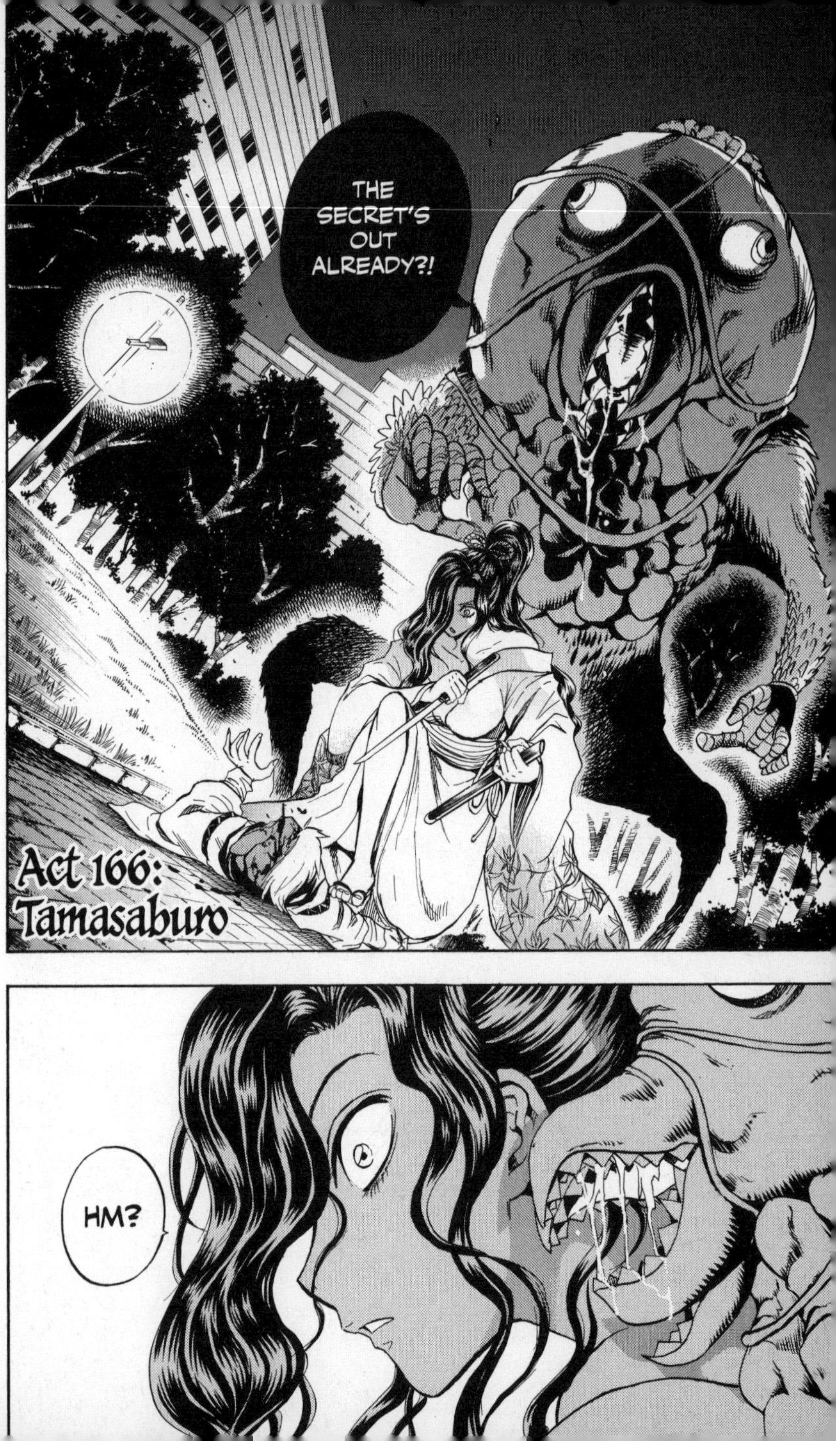
THE SECRET'S OUT ALREADY?!
Act 166: Tamasaburo
HM?

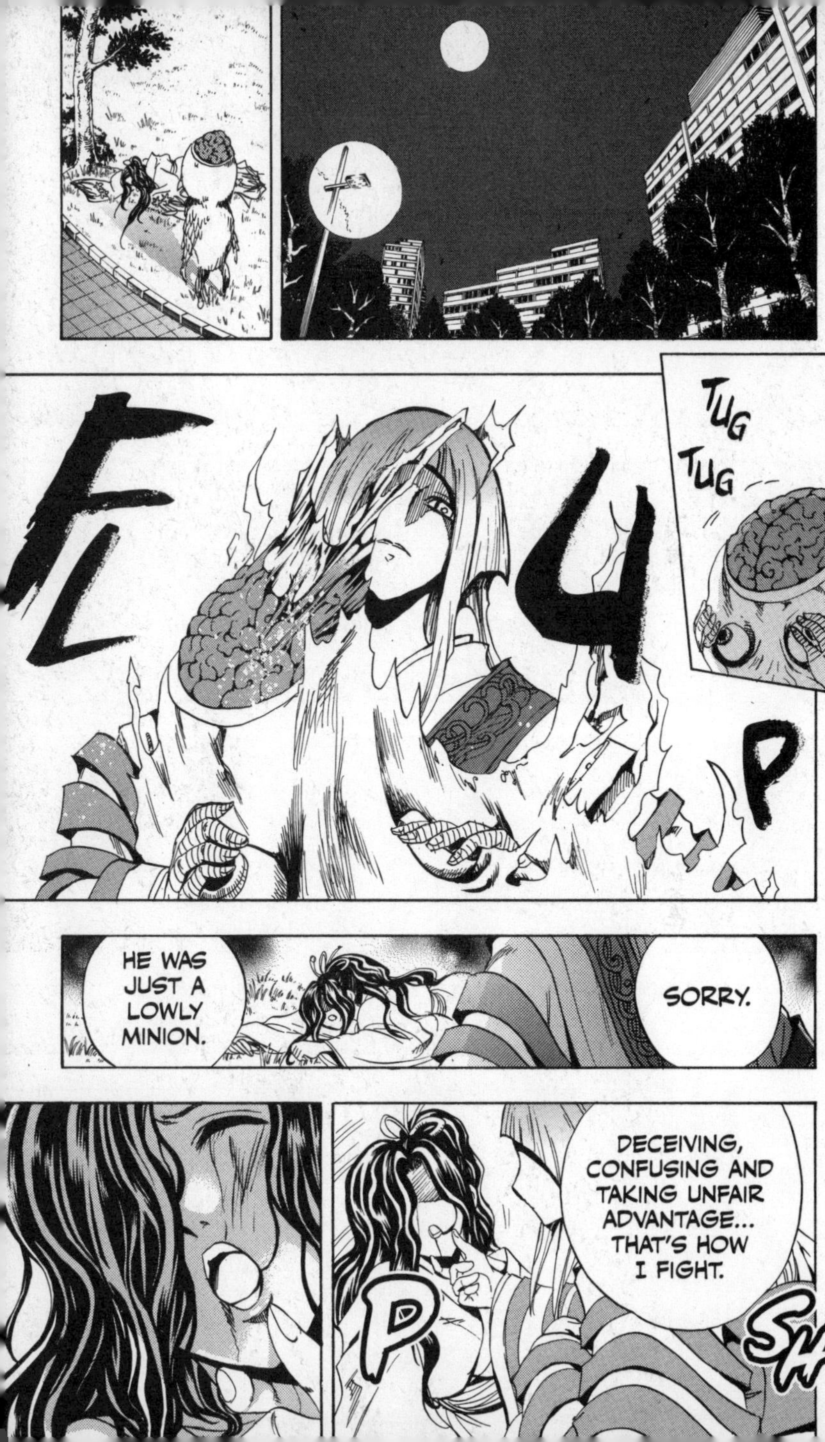
TUG TUG
FLAP
SORRY.
HE WAS JUST A LOWLY MINION.
DECEIVING, CONFUSING AND TAKING UNFAIR ADVANTAGE... THAT'S HOW I FIGHT.
SH
P

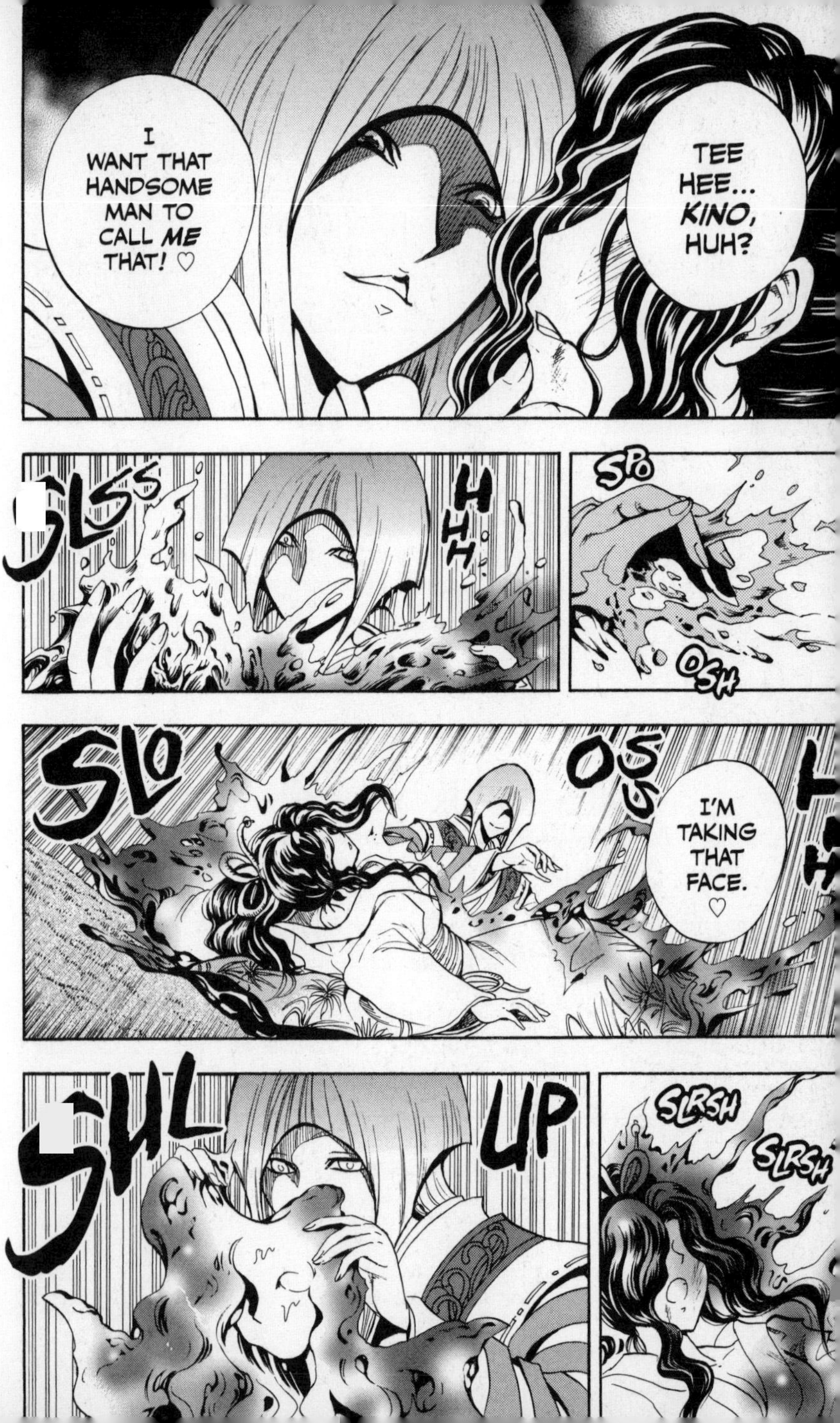
TEE HEE... *KINO*, HUH?
I WANT THAT HANDSOME MAN TO CALL *ME* THAT! ♡
SPO
OSH
SLSS
HHH
I'M TAKING THAT FACE. ♡
OS
SLO
SLRSH
SLRSH
SHL
UP

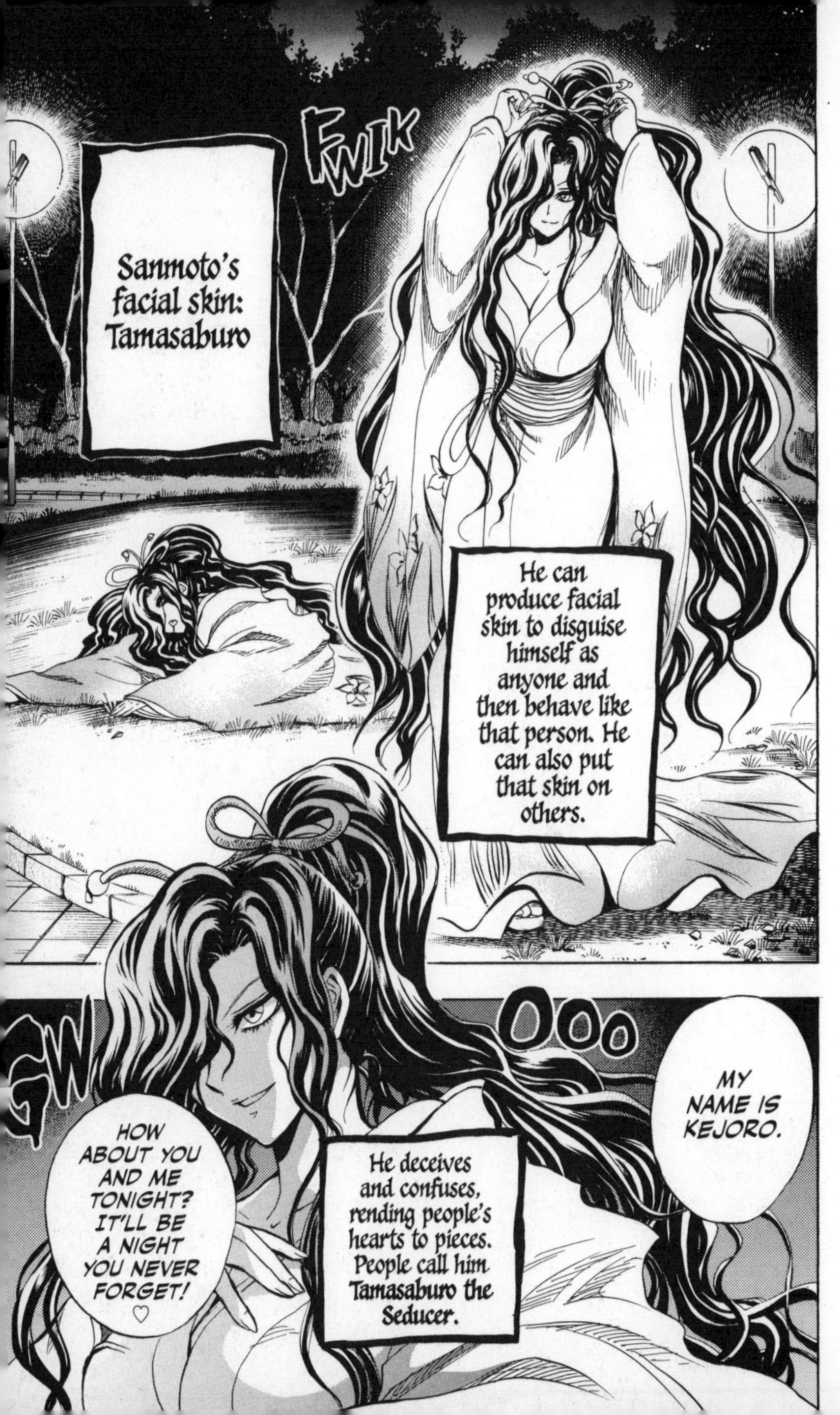
FWIK
Sanmoto's facial skin: Tamasaburo
He can produce facial skin to disguise himself as anyone and then behave like that person. He can also put that skin on others.
GWOOO
MY NAME IS KEJORO.
He deceives and confuses, rending people's hearts to pieces. People call him Tamasaburo the Seducer.
HOW ABOUT YOU AND ME TONIGHT? IT'LL BE A NIGHT YOU NEVER FORGET! ♡

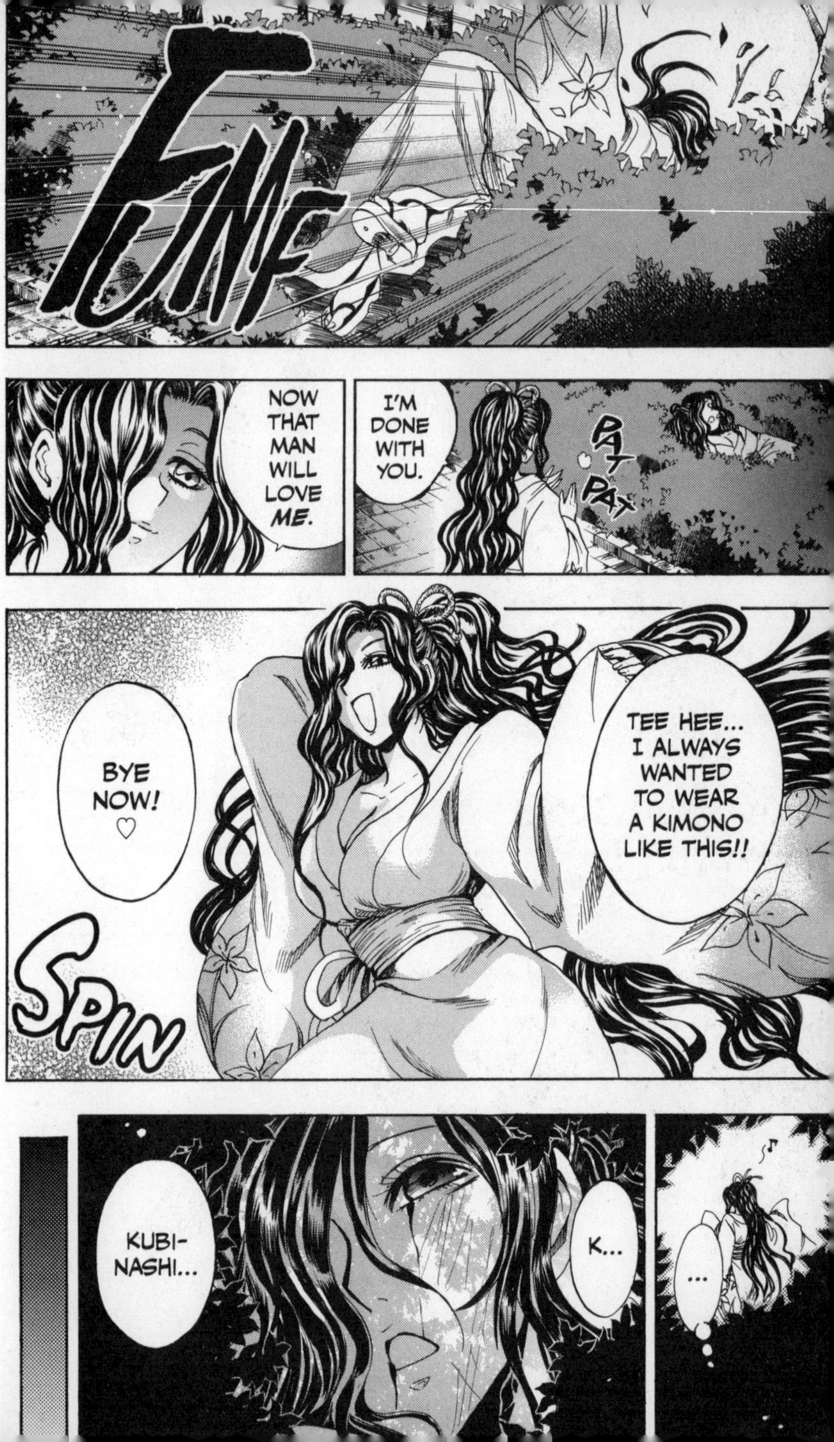
I'M DONE WITH YOU.
PAT PAT
NOW THAT MAN WILL LOVE *ME*.
TEE HEE... I ALWAYS WANTED TO WEAR A KIMONO LIKE THIS!!
BYE NOW! ♡
SPIN
...
K...
KUBI-NASHI...

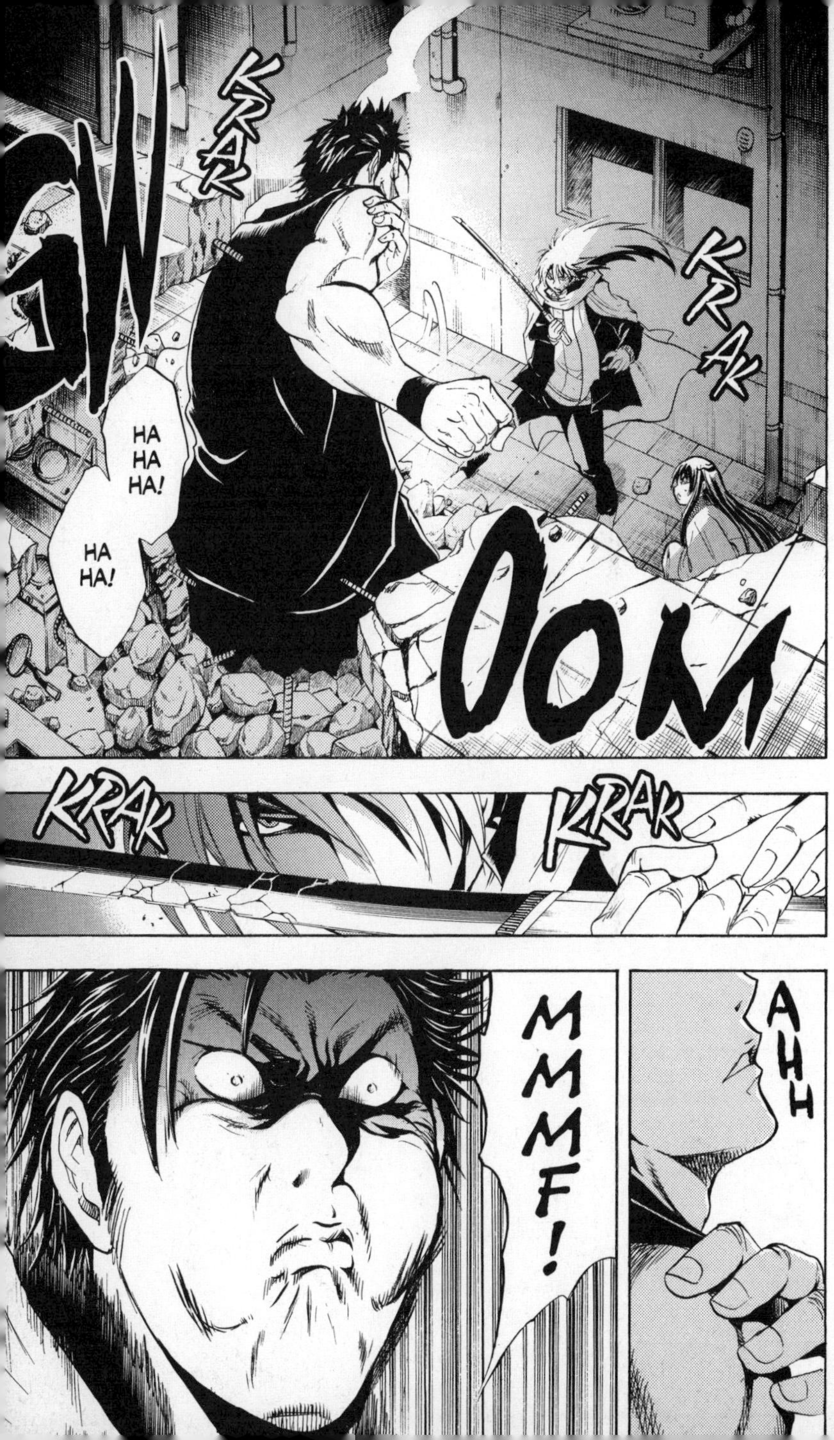
KRAK
KRAK
GW
HA HA HA!
HA HA!
OOM
KRAK
KRAK
AHH
MMMF!

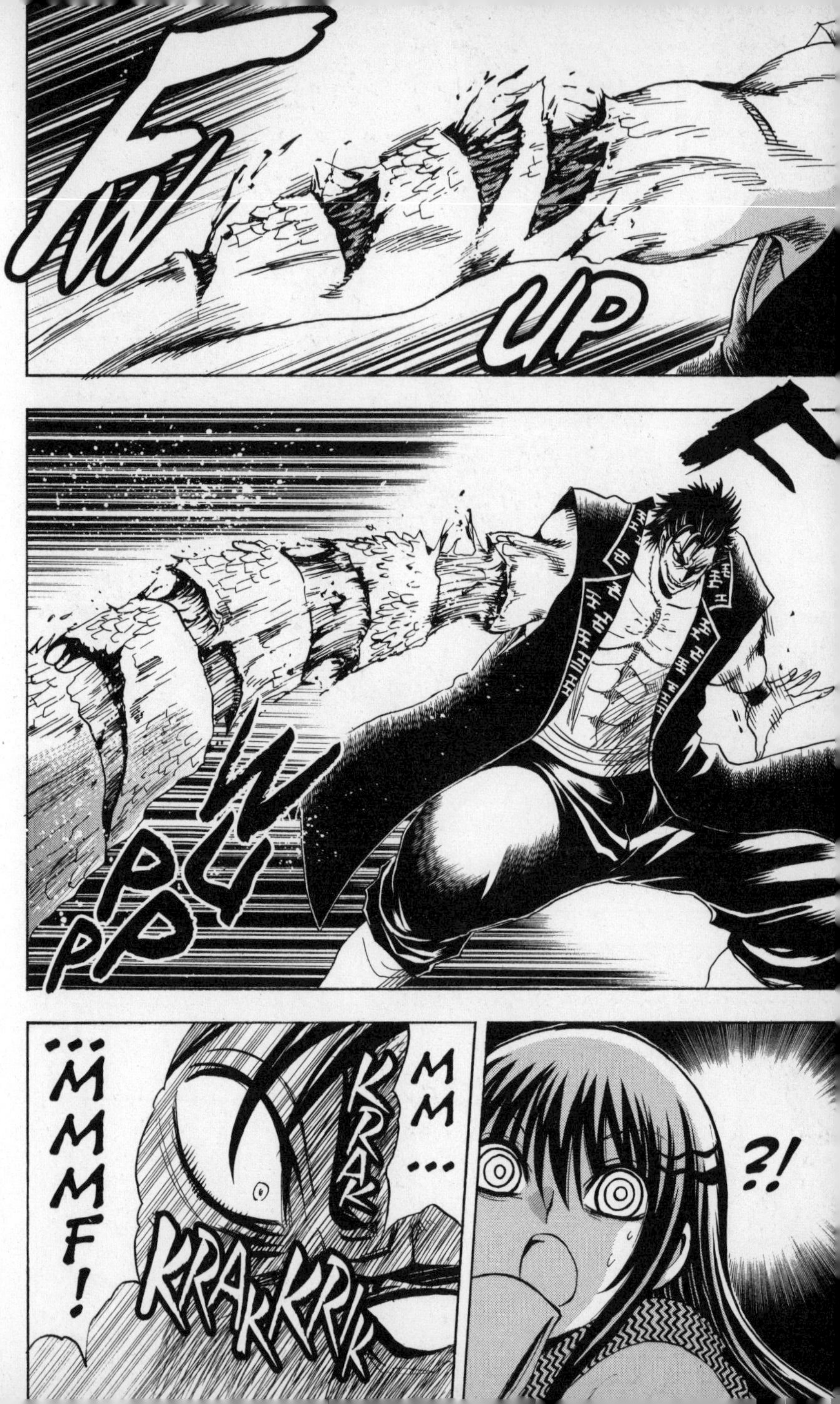
FWUP
FWUPPP
?!
MM...
KRAK
KRRAKKRRK
...MMMMF!

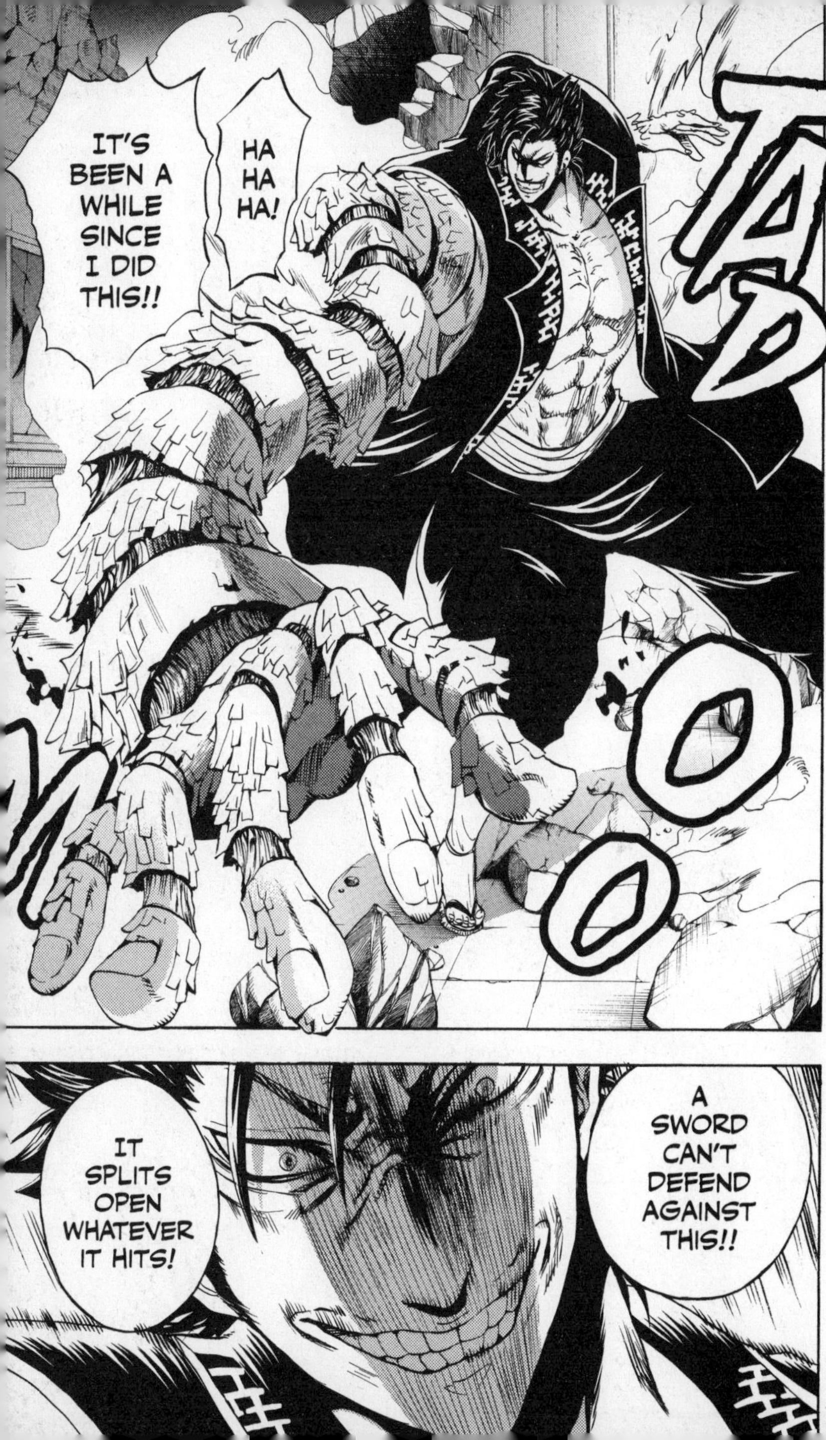
HA HA HA!
IT'S BEEN A WHILE SINCE I DID THIS!!
TADOOM
A SWORD CAN'T DEFEND AGAINST THIS!!
IT SPLITS OPEN WHATEVER IT HITS!

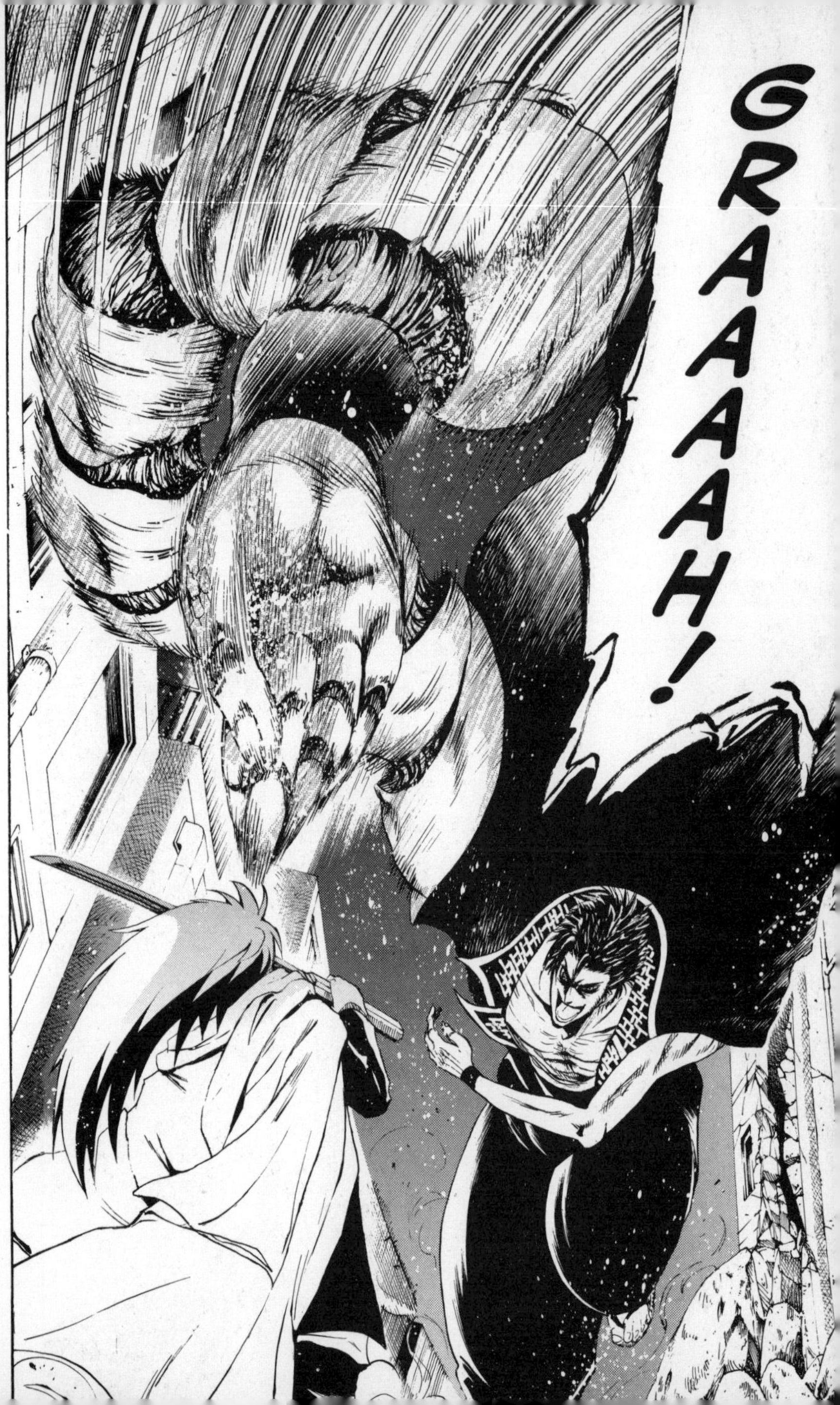
GRAAAAH!

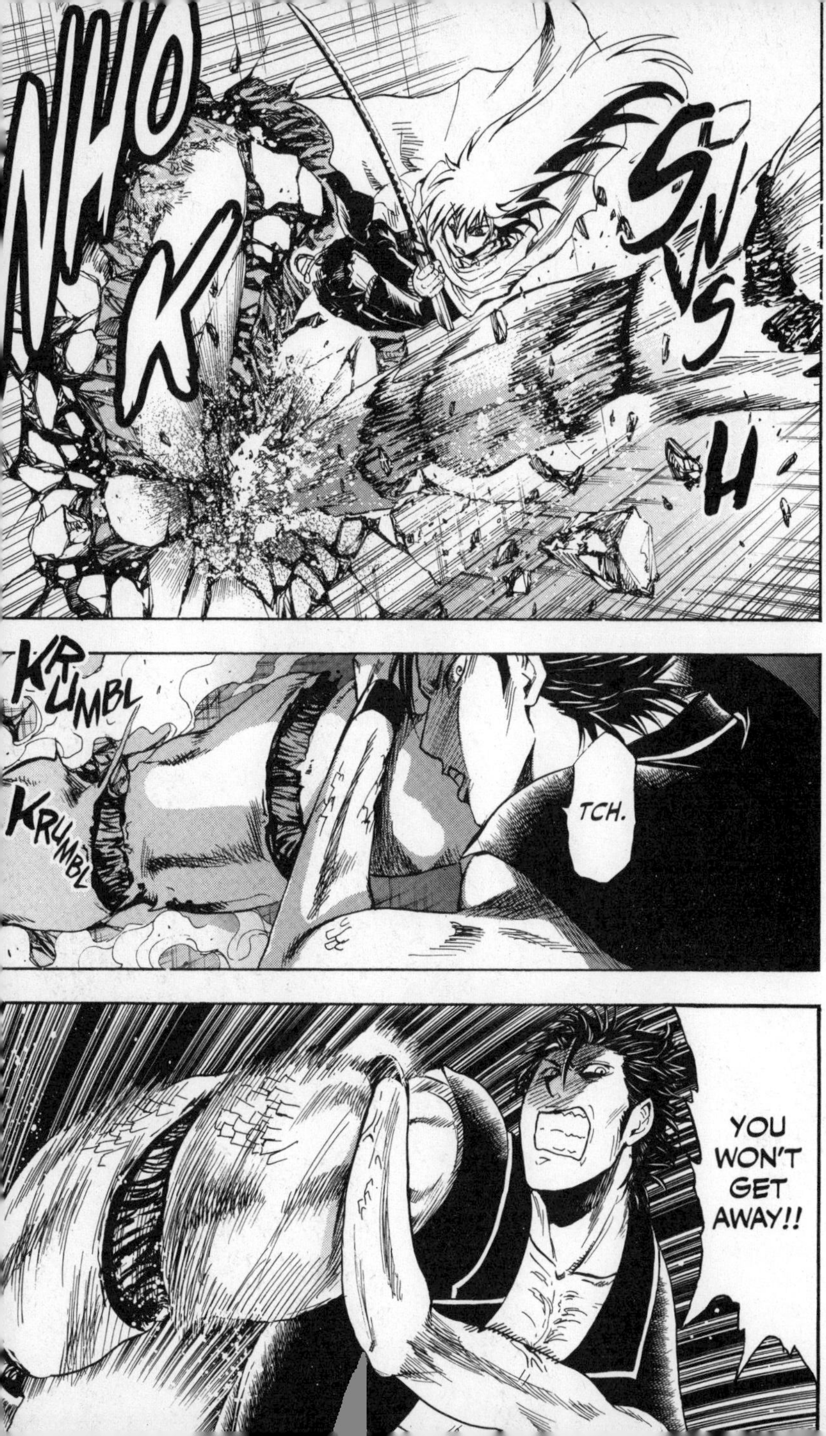
SNSH
NHOK
KRUMBL
KRUMBL
TCH.
YOU WON'T GET AWAY!!

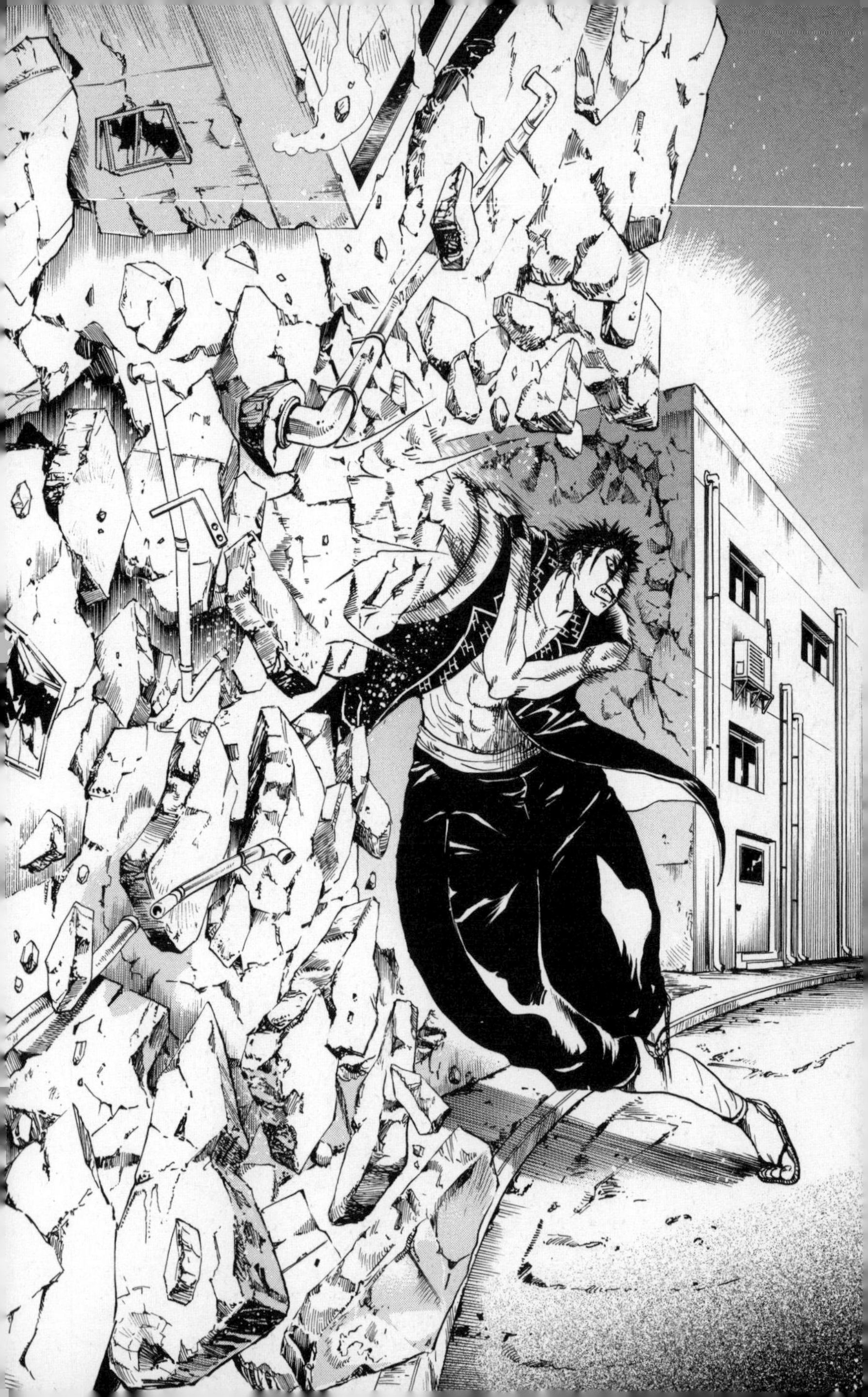

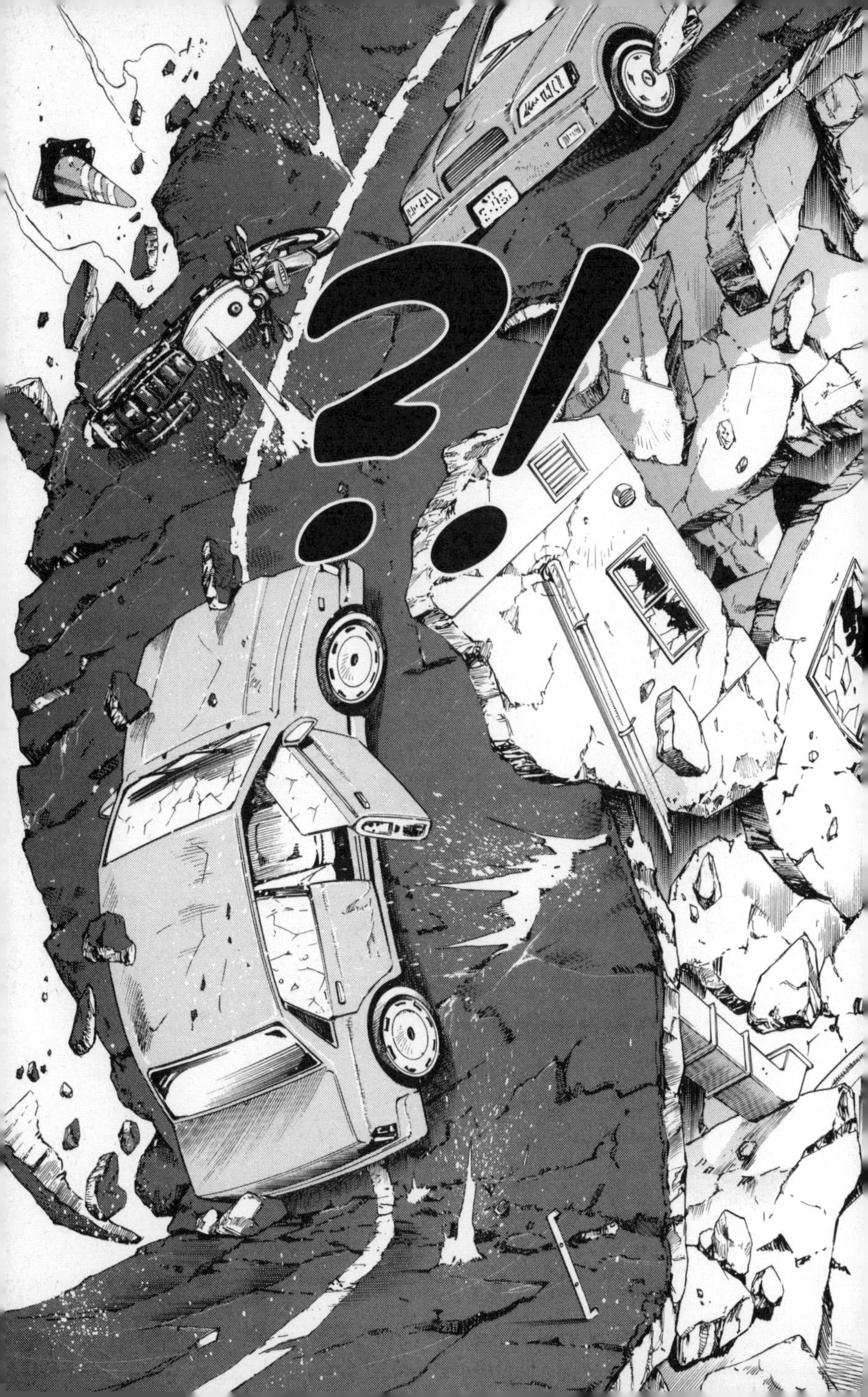
?!

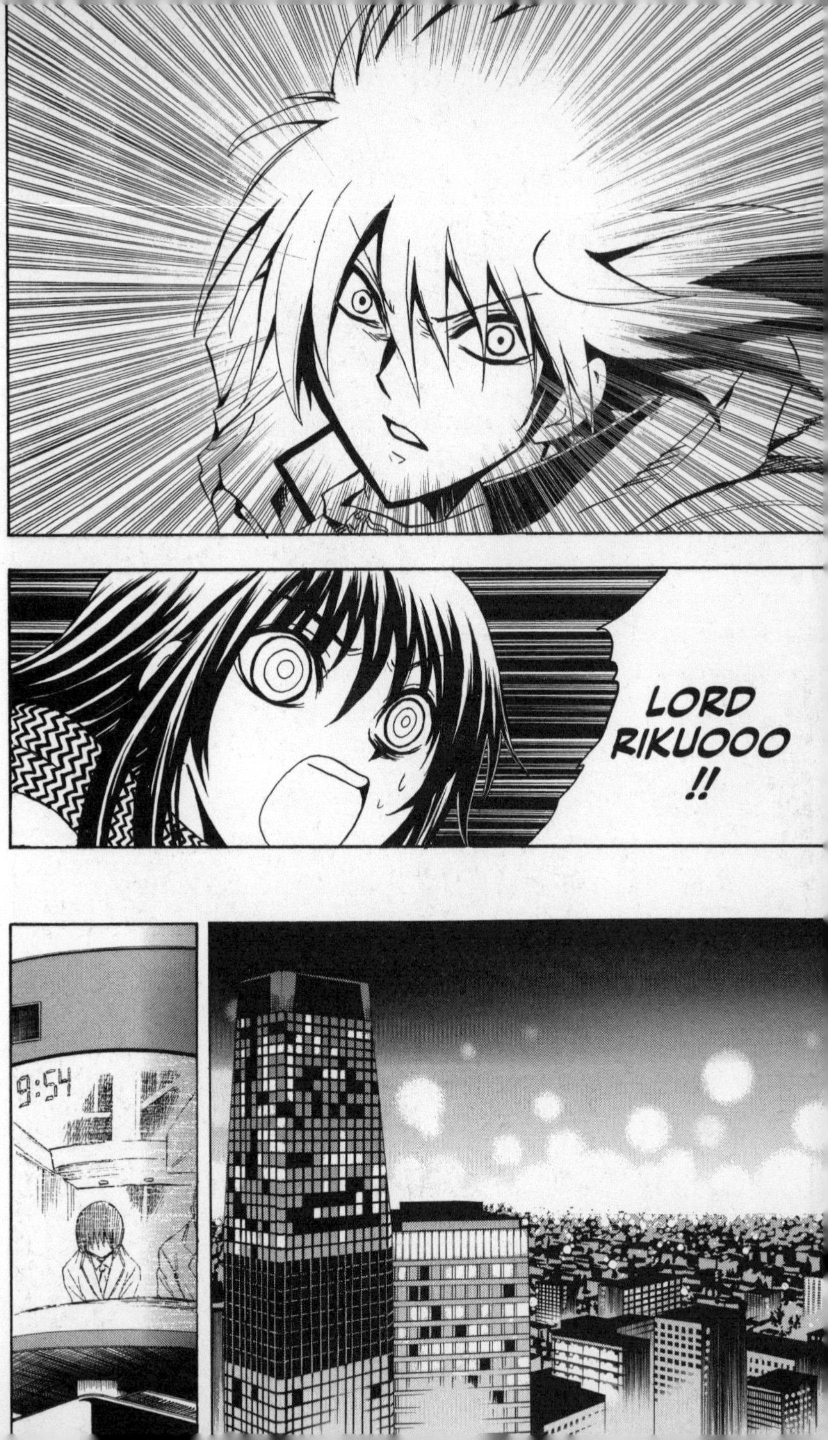
LORD RIKUOOO !!
9:54

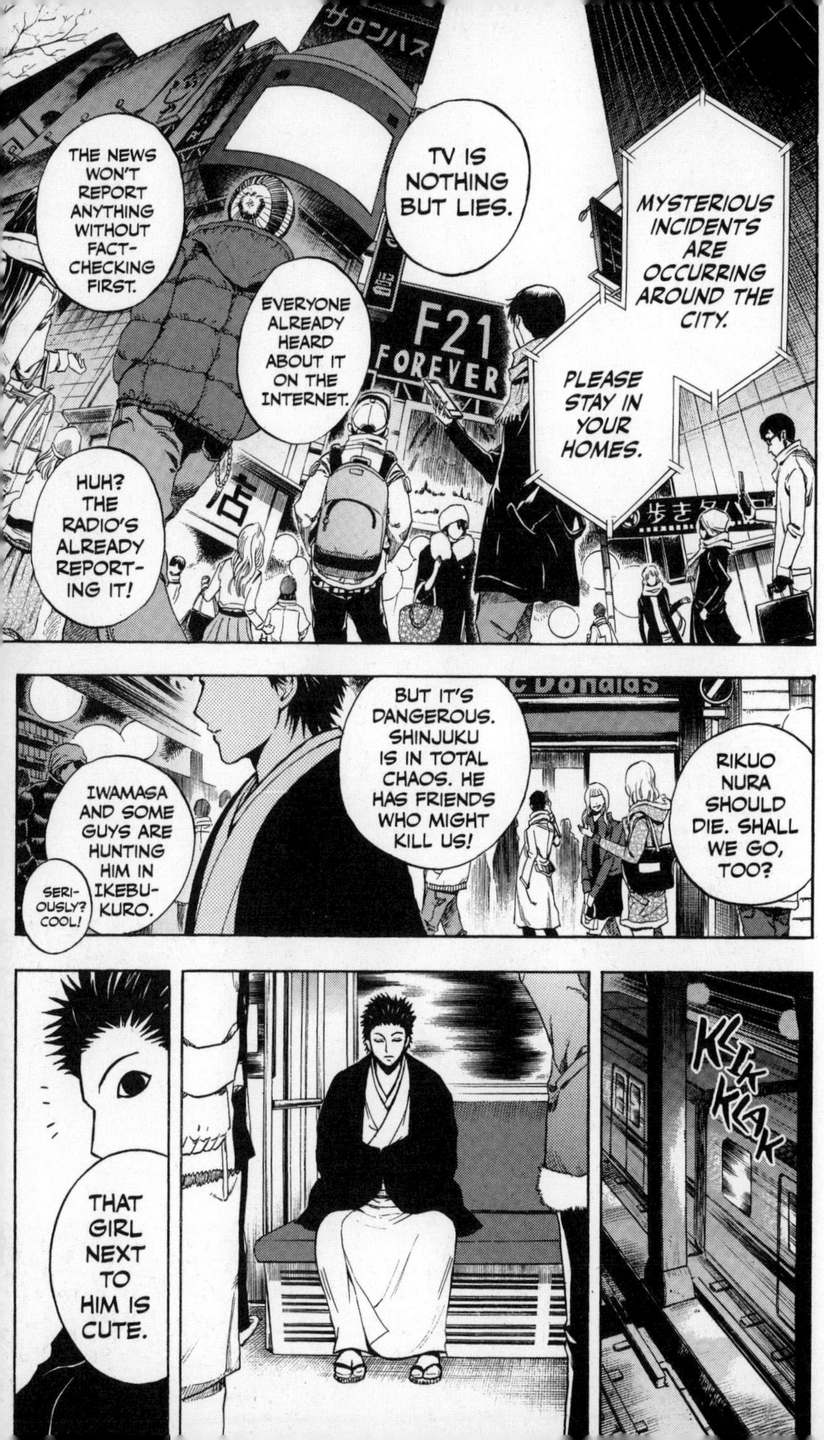
MYSTERIOUS INCIDENTS ARE OCCURRING AROUND THE CITY.
PLEASE STAY IN YOUR HOMES.
TV IS NOTHING BUT LIES.
F21 FOREVER
EVERYONE ALREADY HEARD ABOUT IT ON THE INTERNET.
THE NEWS WON'T REPORT ANYTHING WITHOUT FACT-CHECKING FIRST.
HUH? THE RADIO'S ALREADY REPORTING IT!
RIKUO NURA SHOULD DIE. SHALL WE GO, TOO?
BUT IT'S DANGEROUS. SHINJUKU IS IN TOTAL CHAOS. HE HAS FRIENDS WHO MIGHT KILL US!
IWAMASA AND SOME GUYS ARE HUNTING HIM IN IKEBUKURO.
SERIOUSLY? COOL!
KLIK KLAK
THAT GIRL NEXT TO HIM IS CUTE.

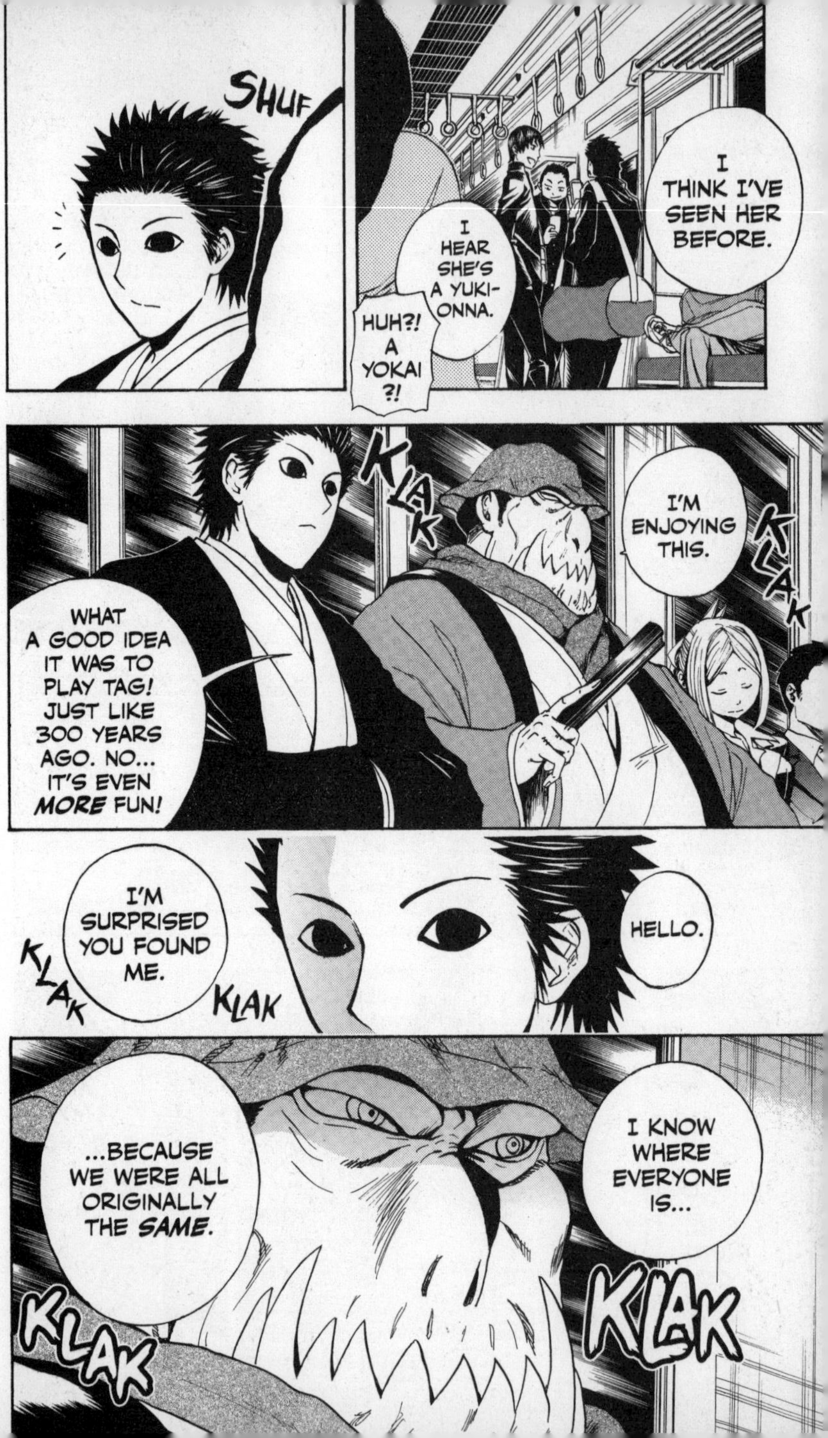
I THINK I'VE SEEN HER BEFORE.
I HEAR SHE'S A YUKI-ONNA.
HUH?! A YOKAI ?!
SHUF
KLAK
I'M ENJOYING THIS.
KLAK
WHAT A GOOD IDEA IT WAS TO PLAY TAG! JUST LIKE 300 YEARS AGO. NO... IT'S EVEN *MORE* FUN!
HELLO.
I'M SURPRISED YOU FOUND ME.
KLAK
KLAK
I KNOW WHERE EVERYONE IS...
...BECAUSE WE WERE ALL ORIGINALLY THE *SAME*.
KLAK
KLAK

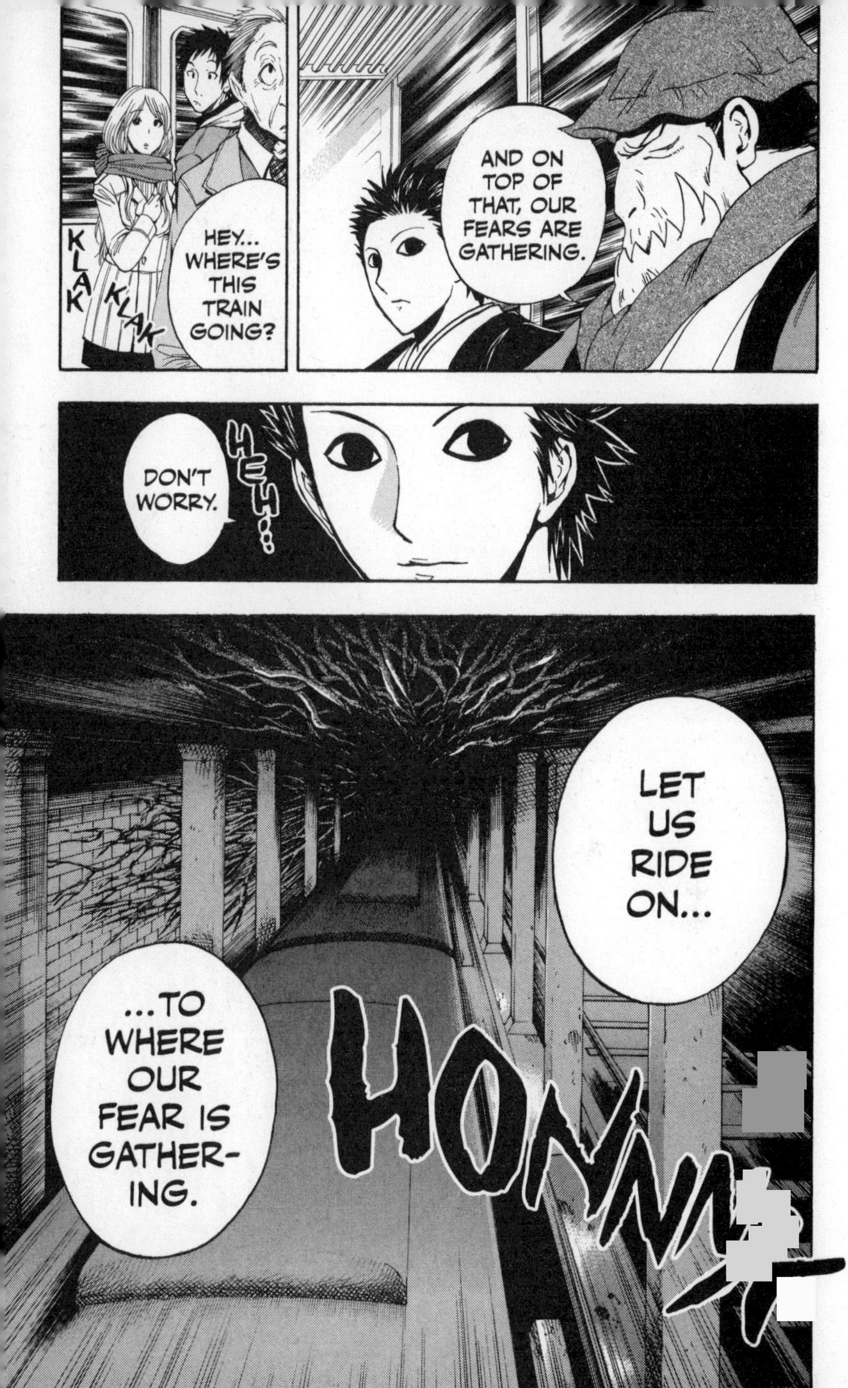
AND ON TOP OF THAT, OUR FEARS ARE GATHERING.
HEY... WHERE'S THIS TRAIN GOING?
KLAK KLAK
HEH...
DON'T WORRY.
LET US RIDE ON...
...TO WHERE OUR FEAR IS GATHER-ING.

NURA: RISE OF THE YOKAI CLAN

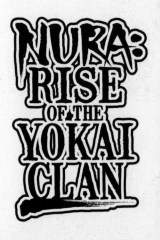

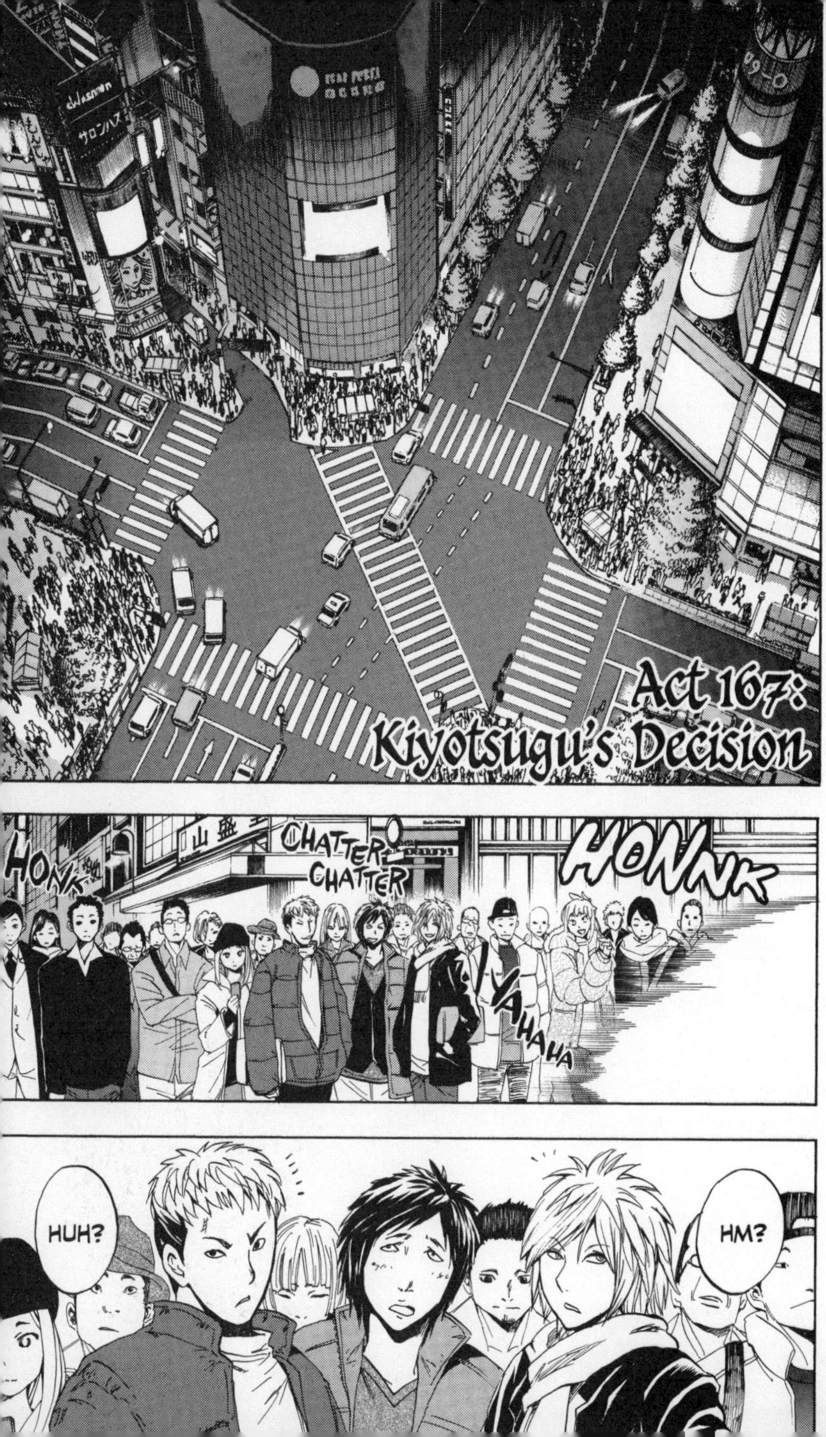
Act 167:
Kiyotsugu's Decision
HONNK
YAHAHAHA
CHATTER CHATTER
HONK
HM?
HUH?

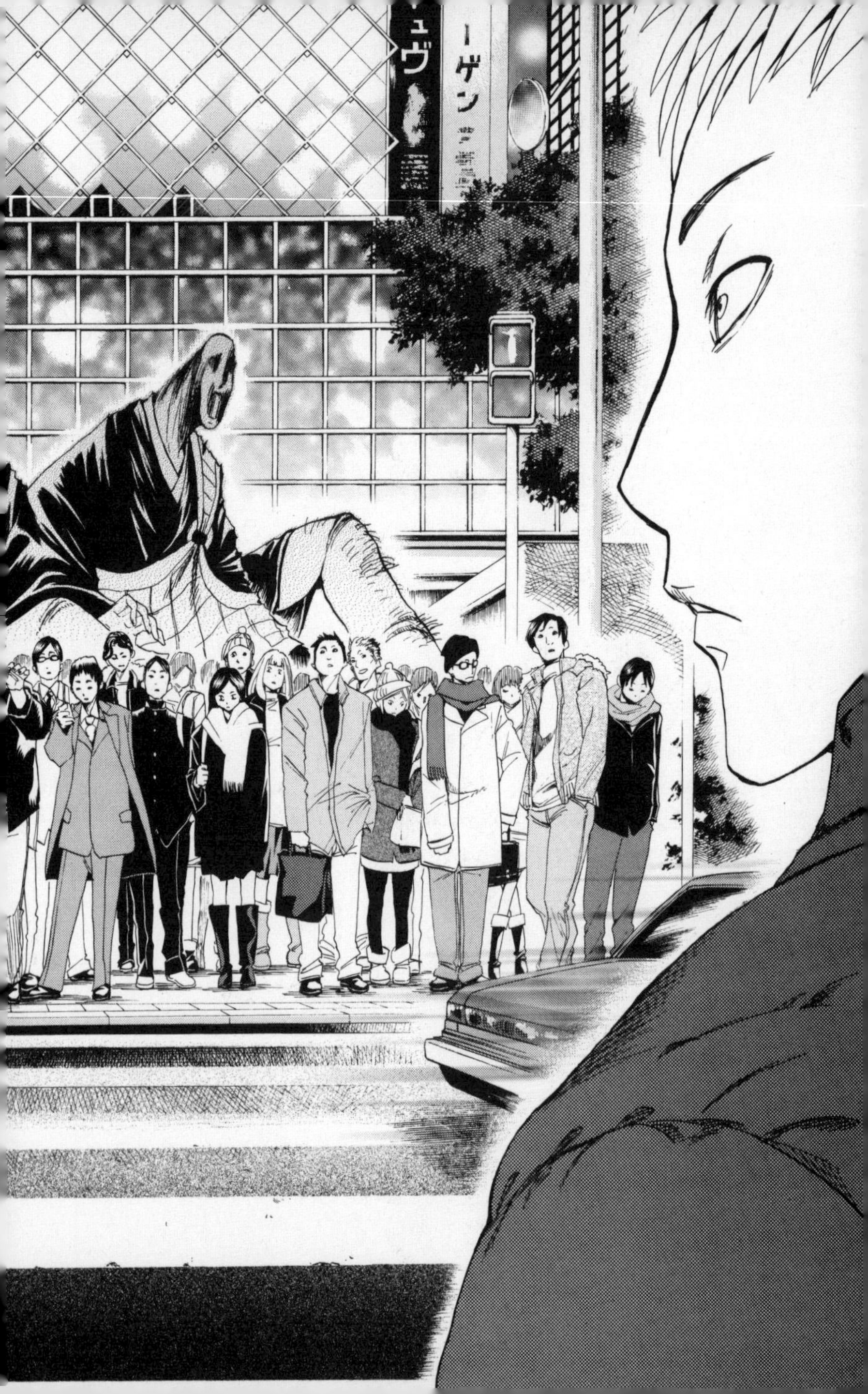
ュヴ
ーゲン

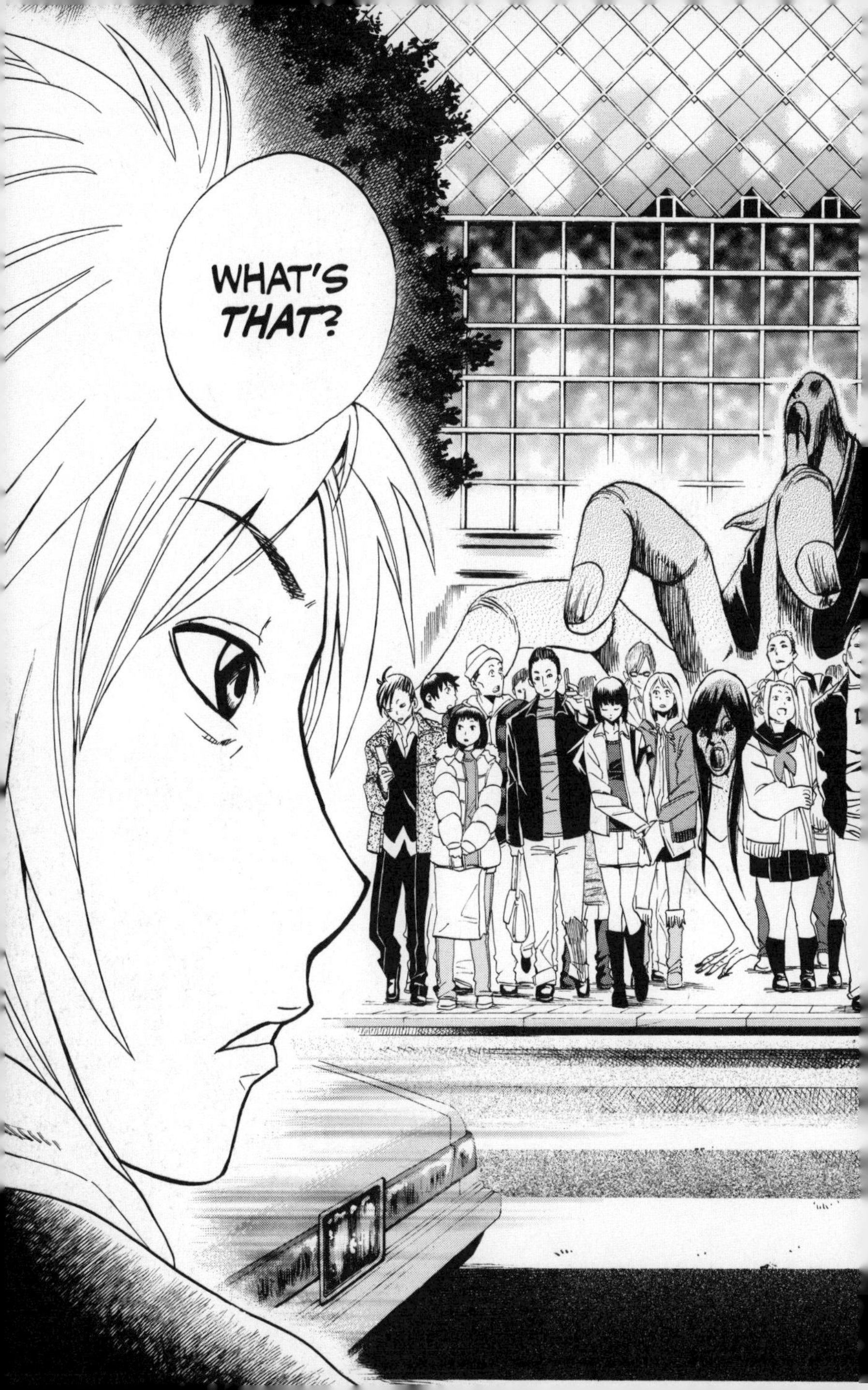
WHAT'S THAT?

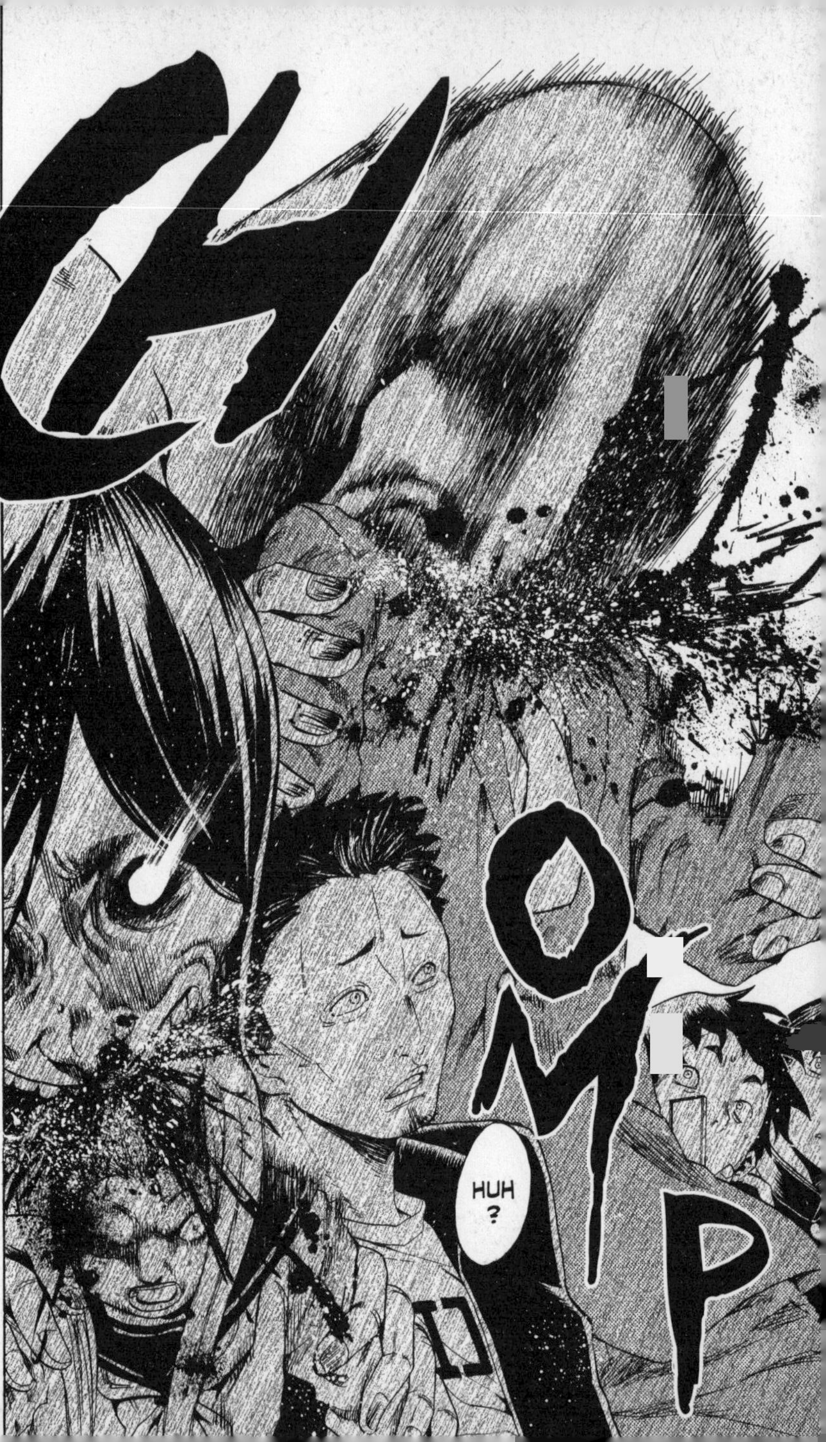
GL
OMP
HUH ?

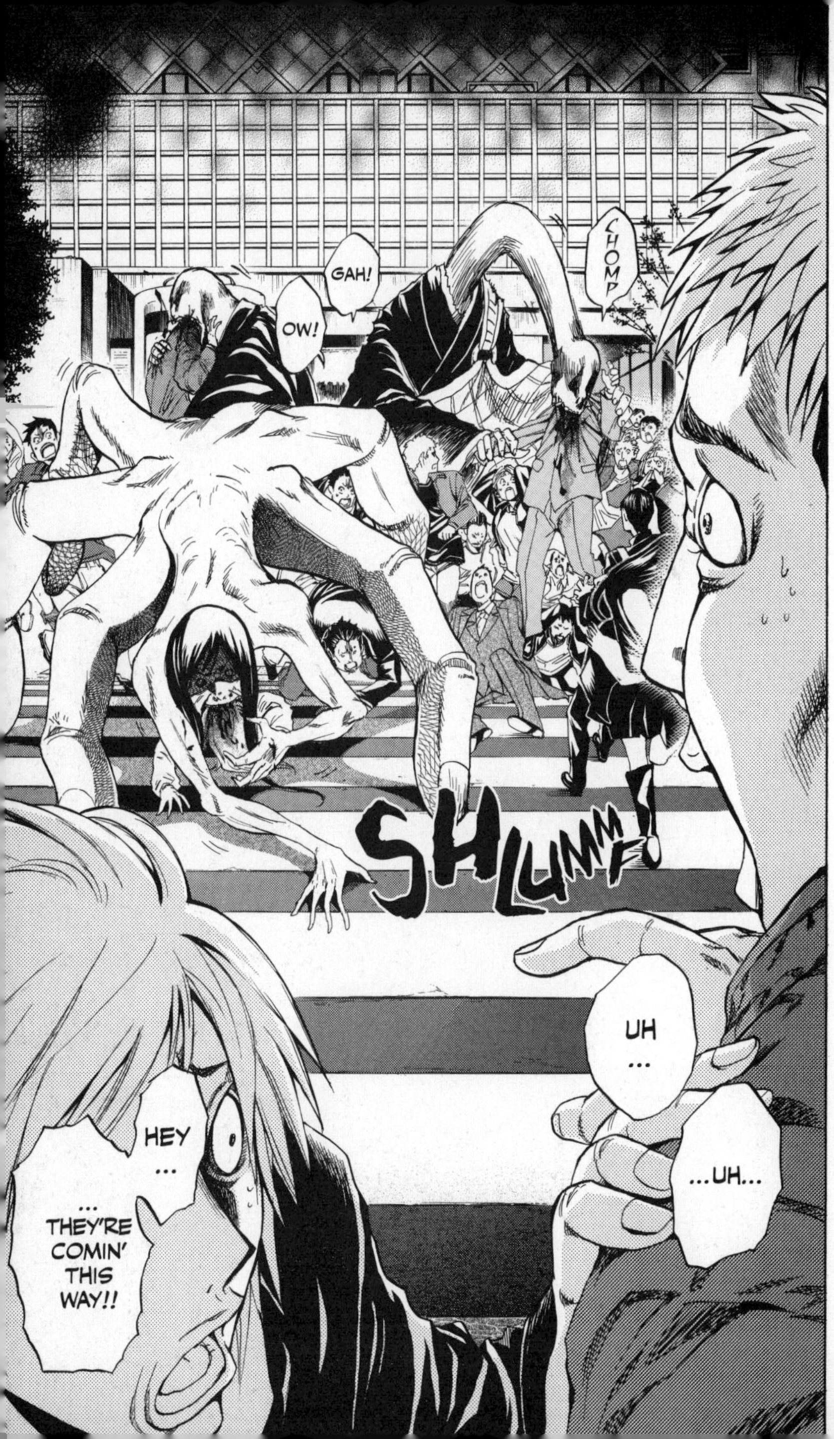
CHOMP
GAH!
OW!
SHLUMMF
UH ...
...UH...
HEY ...
... THEY'RE COMIN' THIS WAY!!

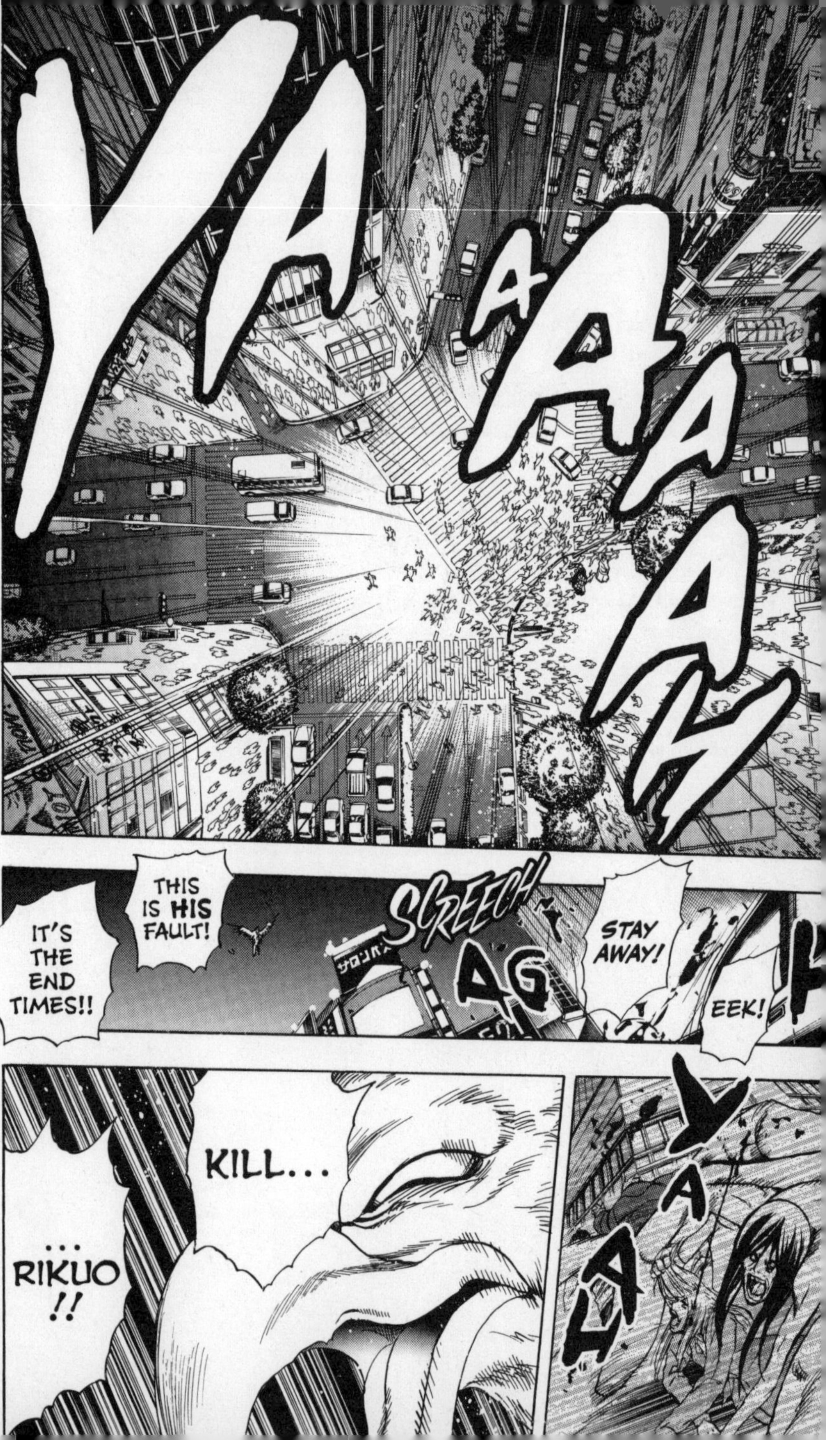
YAAAAAH
EEK!
STAY AWAY!
SCREECH
AG
THIS IS HIS FAULT!
IT'S THE END TIMES!!
YAAAH
KILL...
...RIKUO!!

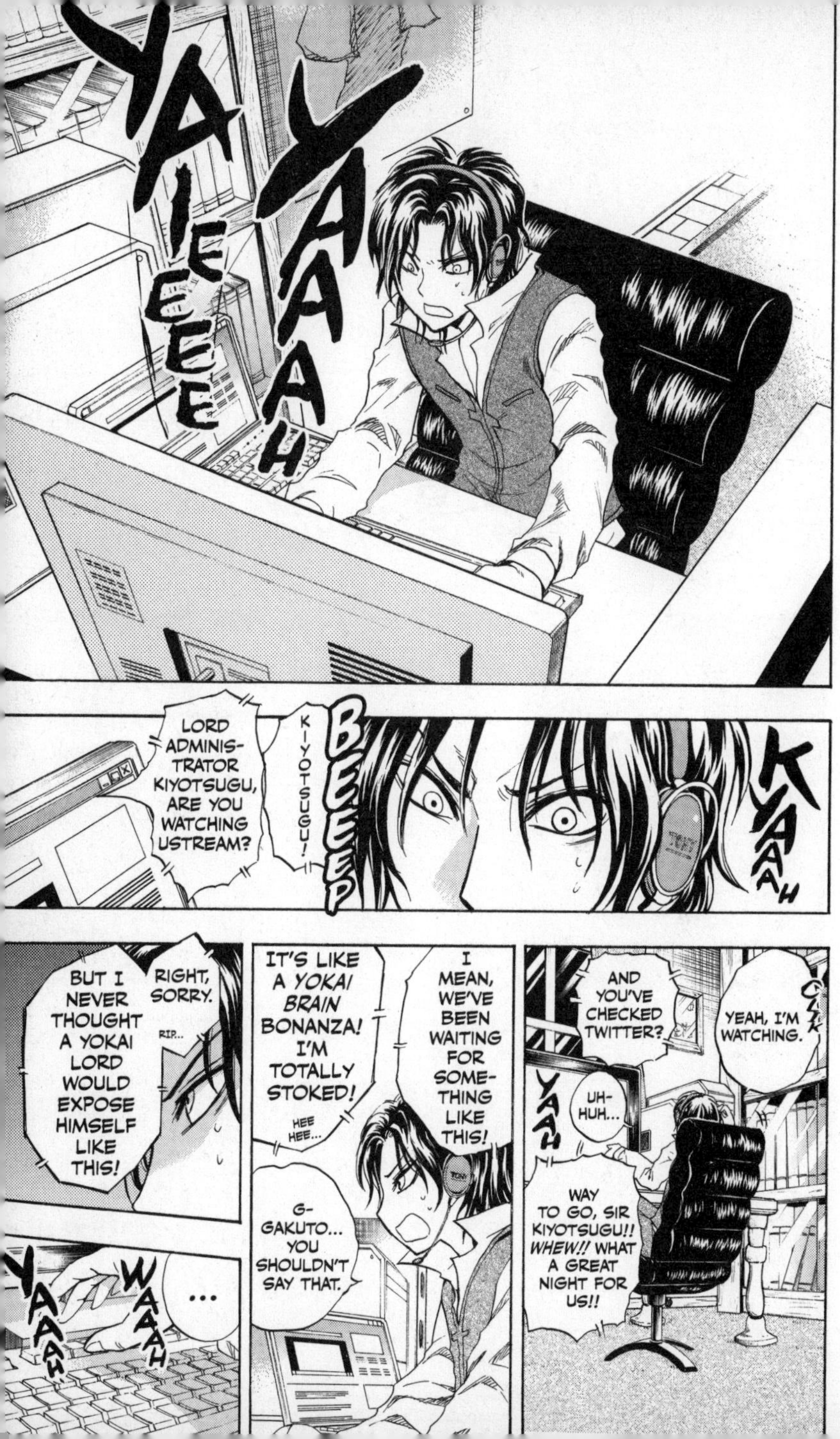

YAAAAAH
YAIEEEEE
KYAAAAH
BEEEEP
KIYOTSUGU!
LORD ADMINISTRATOR KIYOTSUGU, ARE YOU WATCHING USTREAM?
CLICK
YEAH, I'M WATCHING.
AND YOU'VE CHECKED TWITTER?
UH-HUH...
YAAAH
WAY TO GO, SIR KIYOTSUGU!! *WHEW!!* WHAT A GREAT NIGHT FOR US!!
I MEAN, WE'VE BEEN WAITING FOR SOMETHING LIKE THIS!
IT'S LIKE A *YOKAI BRAIN* BONANZA! I'M TOTALLY STOKED!
HEE HEE...
G-GAKUTO... YOU SHOULDN'T SAY THAT.
RIGHT, SORRY.
RIP...
BUT I NEVER THOUGHT A YOKAI LORD WOULD EXPOSE HIMSELF LIKE THIS!
WAAAH
YAAAAH
...

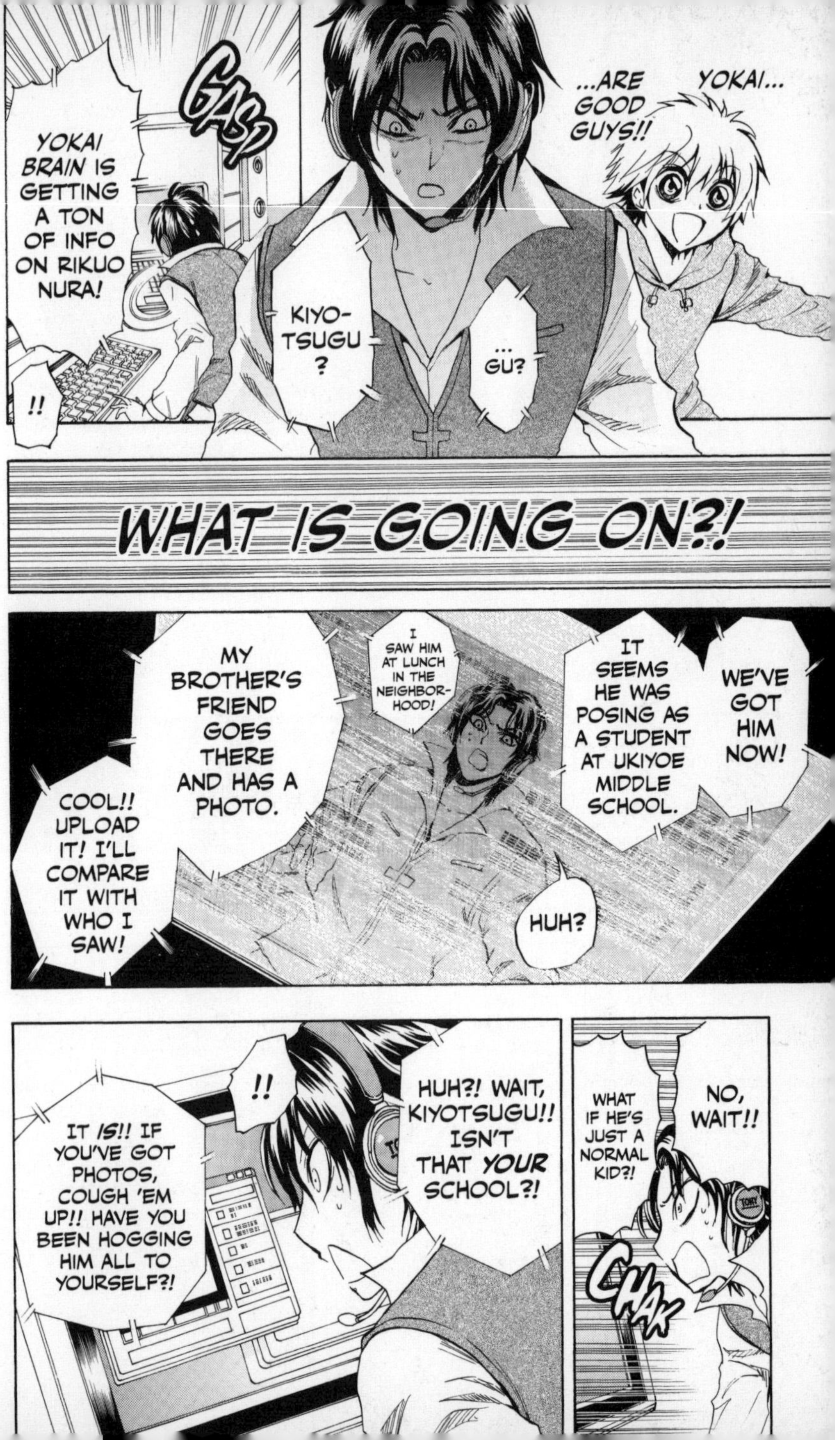
YOKAI...
...ARE GOOD GUYS!!
GASP
KIYO-TSUGU?
...GU?
YOKAI BRAIN IS GETTING A TON OF INFO ON RIKUO NURA!
!!
WHAT IS GOING ON?!
WE'VE GOT HIM NOW!
IT SEEMS HE WAS POSING AS A STUDENT AT UKIYOE MIDDLE SCHOOL.
I SAW HIM AT LUNCH IN THE NEIGHBOR-HOOD!
MY BROTHER'S FRIEND GOES THERE AND HAS A PHOTO.
COOL!! UPLOAD IT! I'LL COMPARE IT WITH WHO I SAW!
HUH?
NO, WAIT!!
WHAT IF HE'S JUST A NORMAL KID?!
CHAK
HUH?! WAIT, KIYOTSUGU!! ISN'T THAT YOUR SCHOOL?!
!!
IT IS!! IF YOU'VE GOT PHOTOS, COUGH 'EM UP!! HAVE YOU BEEN HOGGING HIM ALL TO YOURSELF?!

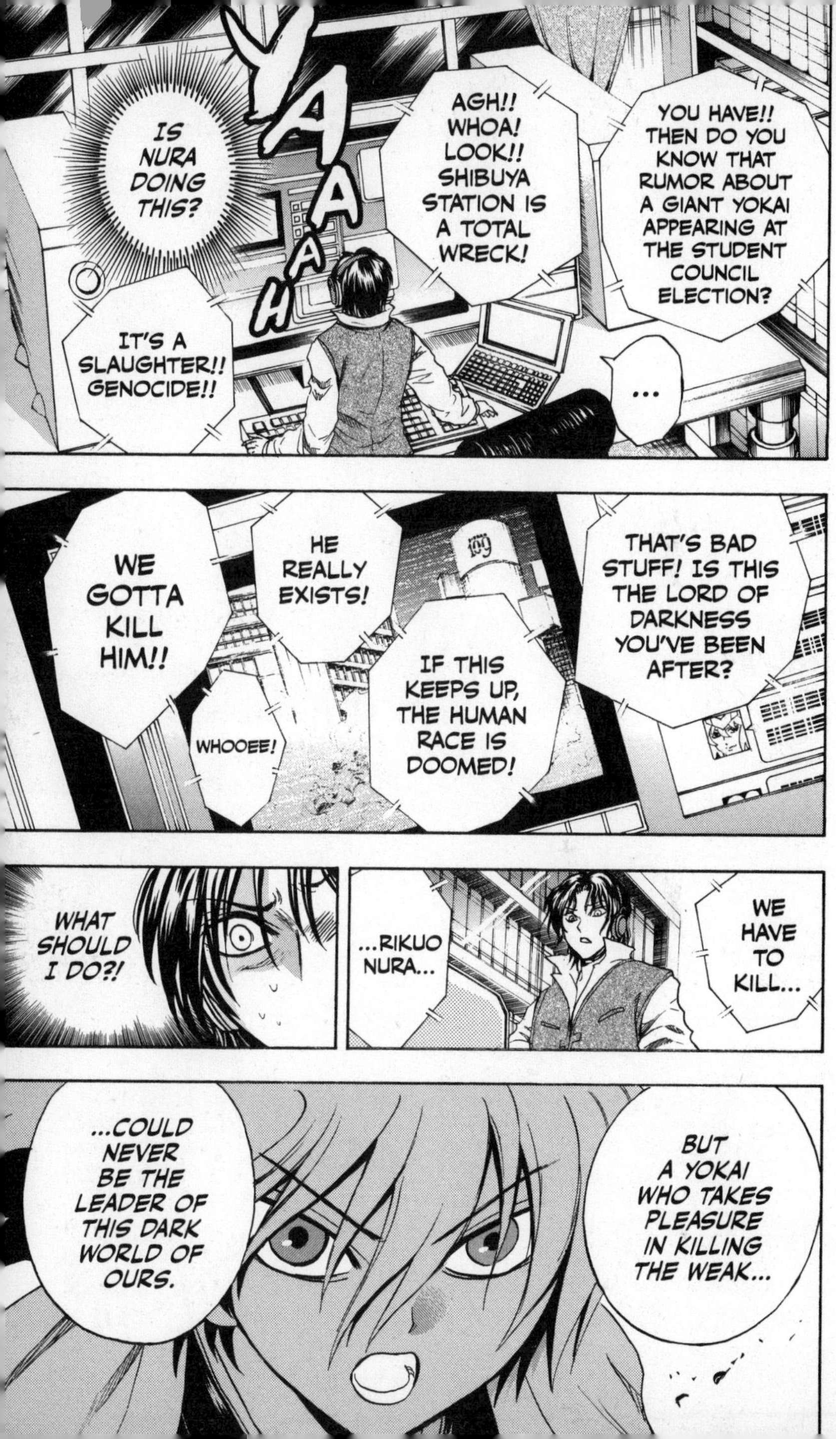
YOU HAVE!! THEN DO YOU KNOW THAT RUMOR ABOUT A GIANT YOKAI APPEARING AT THE STUDENT COUNCIL ELECTION?
...
AGH!! WHOA! LOOK!! SHIBUYA STATION IS A TOTAL WRECK!
YAAAAH
IS NURA DOING THIS?
IT'S A SLAUGHTER!! GENOCIDE!!
THAT'S BAD STUFF! IS THIS THE LORD OF DARKNESS YOU'VE BEEN AFTER?
HE REALLY EXISTS!
IF THIS KEEPS UP, THE HUMAN RACE IS DOOMED!
WE GOTTA KILL HIM!!
WHOOEE!
WE HAVE TO KILL...
...RIKUO NURA...
WHAT SHOULD I DO?!
BUT A YOKAI WHO TAKES PLEASURE IN KILLING THE WEAK...
...COULD NEVER BE THE LEADER OF THIS DARK WORLD OF OURS.

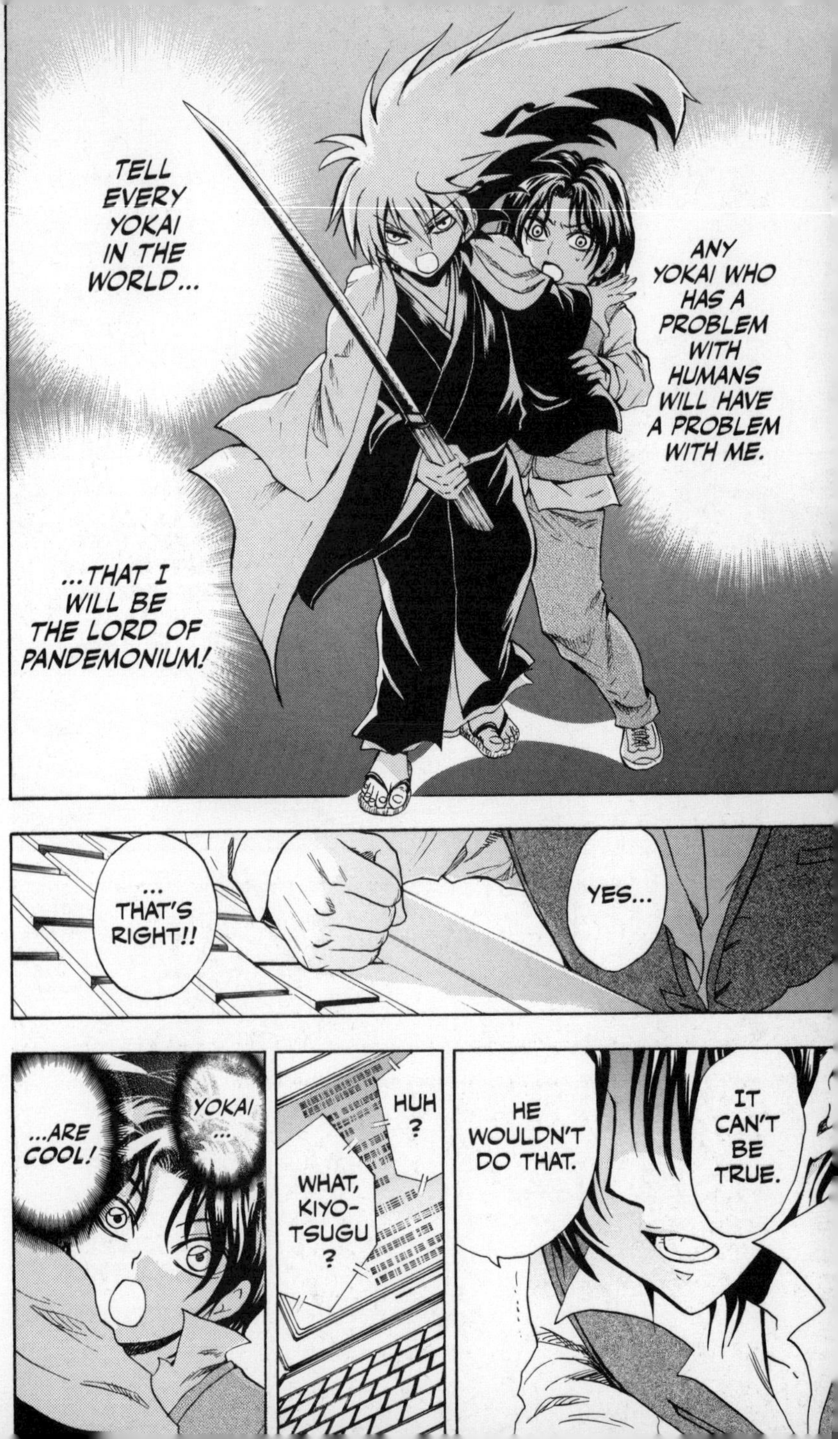
TELL EVERY YOKAI IN THE WORLD...
...THAT I WILL BE THE LORD OF PANDEMONIUM!
ANY YOKAI WHO HAS A PROBLEM WITH HUMANS WILL HAVE A PROBLEM WITH ME.
YES...
...THAT'S RIGHT!!
IT CAN'T BE TRUE.
HE WOULDN'T DO THAT.
HUH?
WHAT, KIYO-TSUGU?
YOKAI...
...ARE COOL!

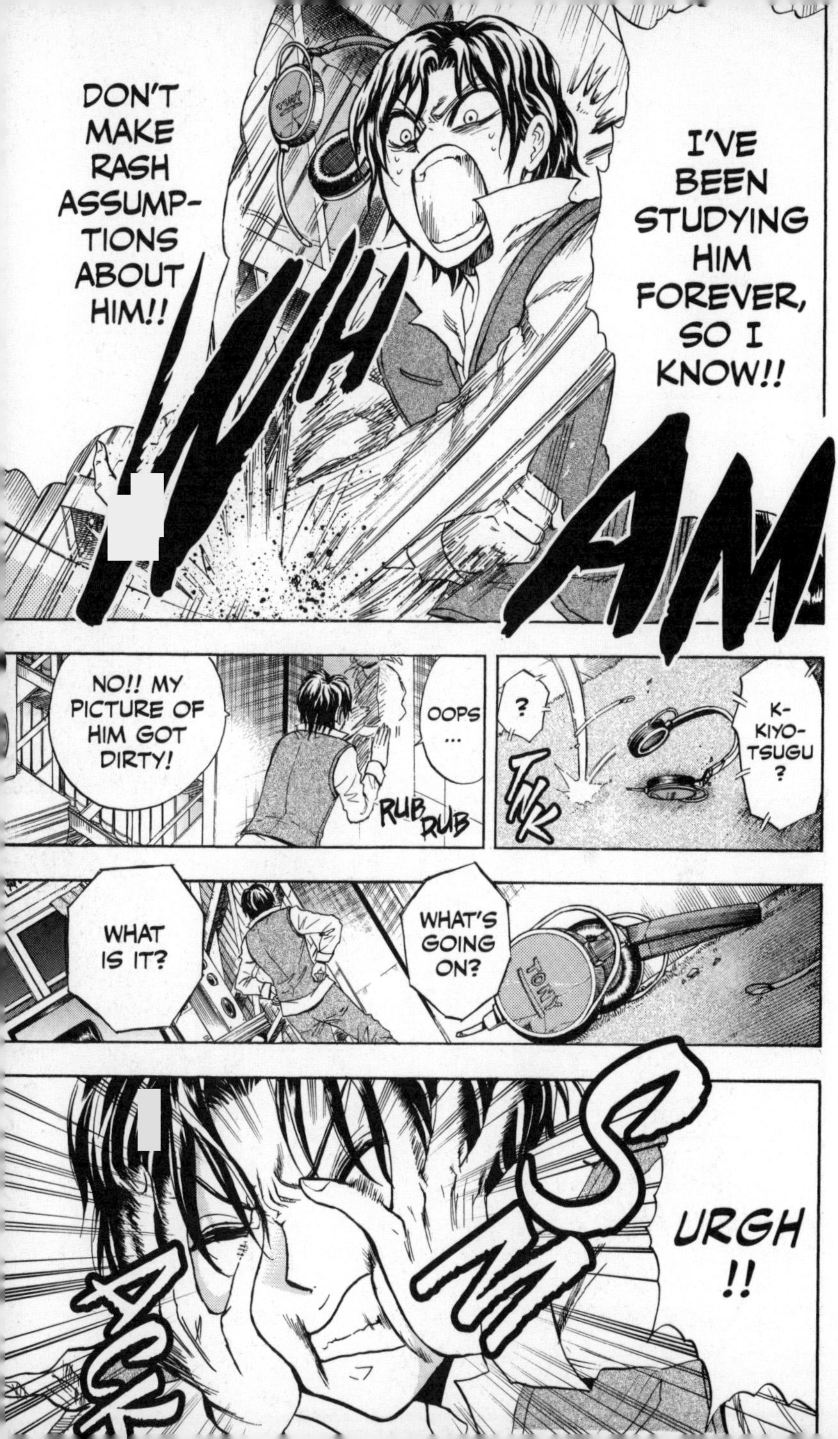
I'VE BEEN STUDYING HIM FOREVER, SO I KNOW!!
DON'T MAKE RASH ASSUMPTIONS ABOUT HIM!!
WHAM
?
K-KIYOTSUGU?
TINK
OOPS...
NO!! MY PICTURE OF HIM GOT DIRTY!
RUB RUB
WHAT'S GOING ON?
WHAT IS IT?
URGH!!
SMACK

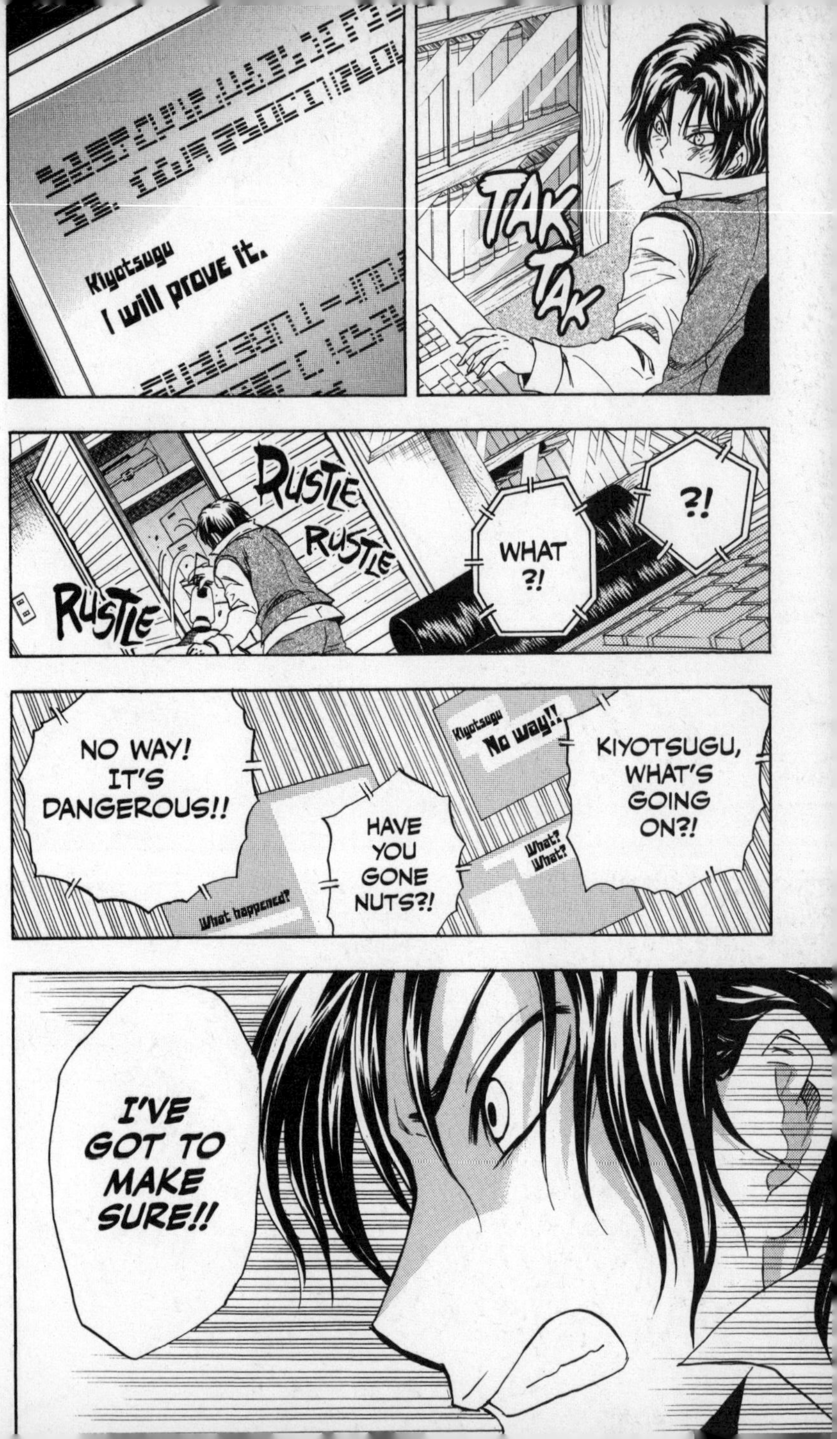
TAK TAK
Kiyotsugu
I will prove it.
?!
WHAT ?!
RUSTLE RUSTLE
RUSTLE
KIYOTSUGU, WHAT'S GOING ON?!
Kiyotsugu
No way!!
What? What?
HAVE YOU GONE NUTS?!
NO WAY! IT'S DANGEROUS!!
What happened?
I'VE GOT TO MAKE SURE!!

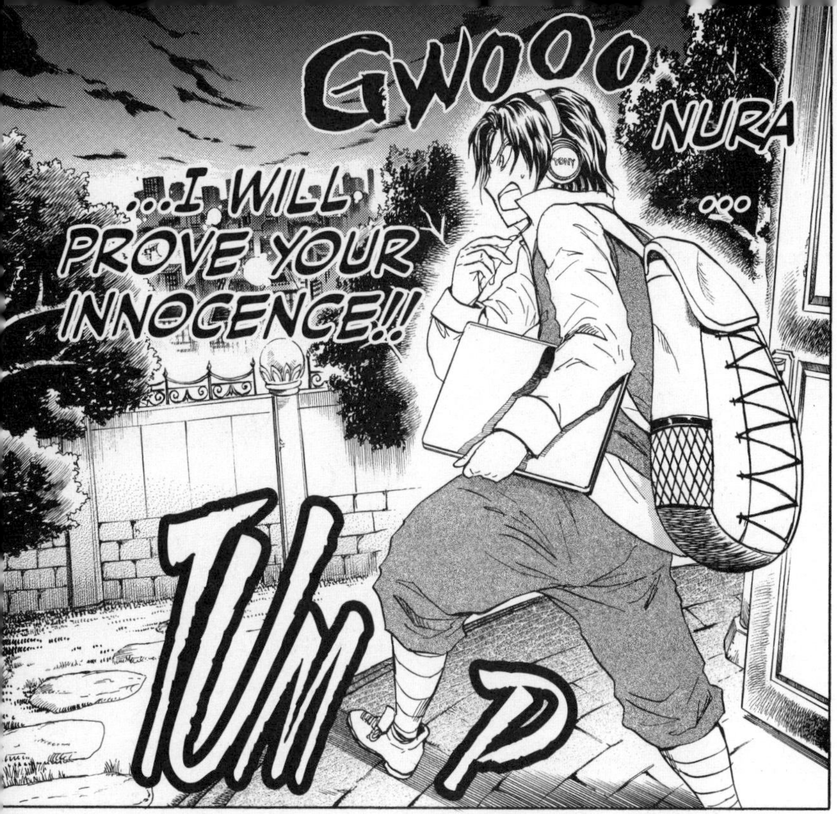
GWOOO
NURA
...
...I WILL PROVE YOUR INNOCENCE!!
TUMP
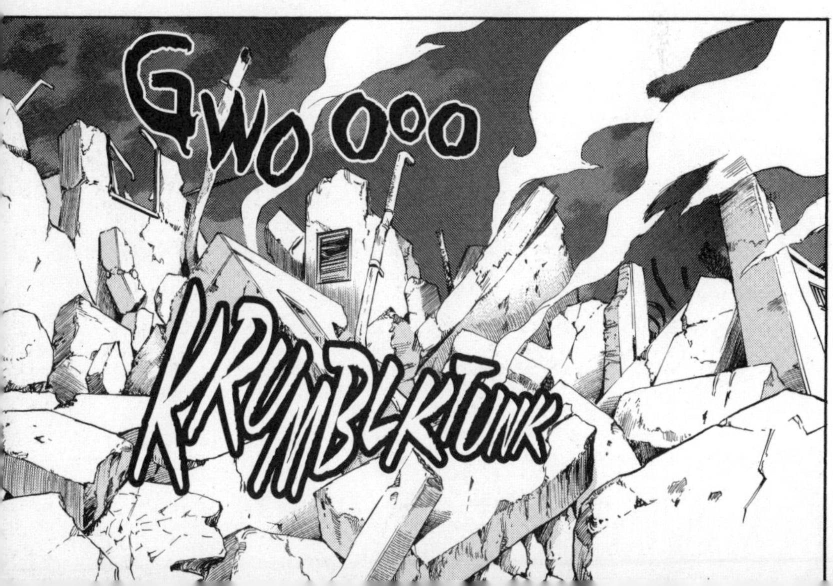
GWOOOO
KRUMBLKRUNK

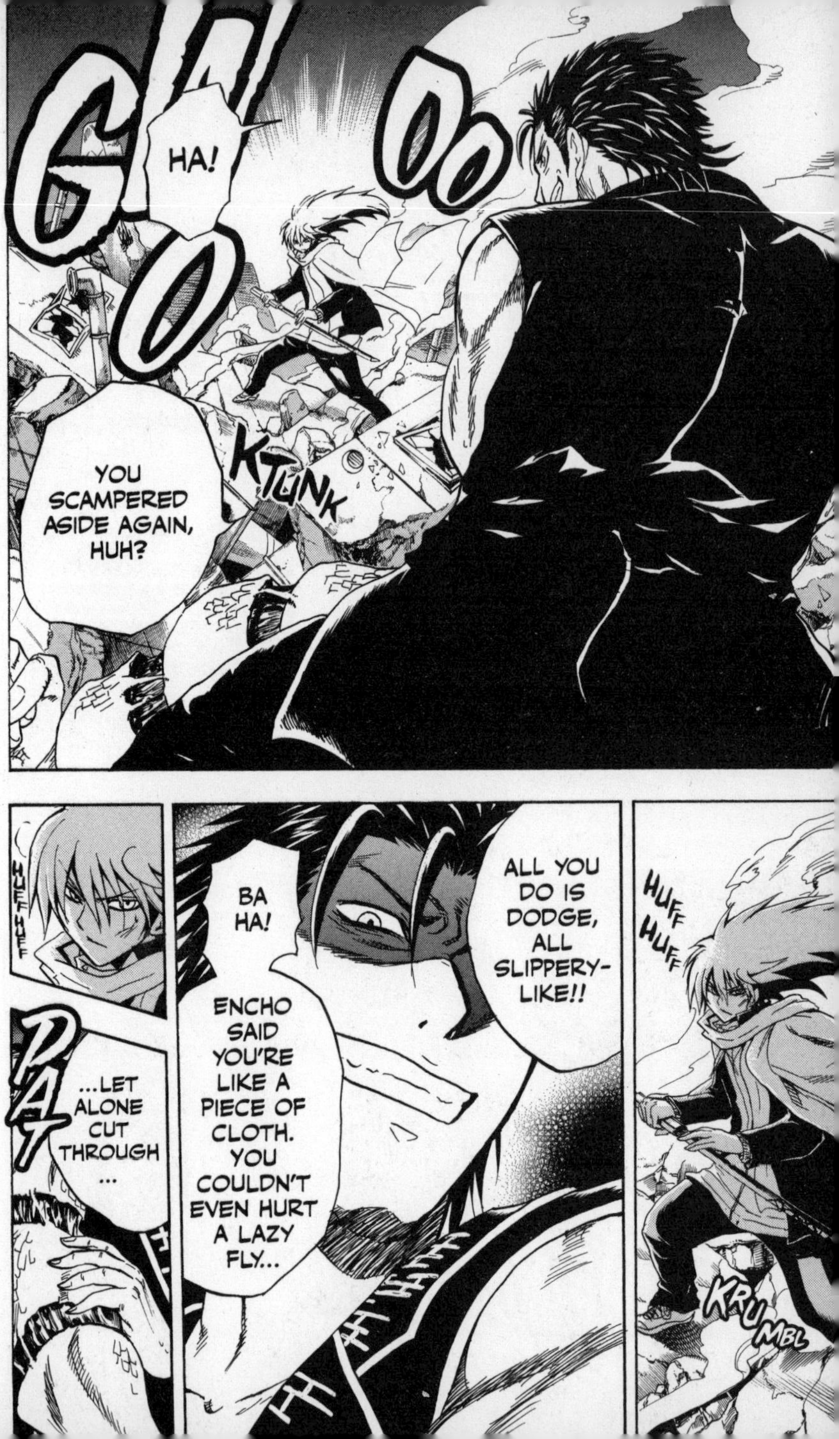
HA!
KTUNK
YOU SCAMPERED ASIDE AGAIN, HUH?
HUFF HUFF
KRUMBL
ALL YOU DO IS DODGE, ALL SLIPPERY-LIKE!!
BA HA!
ENCHO SAID YOU'RE LIKE A PIECE OF CLOTH. YOU COULDN'T EVEN HURT A LAZY FLY...
HUFF HUFF
DAT
...LET ALONE CUT THROUGH ...

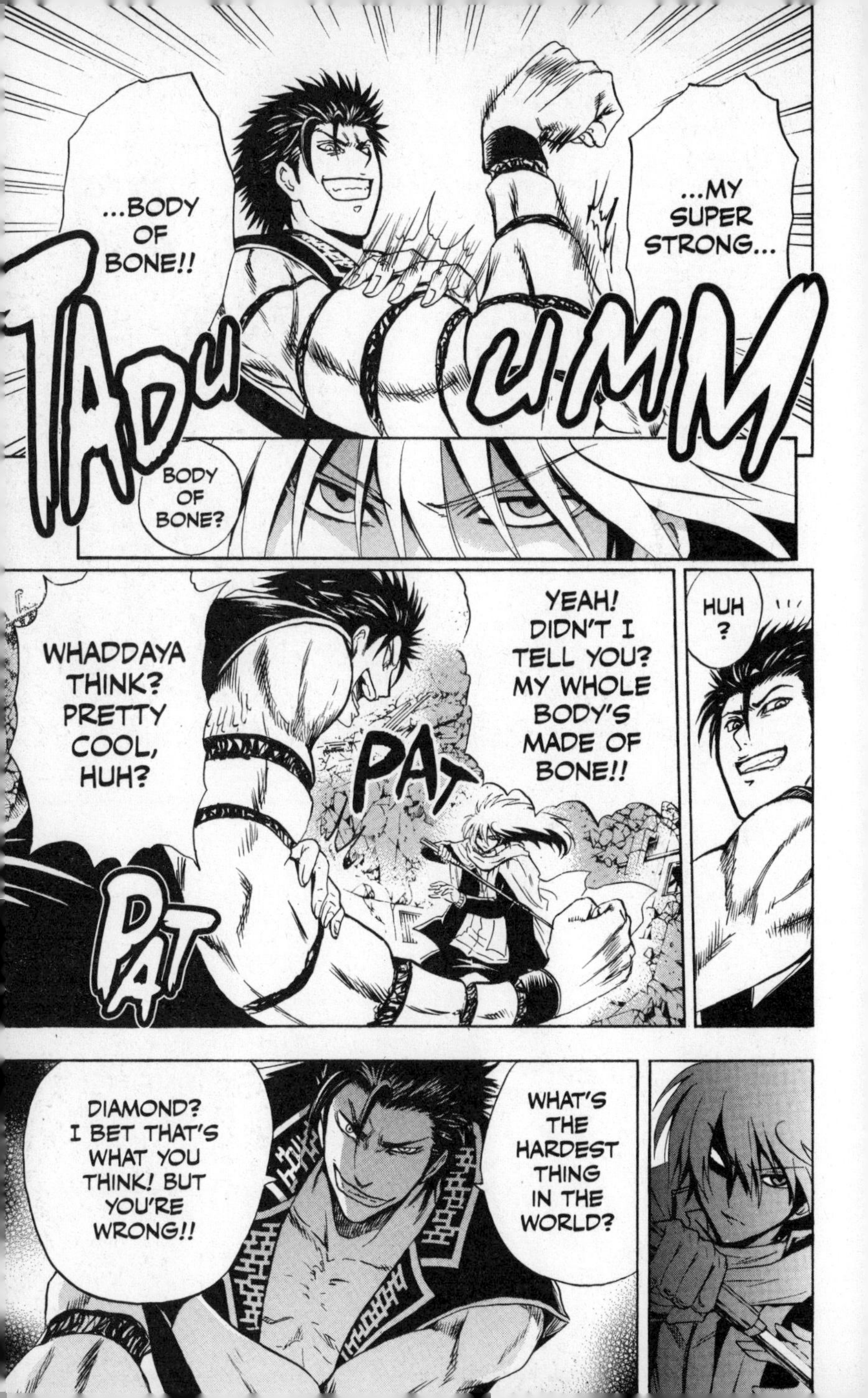
...MY SUPER STRONG...
...BODY OF BONE!!
TADUUMM
BODY OF BONE?
HUH ?
YEAH! DIDN'T I TELL YOU? MY WHOLE BODY'S MADE OF BONE!!
PAT
WHADDAYA THINK? PRETTY COOL, HUH?
PAT
WHAT'S THE HARDEST THING IN THE WORLD?
DIAMOND? I BET THAT'S WHAT YOU THINK! BUT YOU'RE WRONG!!

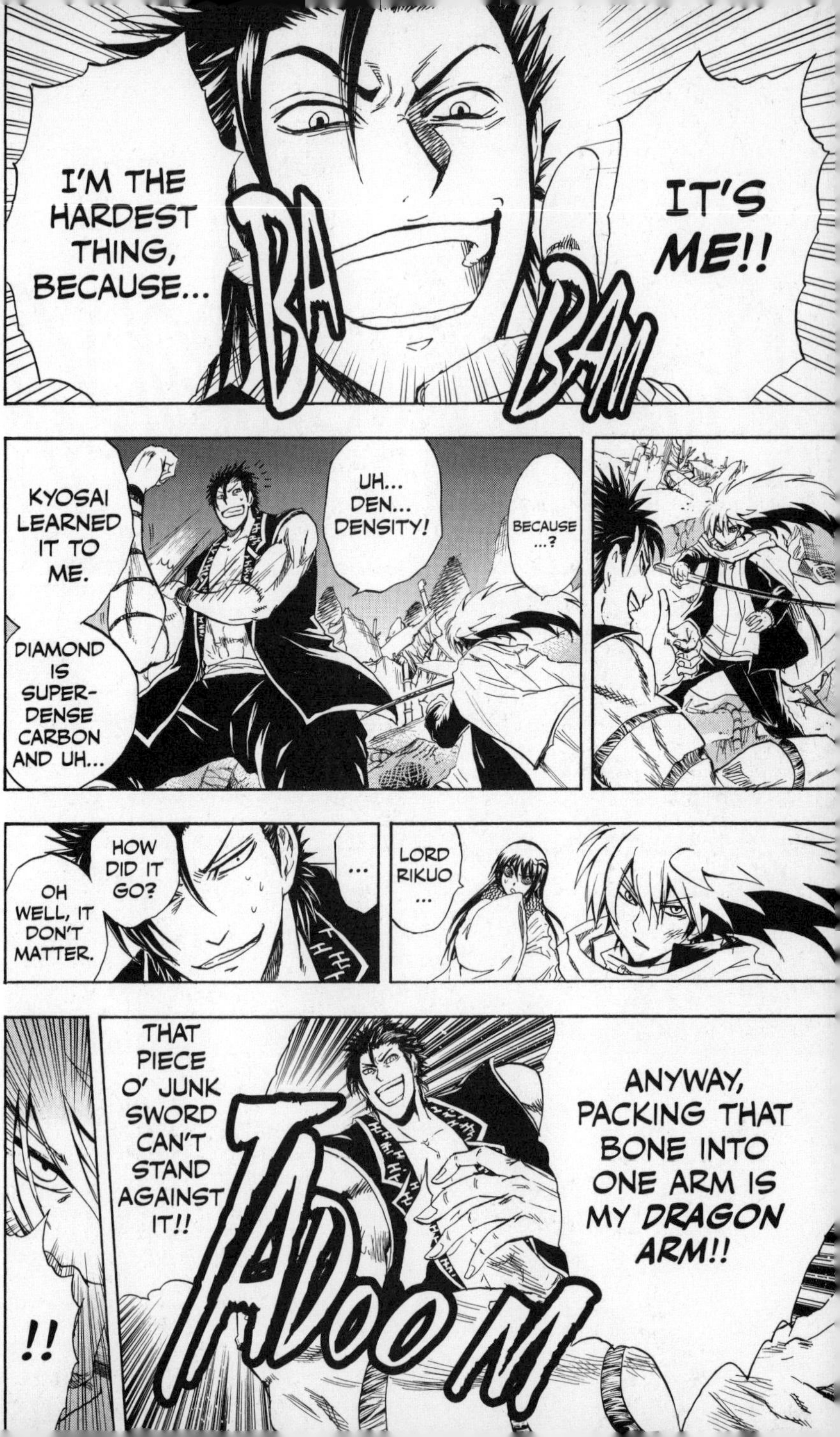
I'M THE HARDEST THING, BECAUSE...
IT'S ME!!
BA
BAM
KYOSAI LEARNED IT TO ME.
DIAMOND IS SUPER-DENSE CARBON AND UH...
BECAUSE ...?
UH... DEN... DENSITY!
LORD RIKUO ...
...
HOW DID IT GO?
OH WELL, IT DON'T MATTER.
ANYWAY, PACKING THAT BONE INTO ONE ARM IS MY DRAGON ARM!!
THAT PIECE O' JUNK SWORD CAN'T STAND AGAINST IT!!
ADOOM
!!

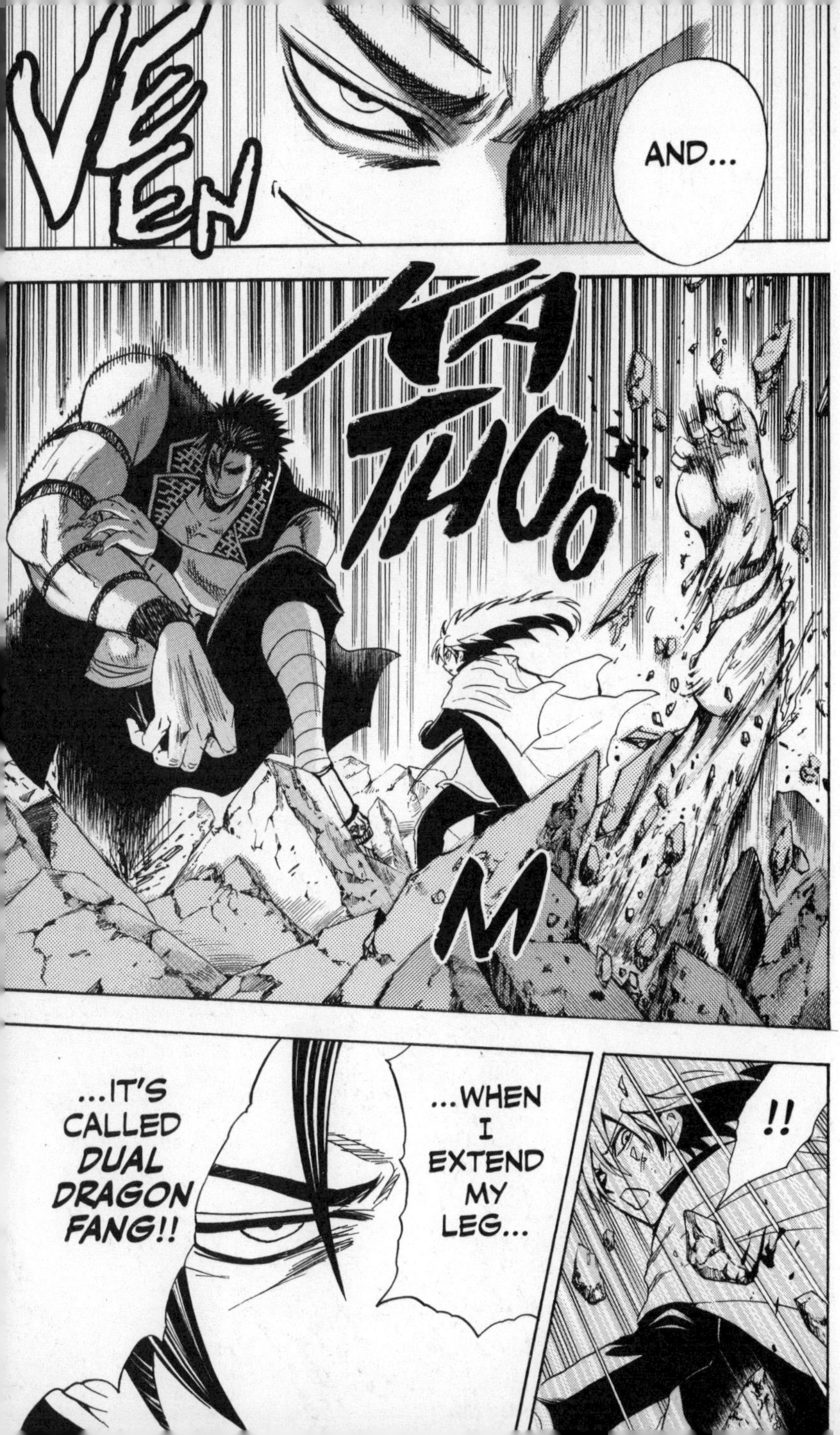
AND...
VEEN
KATHOOM
!!
...WHEN I EXTEND MY LEG...
...IT'S CALLED DUAL DRAGON FANG!!

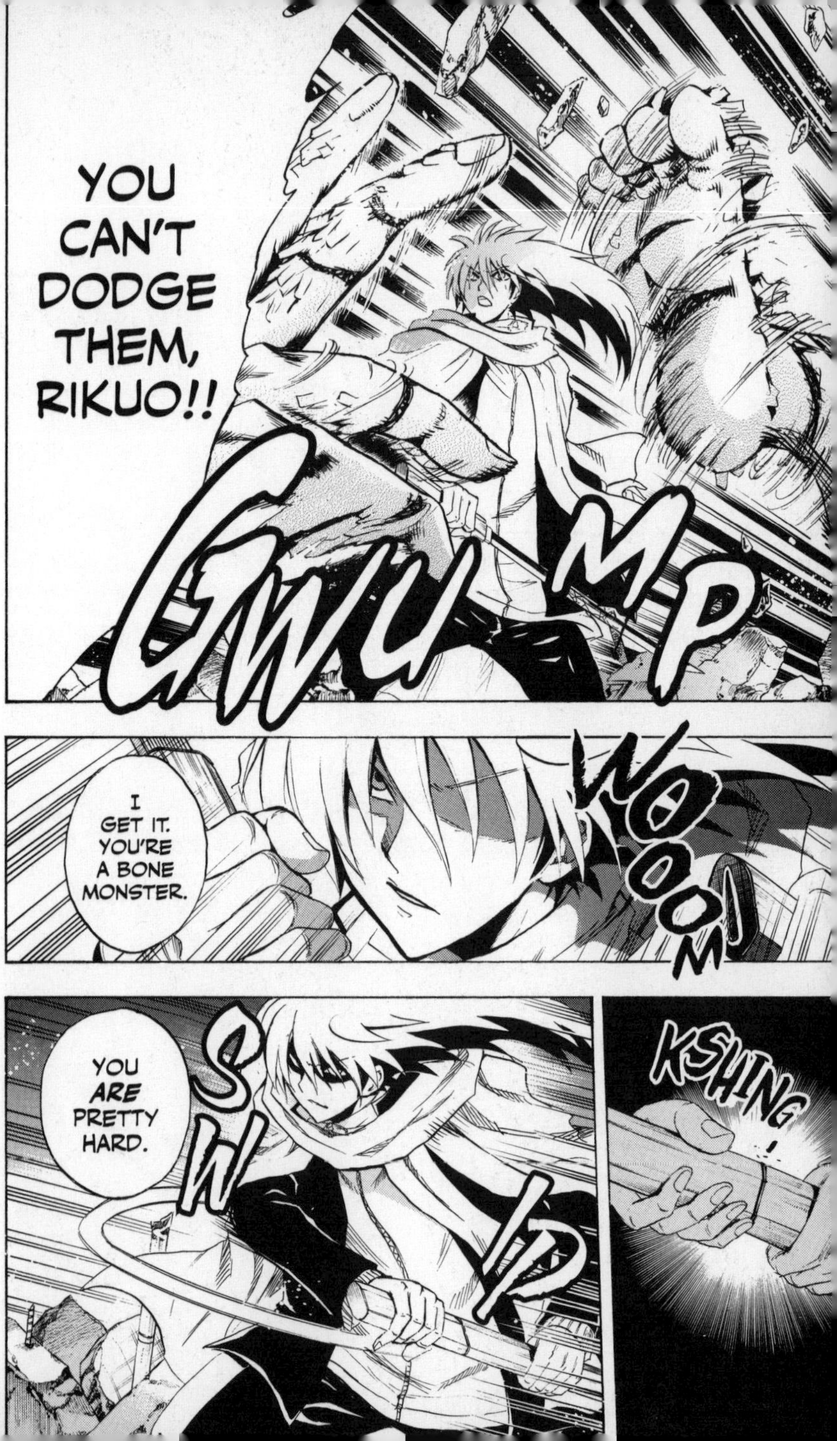
YOU CAN'T DODGE THEM, RIKUO!!
GWUMP
WOOOM
I GET IT. YOU'RE A BONE MONSTER.
KSHING
SWIP
YOU ARE PRETTY HARD.

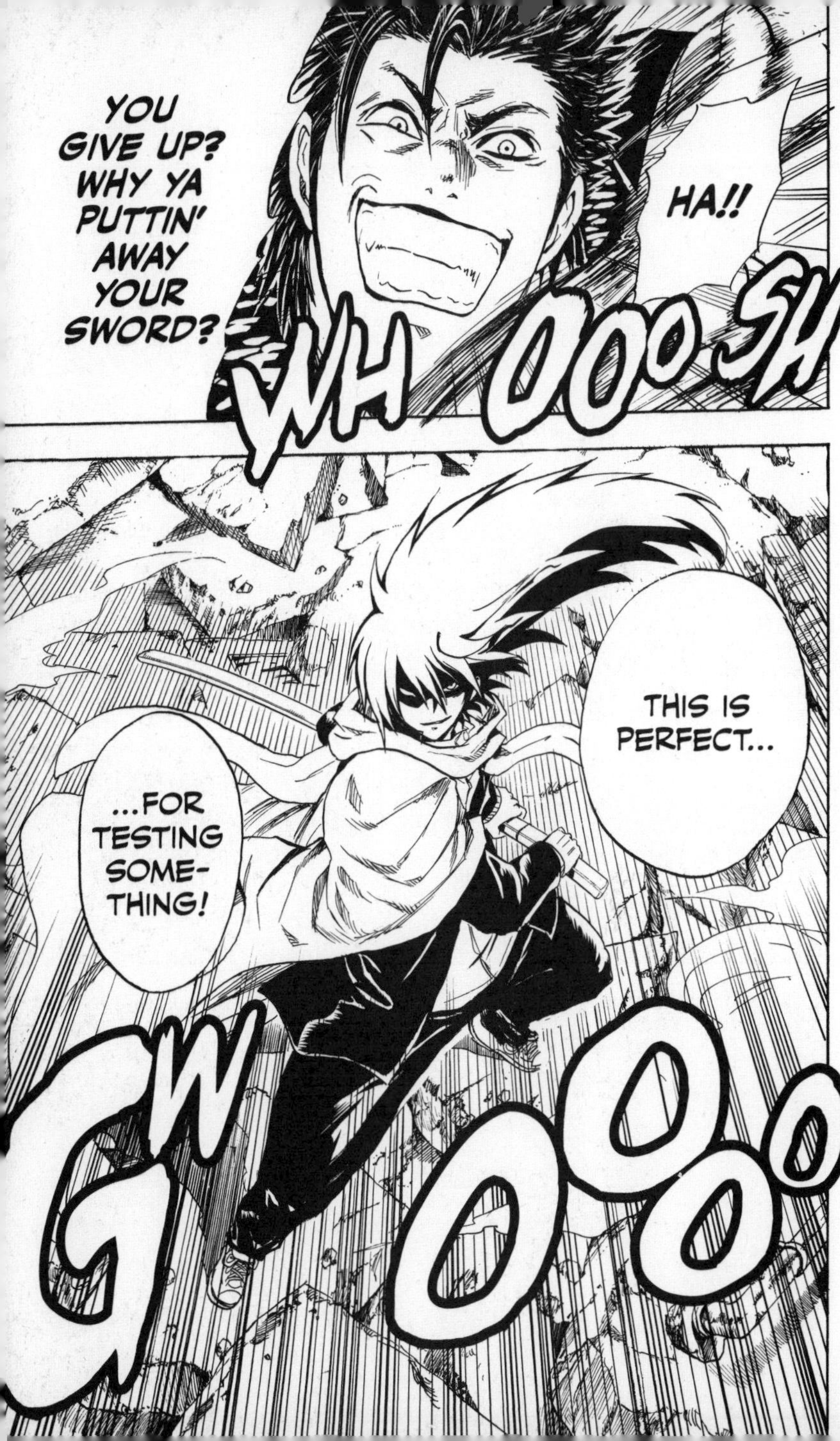
HA!!
YOU GIVE UP? WHY YA PUTTIN' AWAY YOUR SWORD?
WHOOOSH
THIS IS PERFECT...
...FOR TESTING SOME-THING!
GWOOOO

A bonus manga that's totally the opposite of the real story.

We're in the Nura Fan Club! Part 1

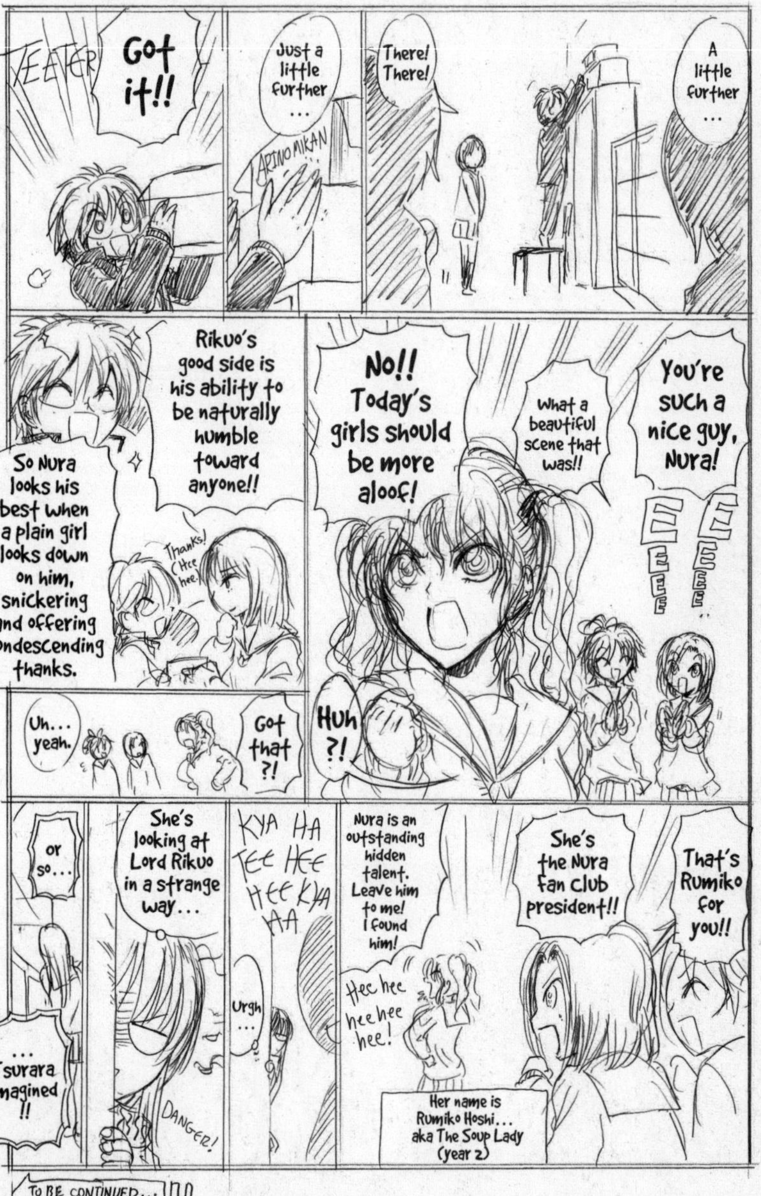
A little further...
There! There!
Just a little further...
ARINO MIKAN
Got it!!
TEETER
You're such a nice guy, Nura!
What a beautiful scene that was!!
No!! Today's girls should be more aloof!
EEEEE
EEEEE
Huh?!
Rikuo's good side is his ability to be naturally humble toward anyone!!
So Nura looks his best when a plain girl looks down on him, snickering and offering condescending thanks.
Thanks! (Hee hee.)
Got that?!
Uh... yeah.
That's Rumiko for you!!
She's the Nura fan club president!!
Nura is an outstanding hidden talent. Leave him to me! I found him!
Hee hee hee hee hee!
Her name is Rumiko Hoshi... aka The Soup Lady (year 2)
KYA HA TEE HEE HEE KYA HA
Urgh...
She's looking at Lord Rikuo in a strange way...
DANGER!
or so...
...Tsurara imagined!!

TO BE CONTINUED... 100

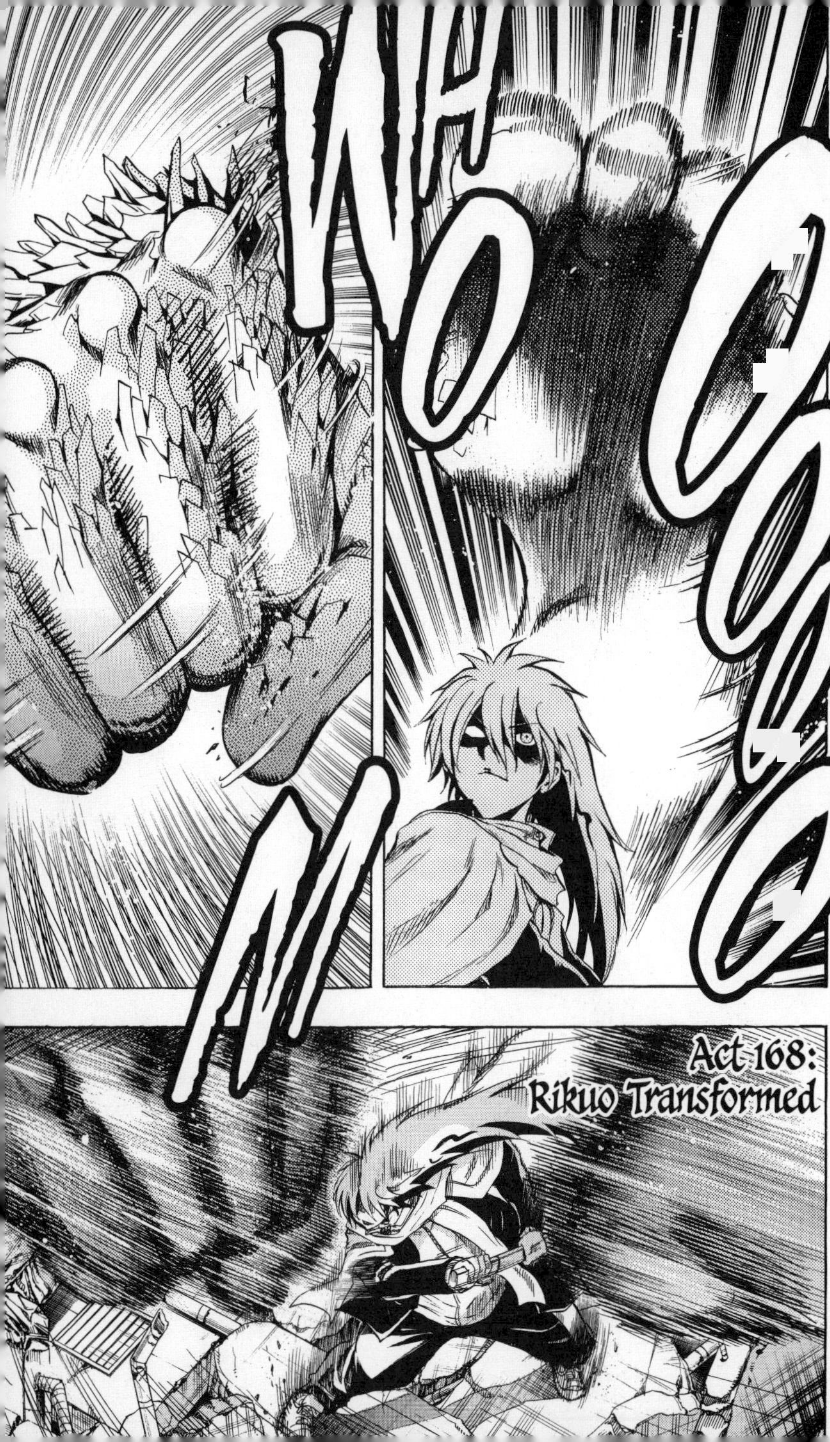
WHOOOOOOM
Act 168:
Rikuo Transformed

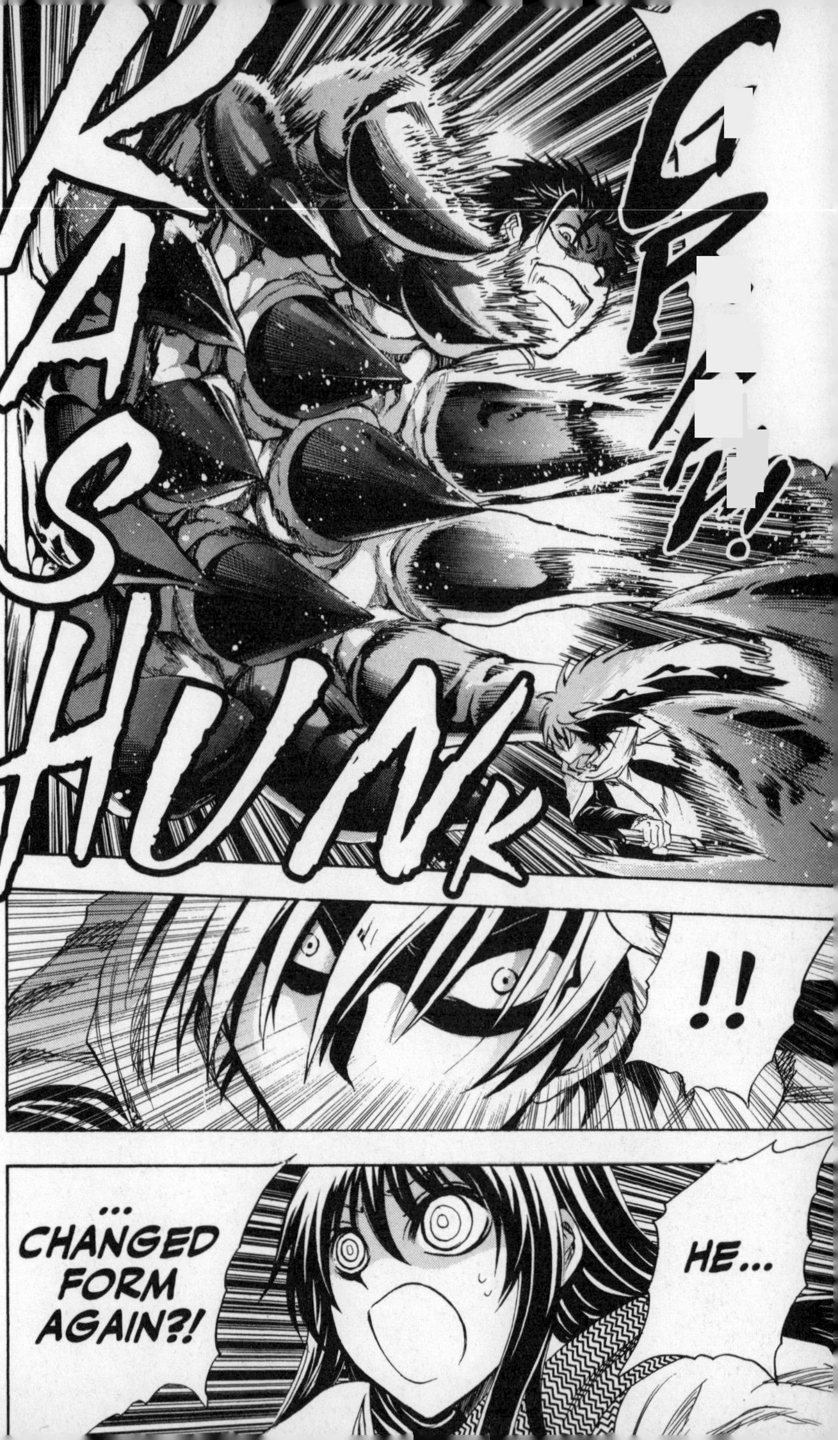
KASHUNK
!!
HE...
...CHANGED FORM AGAIN?!

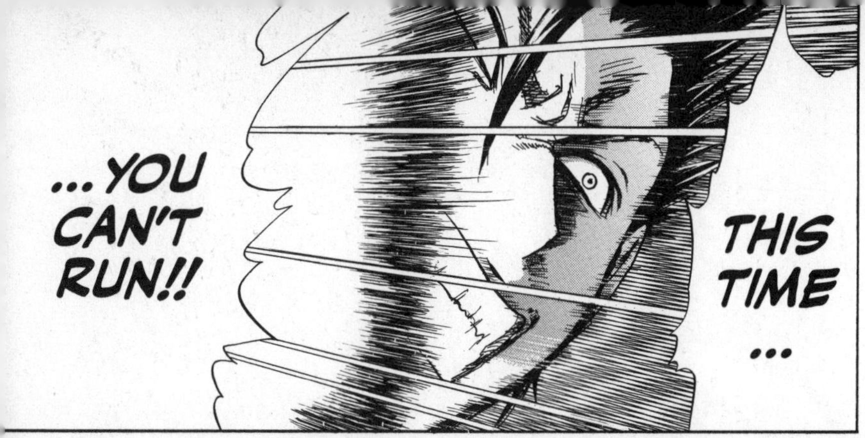
THIS TIME ...
...YOU CAN'T RUN!!
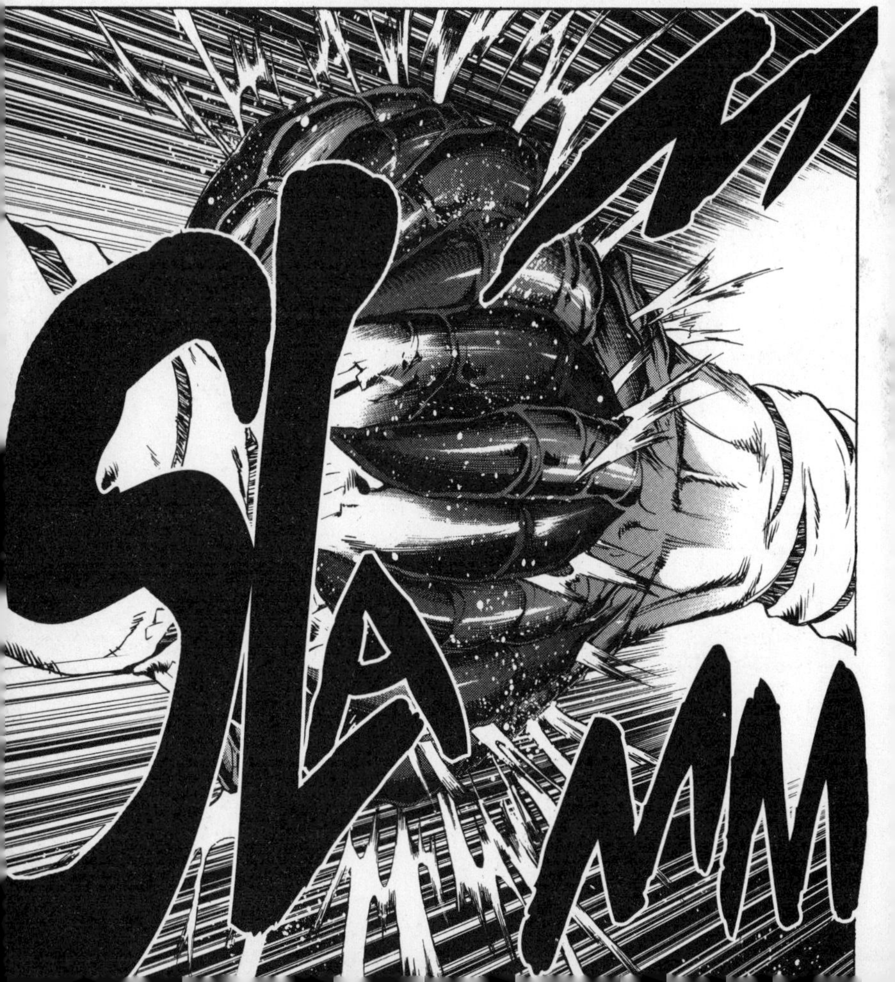
SLAMM

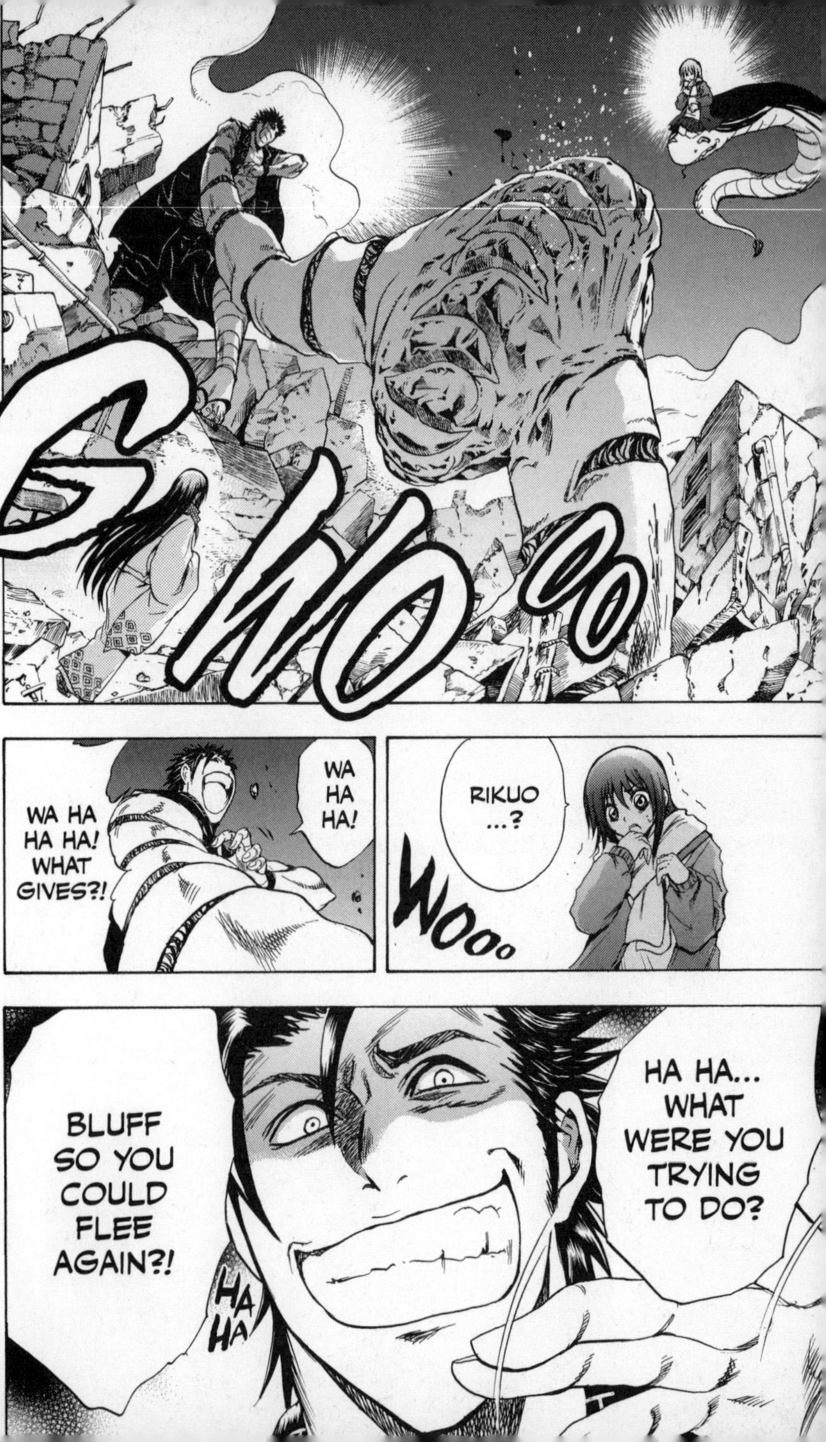
GWOo
RIKUO ...?
WOOo
WA HA HA!
WA HA HA HA! WHAT GIVES?!
HA HA... WHAT WERE YOU TRYING TO DO?
BLUFF SO YOU COULD FLEE AGAIN?!
HA HA

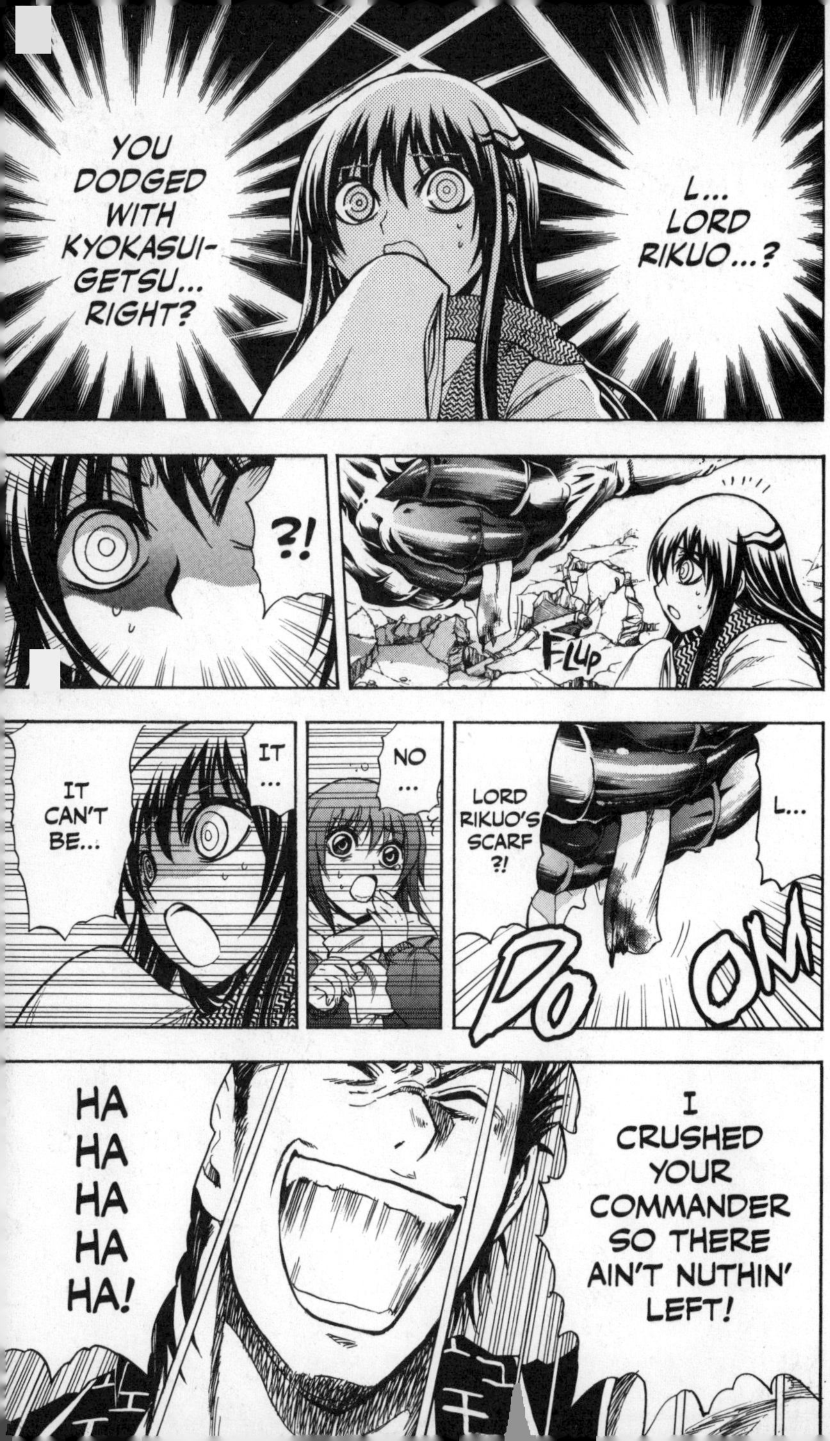

L... LORD RIKUO...?
YOU DODGED WITH KYOKASUI-GETSU... RIGHT?
FLLUP
?!
L...
LORD RIKUO'S SCARF ?!
DOOM
NO ...
IT ...
IT CAN'T BE...
I CRUSHED YOUR COMMANDER SO THERE AIN'T NUTHIN' LEFT!
HA HA HA HA HA HA!

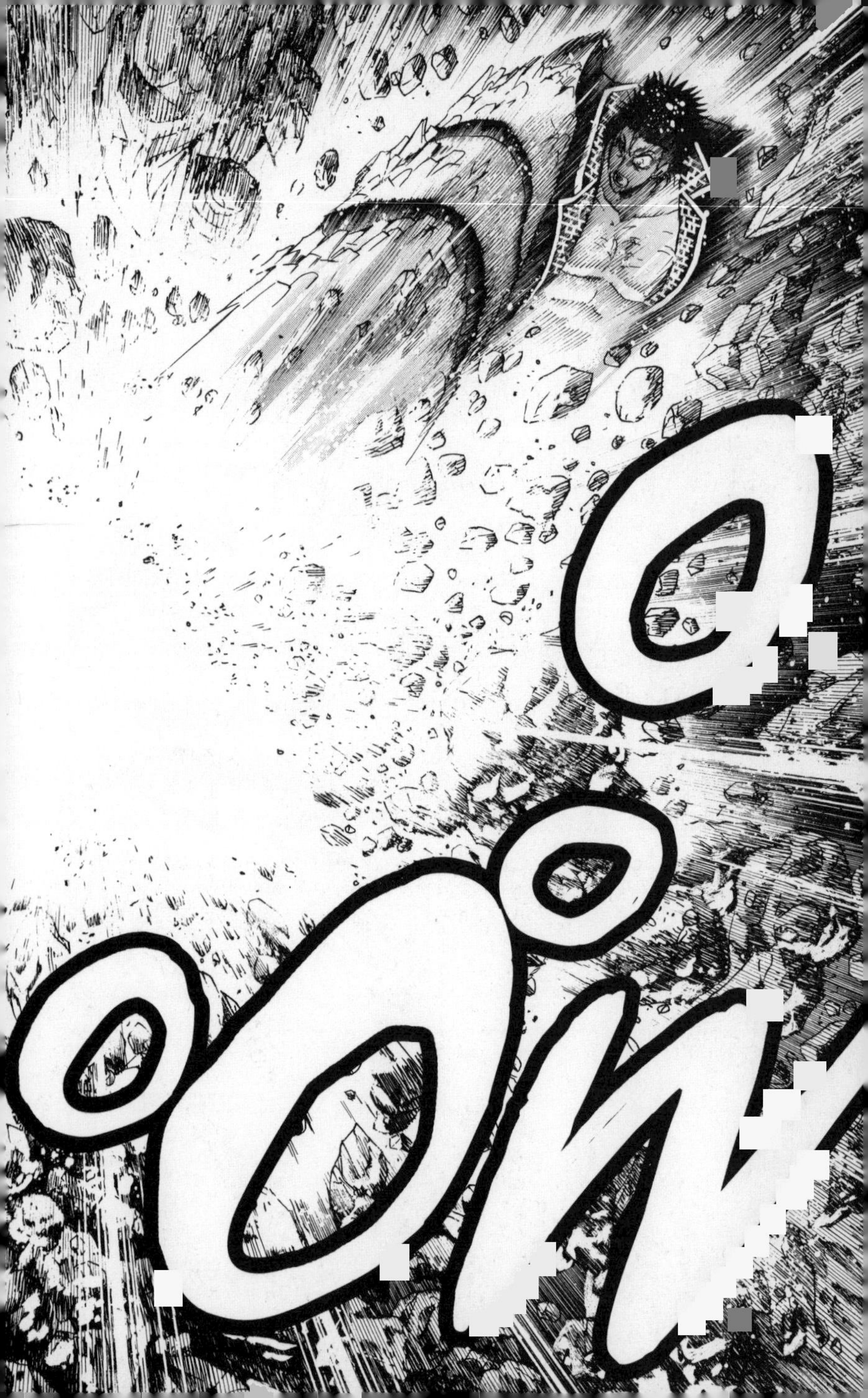

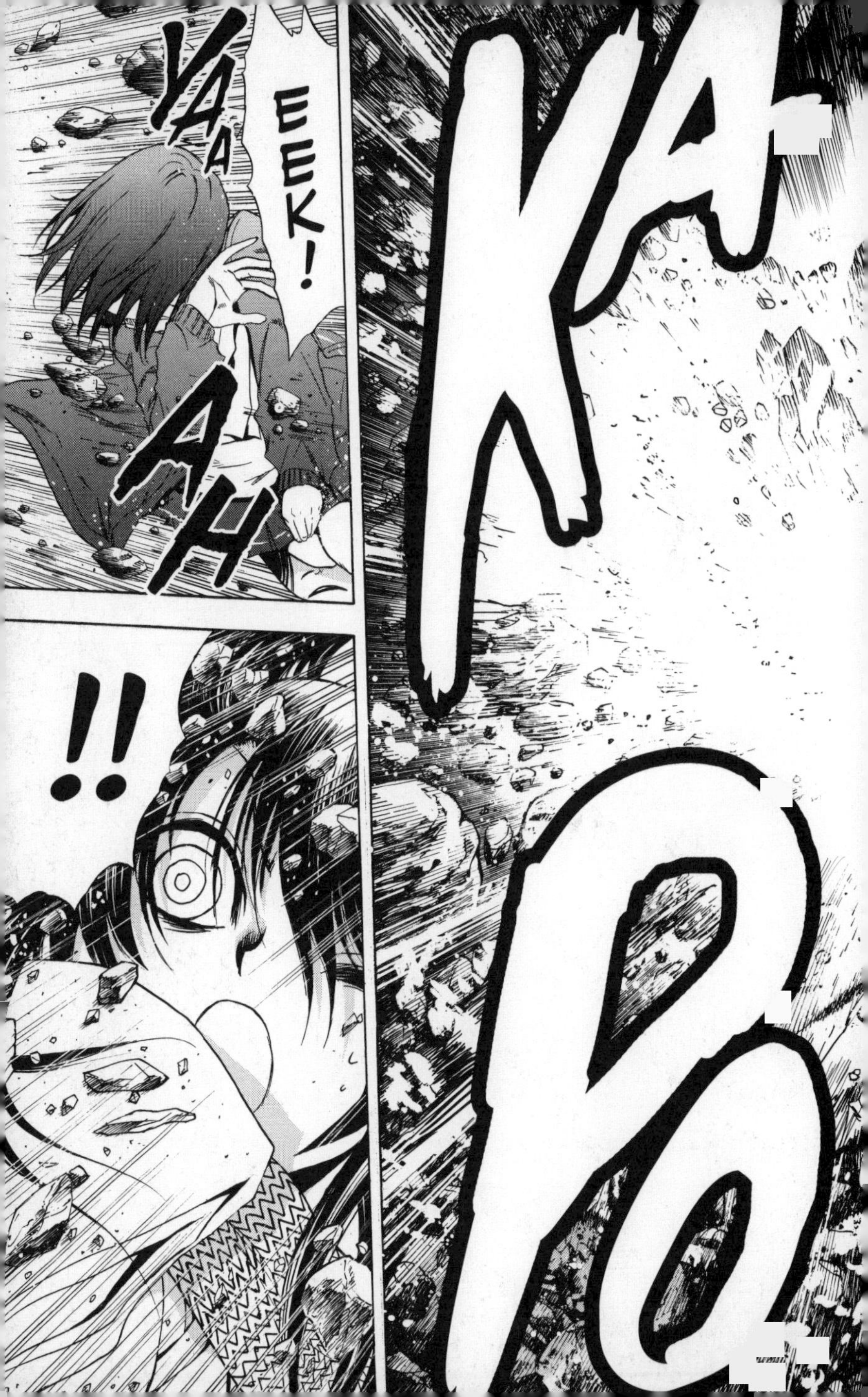
KA
BO
EEK!
YAAAH
!!

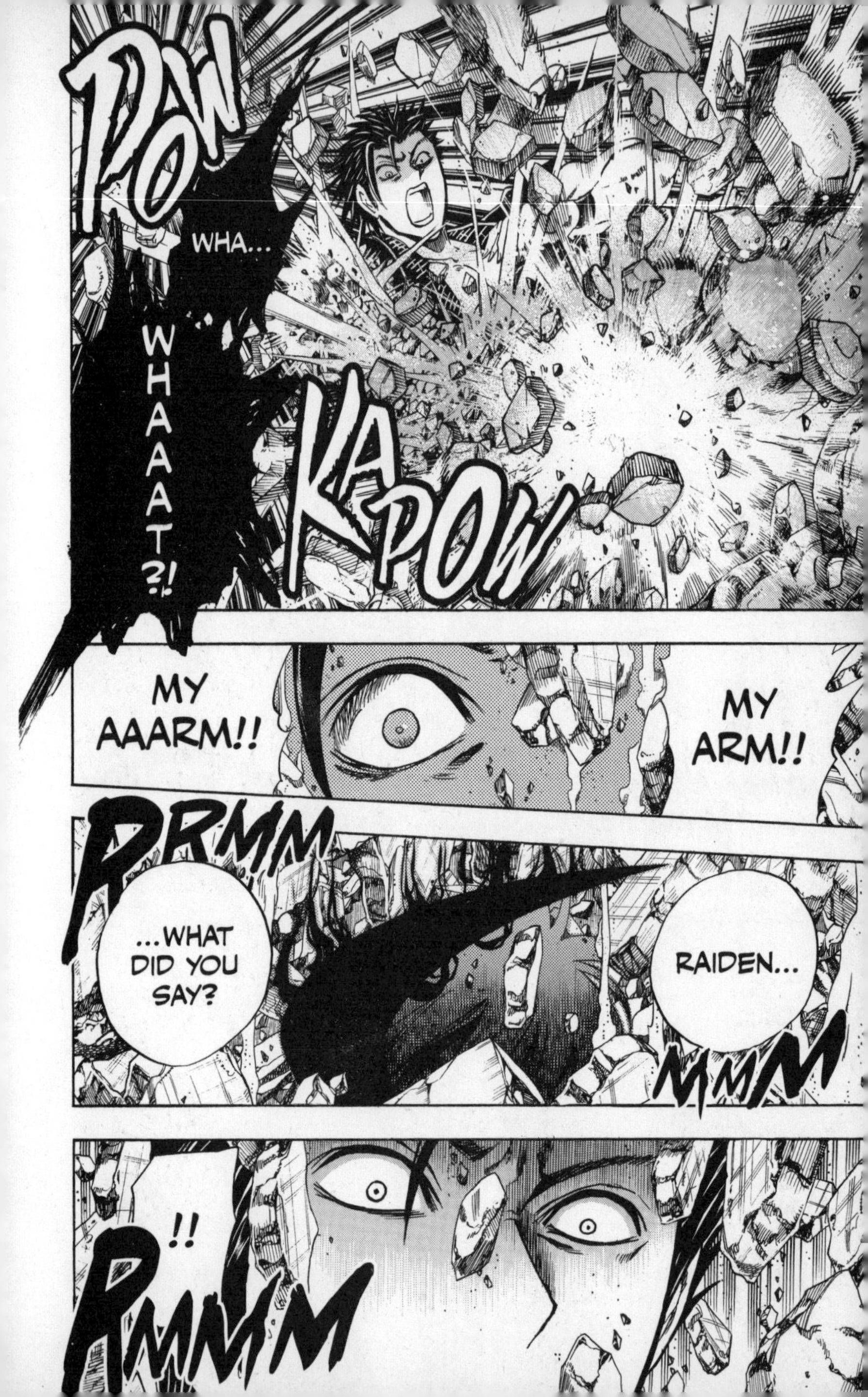
POW
WHA...
WHAAAAT?!
KA POW
MY ARM!!
MY AAARM!!
RAIDEN...
...WHAT DID YOU SAY?
RRMM
MMM
!!
RMMM

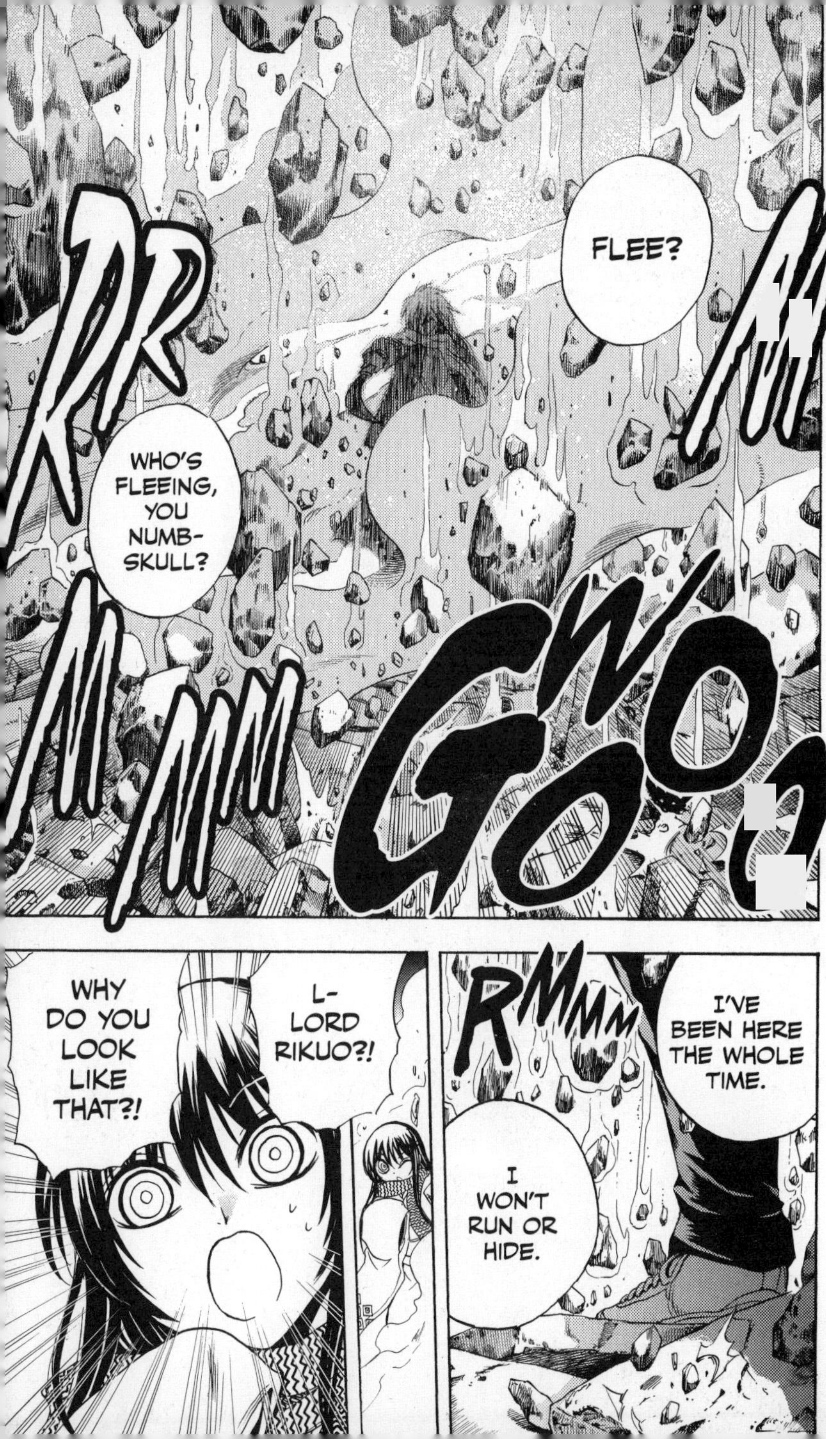
FLEE?
WHO'S FLEEING, YOU NUMB-SKULL?
I'VE BEEN HERE THE WHOLE TIME.
I WON'T RUN OR HIDE.
L-LORD RIKUO?!
WHY DO YOU LOOK LIKE THAT?!

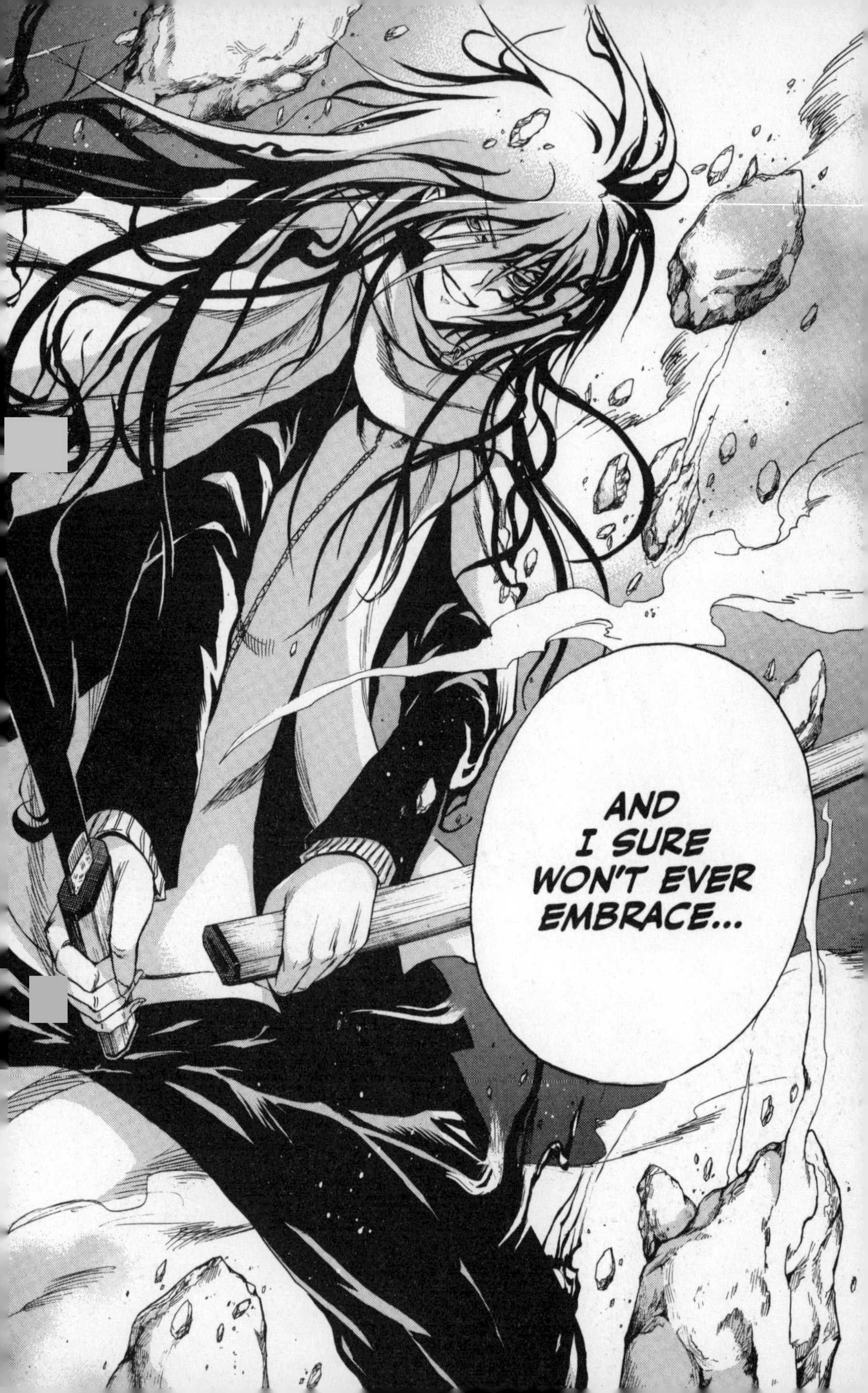
AND I SURE WON'T EVER EMBRACE...

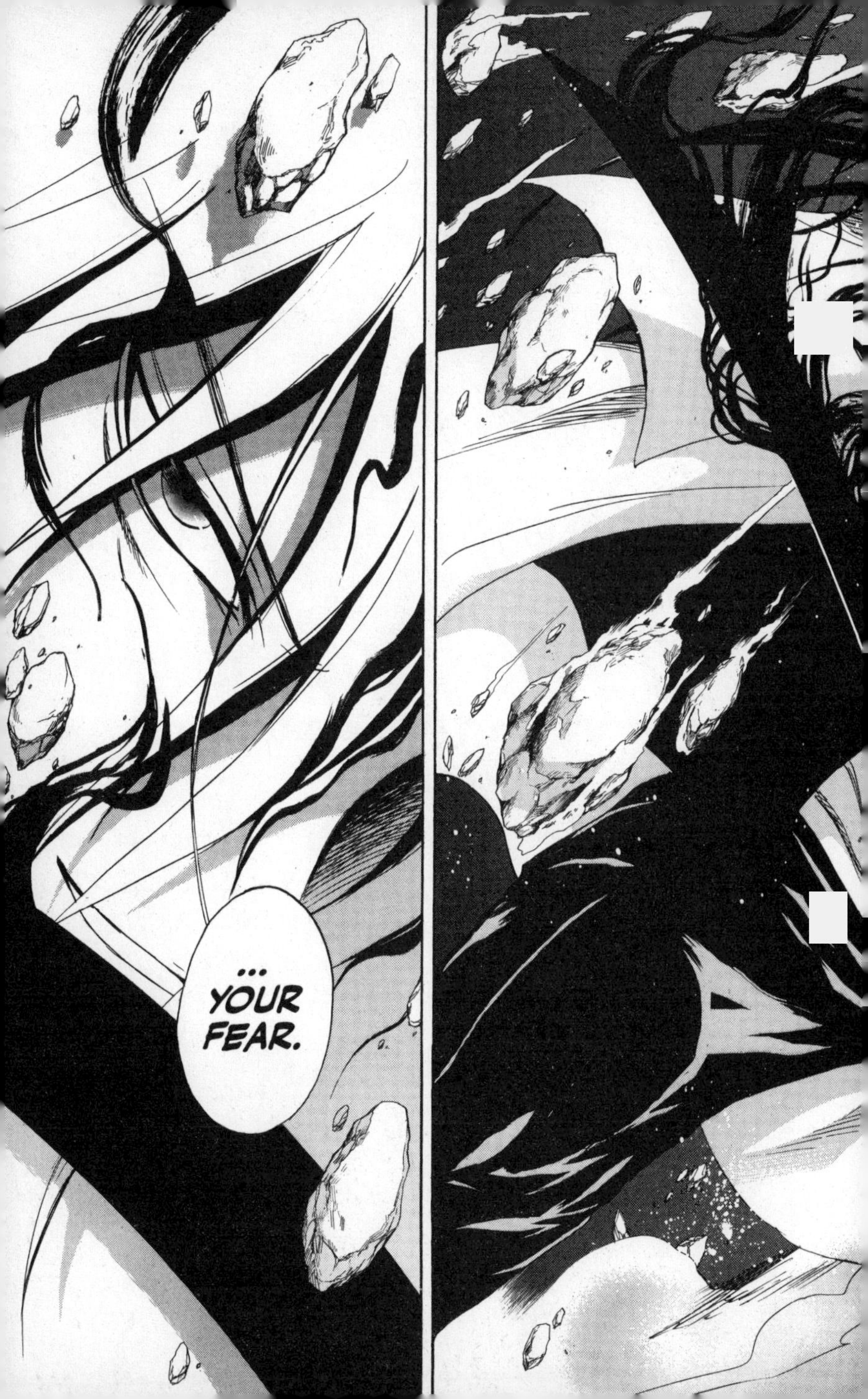
... YOUR FEAR.

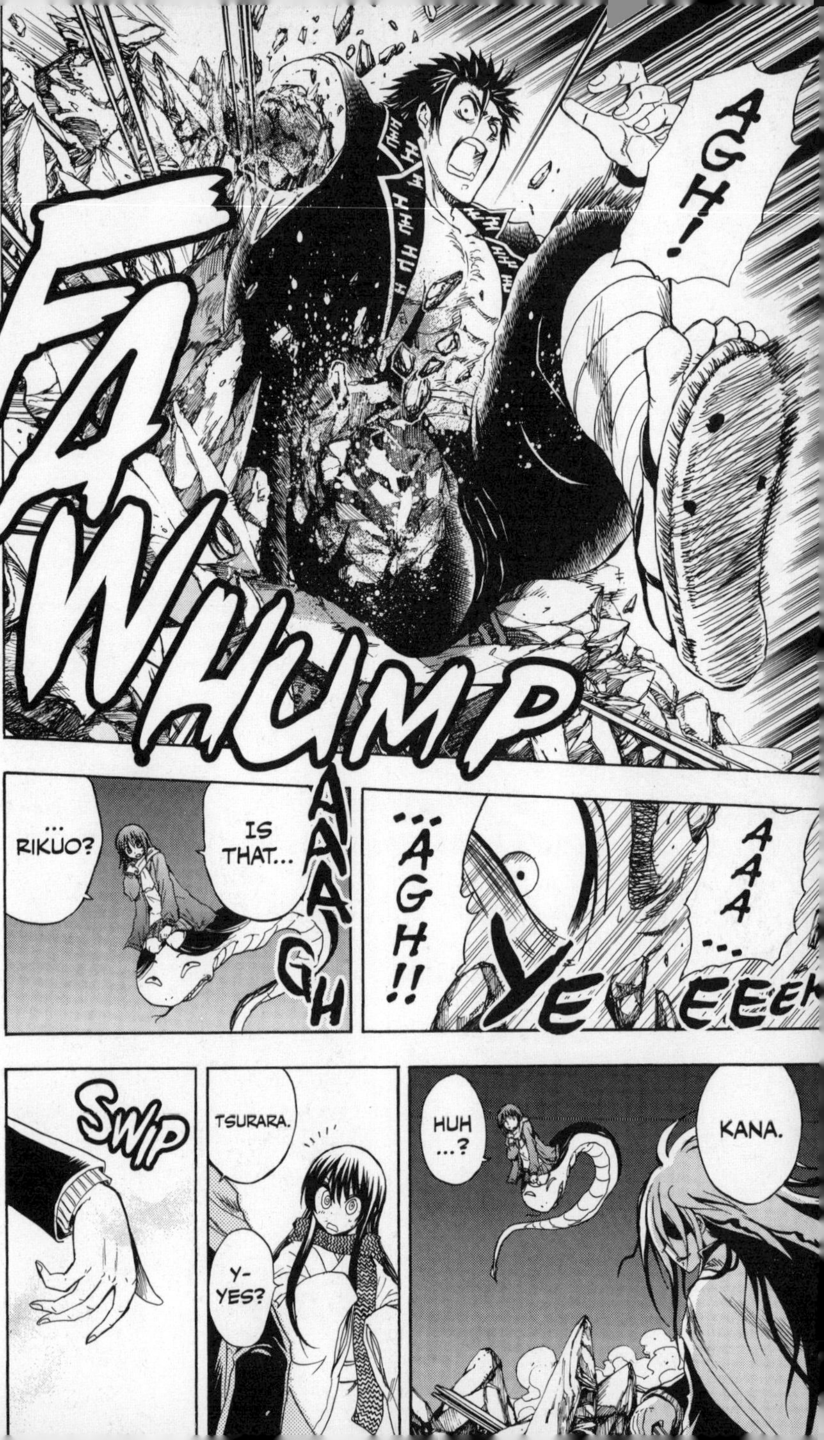
AGH!
WHUMP
AAA...
...ÄGH!!
YEEEE
IS THAT...
...RIKUO?
AAAAGH
KANA.
HUH...?
TSURARA.
Y-YES?
SWIP

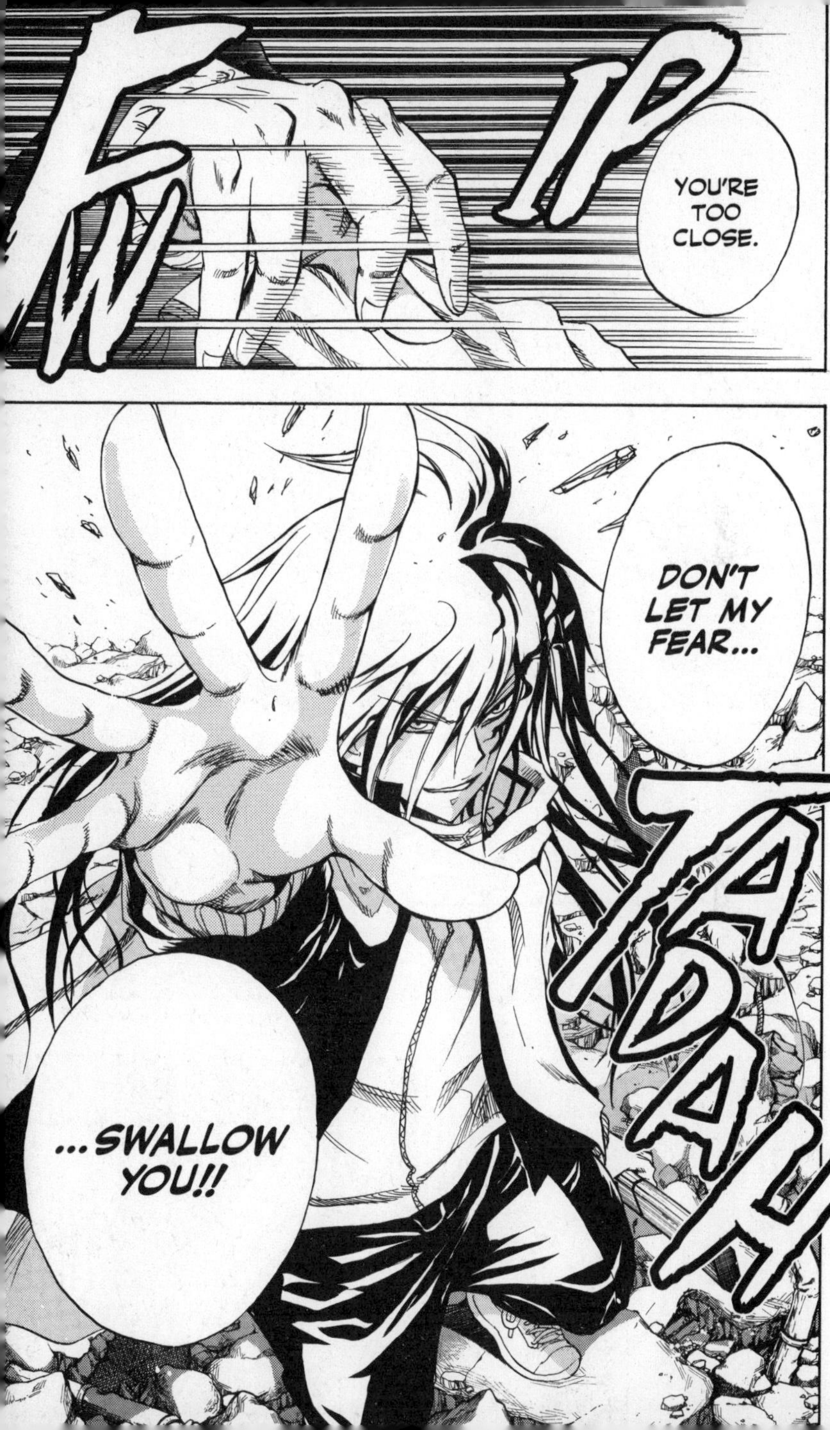

FWIP
YOU'RE TOO CLOSE.
DON'T LET MY FEAR...
TADAH
...SWALLOW YOU!!

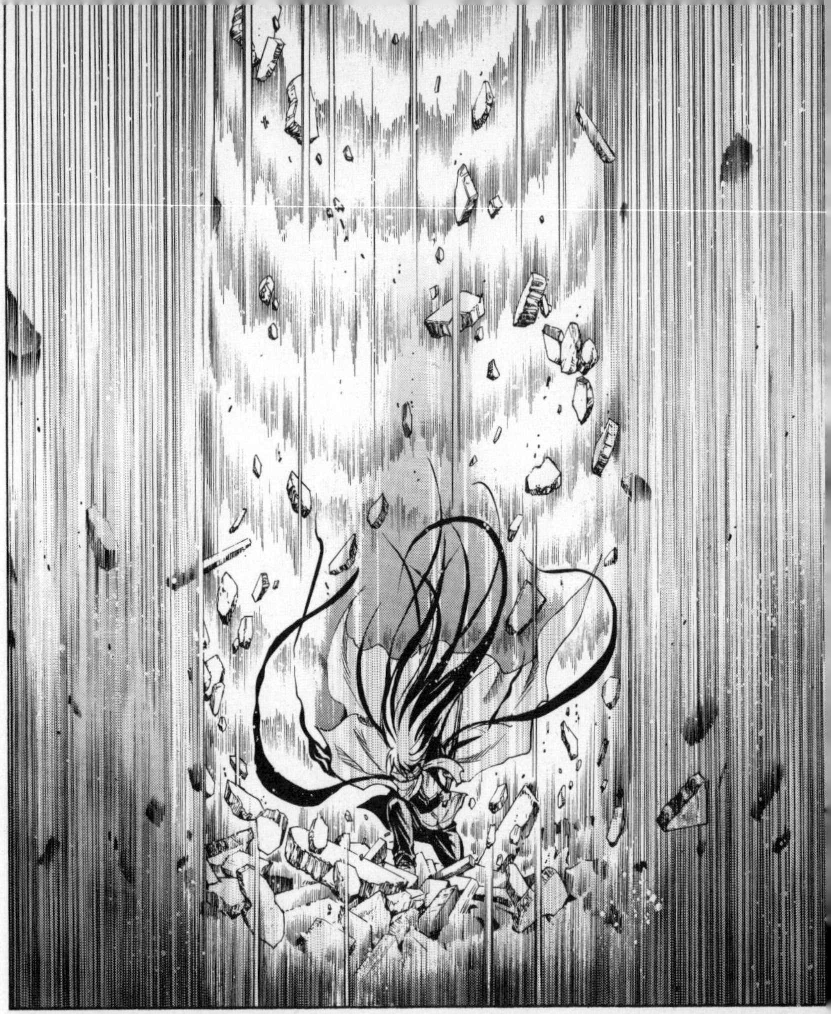
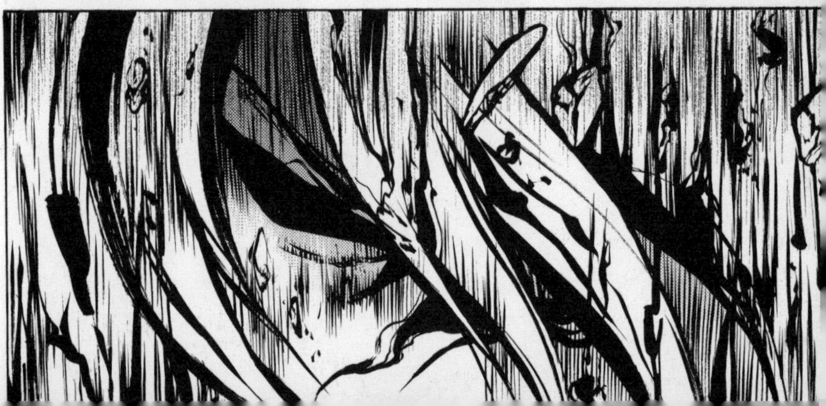

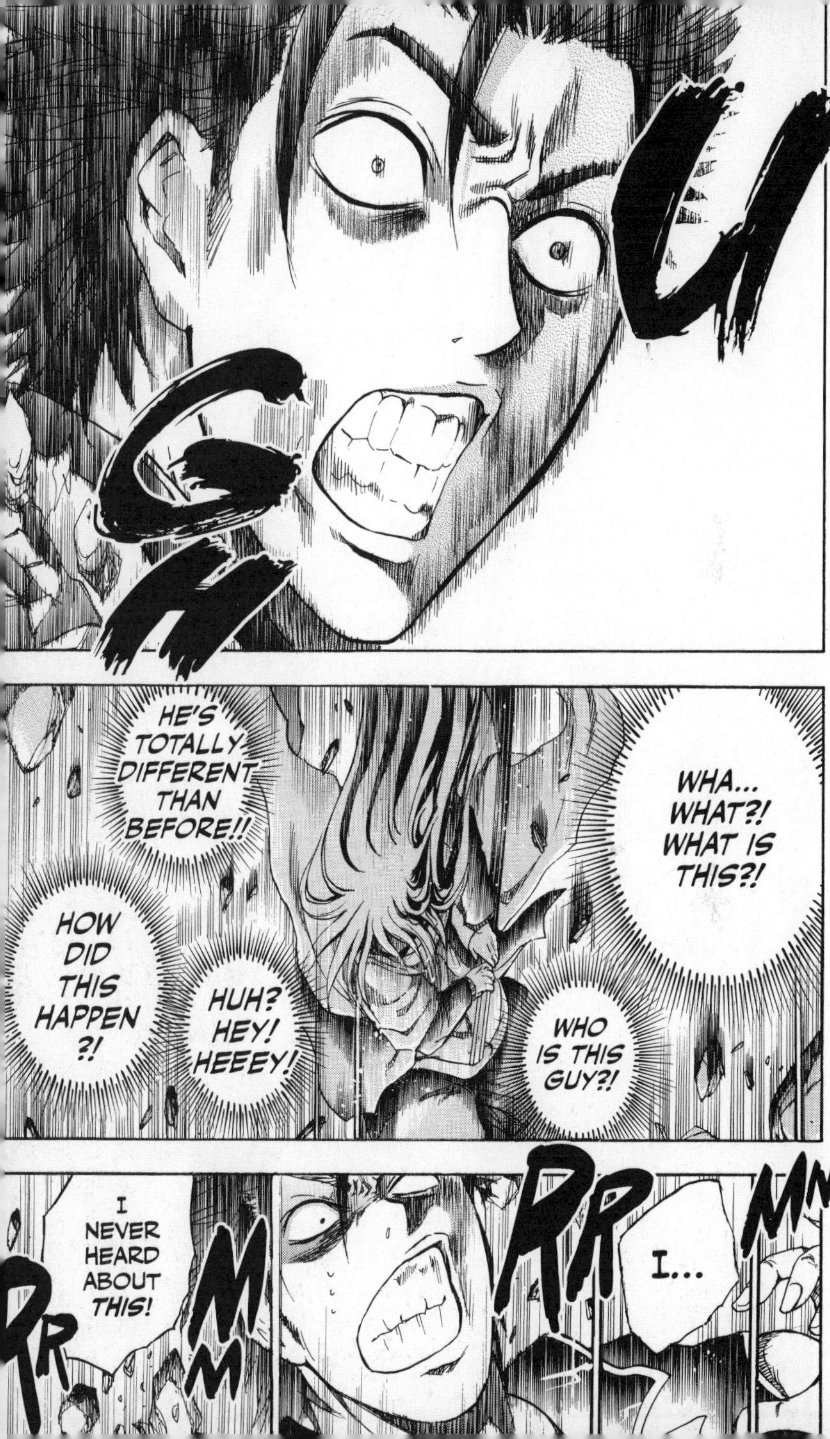
WHA... WHAT?! WHAT IS THIS?!
HE'S TOTALLY DIFFERENT THAN BEFORE!!
WHO IS THIS GUY?!
HUH? HEY! HEEEY!
HOW DID THIS HAPPEN?!
I...
I NEVER HEARD ABOUT THIS!

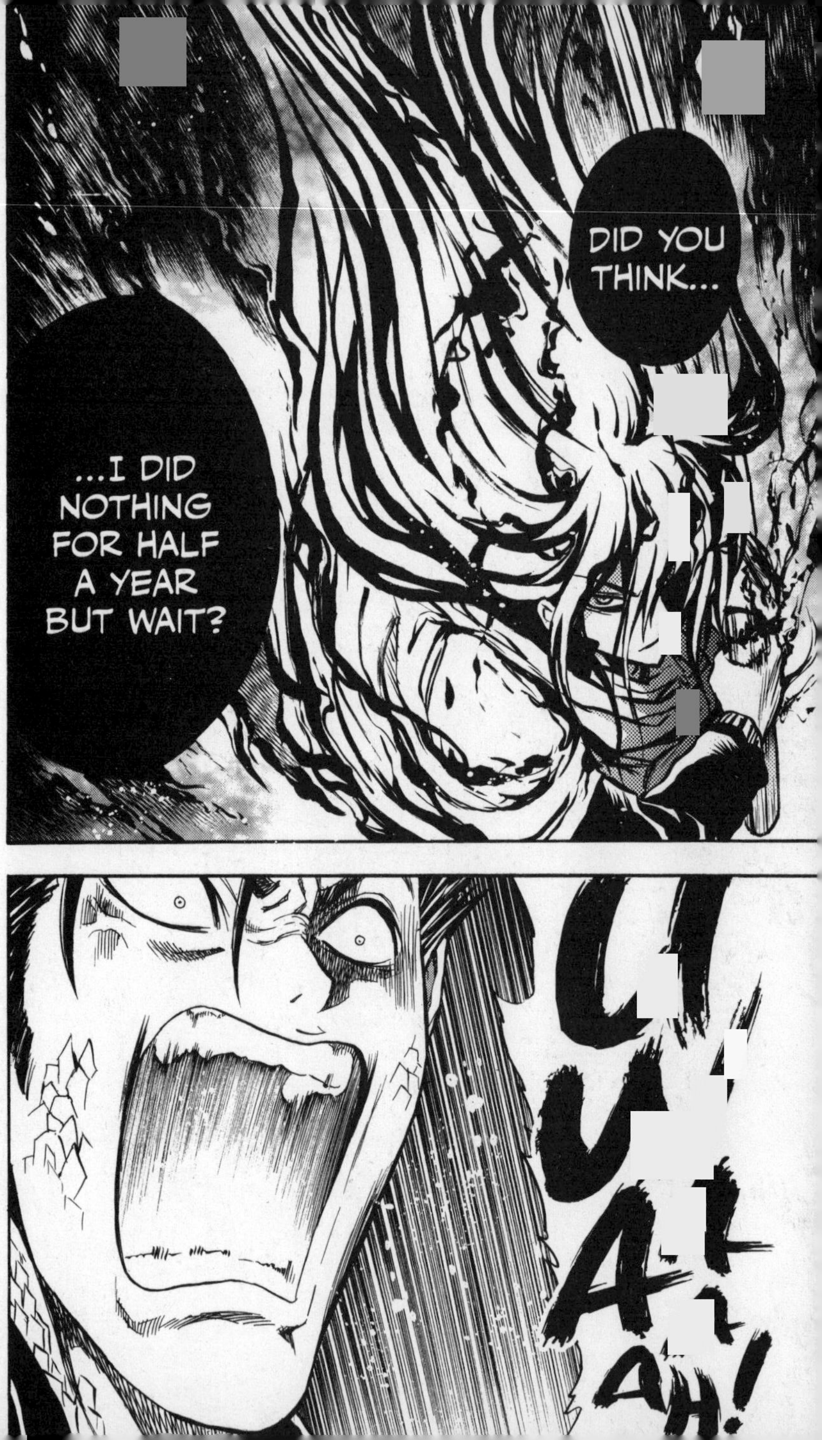
DID YOU THINK...
...I DID NOTHING FOR HALF A YEAR BUT WAIT?

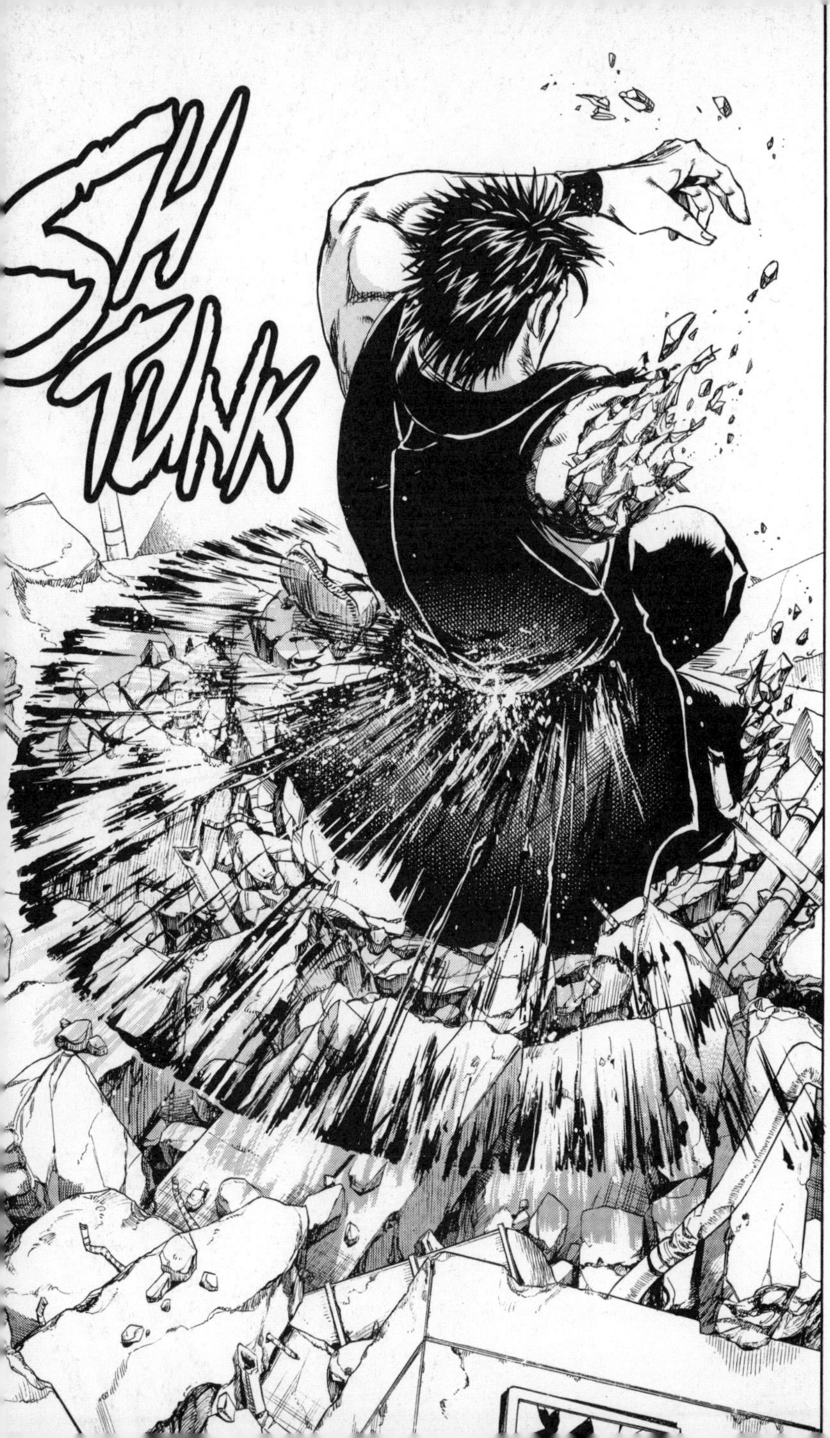
SHUNK

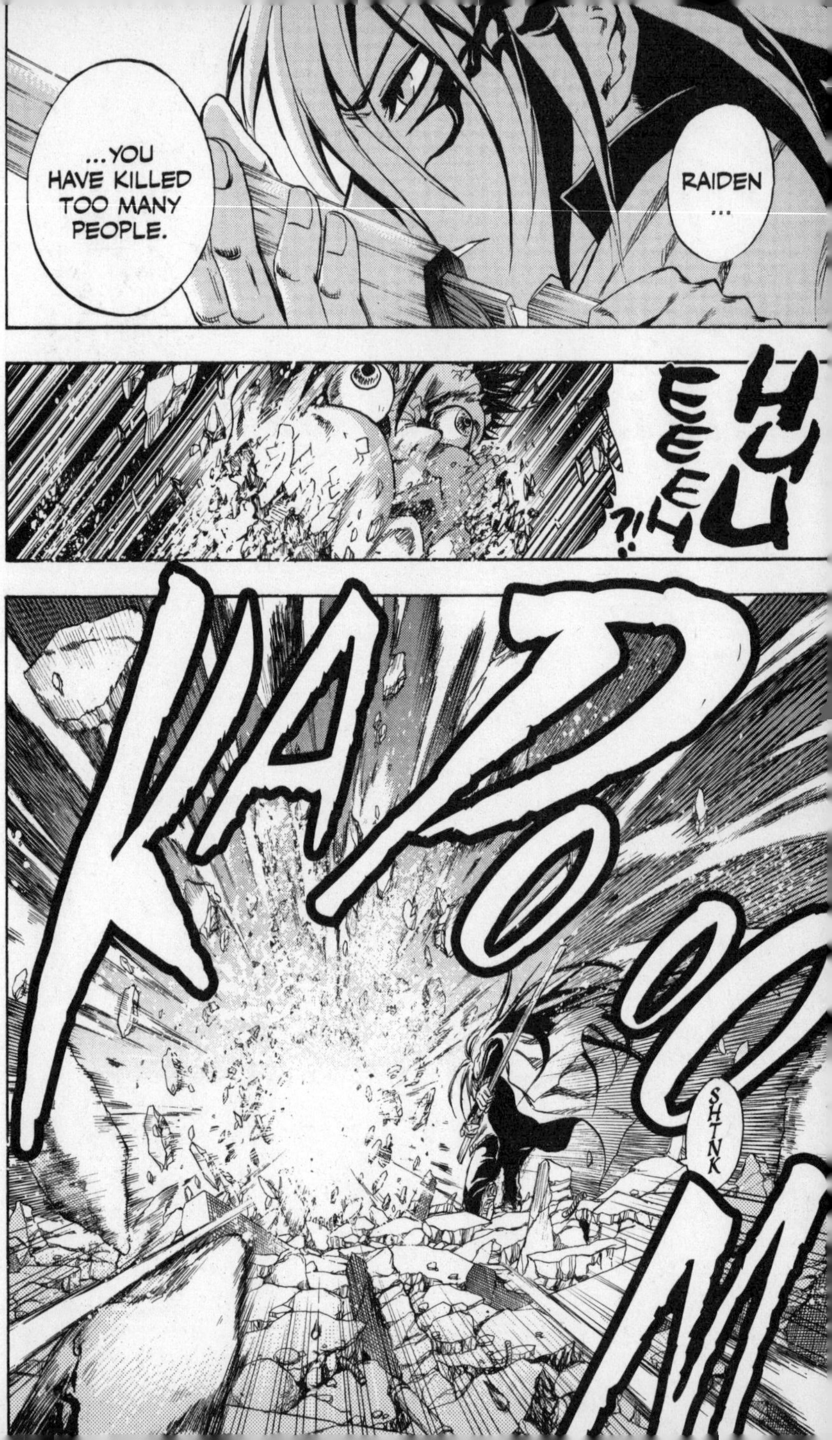
RAIDEN...
...YOU HAVE KILLED TOO MANY PEOPLE.
HUUEEEEH?!
KA-BOOM
SHTNK

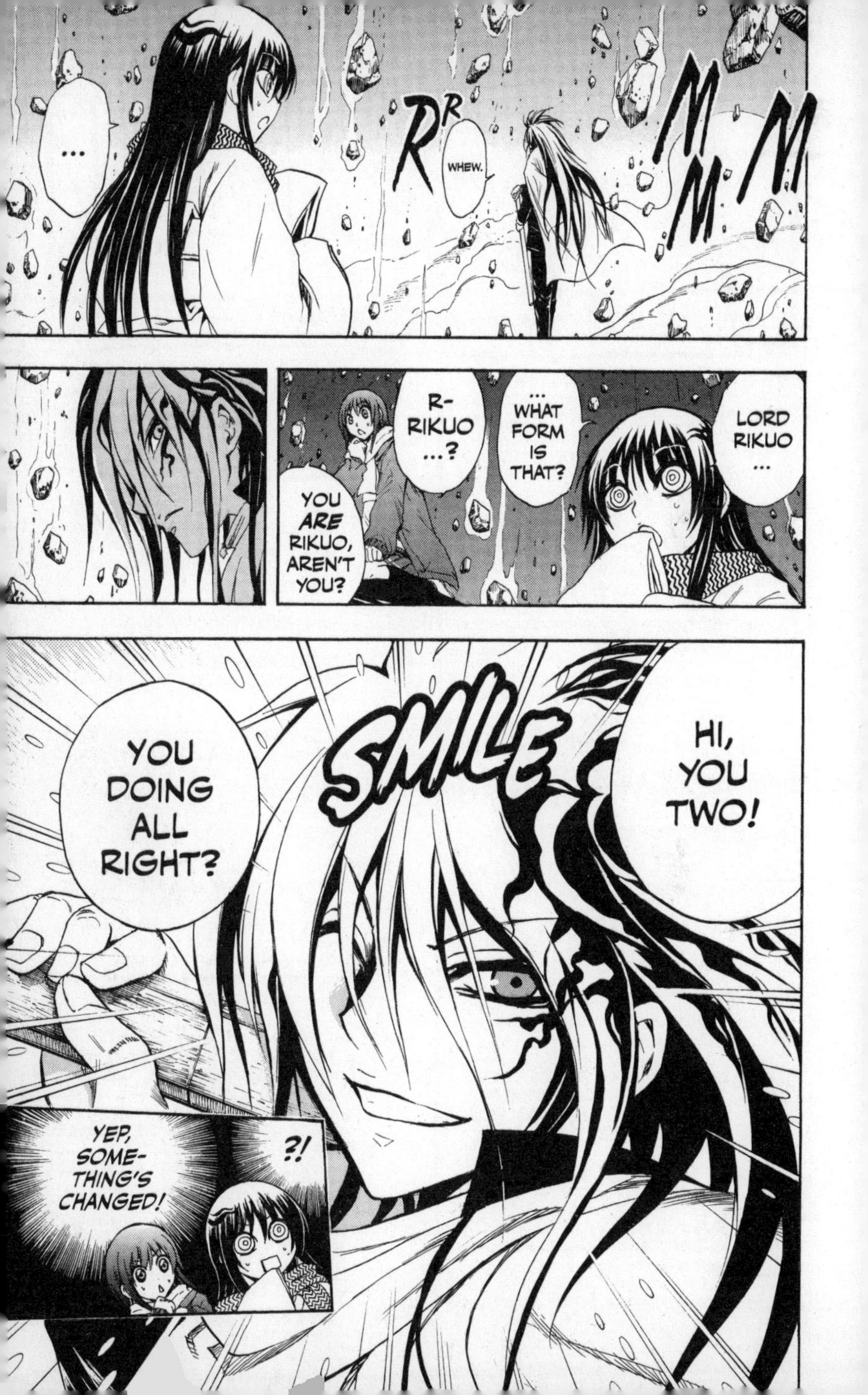

RRMMMM
WHEW.
...
LORD RIKUO ...
... WHAT FORM IS THAT?
R-RIKUO ...?
YOU *ARE* RIKUO, AREN'T YOU?
HI, YOU TWO!
SMILE
YOU DOING ALL RIGHT?
?!
YEP, SOME-THING'S CHANGED!

KIYOTSUGU's YOKAI BRAIN #20

COME TO SADO ☆ SPECIAL

Q: I LIVE ON THE ISLAND OF SADO-GASHIMA IN NIIGATA PREFECTURE. THERE ARE LOTS OF LEGENDS ON SADOGASHIMA! RIKUO AND TSURARA, PLEASE COME TO SADO SOMETIME! ☆ -HAANYAN, NIIGATA PREFECTURE

TSURARA: I KNOW THE FOLK SONG "SADO OKESA" AND THE FISHING BOATS CALLED TARAI BUNE! LORD RIKUO, LET'S GO TO SADO! ☆

NATTO-KOZO: IS THERE A CRESTED IBIS YOKAI THERE?

Q: RIKUO'S HEIGHT CHANGES A LOT FROM HUMAN TO YOKAI FORM. DOESN'T HIS KIMONO RIP? -KOYUKI ♪, SAITAMA PREFECTURE

TSURARA: I'VE ALWAYS WONDERED ABOUT THAT! HOW DOES THAT WORK?

RIKUO: IT'S PROBABLY BEST NOT TO THINK ABOUT IT TOO HARD, BUT I GUESS WHEN I TRANSFORM MY CLOTHES DO TOO!

TSURARA: AHA! YOUR FEAR DOES THAT! IT'S TRUE THAT WHEN I WASH YOUR KIMONO AT NIGHT, IT'S SHRUNK BY MORNING!

RIKUO: NO, YOU JUST MESS UP THE WASHING!

Q: WHAT DOES KAPPA HAVE ON HIS HEAD? A DISH? OR IS THAT A BONE? -OOKAMI DAISUKI, NAGANO PREFECTURE

KAPPA: IT'S A DISH! IT'S PRETTY BIG, RIGHT?

Q: WHAT SUBJECTS IS RIKUO GOOD OR BAD AT IN SCHOOL? -OKA, HOKKAIDO

RIKUO: I'M NOT VERY GOOD AT ENGLISH.

AND NONE OF THE YOKAI AT THE MAIN HOUSE KNOW ENGLISH, SO THEY CAN'T HELP ME. BUT I LIKE MATH! AND NUMERICAL FORMULAS ARE MORE LIKE WORDS THAN CALCULATION!

Q: THIS IS A QUESTION FOR TSURARA AND KUBINASHI! WHAT WAS SHOEI LIKE WHEN HE WAS LITTLE? -SHIGURE SHIMOTSUKI, IWATE PREFECTURE

KUBINASHI: HE THOUGHT HE WAS HUMAN.

TSURARA: RIGHT! HIHI WAS RAISED THAT WAY TOO. THEY WERE SO SMALL THEN...

Q: I LOVE REIRA SO SUPER DUPER DUPER DUPER MUCH THAT I COULD MARRY HER!! WHAT ARE HER MEASUREMENTS? (IN CENTIMETERS, PLEASE) -REIRA'S LEMON SLICE, SHIZUOKA PREFECTURE

REIRA: I NEVER REALLY KNOW WHY, BUT LOTS OF GUYS LIKE ME! TEE HEE HEE! YOU'RE 12 YEARS OLD? HEH HEH... THEN I WON'T TELL YOU!

Q: WHAT WAS YANAGIDA DOING THE NIGHT SANMOTO BECAME A DEVIL? -HEITARO, HOKKAIDO

YANAGIDA: I WAS AFRAID WHEN SANMOTO FELL FROM THE ROOF, BUT WHEN HE CAME BACK I WAS LIKE, "ALRIGHT!"

Q: THIS IS FOR KIYOTSUGU. WHAT KINDS OF THINGS DO THE MEMBERS OF THE KIYOJUJI PARANORMAL PATROL USUALLY DO? -YUKINOSHITA, IBARAKI PREFECTURE

KIYOTSUGU: UPDATING YOKAI BRAIN LIKE THIS IS ONE THING WE DO!! COME TO THINK OF IT, IT'S BEEN A LONG TIME SINCE I WROTE ANYTHING!!

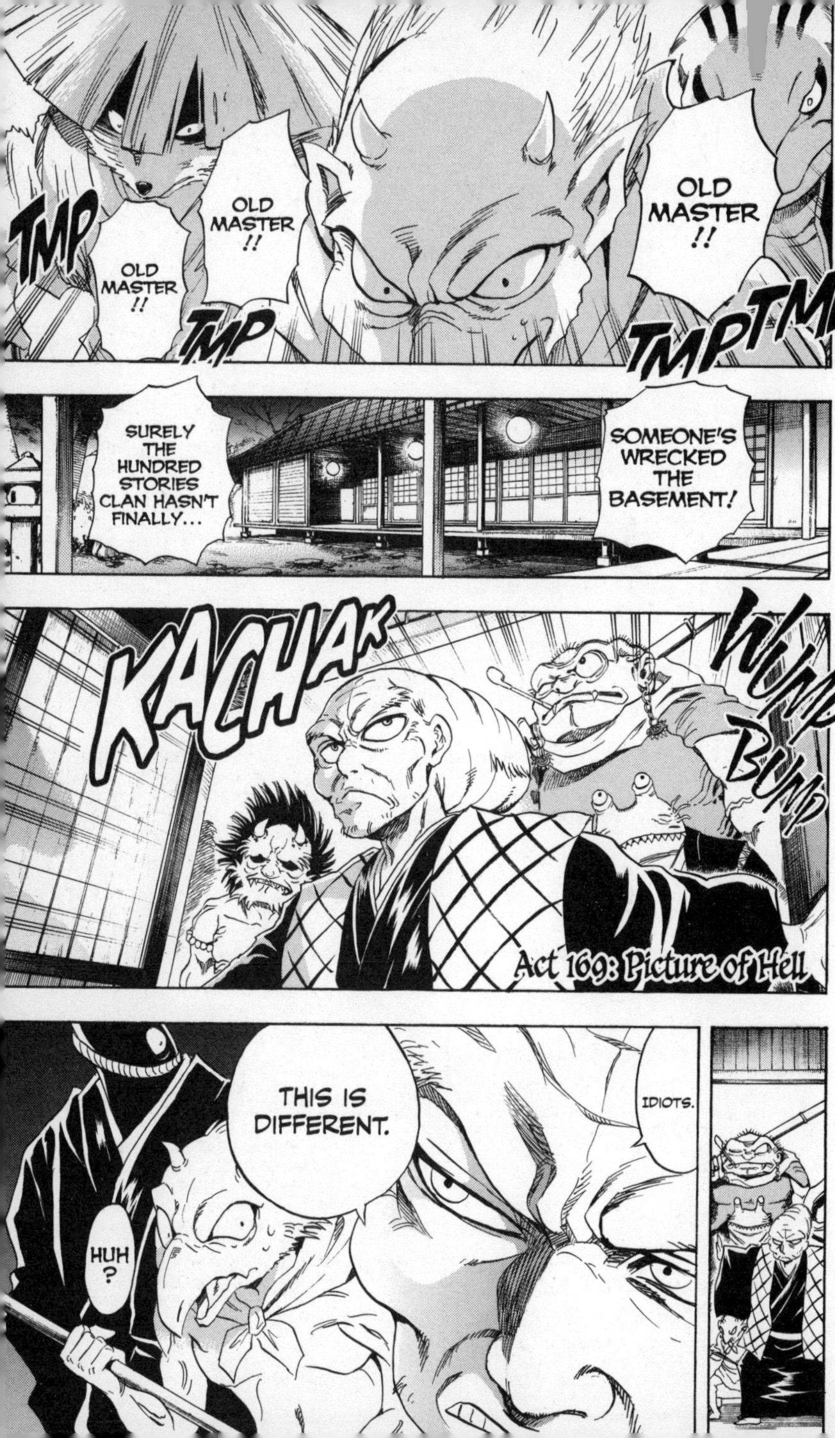
OLD MASTER!!
TMPTMP
OLD MASTER!!
TMP
OLD MASTER!!
TMP
SOMEONE'S WRECKED THE BASEMENT!
SURELY THE HUNDRED STORIES CLAN HASN'T FINALLY...
WUMP BUMP
KACHAK
Act 169: Picture of Hell
IDIOTS.
THIS IS DIFFERENT.
HUH?

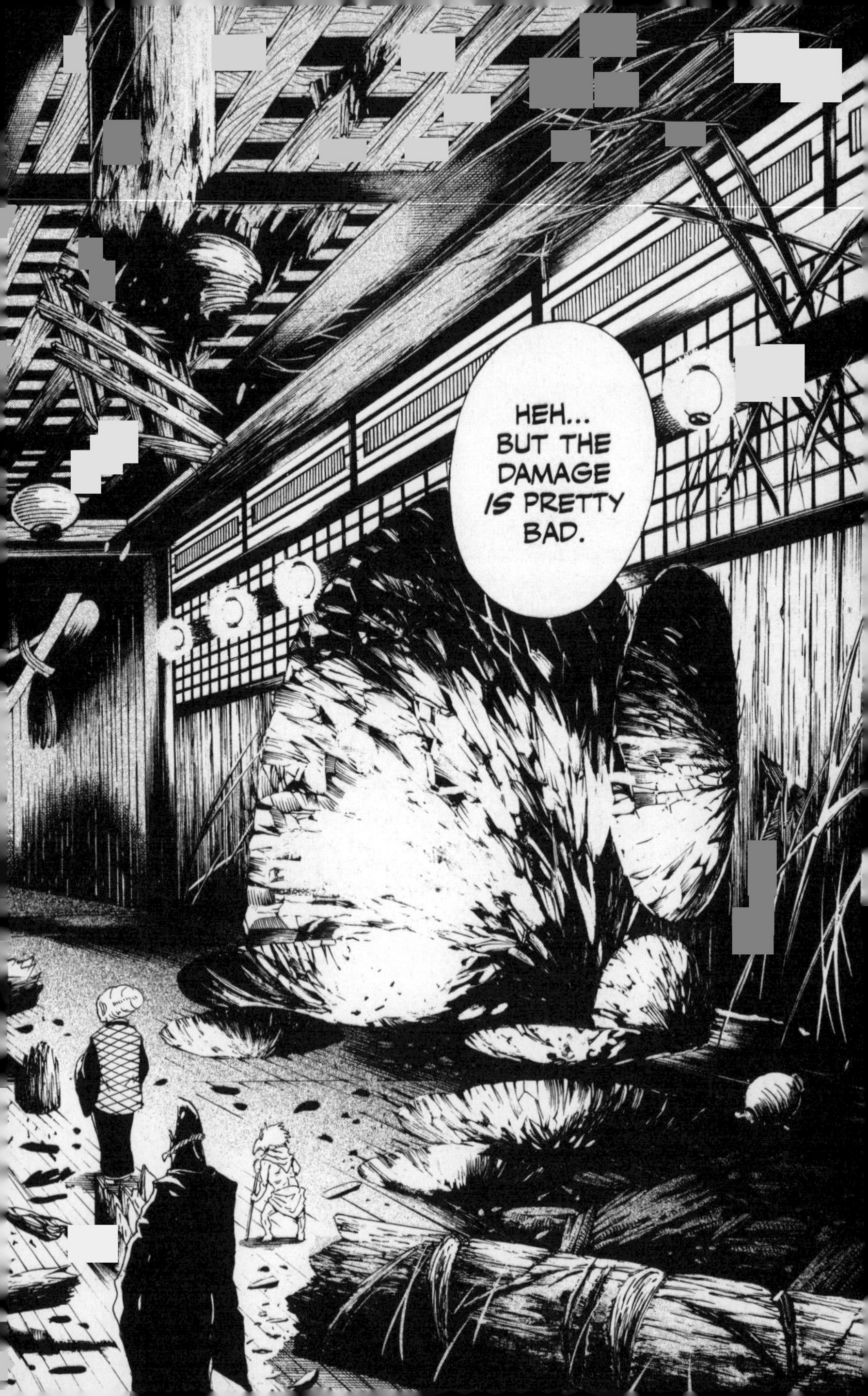
HEH... BUT THE DAMAGE *IS* PRETTY BAD.

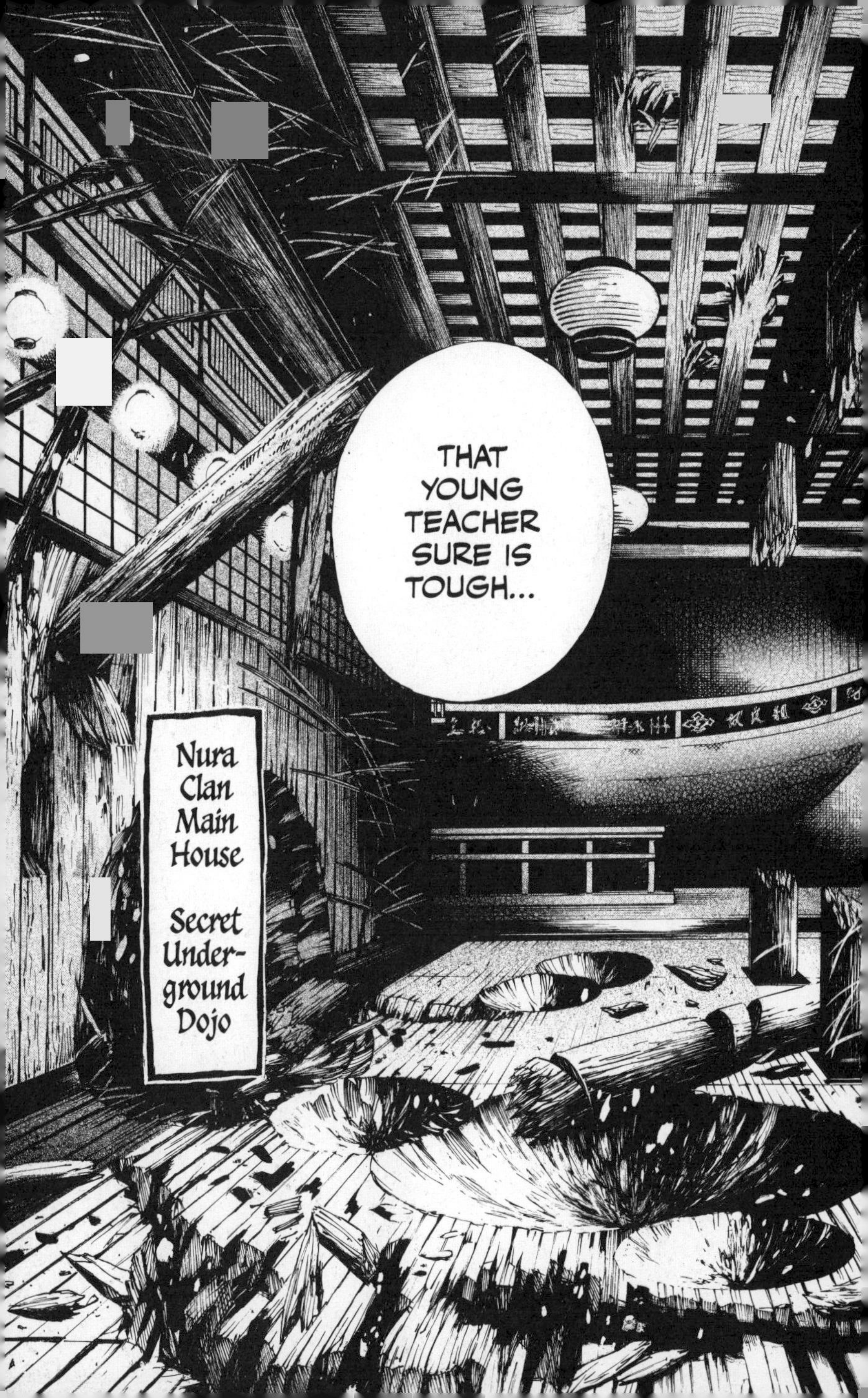
THAT YOUNG TEACHER SURE IS TOUGH...
Nura Clan Main House
Secret Underground Dojo

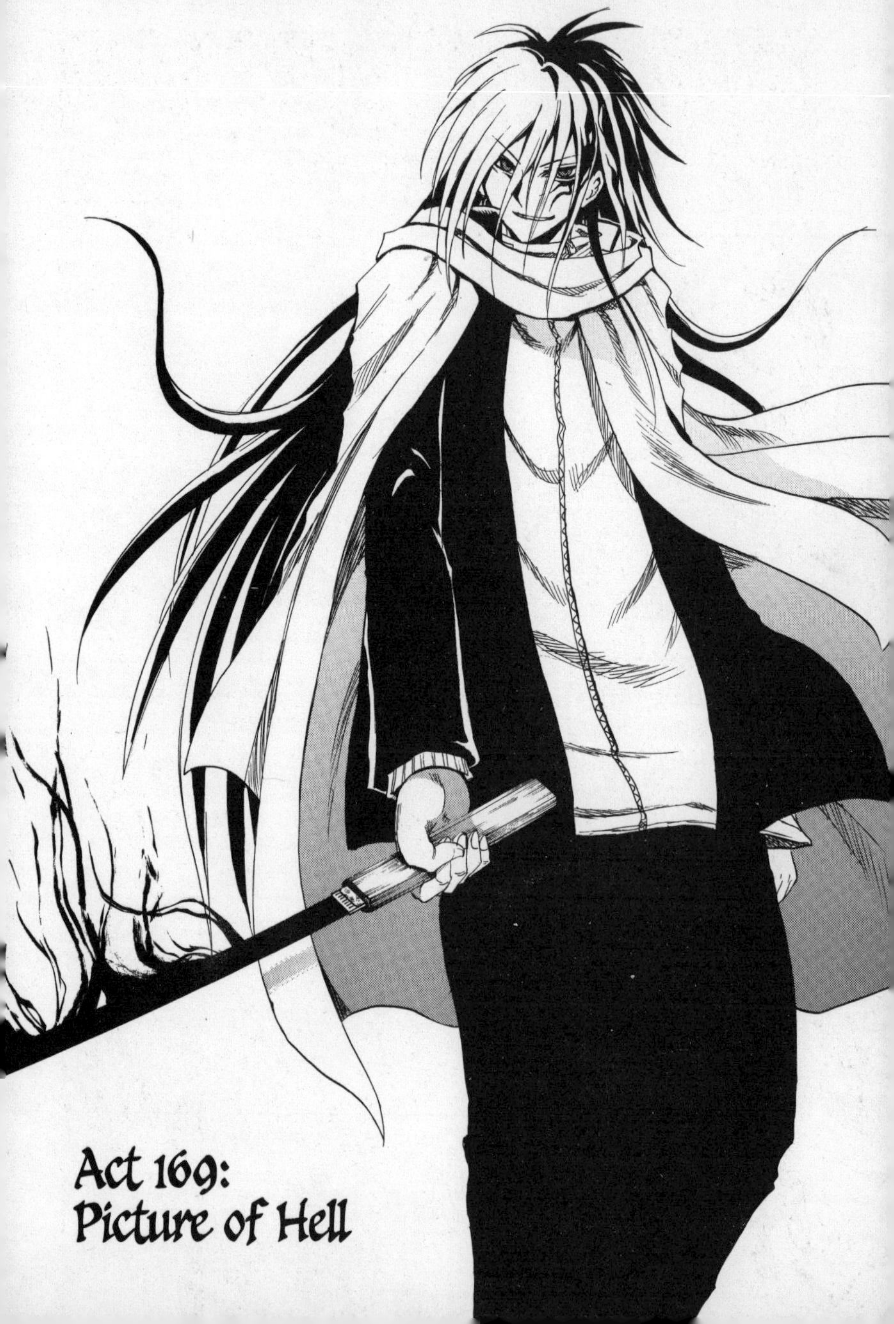

Act 169: Picture of Hell

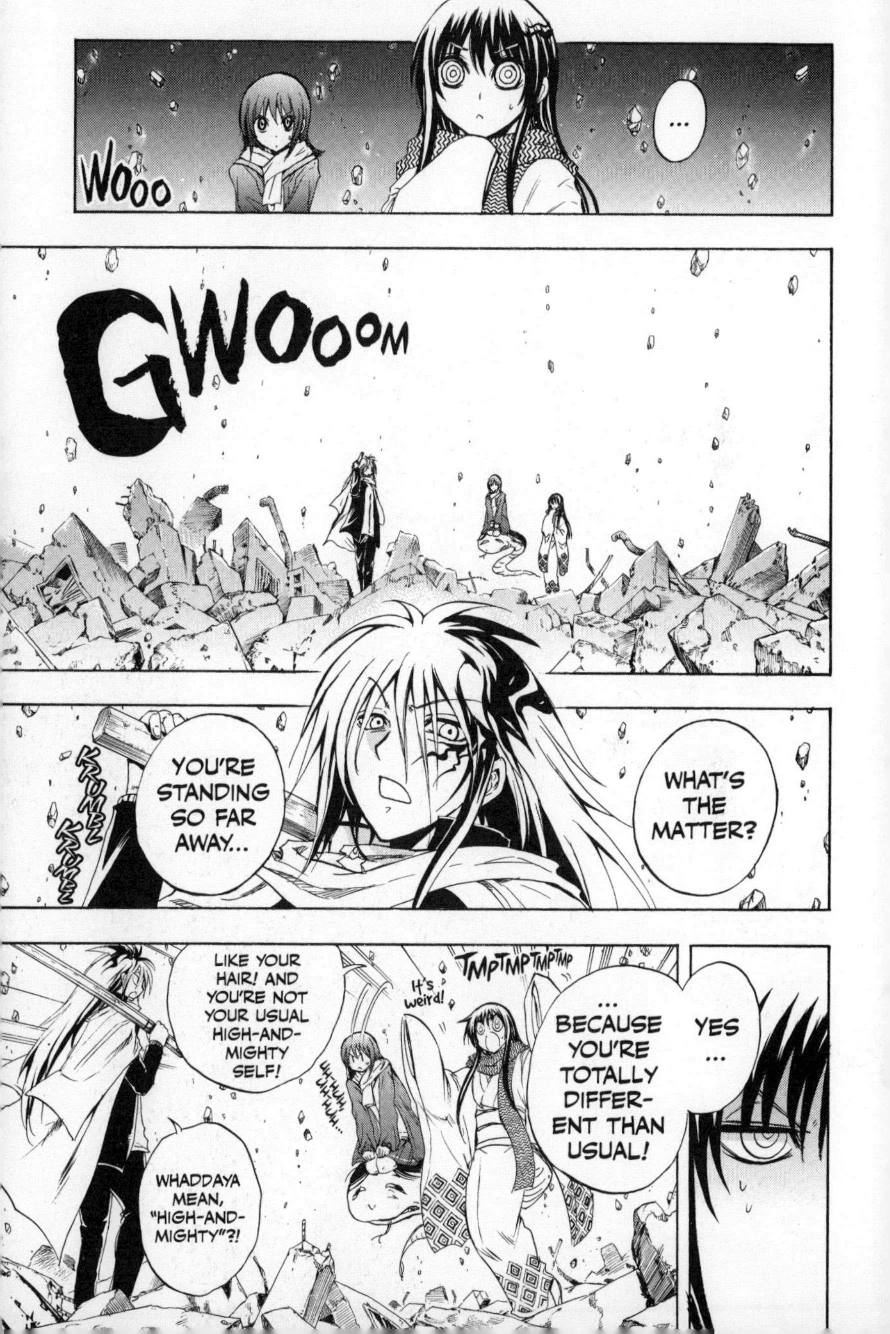
...
WOOO
GWOOOM
WHAT'S THE MATTER?
YOU'RE STANDING SO FAR AWAY...
KRUMBL KRUMBL
YES ...
... BECAUSE YOU'RE TOTALLY DIFFERENT THAN USUAL!
TMPTMPTMPTMP
It's weird!
LIKE YOUR HAIR! AND YOU'RE NOT YOUR USUAL HIGH-AND-MIGHTY SELF!
UH-HUH UH-HUH...
WHADDAYA MEAN, "HIGH-AND-MIGHTY"?!

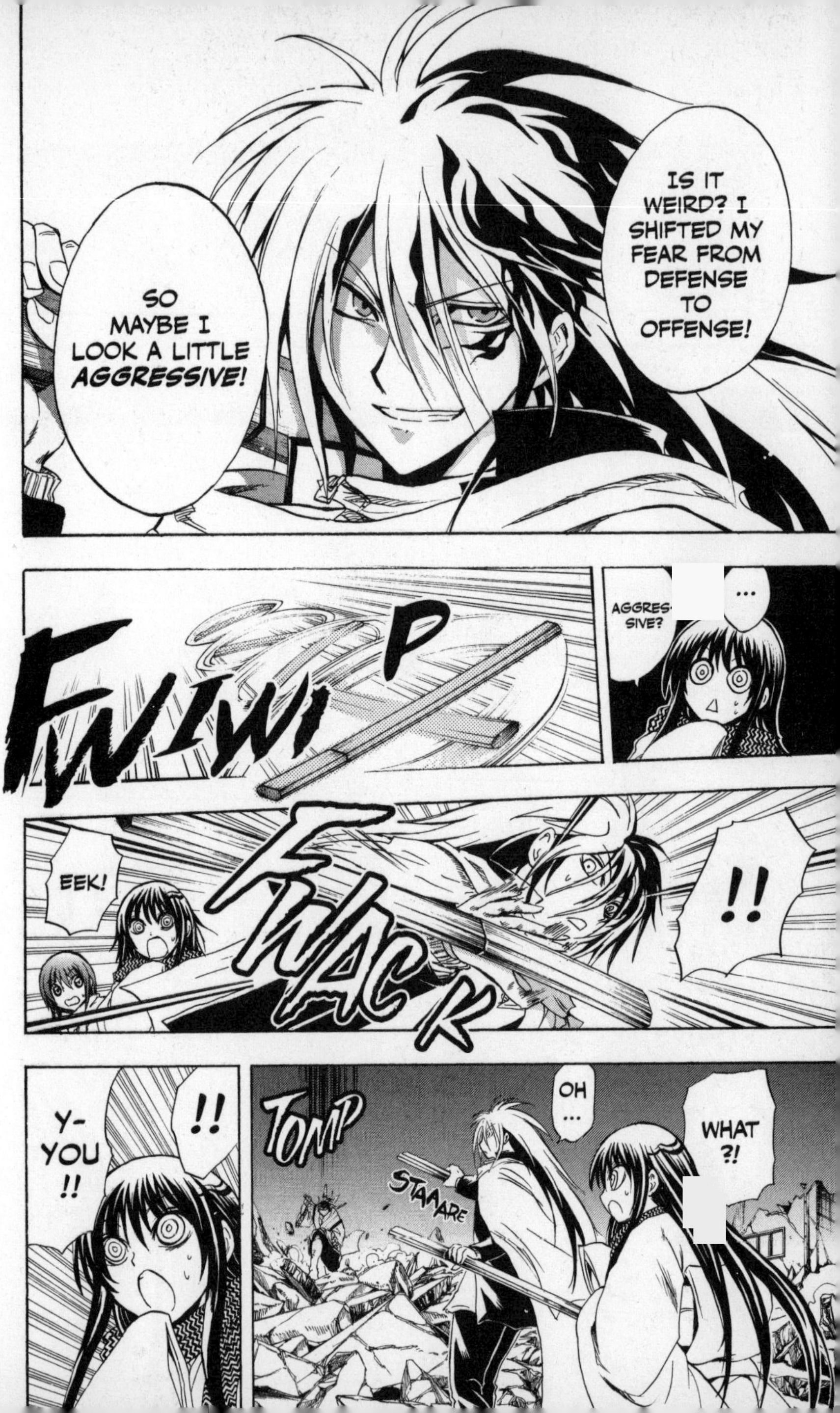
IS IT WEIRD? I SHIFTED MY FEAR FROM DEFENSE TO OFFENSE!
SO MAYBE I LOOK A LITTLE *AGGRESSIVE!*
...
AGGRES-SIVE?
FWIWIP
!!
FWACK
EEK!
WHAT?!
OH ...
STAAARE
TOMP
!!
Y-YOU !!

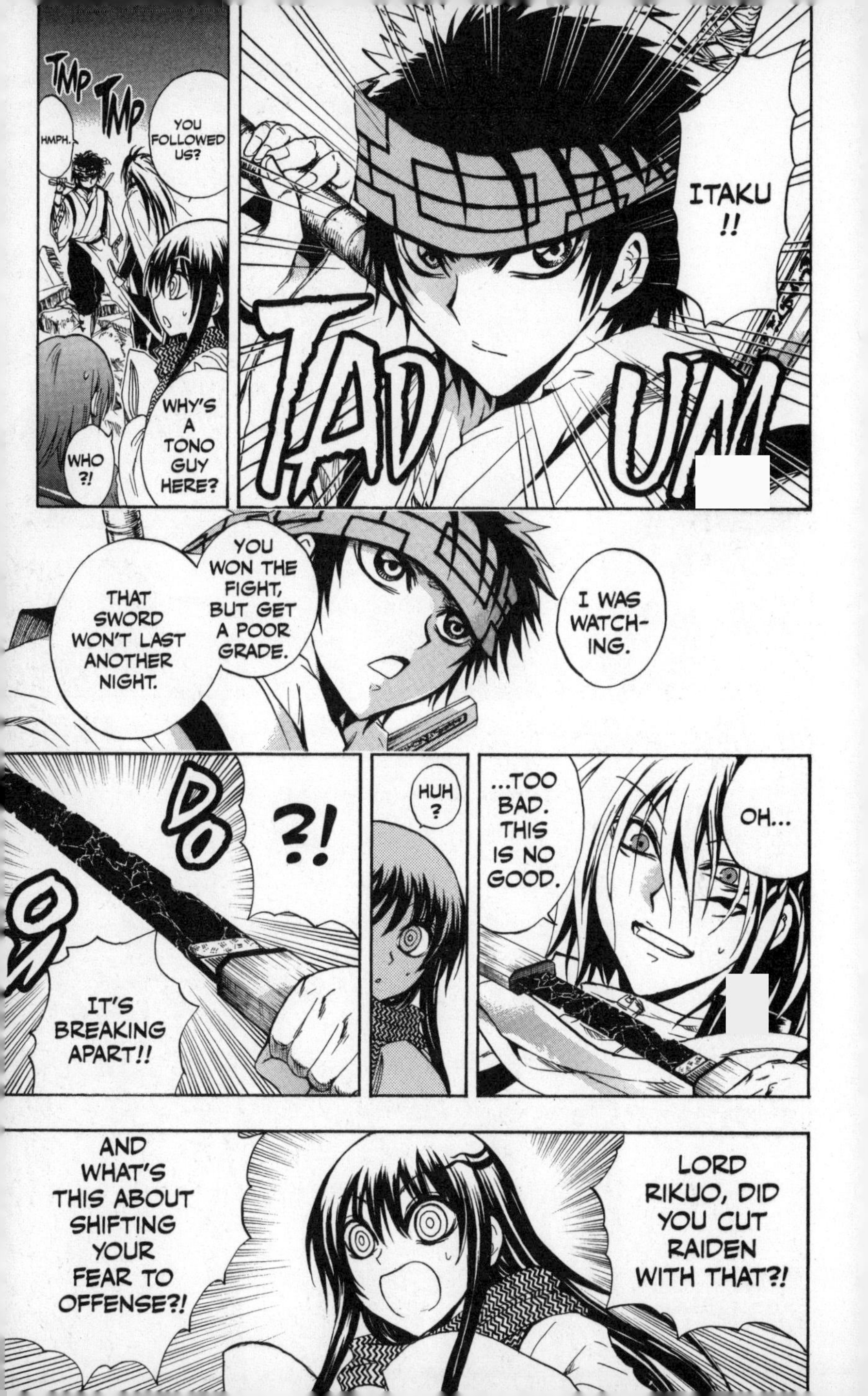
ITAKU!!
TAD UM
TMP TMP
YOU FOLLOWED US?
HMPH.
WHY'S A TONO GUY HERE?
WHO?!
I WAS WATCHING.
YOU WON THE FIGHT, BUT GET A POOR GRADE.
THAT SWORD WON'T LAST ANOTHER NIGHT.
OH...
...TOO BAD. THIS IS NO GOOD.
HUH?
DO
?!
O
IT'S BREAKING APART!!
LORD RIKUO, DID YOU CUT RAIDEN WITH THAT?!
AND WHAT'S THIS ABOUT SHIFTING YOUR FEAR TO OFFENSE?!

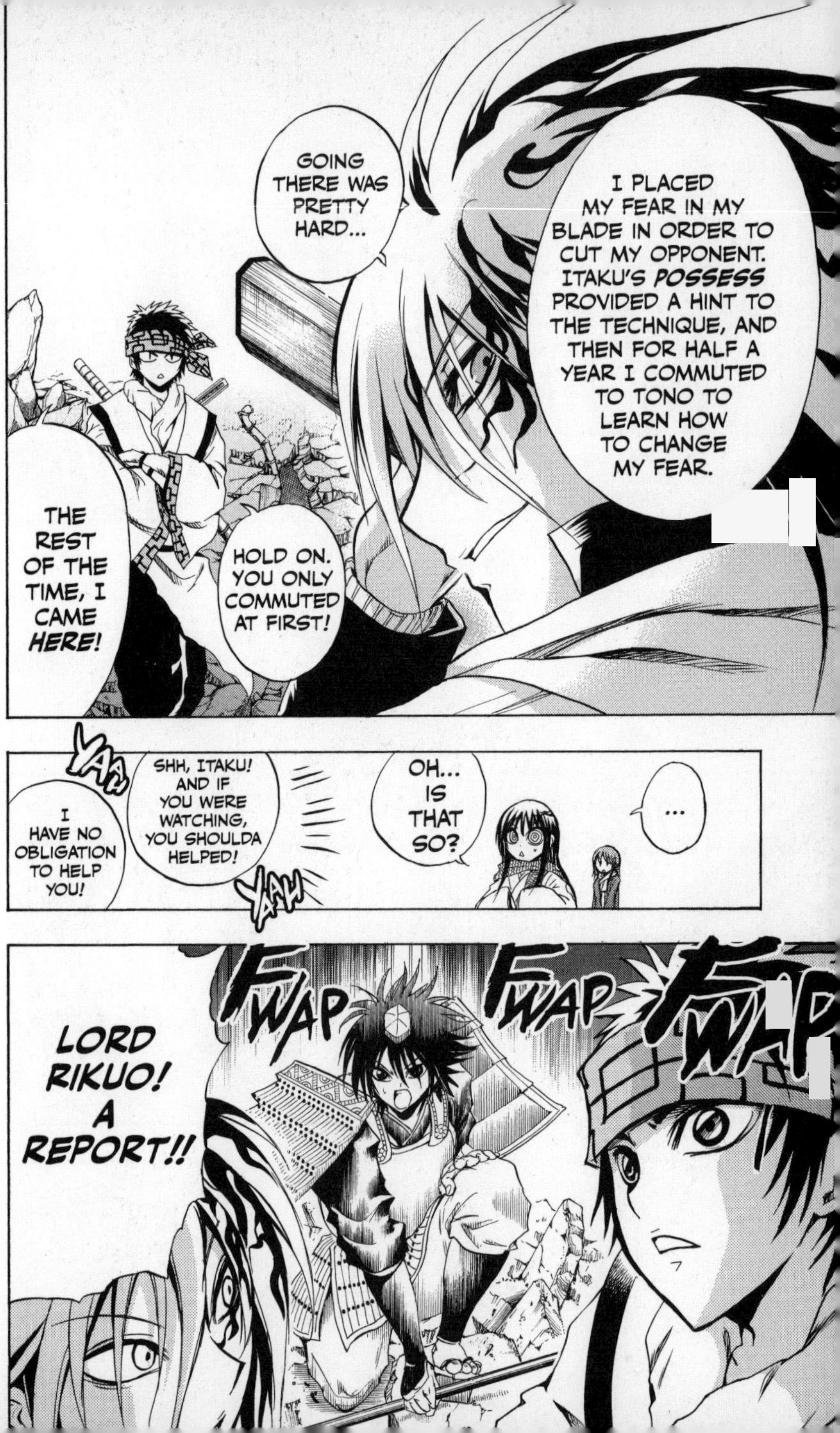
I PLACED MY FEAR IN MY BLADE IN ORDER TO CUT MY OPPONENT. ITAKU'S *POSSESS* PROVIDED A HINT TO THE TECHNIQUE, AND THEN FOR HALF A YEAR I COMMUTED TO TONO TO LEARN HOW TO CHANGE MY FEAR.
GOING THERE WAS PRETTY HARD...
HOLD ON. YOU ONLY COMMUTED AT FIRST!
THE REST OF THE TIME, I CAME *HERE*!
...
OH... IS THAT SO?
YAAAH
SHH, ITAKU! AND IF YOU WERE WATCHING, YOU SHOULDA HELPED!
YAAAH
I HAVE NO OBLIGATION TO HELP YOU!
FWAP
FWAP
FWAP
LORD RIKUO! A REPORT!!

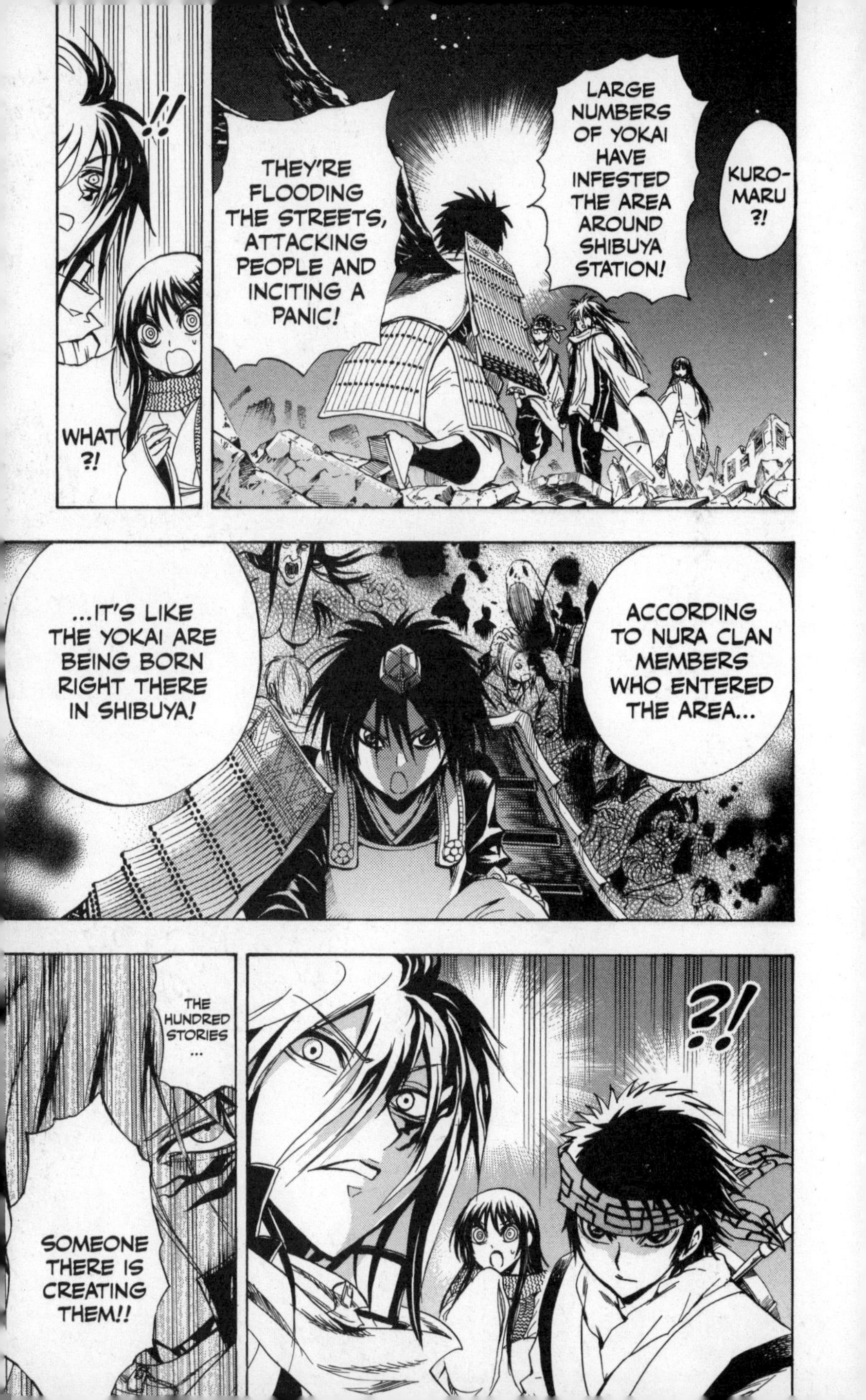
KURO-MARU?!
LARGE NUMBERS OF YOKAI HAVE INFESTED THE AREA AROUND SHIBUYA STATION!
THEY'RE FLOODING THE STREETS, ATTACKING PEOPLE AND INCITING A PANIC!
!!
WHAT?!
ACCORDING TO NURA CLAN MEMBERS WHO ENTERED THE AREA...
...IT'S LIKE THE YOKAI ARE BEING BORN RIGHT THERE IN SHIBUYA!
?!
THE HUNDRED STORIES...
SOMEONE THERE IS CREATING THEM!!

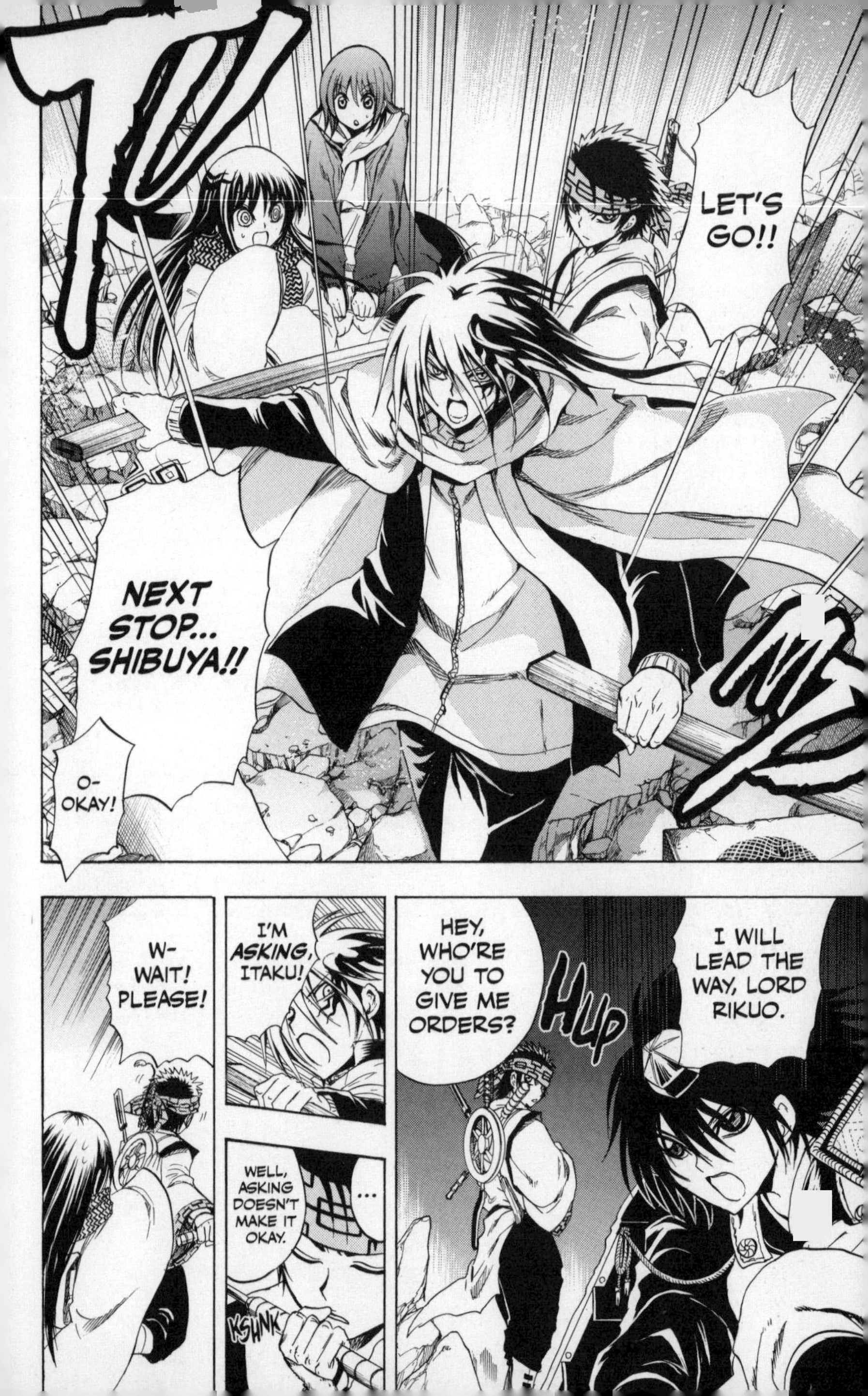
LET'S GO!!
NEXT STOP... SHIBUYA!!
O- OKAY!
I WILL LEAD THE WAY, LORD RIKUO.
HEY, WHO'RE YOU TO GIVE ME ORDERS?
HUP
I'M ASKING, ITAKU!
...
WELL, ASKING DOESN'T MAKE IT OKAY.
KSHNK
W- WAIT! PLEASE!

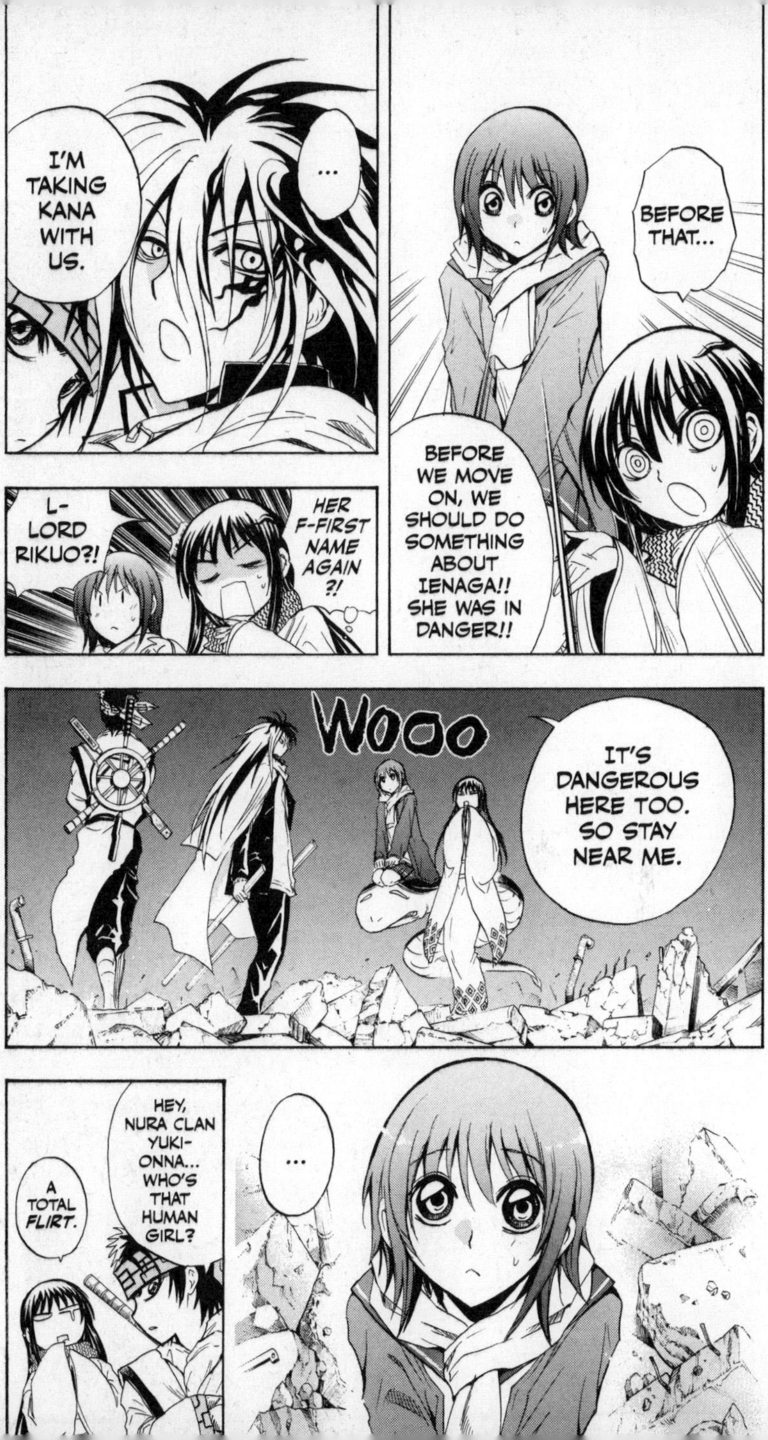

BEFORE THAT...
BEFORE WE MOVE ON, WE SHOULD DO SOMETHING ABOUT IENAGA!! SHE WAS IN DANGER!!
...
I'M TAKING KANA WITH US.
HER F-FIRST NAME AGAIN?!
L-LORD RIKUO?!
WOOO
IT'S DANGEROUS HERE TOO. SO STAY NEAR ME.
...
HEY, NURA CLAN YUKI-ONNA... WHO'S THAT HUMAN GIRL?
A TOTAL *FLIRT*.

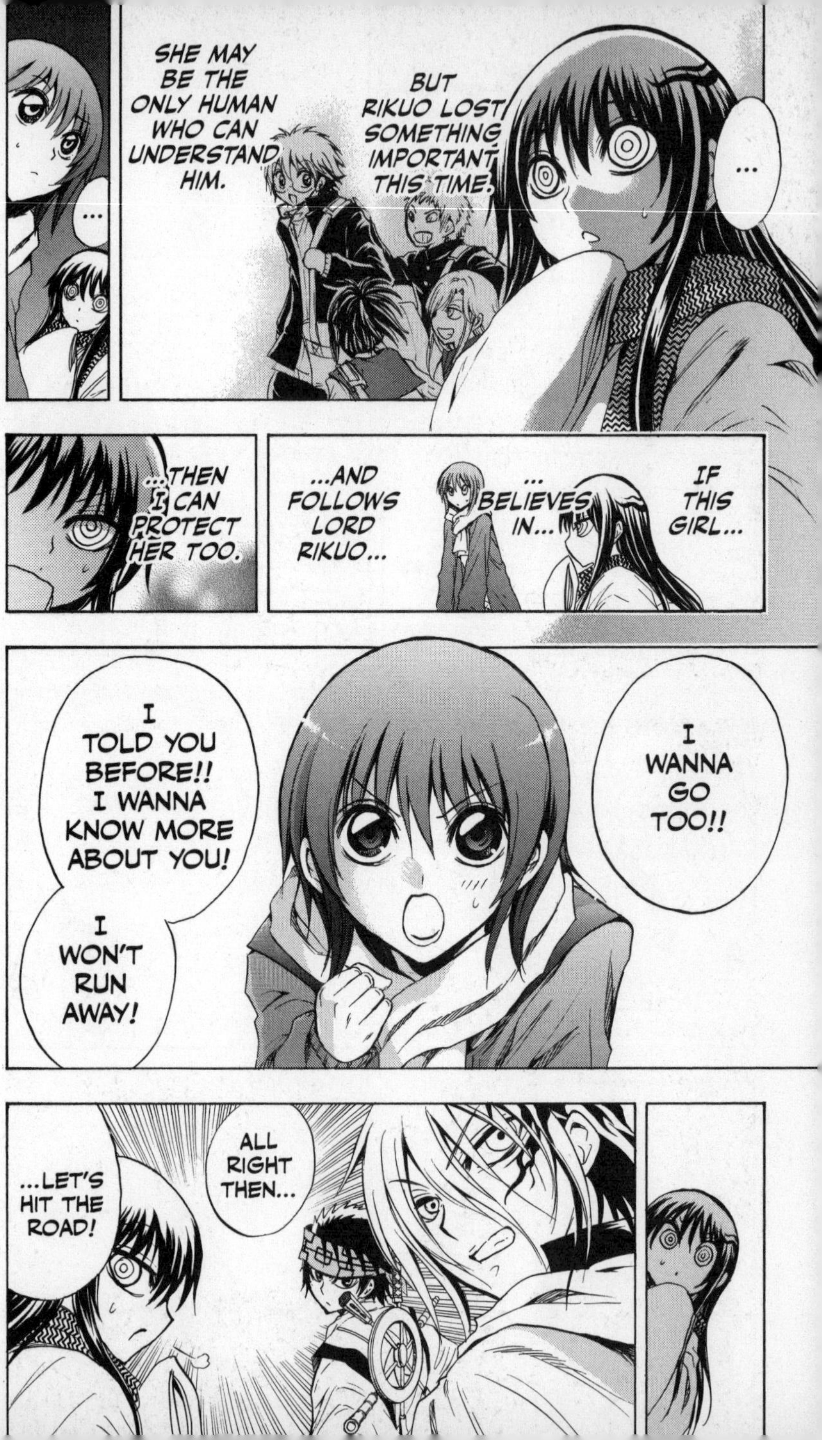
...
SHE MAY BE THE ONLY HUMAN WHO CAN UNDERSTAND HIM.
BUT RIKUO LOST SOMETHING IMPORTANT THIS TIME.
...
IF THIS GIRL...
...BELIEVES IN...
...AND FOLLOWS LORD RIKUO...
...THEN I CAN PROTECT HER TOO.
I WANNA GO TOO!!
I TOLD YOU BEFORE!! I WANNA KNOW MORE ABOUT YOU!
I WON'T RUN AWAY!
ALL RIGHT THEN...
...LET'S HIT THE ROAD!

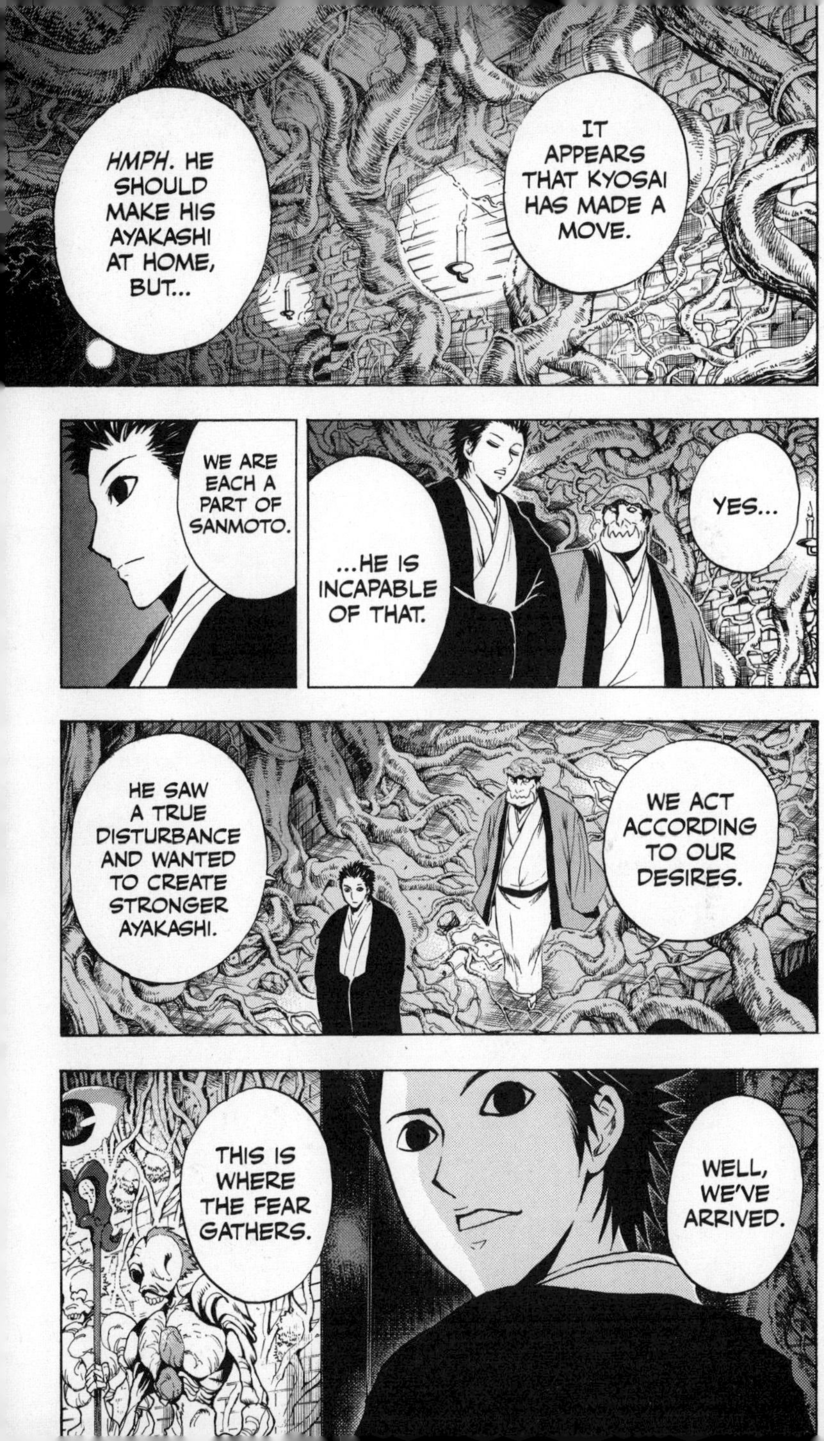
IT APPEARS THAT KYOSAI HAS MADE A MOVE.
HMPH. HE SHOULD MAKE HIS AYAKASHI AT HOME, BUT...
YES...
...HE IS INCAPABLE OF THAT.
WE ARE EACH A PART OF SANMOTO.
WE ACT ACCORDING TO OUR DESIRES.
HE SAW A TRUE DISTURBANCE AND WANTED TO CREATE STRONGER AYAKASHI.
WELL, WE'VE ARRIVED.
THIS IS WHERE THE FEAR GATHERS.

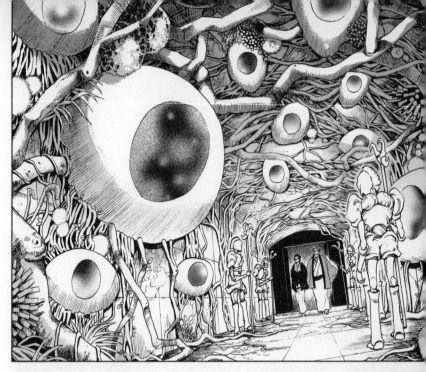

THE FEAR IS GATHERING AS DESIRED.

ENCHO... IS THIS IT?!

HM ?!

WAAH

YAAH

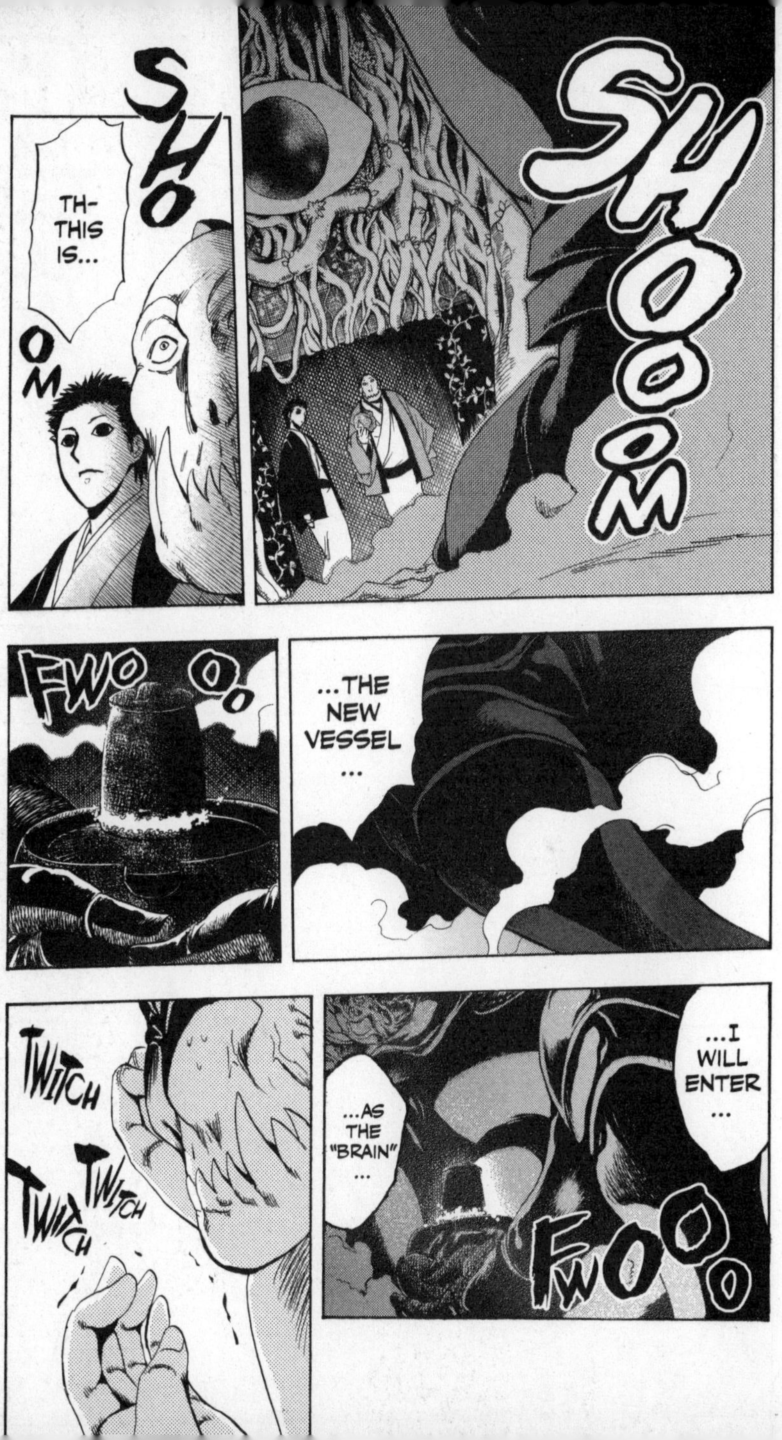
SHOOOOM
SHOOM
TH-THIS IS...
...THE NEW VESSEL...
FWOOO
...I WILL ENTER...
...AS THE "BRAIN"...
FWOOO
TWITCH
TWITCH
TWITCH

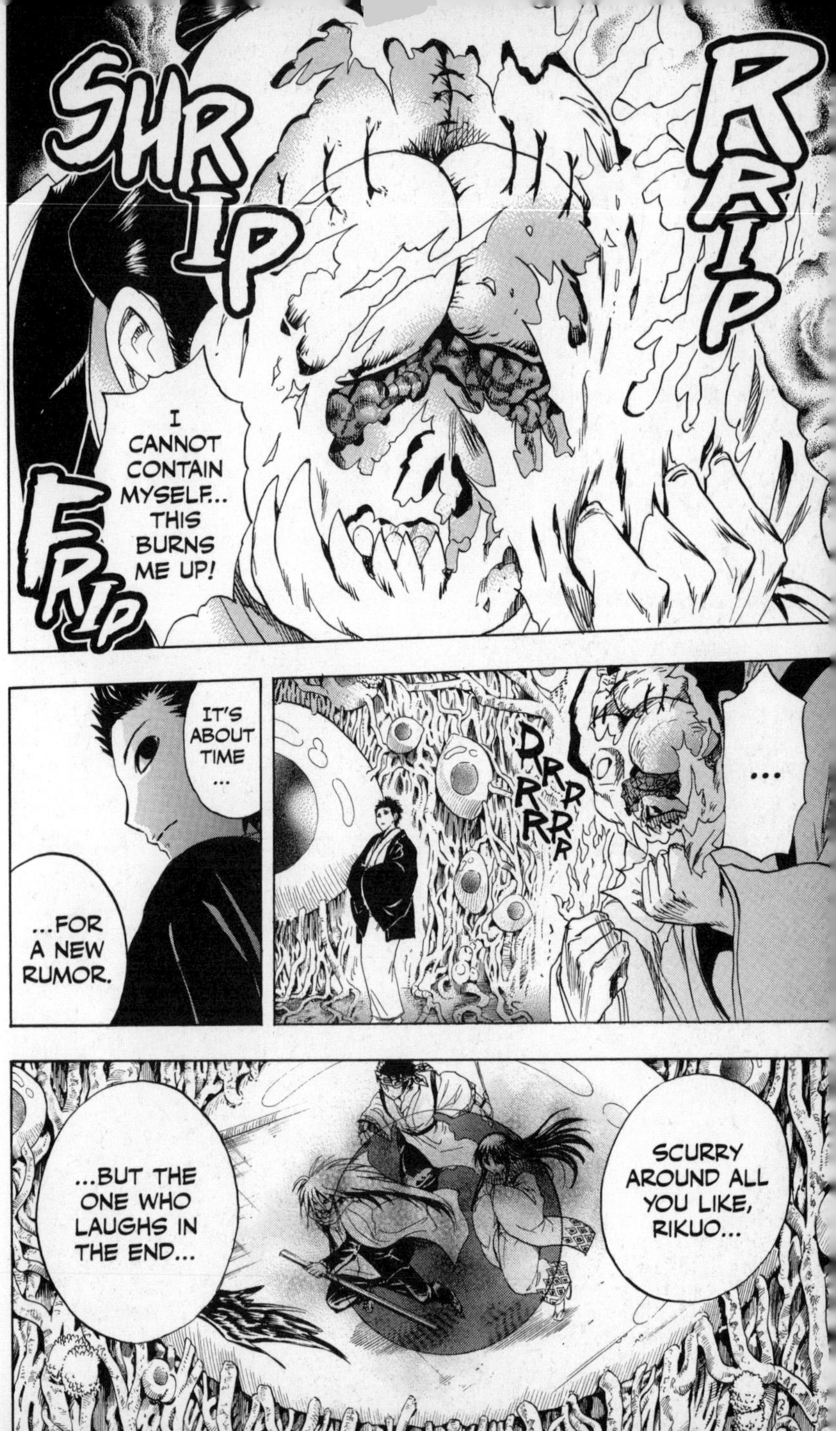
RRIP
SHRIP
I CANNOT CONTAIN MYSELF... THIS BURNS ME UP!
FRIP
...
DRRRRRR
IT'S ABOUT TIME...
...FOR A NEW RUMOR.
SCURRY AROUND ALL YOU LIKE, RIKUO...
...BUT THE ONE WHO LAUGHS IN THE END...

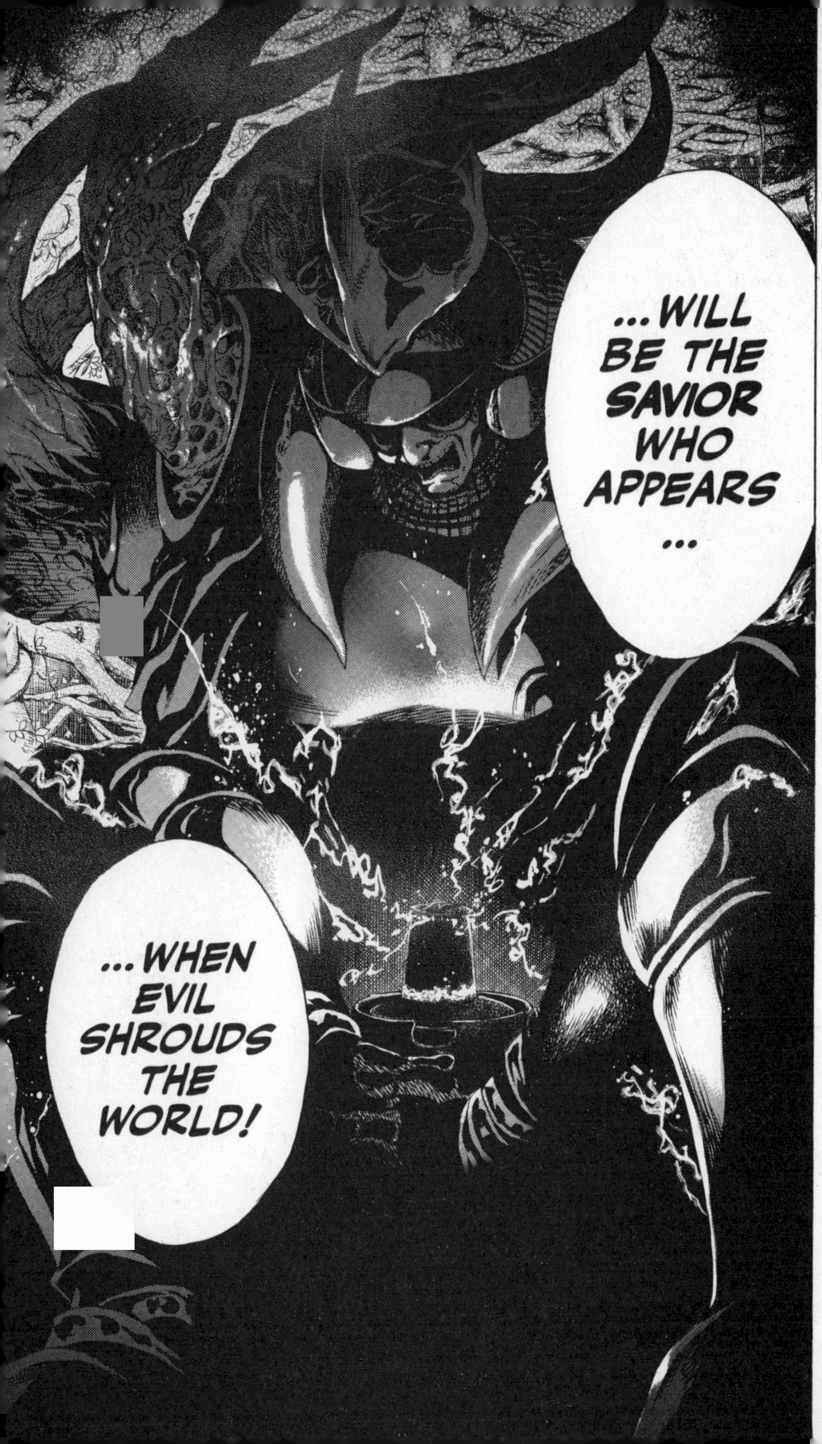
...WILL BE THE SAVIOR WHO APPEARS ...
...WHEN EVIL SHROUDS THE WORLD!

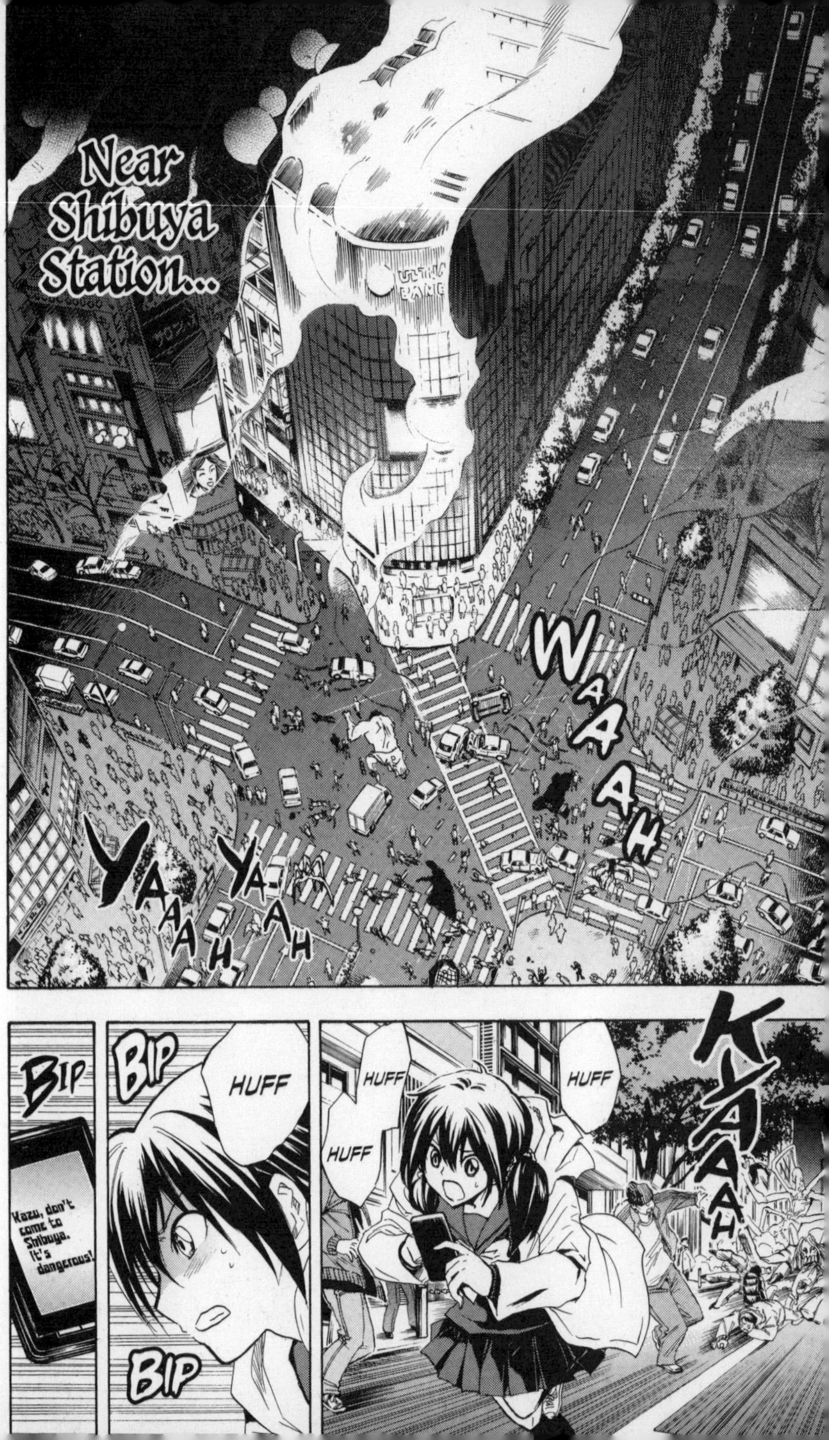
Near Shibuya Station...
WAAAH
YAAH
YAAAH
KYAAAAH
HUFF
HUFF
HUFF
HUFF
BIP
HUFF
BIP
BIP
Kazu, don't come to Shibuya. It's dangerous!

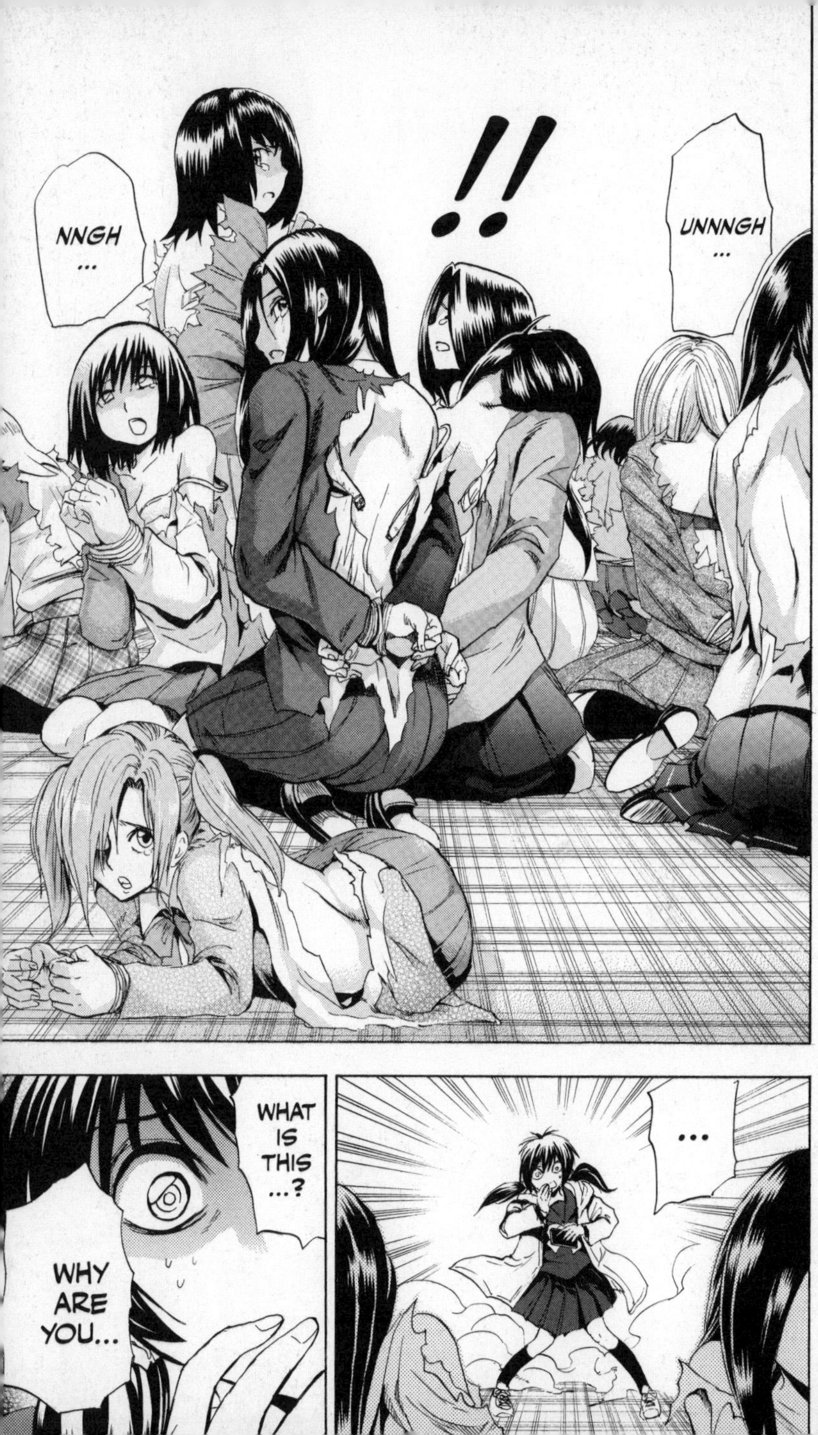
UNNNGH ...
!!
NNGH ...
...
WHAT IS THIS ...?
WHY ARE YOU...

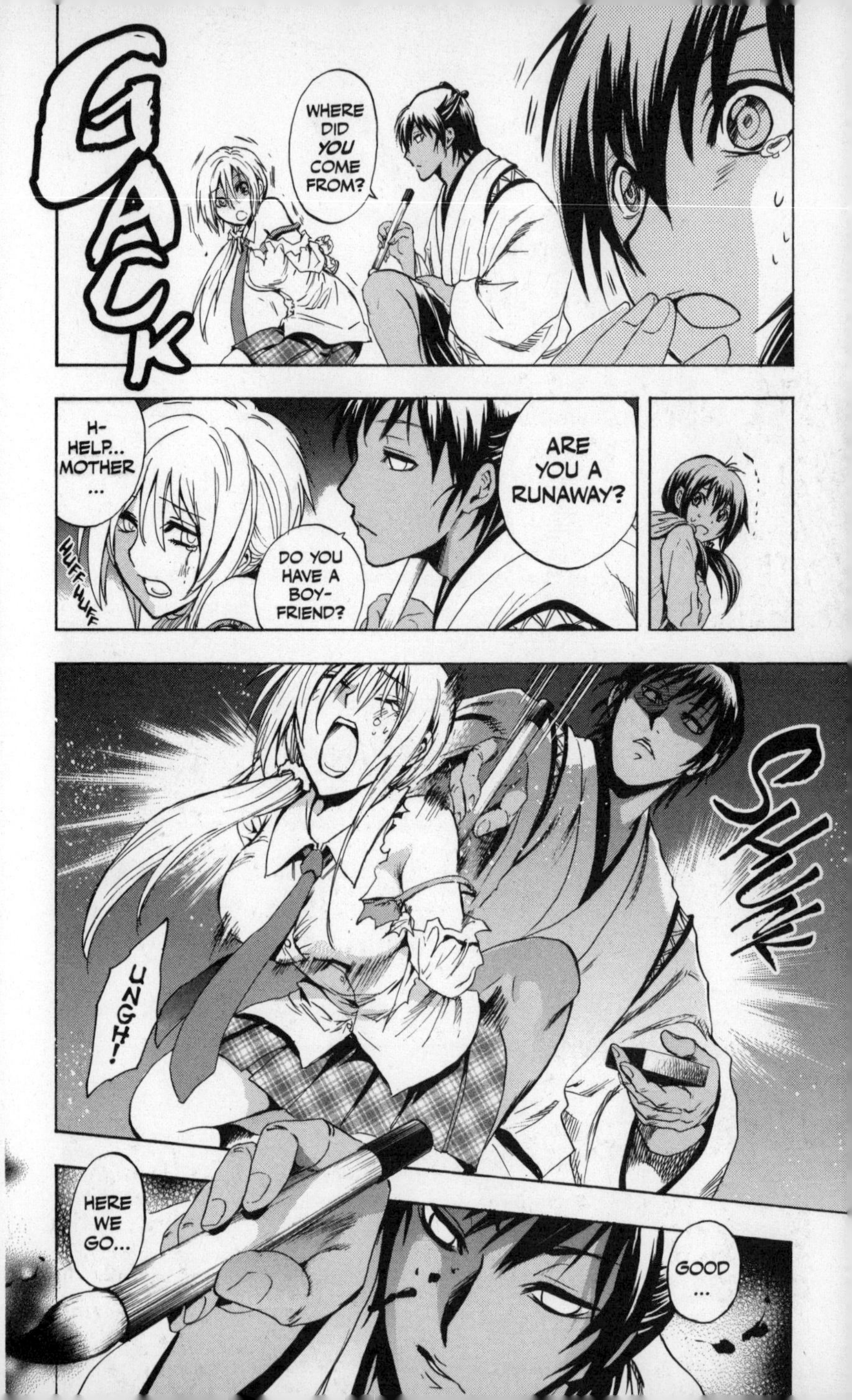
WHERE DID YOU COME FROM?
GACK
ARE YOU A RUNAWAY?
DO YOU HAVE A BOY-FRIEND?
H-HELP... MOTHER ...
HUFF HUFF
SHUNK
UNGH!
GOOD ...
HERE WE GO...

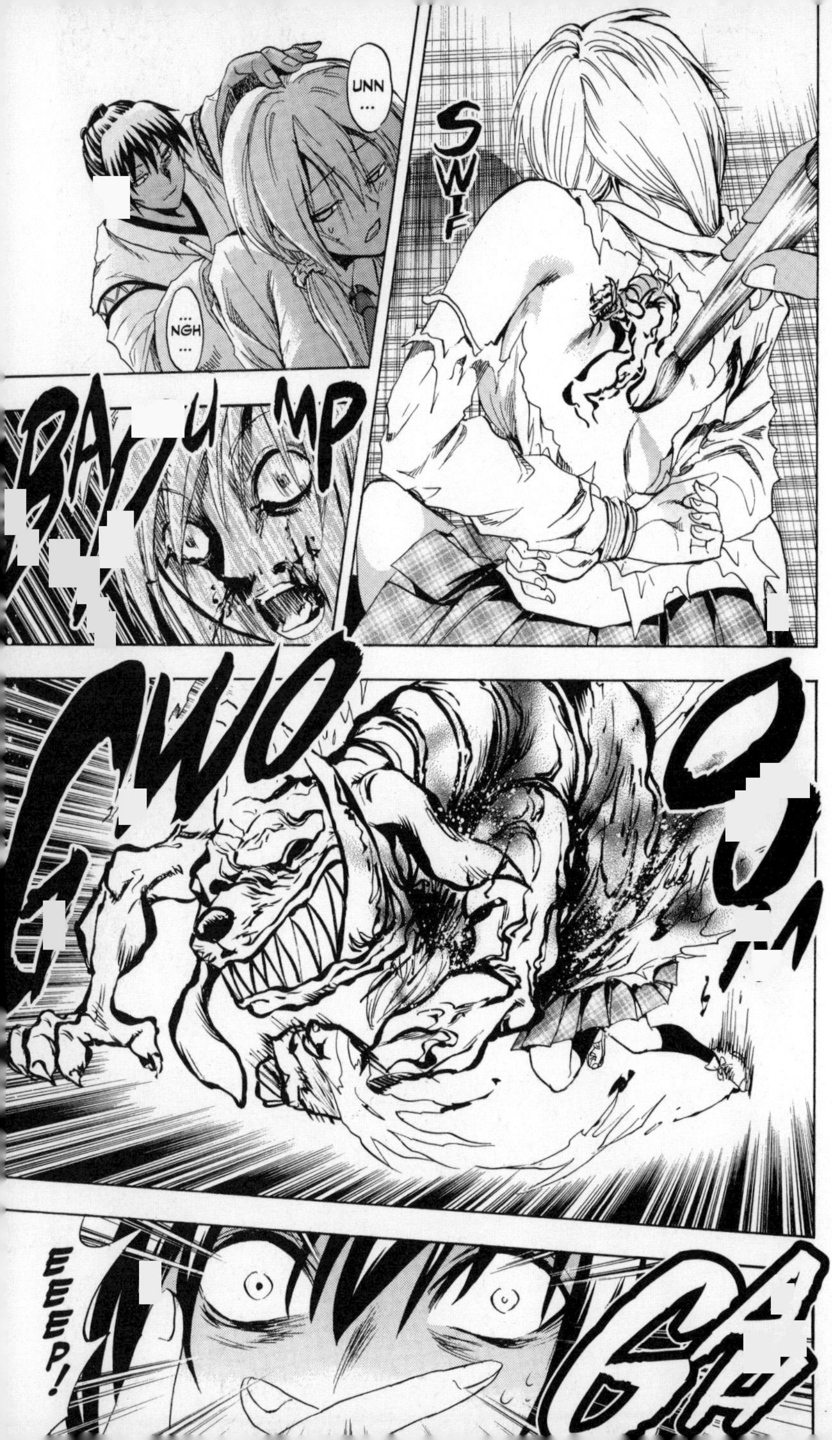
SWIF
UNN ...
... NGH ...
BA UMP
GWOOO
GA
EEEP!

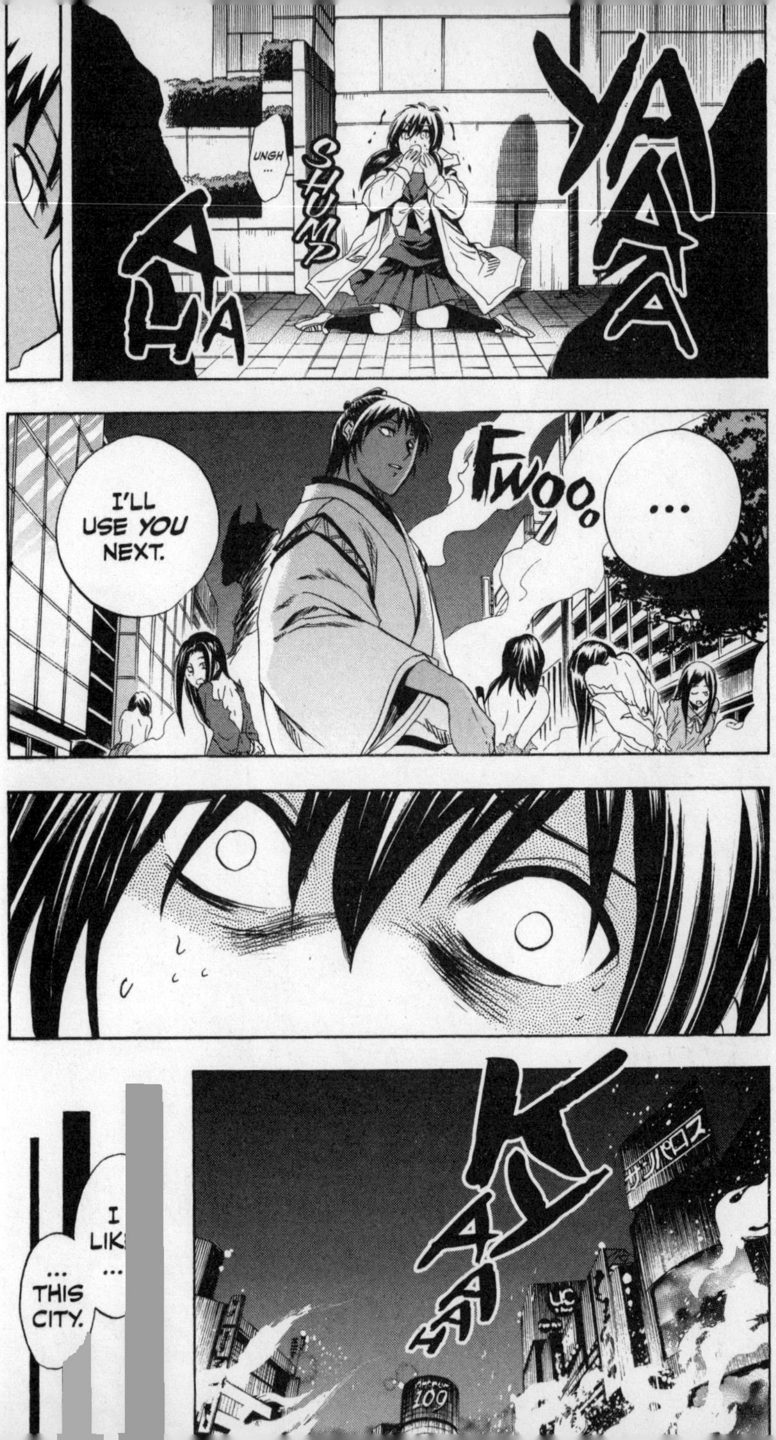
YAAAA
SHUMP
UNGH ...
A HA
...
FWOOo
I'LL USE YOU NEXT.
KYAAAAH
I LIK ...
... THIS CITY.
109

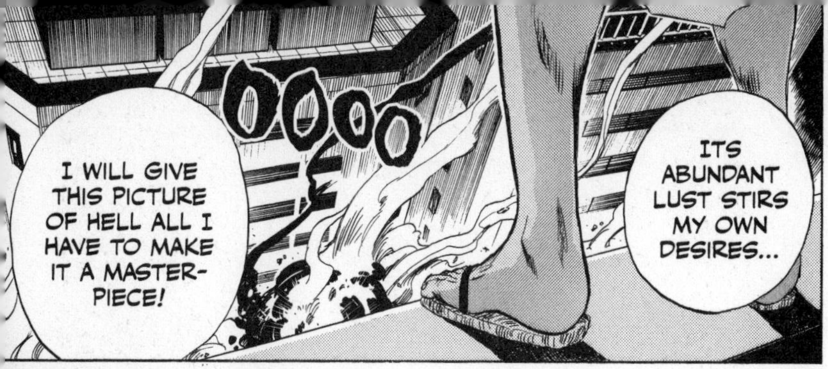
ITS ABUNDANT LUST STIRS MY OWN DESIRES...
OOOO
I WILL GIVE THIS PICTURE OF HELL ALL I HAVE TO MAKE IT A MASTER-PIECE!

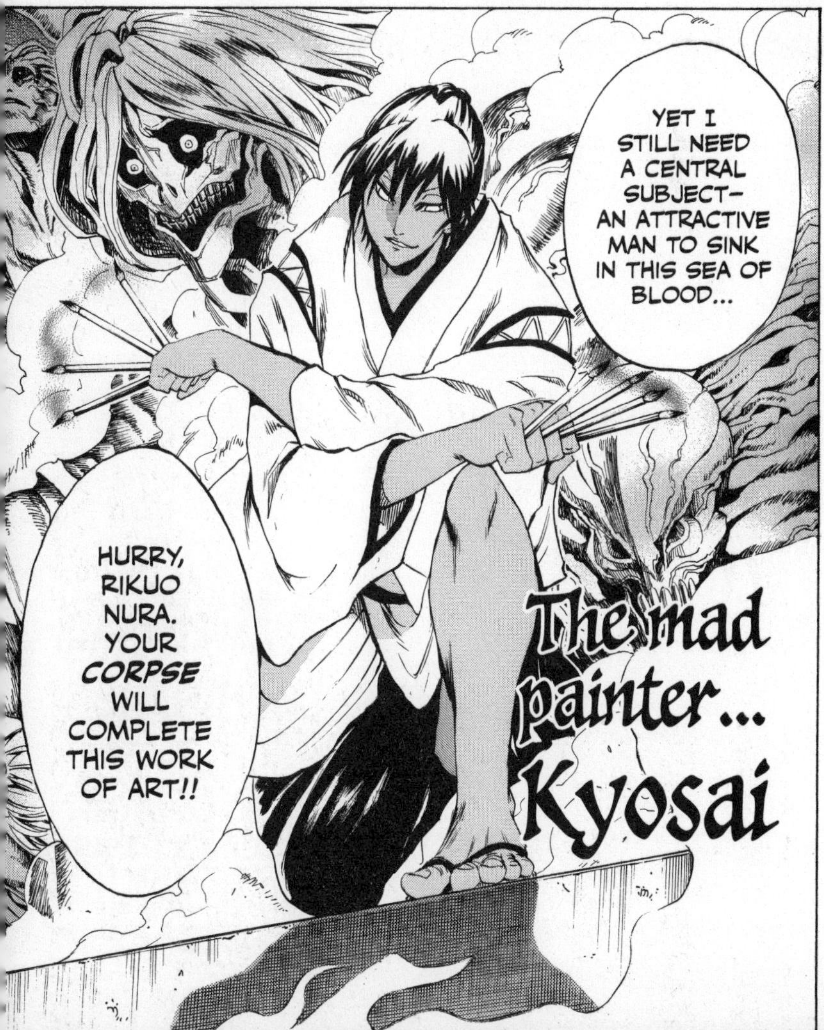
YET I STILL NEED A CENTRAL SUBJECT—AN ATTRACTIVE MAN TO SINK IN THIS SEA OF BLOOD...
The mad painter... Kyosai
HURRY, RIKUO NURA. YOUR *CORPSE* WILL COMPLETE THIS WORK OF ART!!

NURA: RISE OF THE YOKAI CLAN

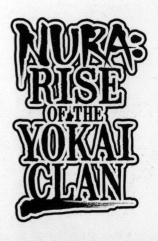

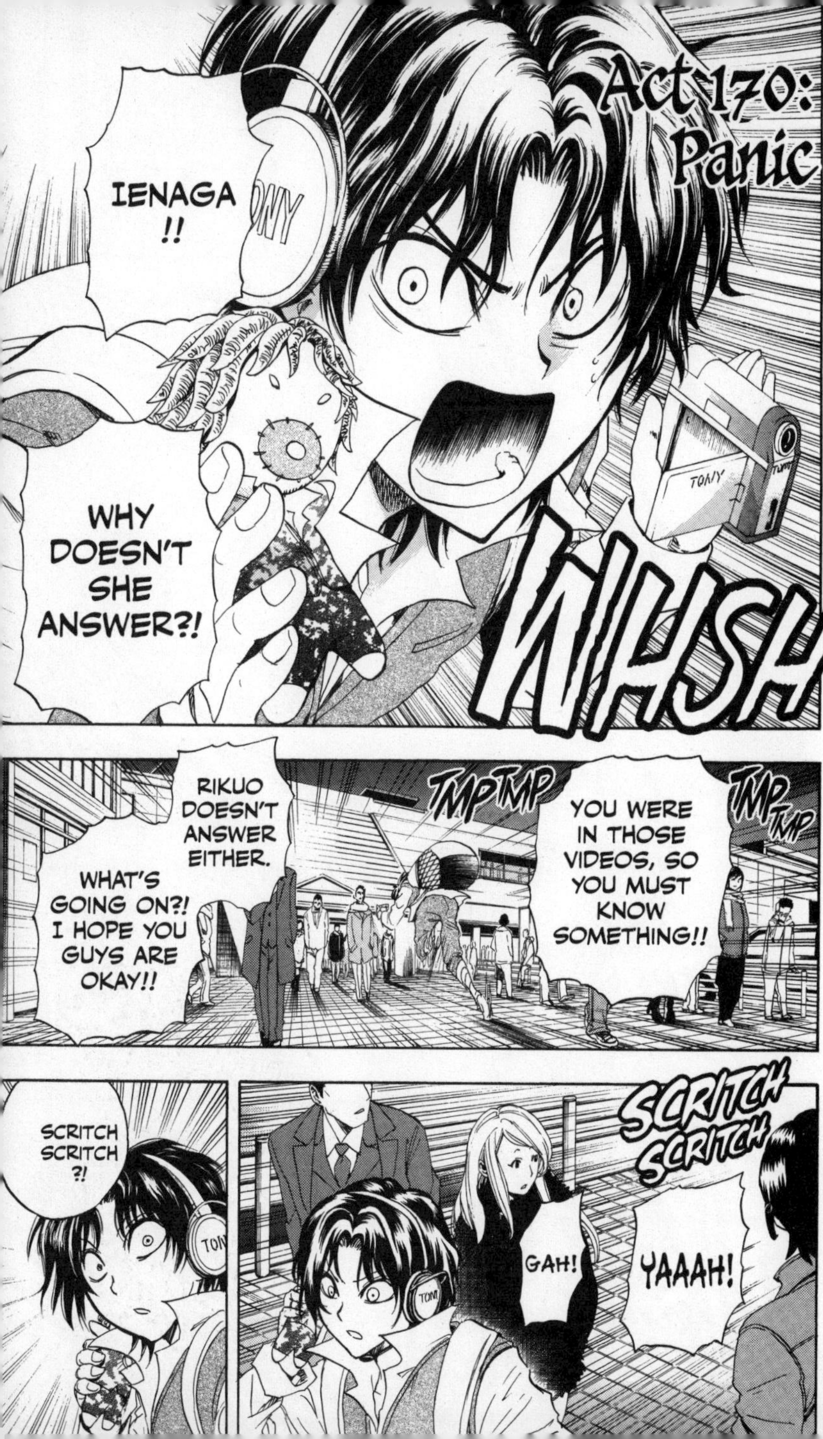
Act 170: Panic
IENAGA !!
WHUSH
WHY DOESN'T SHE ANSWER?!
TMP TMP
YOU WERE IN THOSE VIDEOS, SO YOU MUST KNOW SOMETHING!!
TMP TMP
RIKUO DOESN'T ANSWER EITHER.
WHAT'S GOING ON?! I HOPE YOU GUYS ARE OKAY!!
SCRITCH SCRITCH
YAAAH!
GAH!
SCRITCH SCRITCH ?!

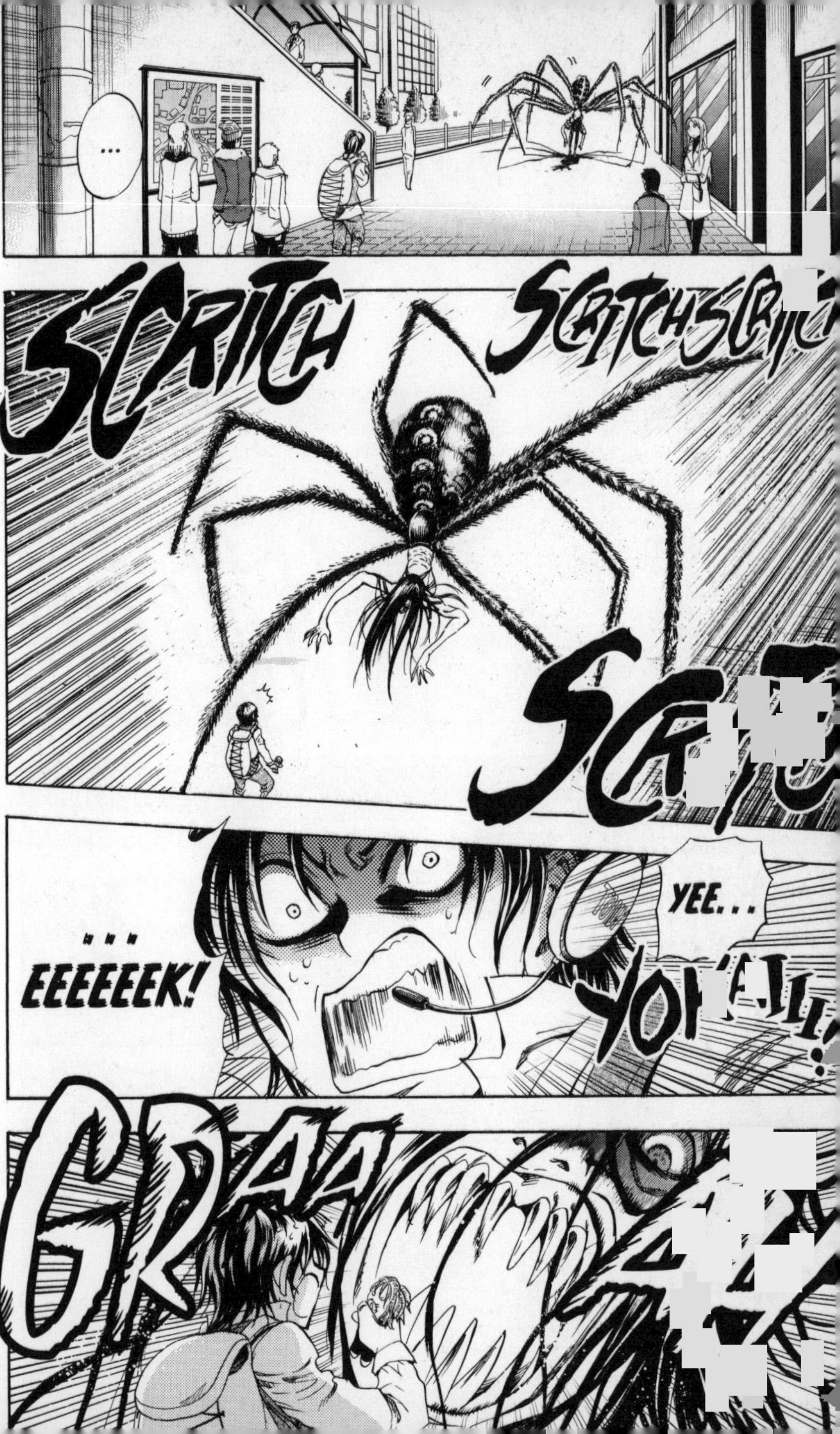
...
SCRITCH
YEE...
... EEEEEEK!

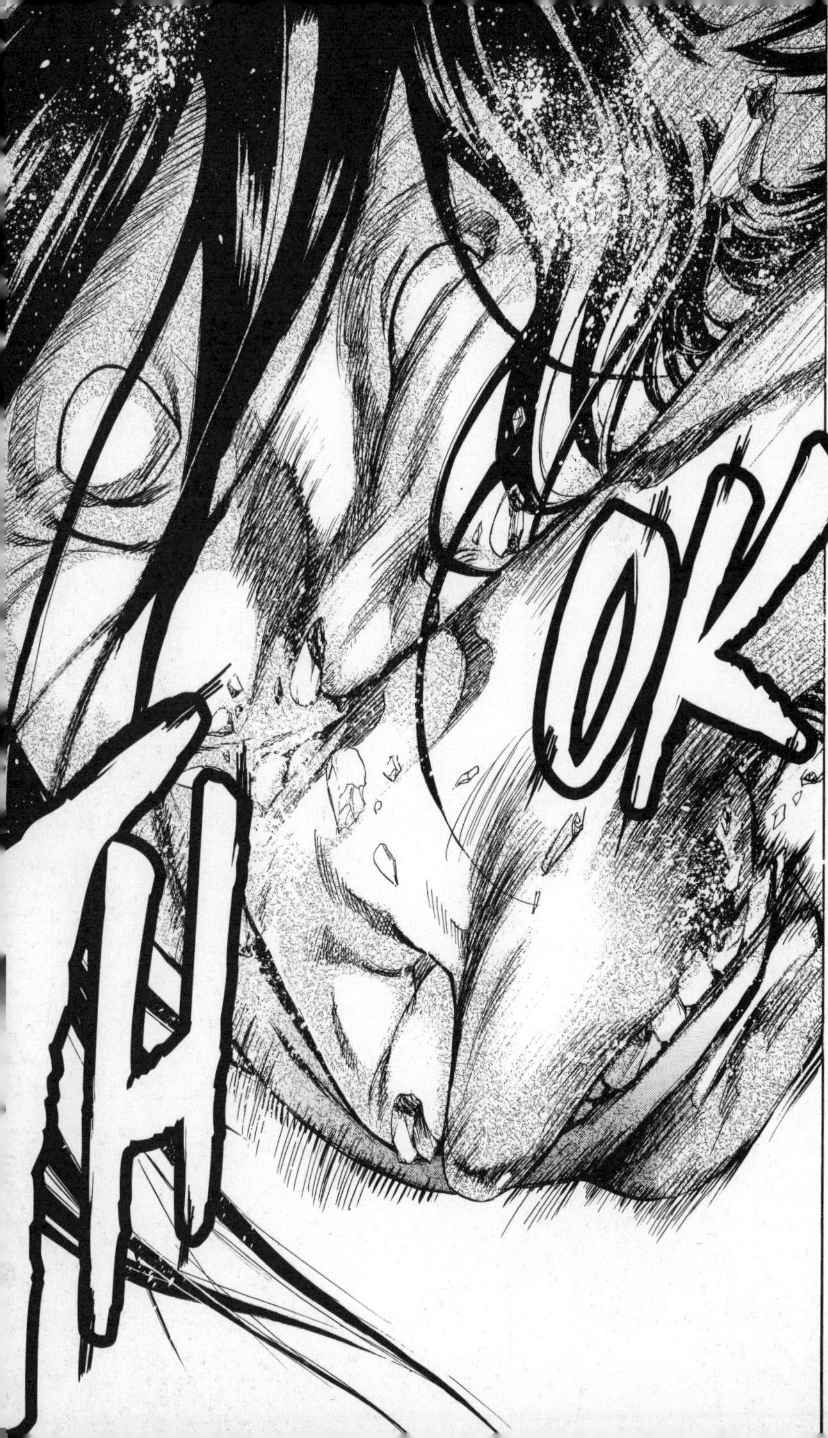
HOK

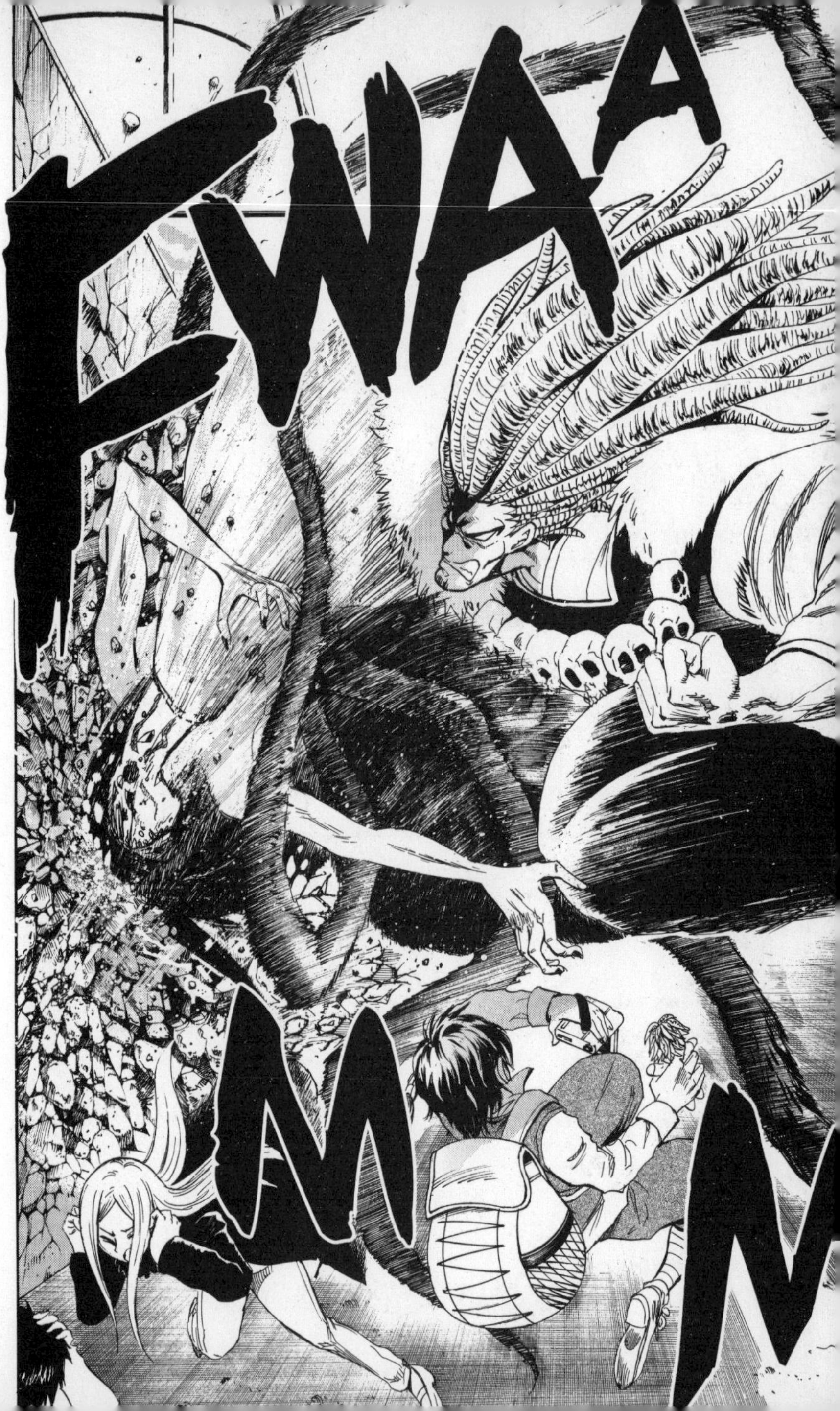
FWAA
MMN

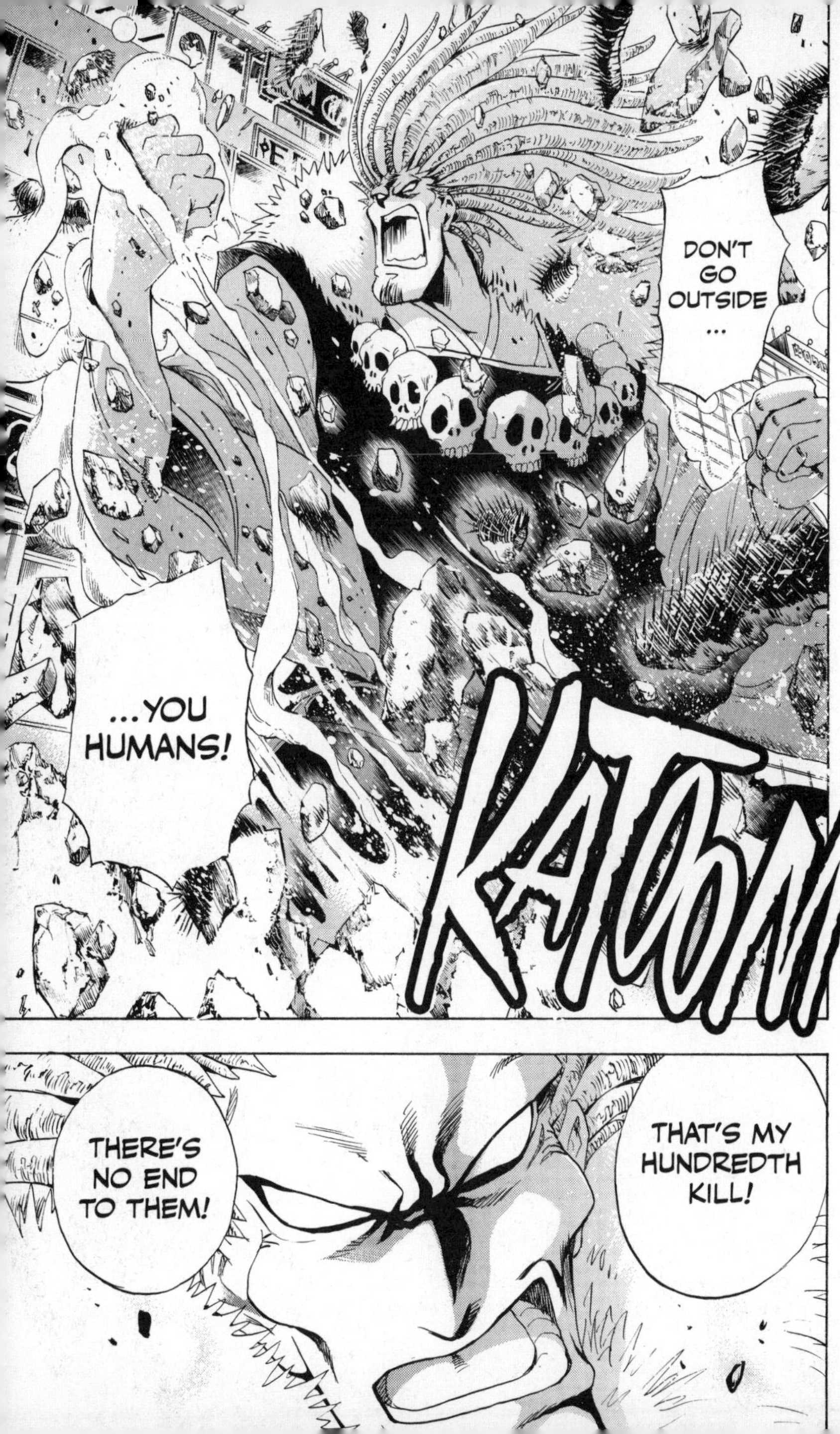
DON'T GO OUTSIDE ...
...YOU HUMANS!
KATOM
THAT'S MY HUNDREDTH KILL!
THERE'S NO END TO THEM!

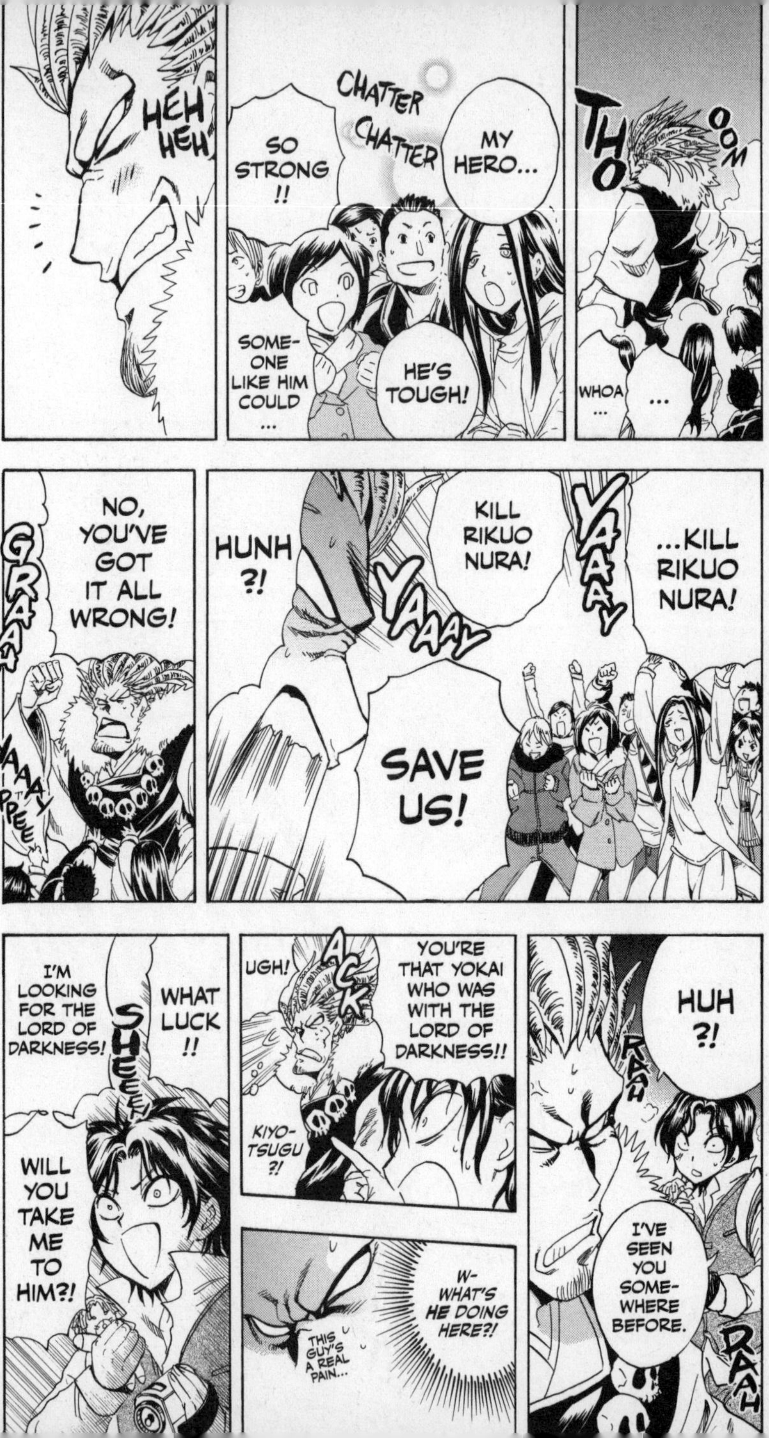
THOOOOM
WHOA...
...
MY HERO...
CHATTER CHATTER
SO STRONG!!
HE'S TOUGH!
SOME-ONE LIKE HIM COULD...
HEH HEH
...KILL RIKUO NURA!
YAAAY
KILL RIKUO NURA!
YAAAY
HUNH?!
SAVE US!
NO, YOU'VE GOT IT ALL WRONG!
GRAAAH
YAAAAY YIPPEE
HUH?!
RAAH
I'VE SEEN YOU SOME-WHERE BEFORE.
DAAAH
YOU'RE THAT YOKAI WHO WAS WITH THE LORD OF DARKNESS!!
ACK
UGH!
KIYO-TSUGU?!
W-WHAT'S HE DOING HERE?!
THIS GUY'S A REAL PAIN...
WHAT LUCK!!
I'M LOOKING FOR THE LORD OF DARKNESS!
SHEEEE
WILL YOU TAKE ME TO HIM?!

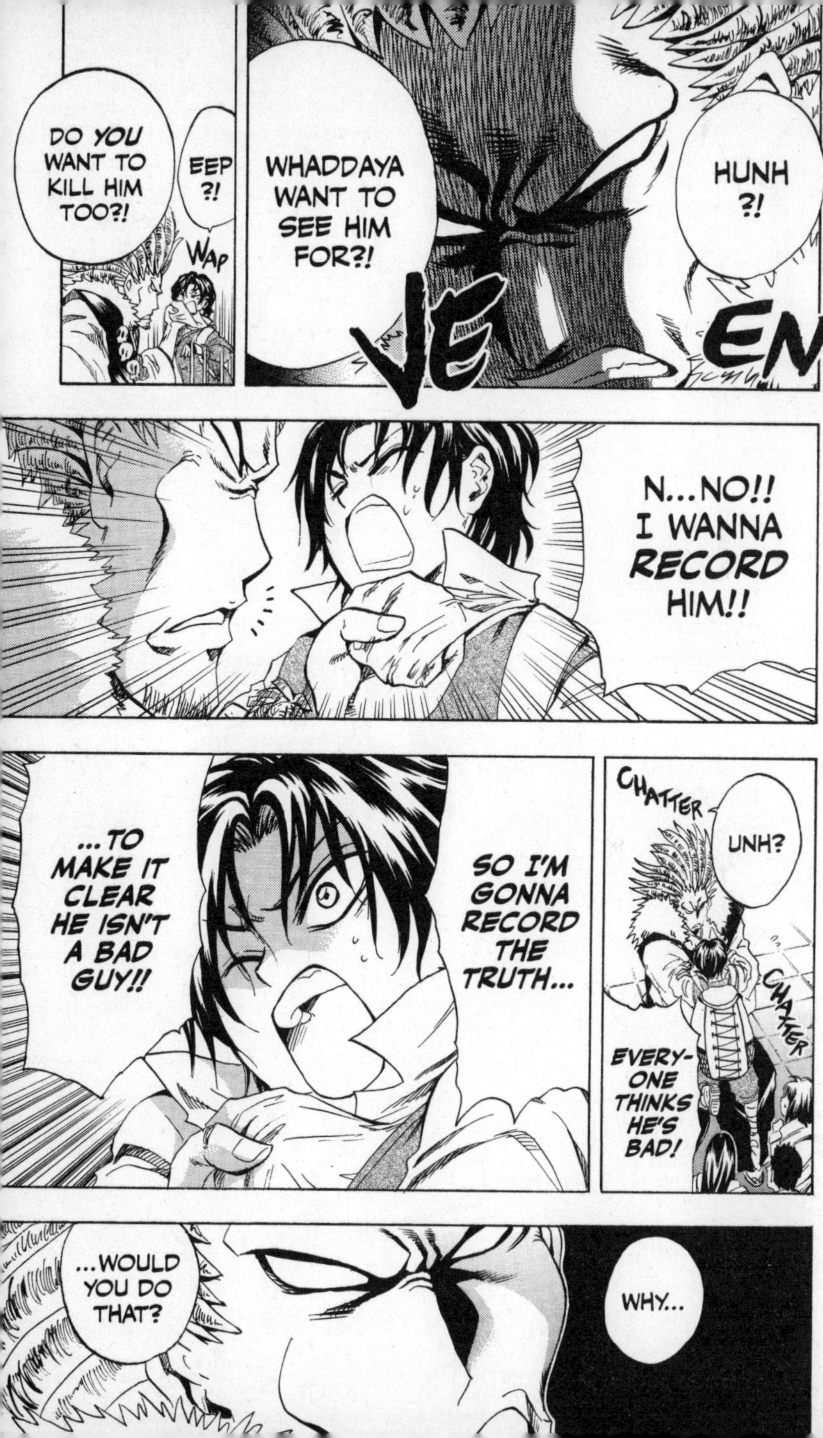
HUNH ?!
EN
WHADDAYA WANT TO SEE HIM FOR?!
VE
EEP ?!
WAP
DO YOU WANT TO KILL HIM TOO?!
N...NO!! I WANNA RECORD HIM!!
CHATTER
UNH?
CHATTER
EVERY-ONE THINKS HE'S BAD!
SO I'M GONNA RECORD THE TRUTH...
...TO MAKE IT CLEAR HE ISN'T A BAD GUY!!
WHY...
...WOULD YOU DO THAT?

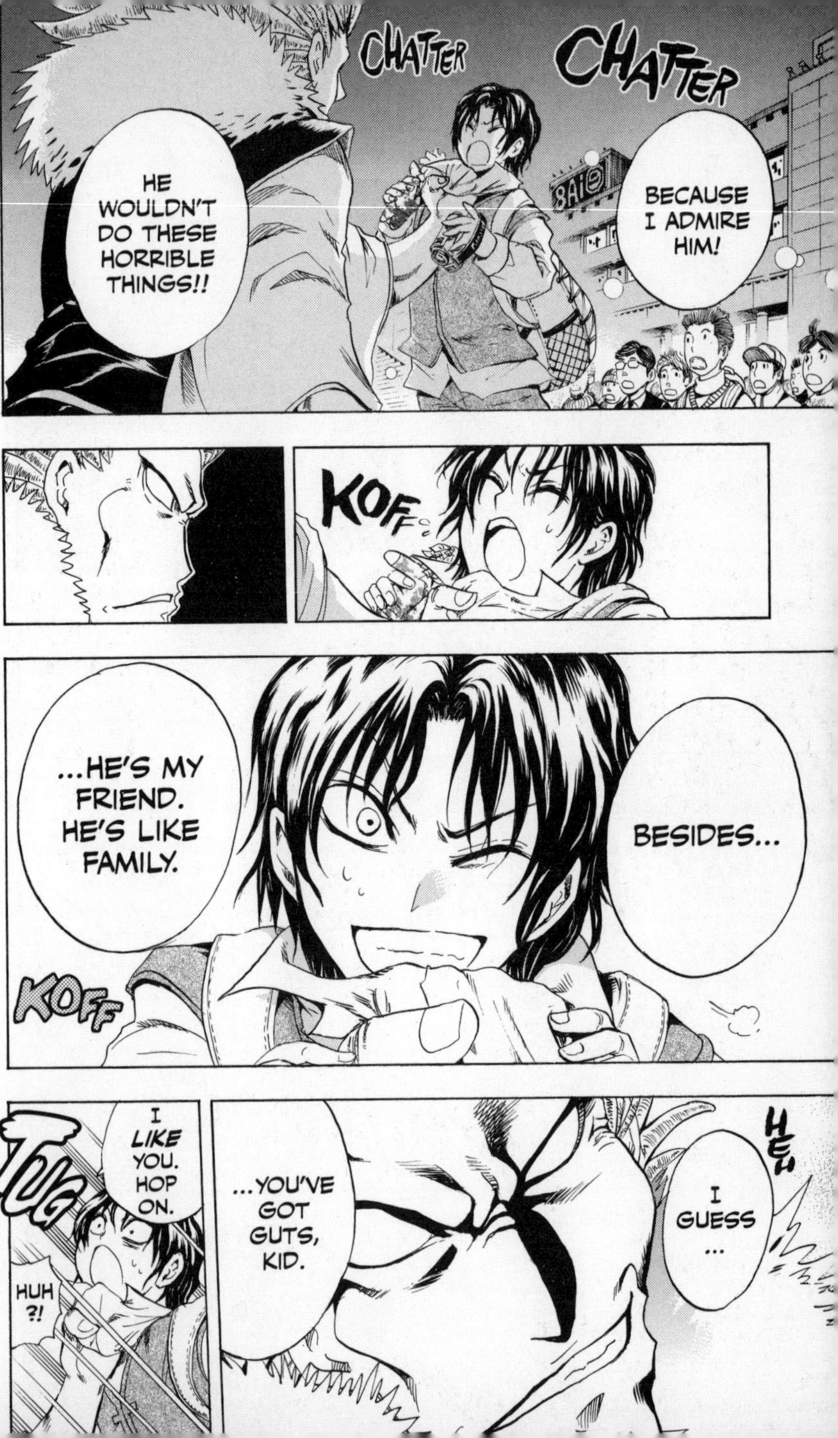
CHATTER
CHATTER
BECAUSE I ADMIRE HIM!
HE WOULDN'T DO THESE HORRIBLE THINGS!!
KOFF
BESIDES...
...HE'S MY FRIEND. HE'S LIKE FAMILY.
KOFF
HEH
I GUESS ...
...YOU'VE GOT GUTS, KID.
TUG
I LIKE YOU. HOP ON.
HUH ?!

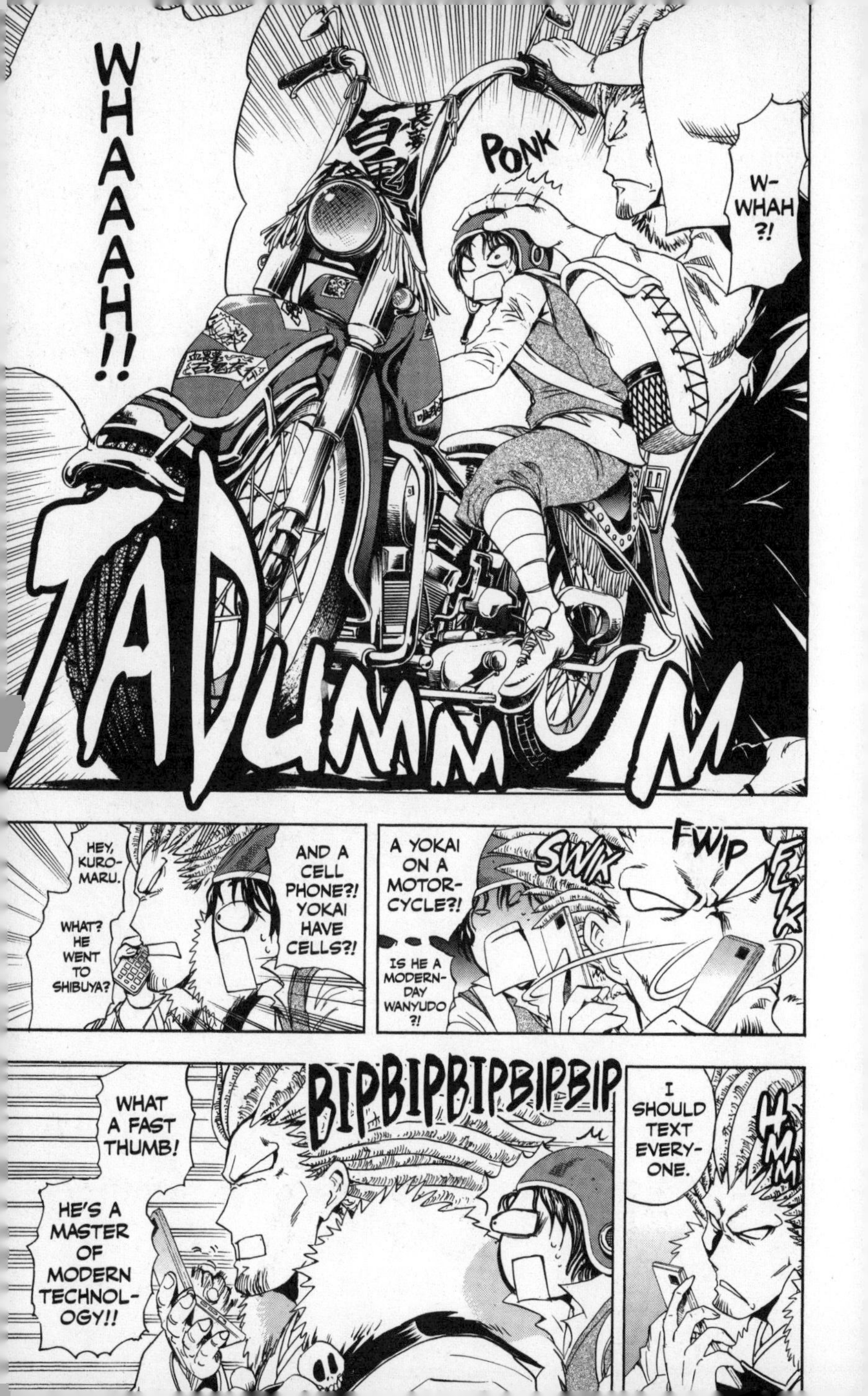
W-WHAH?!
PONK
WHAAAAH!!
TADUMMM
FWIP
SWK
FLIK
A YOKAI ON A MOTORCYCLE?!
IS HE A MODERN-DAY WANYUDO?!
AND A CELL PHONE?! YOKAI HAVE CELLS?!
HEY, KURO-MARU.
WHAT? HE WENT TO SHIBUYA?
HMM
I SHOULD TEXT EVERYONE.
BIPBIPBIPBIPBIP
WHAT A FAST THUMB!
HE'S A MASTER OF MODERN TECHNOLOGY!!

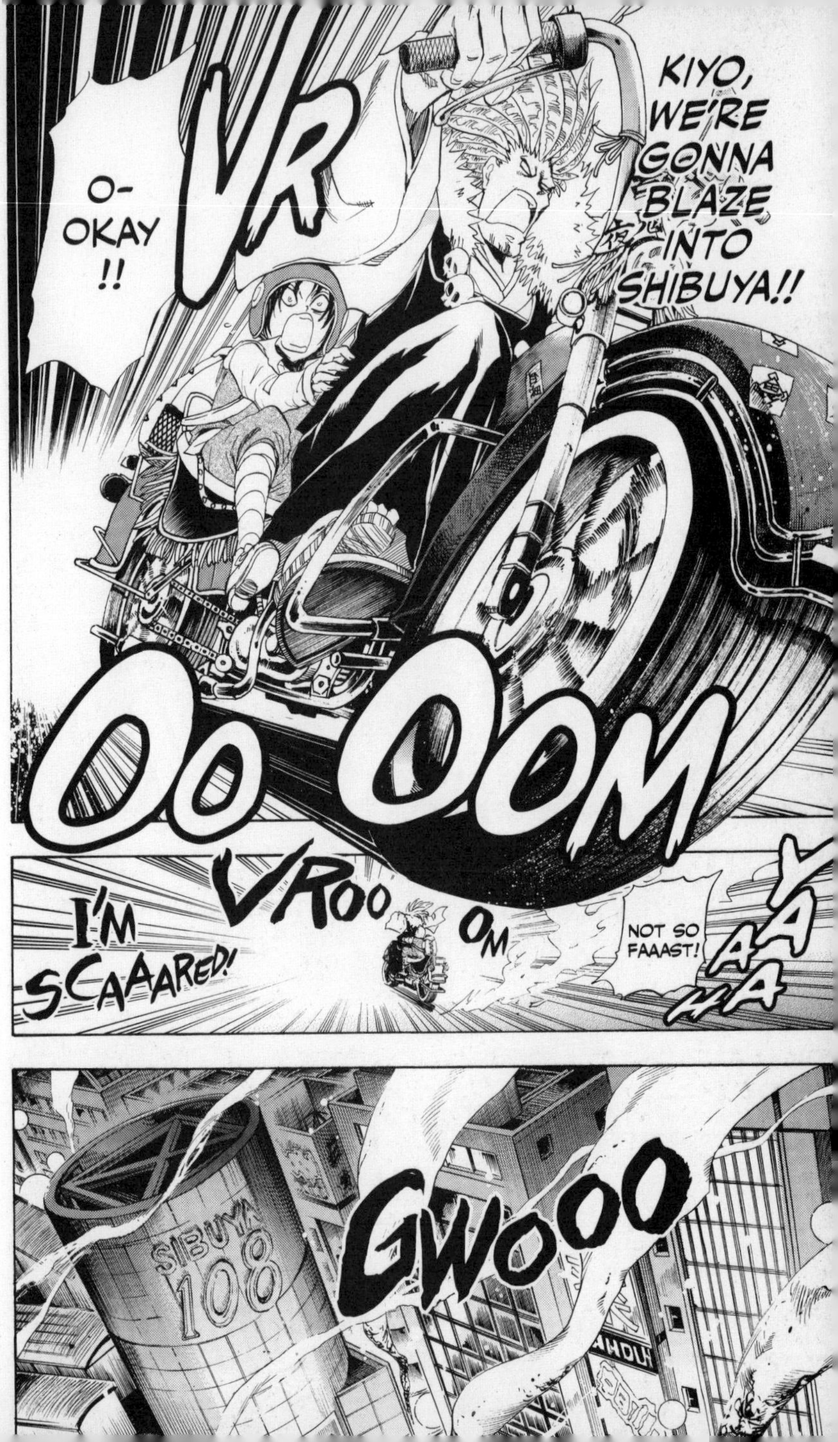
KIYO, WE'RE GONNA BLAZE INTO SHIBUYA!!
VR
O-OKAY!!
OO OOM
YAAAHA
NOT SO FAAAST!
VROO OM
I'M SCAAARED!
GWOOO
SIBUYA 108

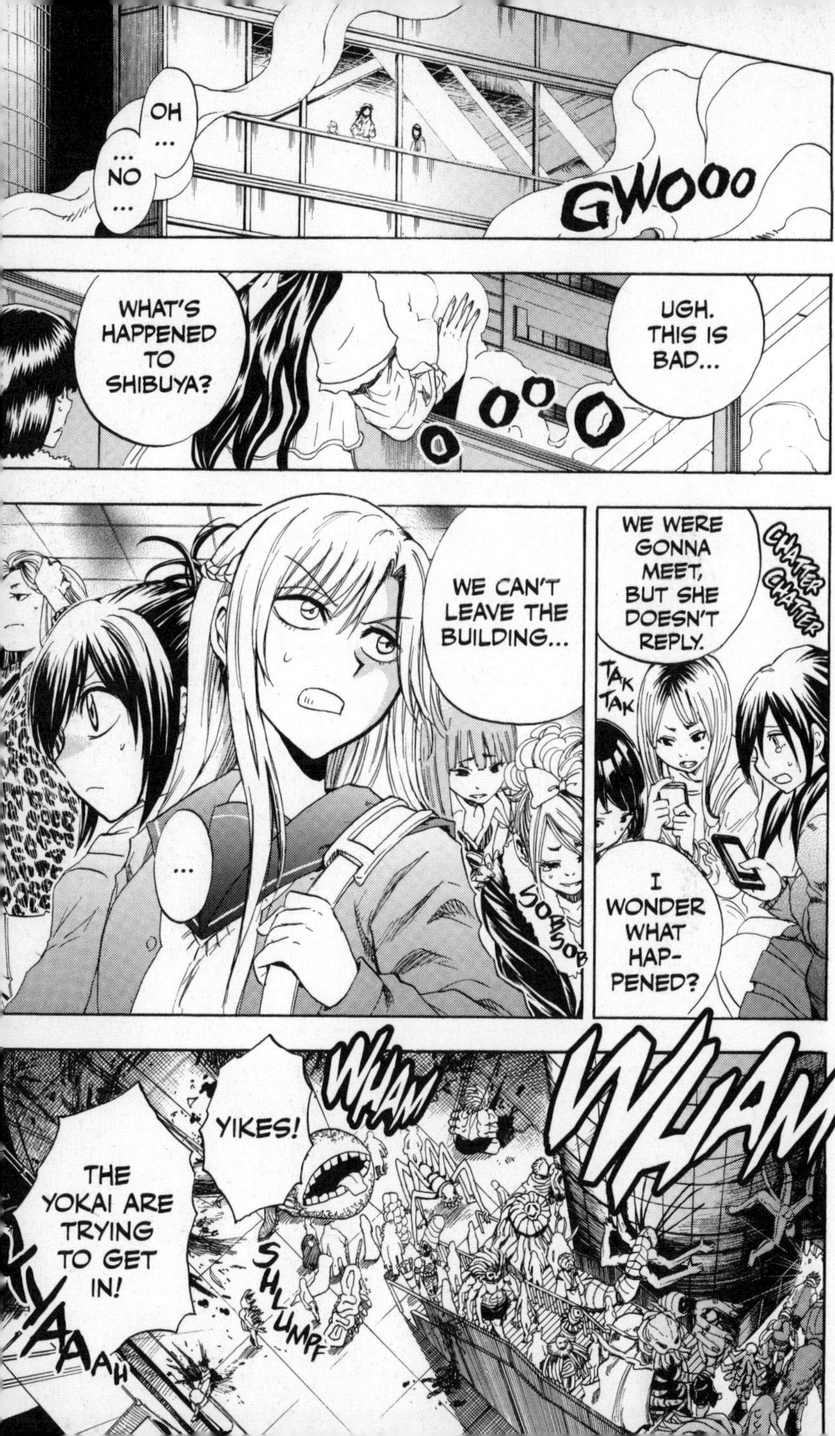
GWOOO
OH ... ... NO ...
UGH. THIS IS BAD...
OOOO
WHAT'S HAPPENED TO SHIBUYA?
WE WERE GONNA MEET, BUT SHE DOESN'T REPLY.
CHATTER CHATTER
TAK TAK
I WONDER WHAT HAP-PENED?
WE CAN'T LEAVE THE BUILDING...
SOB SOB
...
WHAM
WHAM
YIKES!
THE YOKAI ARE TRYING TO GET IN!
SHLUMPF
YAAAAH

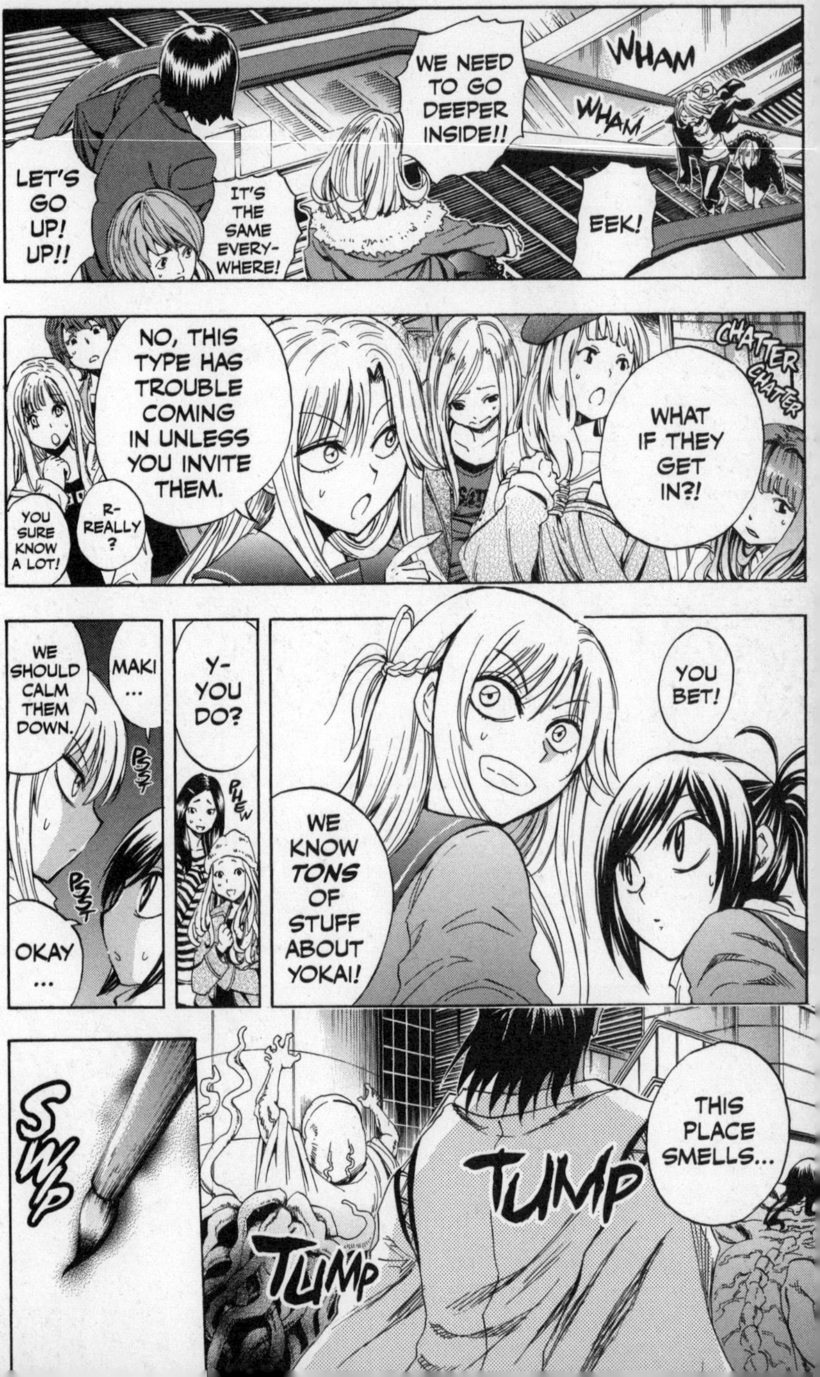
WHAM
WHAM
EEK!
WE NEED TO GO DEEPER INSIDE!!
IT'S THE SAME EVERYWHERE!
LET'S GO UP! UP!!
CHATTER CHATTER
WHAT IF THEY GET IN?!
NO, THIS TYPE HAS TROUBLE COMING IN UNLESS YOU INVITE THEM.
R-REALLY?
YOU SURE KNOW A LOT!
YOU BET!
WE KNOW TONS OF STUFF ABOUT YOKAI!
Y-YOU DO?
PHEW
MAKI...
WE SHOULD CALM THEM DOWN.
PSST
PSST
OKAY...
THIS PLACE SMELLS...
TUMP
TUMP
SWP

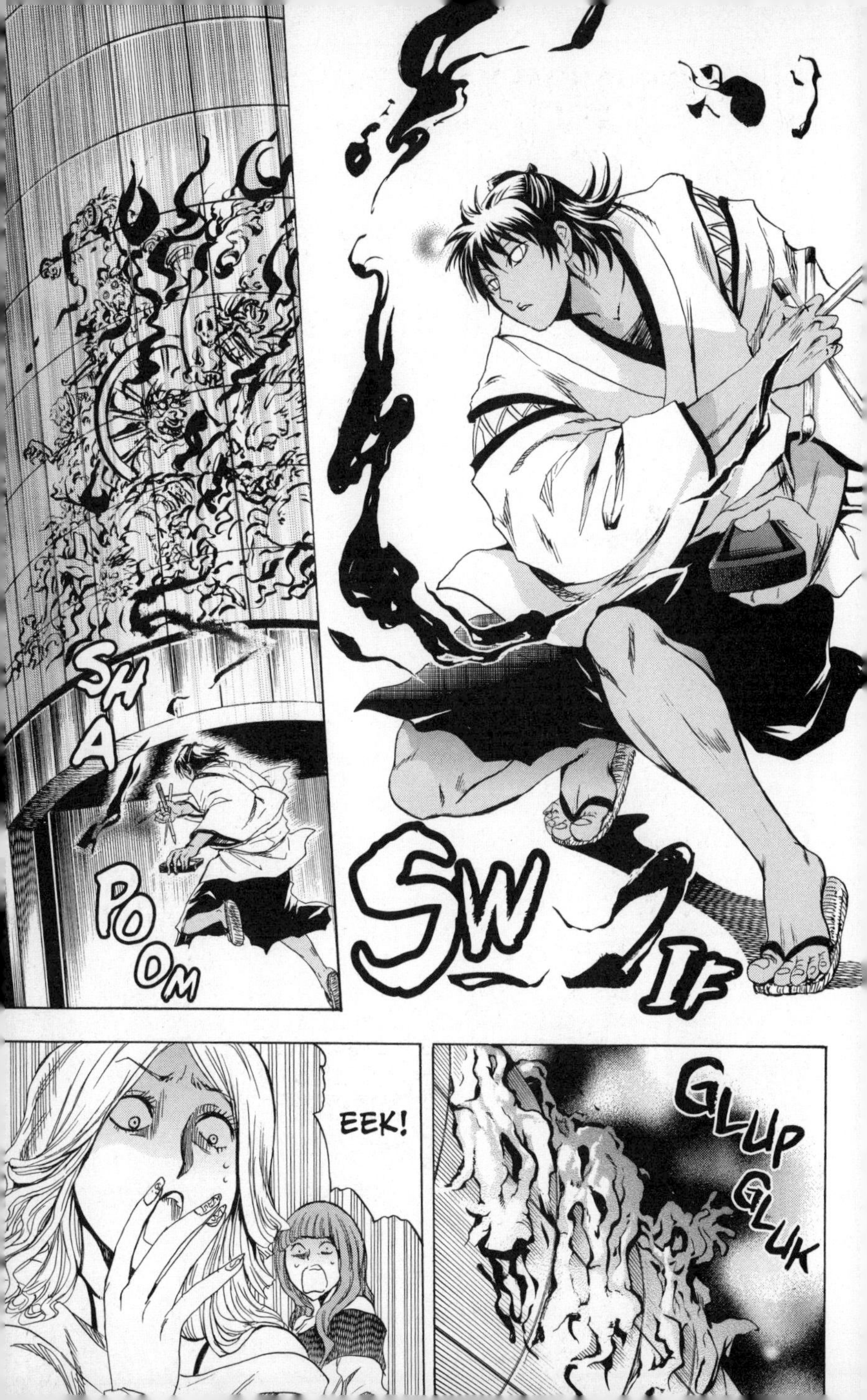
SWIF
SHA
POOM
GLUP
GLUK
EEK!

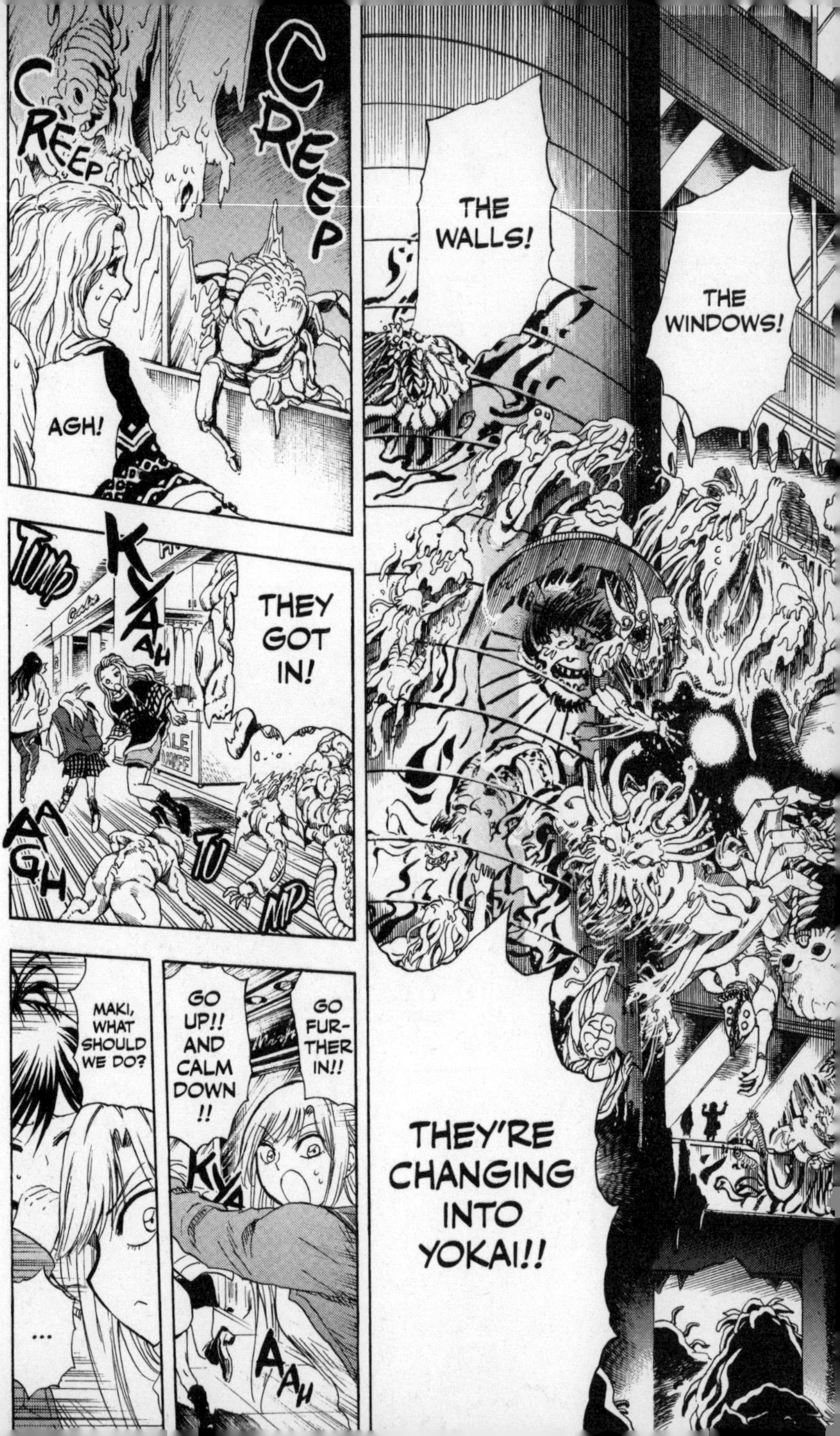
THE WINDOWS!
THE WALLS!
THEY'RE CHANGING INTO YOKAI!!
CREEP
CREEP
AGH!
KYAAH
TUMP
THEY GOT IN!
AAGH
TUMP
GO FURTHER IN!!
GO UP!! AND CALM DOWN!!
KYA
AAH
MAKI, WHAT SHOULD WE DO?
...

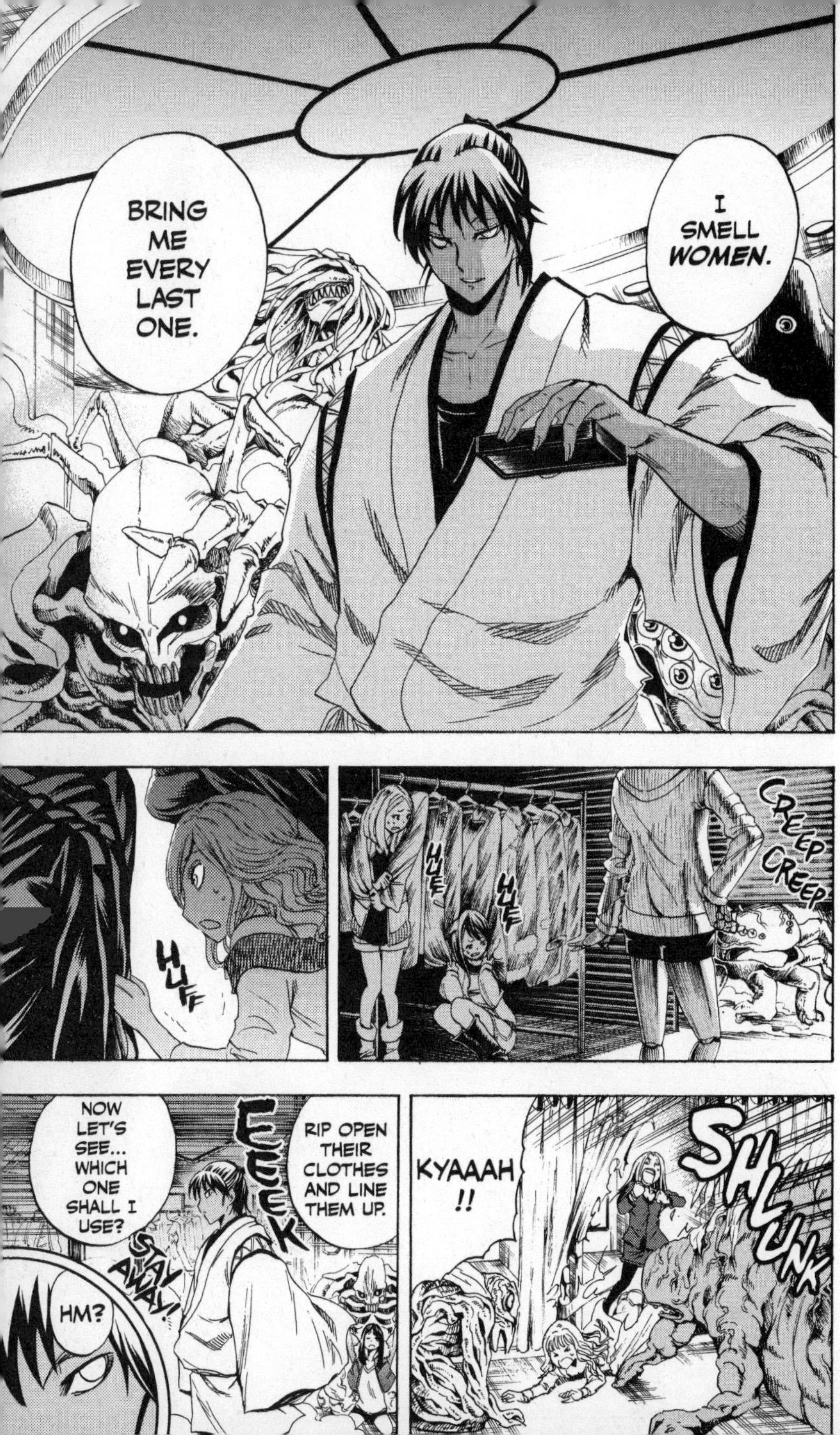
I SMELL WOMEN.
BRING ME EVERY LAST ONE.
CREEP CREEP
HUFF
HUFF
HUFF
SHLUNK
KYAAAH!!
RIP OPEN THEIR CLOTHES AND LINE THEM UP.
EEEEK
NOW LET'S SEE... WHICH ONE SHALL I USE?
STAY AWAY!
HM?

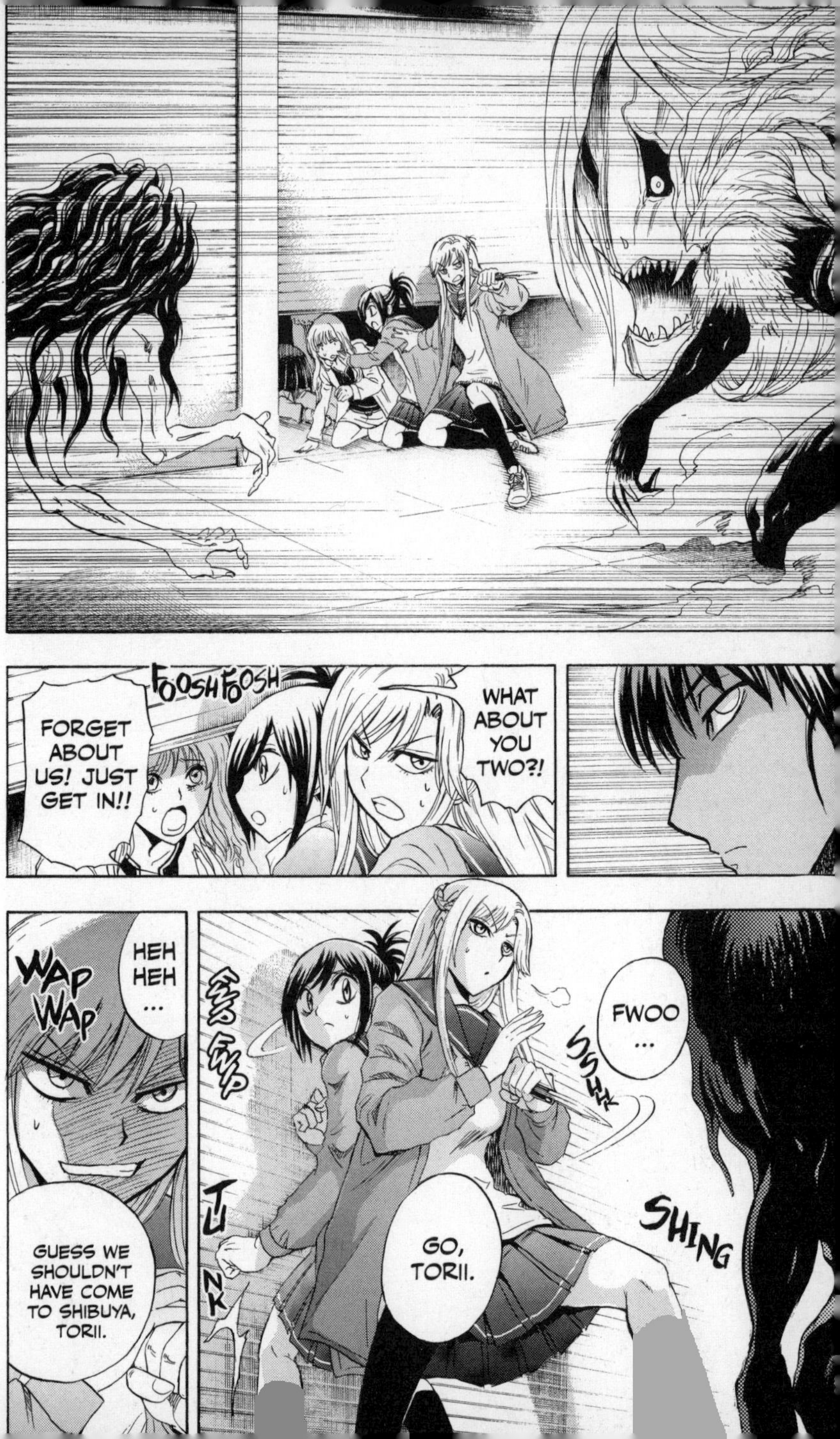
WHAT ABOUT YOU TWO?!
FOOSH FOOSH
FORGET ABOUT US! JUST GET IN!!
FWOO ...
SSHHK
SHING
GO, TORII.
FWIP FWIP
TUNK
HEH HEH ...
WAP WAP
GUESS WE SHOULDN'T HAVE COME TO SHIBUYA, TORII.

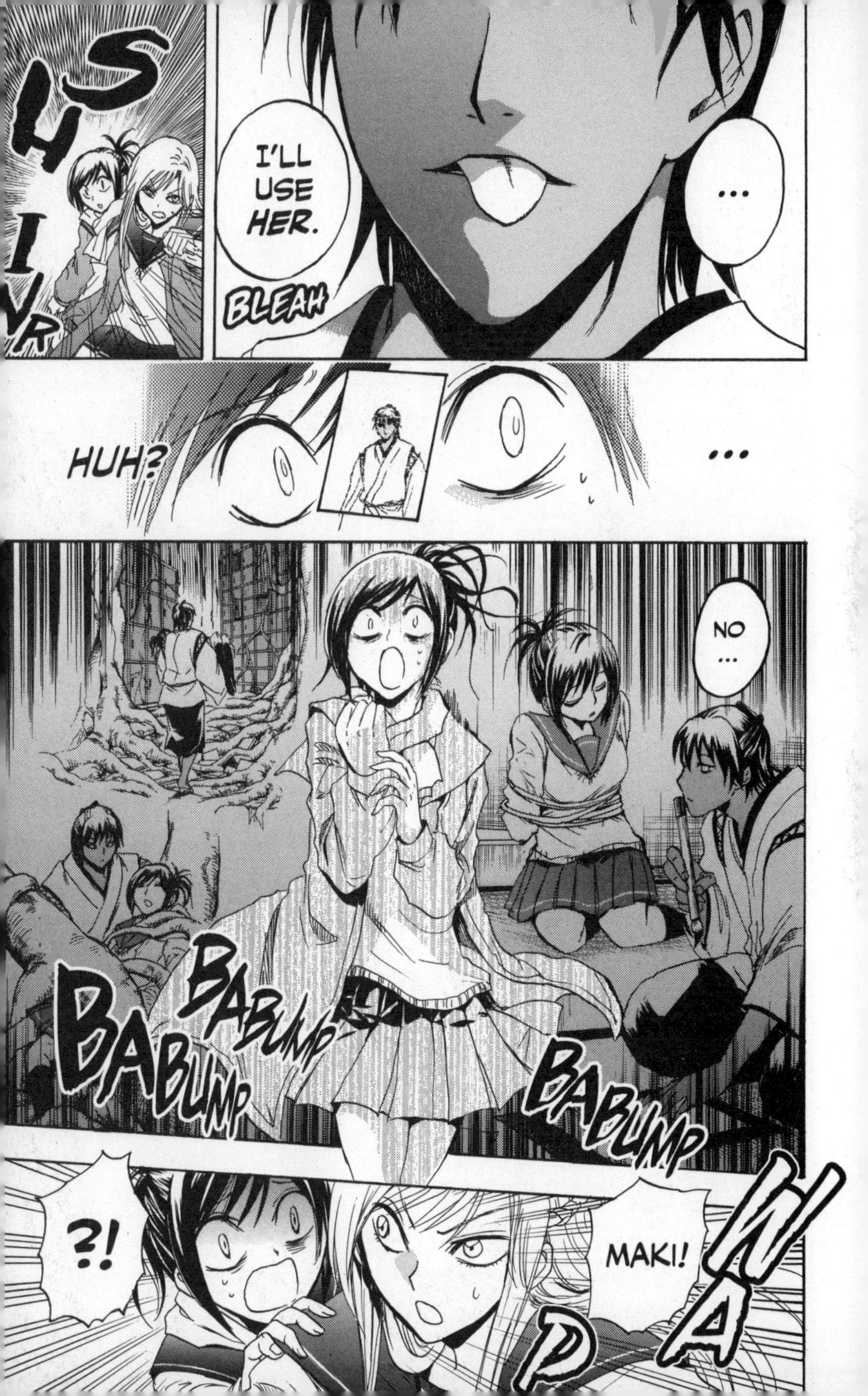
...
I'LL USE HER.
BLEAH
SHIVR
...
HUH?
NO ...
BABUMP
BABUMP
BABUMP
WHAP
MAKI!
?!

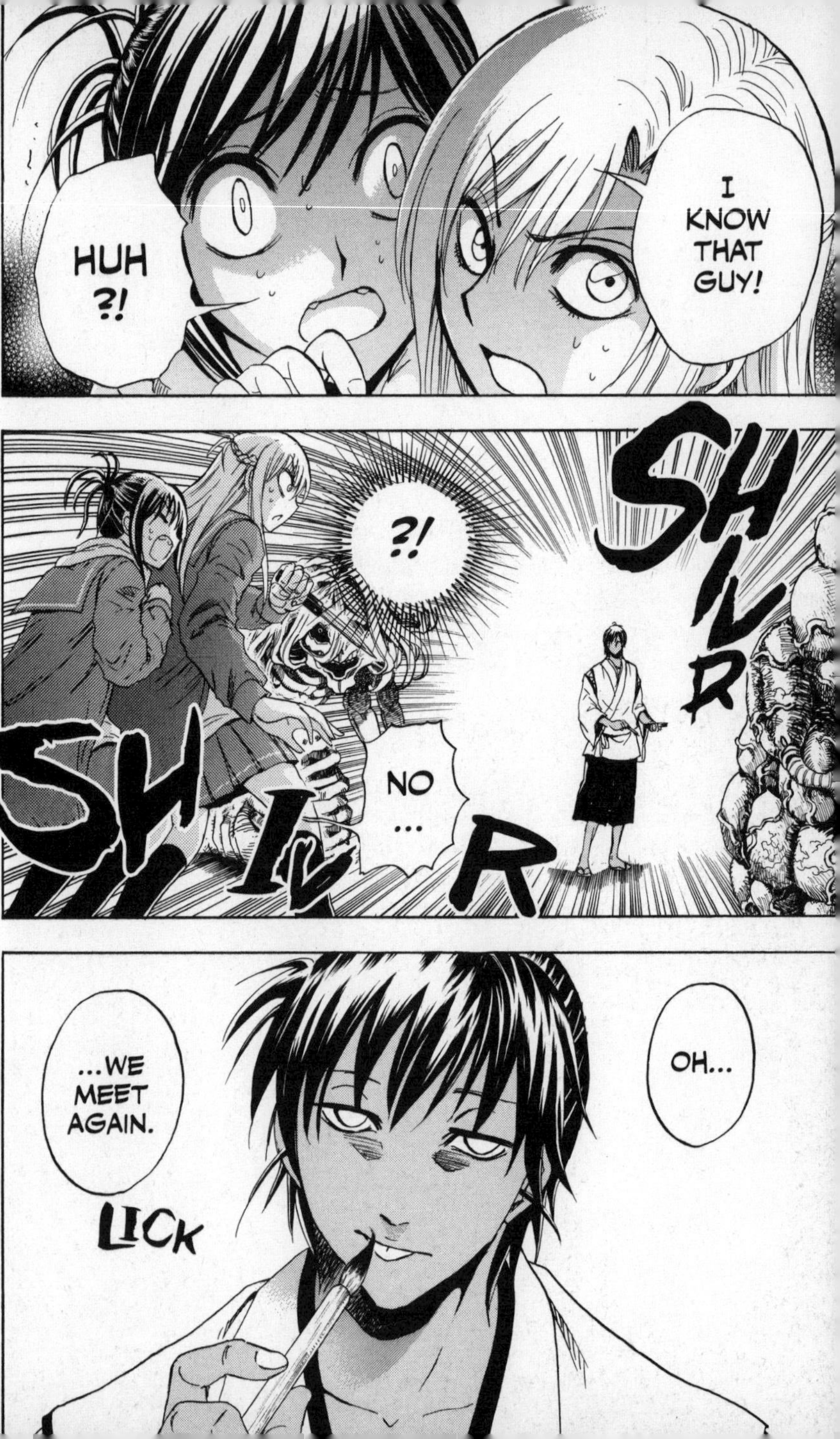
I KNOW THAT GUY!
HUH ?!
?!
NO ...
OH...
...WE MEET AGAIN.
LICK

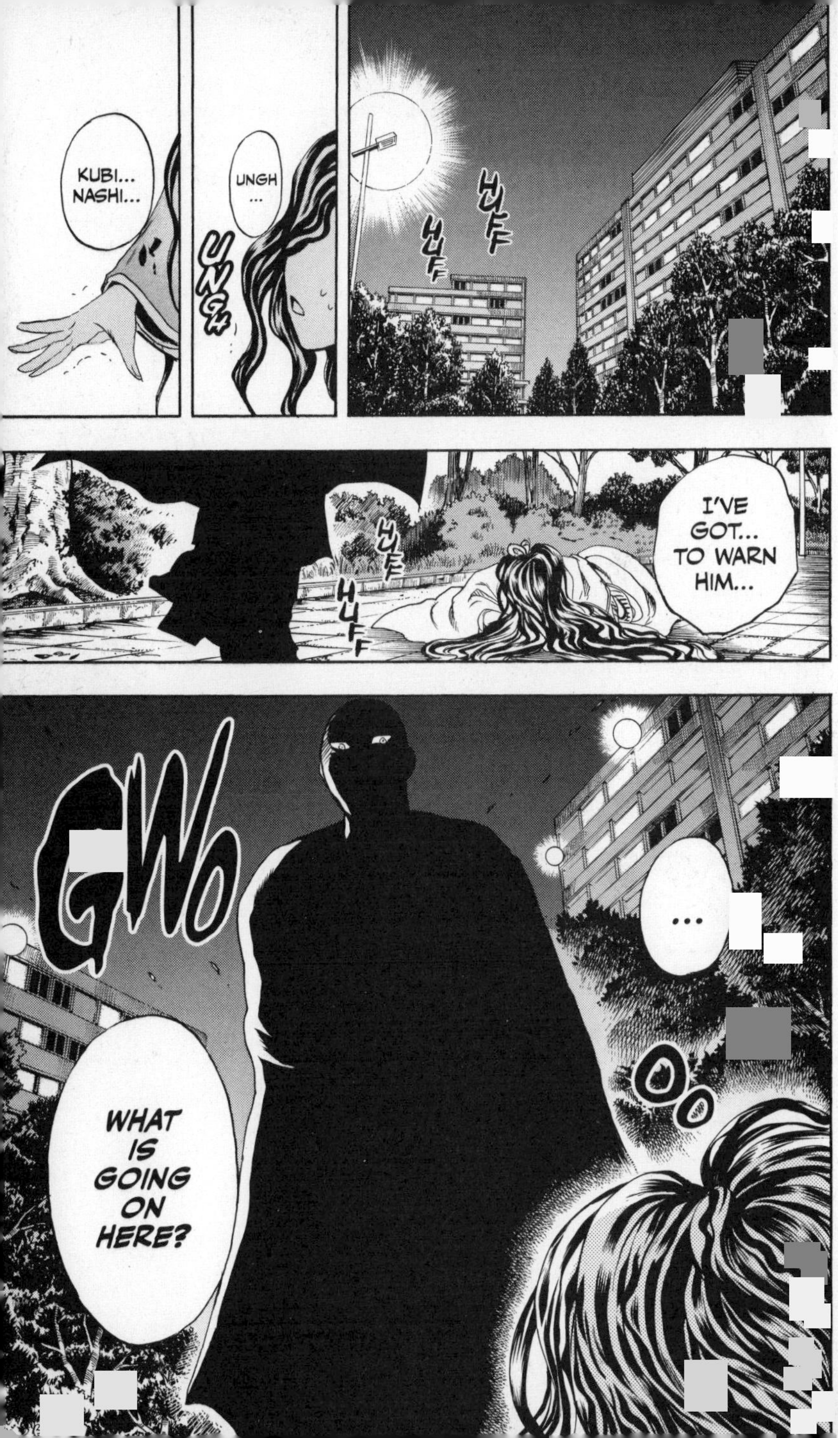
HUFF
HUFF
UNGH
...
UNGH
KUBI... NASHI...
I'VE GOT... TO WARN HIM...
HUFF
HUFF
...
GWO
WHAT IS GOING ON HERE?

Kya ha!
Tee hee hee! Manga

We're in the Nura Fan Club! Part 2

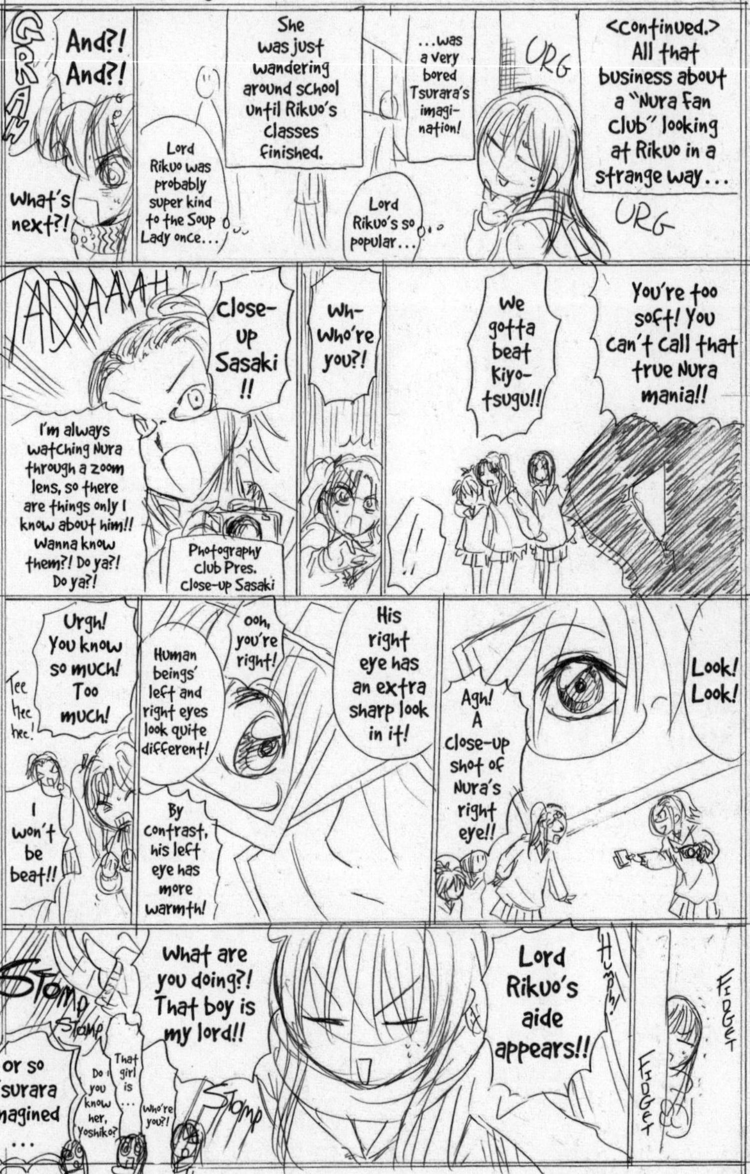
<continued.> All that business about a "Nura fan club" looking at Rikuo in a strange way...
URG
URG
...was a very bored Tsurara's imagination!
Lord Rikuo's so popular...
She was just wandering around school until Rikuo's classes finished.
Lord Rikuo was probably super kind to the Soup Lady once...
GRAAH
And?! And?!
What's next?!
You're too soft! You can't call that true Nura mania!!
We gotta beat Kiyotsugu!!
!!
Wh-who're you?!
TADAAAAH
Close-up Sasaki!!
I'm always watching Nura through a zoom lens, so there are things only I know about him!! Wanna know them?! Do ya?! Do ya?!
Photography club Pres. close-up Sasaki
Look! Look!
Agh! A close-up shot of Nura's right eye!!
His right eye has an extra sharp look in it!
ooh, you're right!
Human beings' left and right eyes look quite different!
By contrast, his left eye has more warmth!
Urgh! You know so much! Too much!
Tee hee hee!
I won't be beat!!
FIDGET
FIDGET
Lord Rikuo's aide appears!!
HUMPH
What are you doing?! That boy is my lord!!
STOMP
STOMP
STOMP
Who're you?!
That girl is...
Do you know her, Yoshiko?
or so Tsurara imagined...

TO BE CONTINUED....

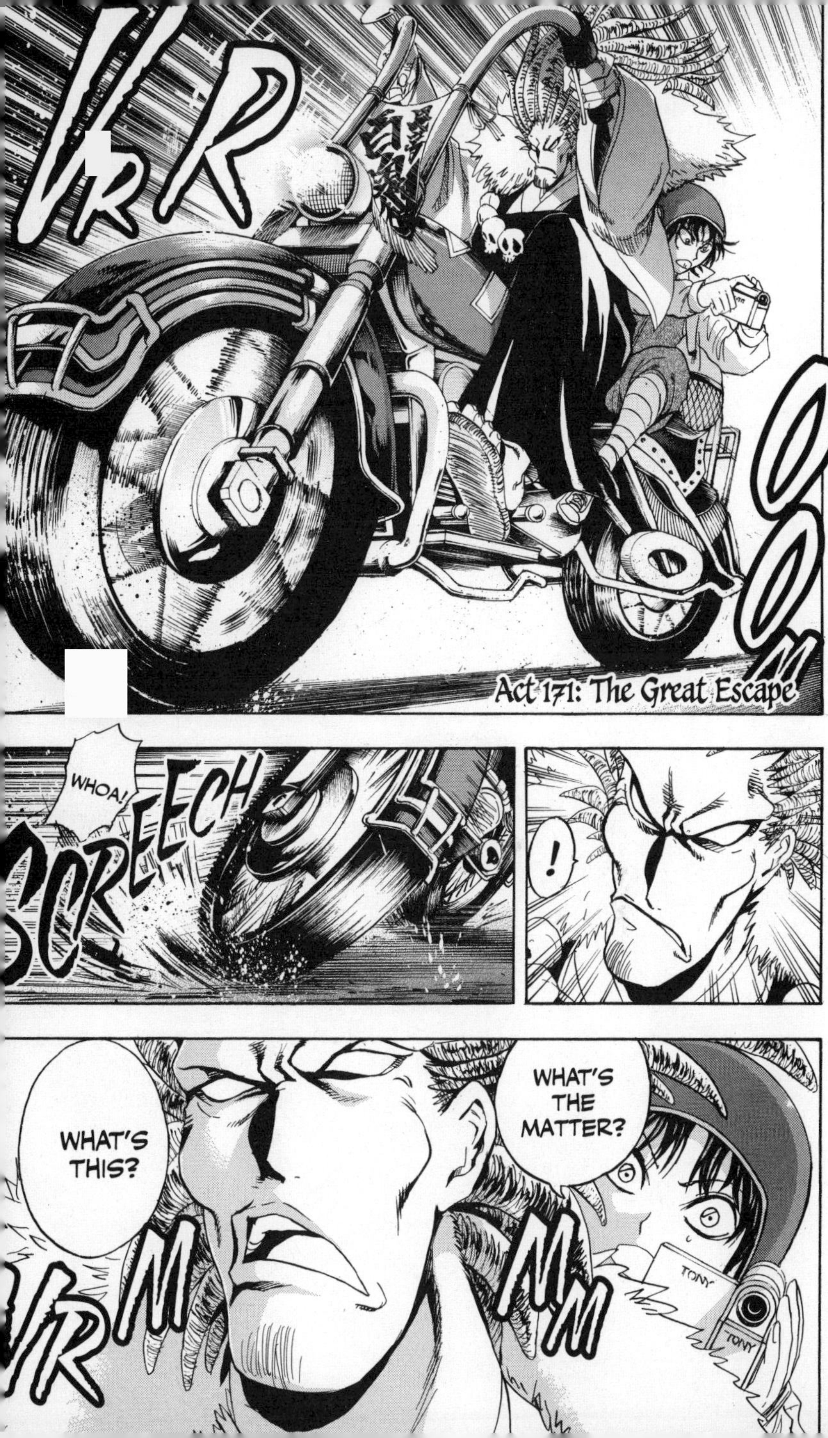
VRR
OOOM
Act 171: The Great Escape
!
WHOA!
SCREECH
WHAT'S THE MATTER?
WHAT'S THIS?
VRMMM
TONY
TONY

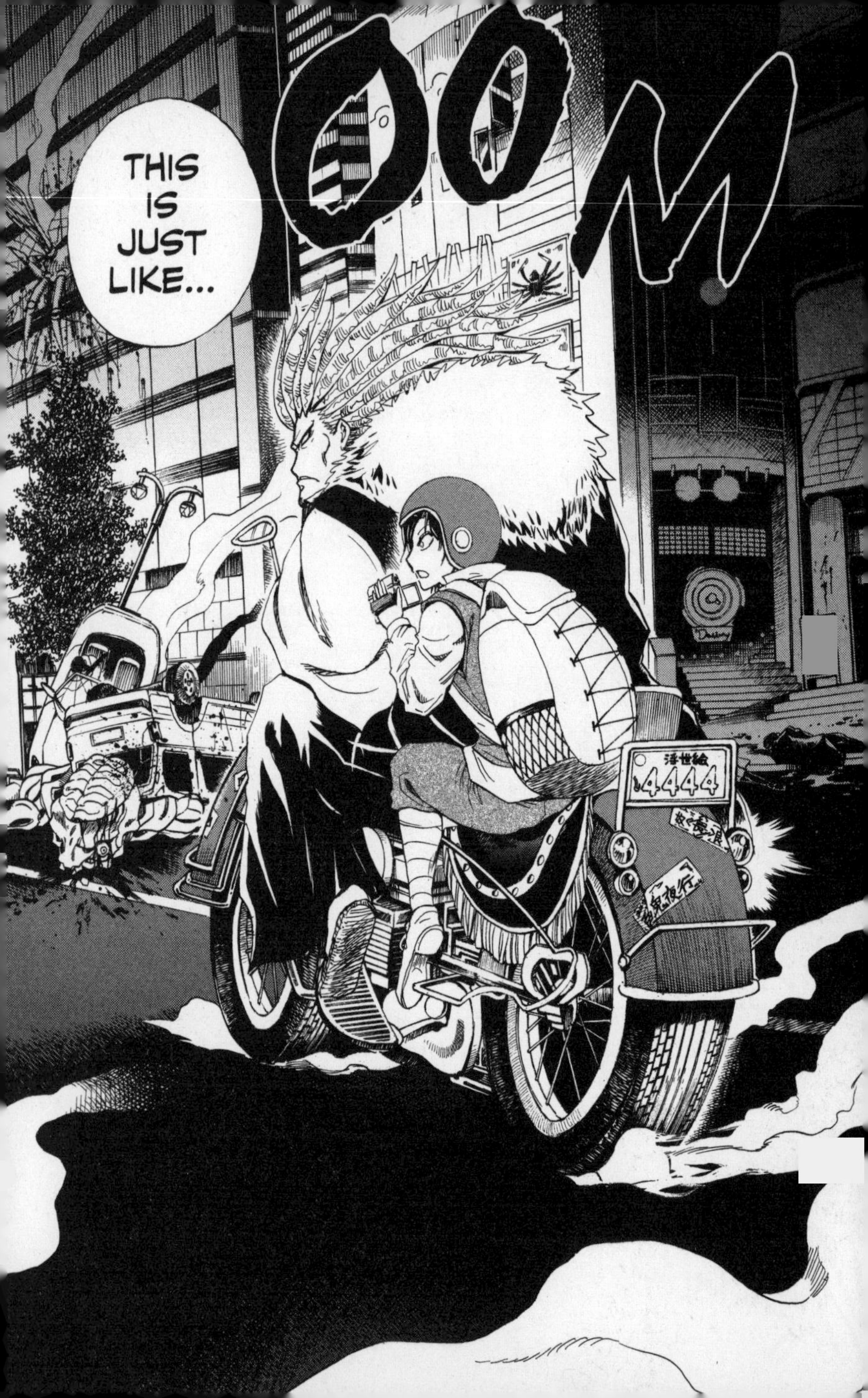
OOM
THIS IS JUST LIKE...
活世絵
4444

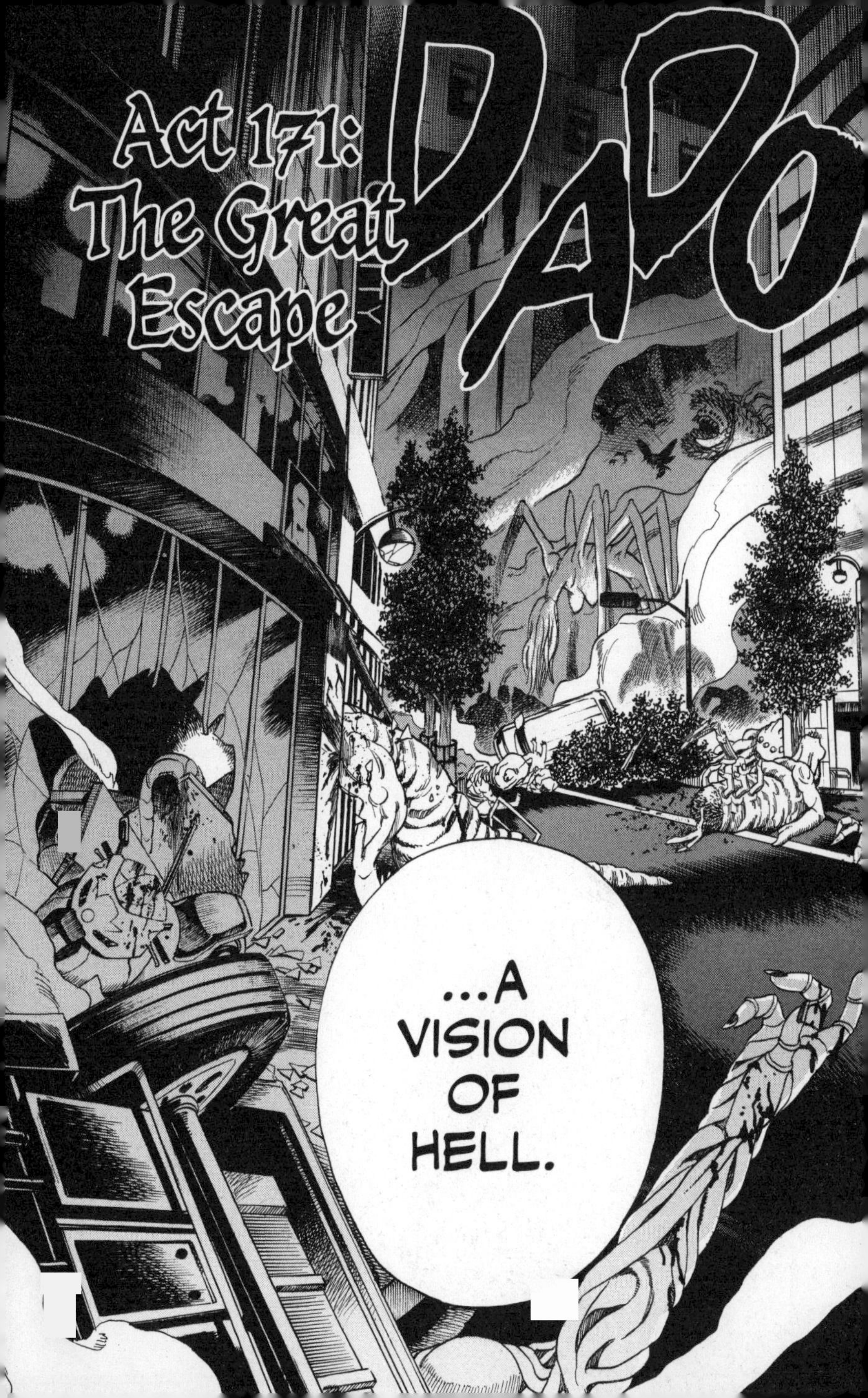
Act 171: The Great Escape
DADO
...A VISION OF HELL.

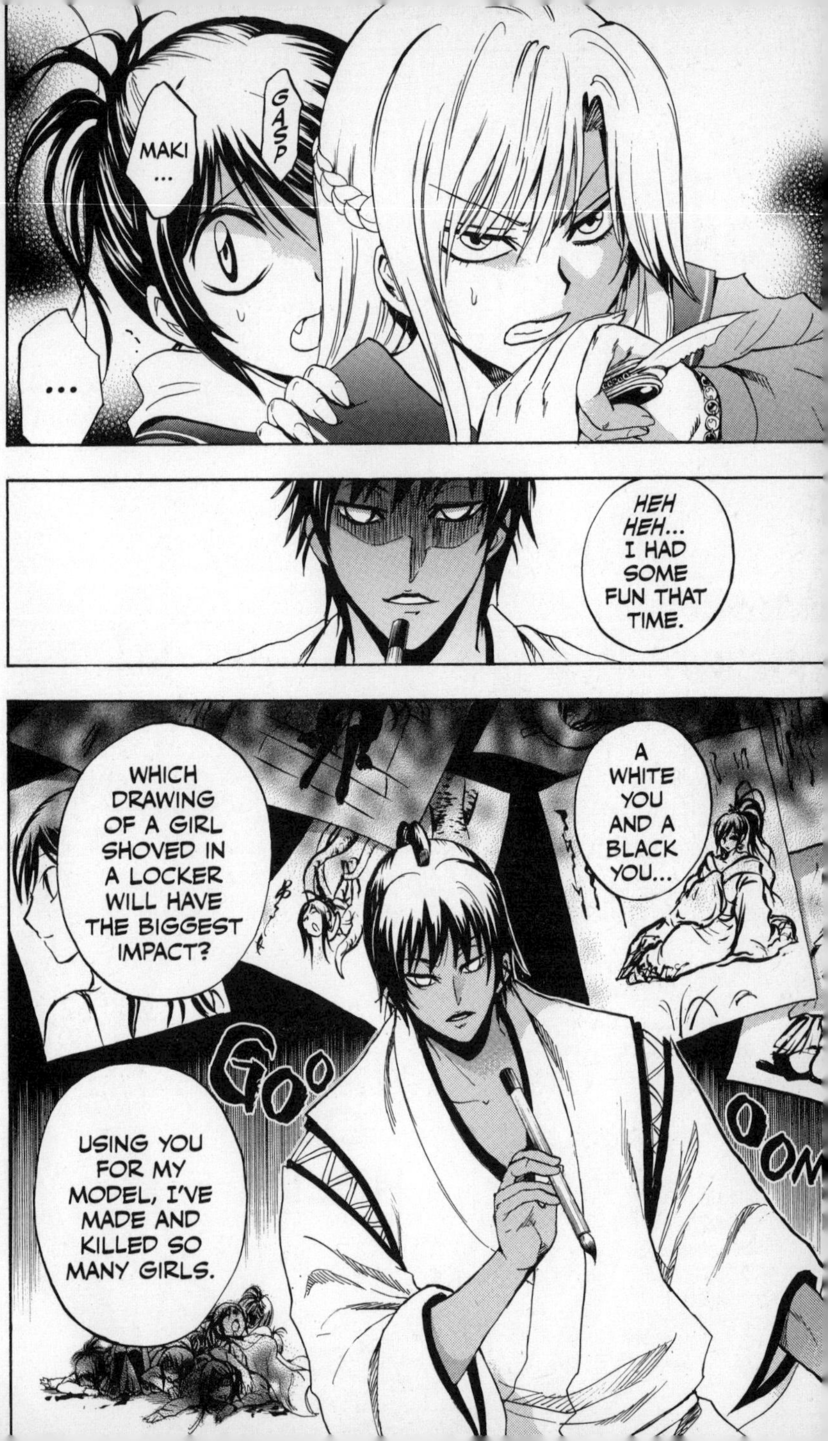
GASP
MAKI ...
...
HEH HEH... I HAD SOME FUN THAT TIME.
A WHITE YOU AND A BLACK YOU...
WHICH DRAWING OF A GIRL SHOVED IN A LOCKER WILL HAVE THE BIGGEST IMPACT?
GOO OOM
USING YOU FOR MY MODEL, I'VE MADE AND KILLED SO MANY GIRLS.

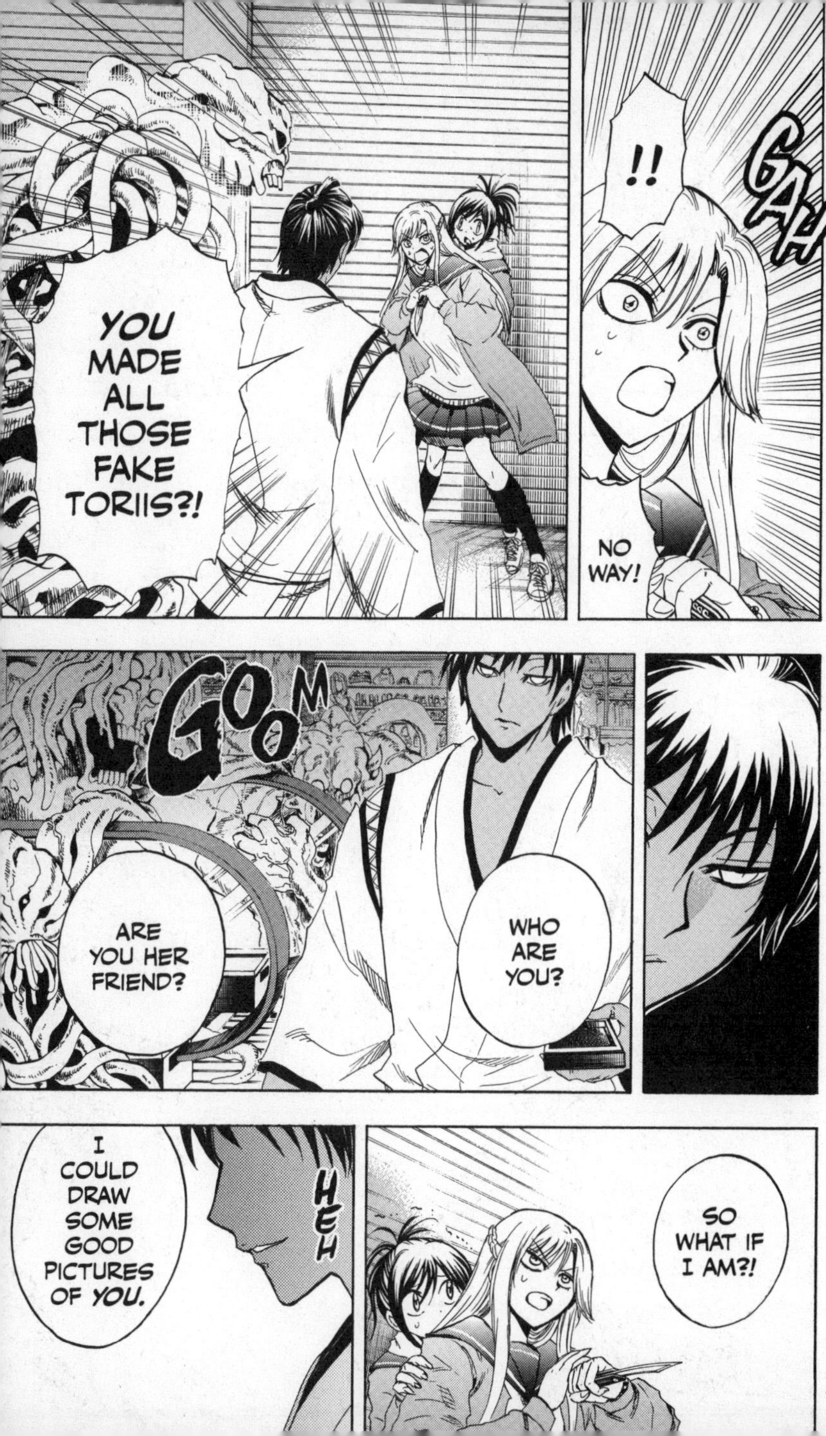
!!
GAH
NO WAY!
YOU MADE ALL THOSE FAKE TORIIS?!
GOOM
WHO ARE YOU?
ARE YOU HER FRIEND?
SO WHAT IF I AM?!
HEH
I COULD DRAW SOME GOOD PICTURES OF YOU.

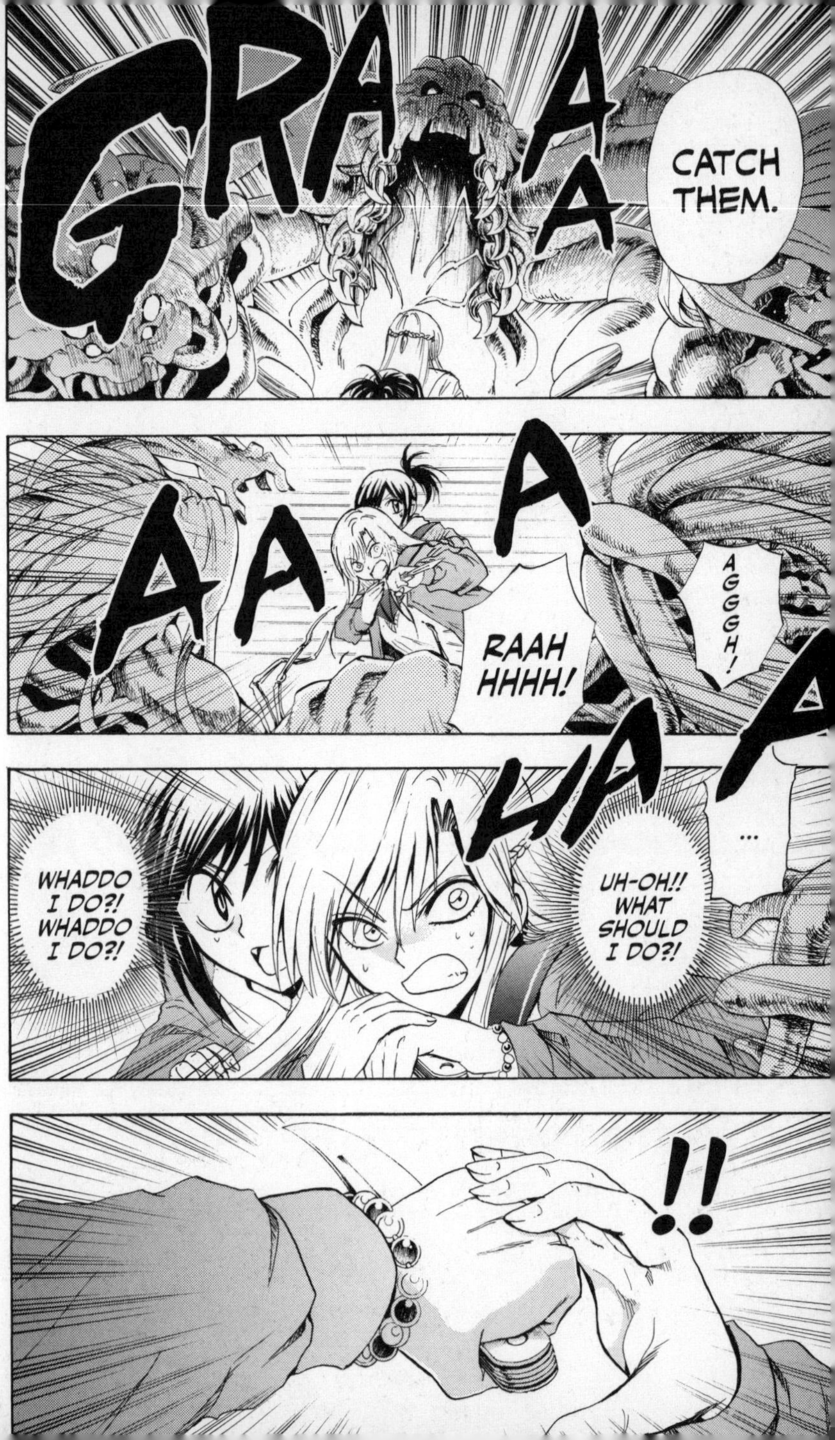
CATCH THEM.
GRAAA
AGGGH!
RAAH HHHH!
AAA
AAA
...
UH-OH!! WHAT SHOULD I DO?!
WHADDO I DO?! WHADDO I DO?!
!!

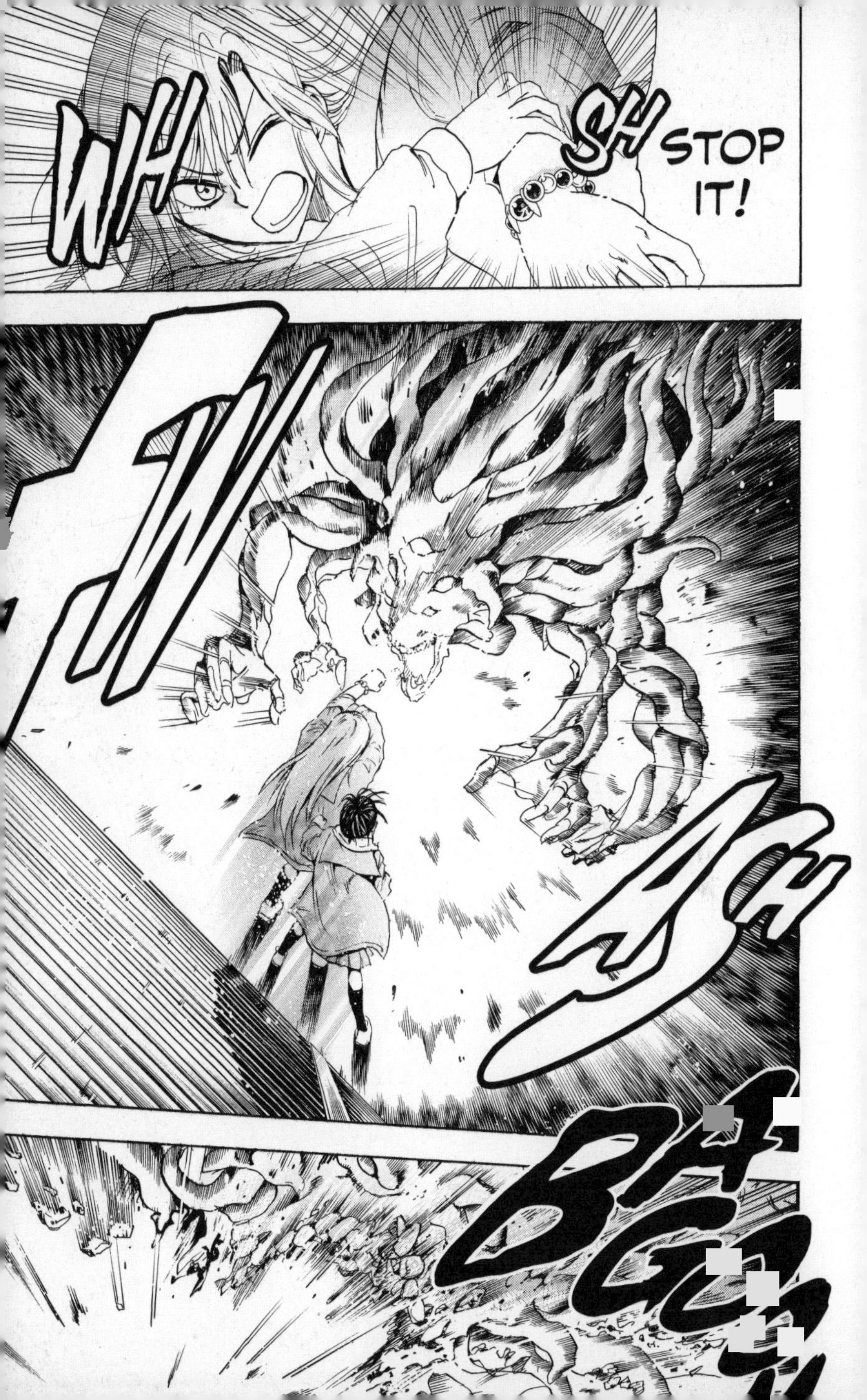
STOP IT!
SH
WH

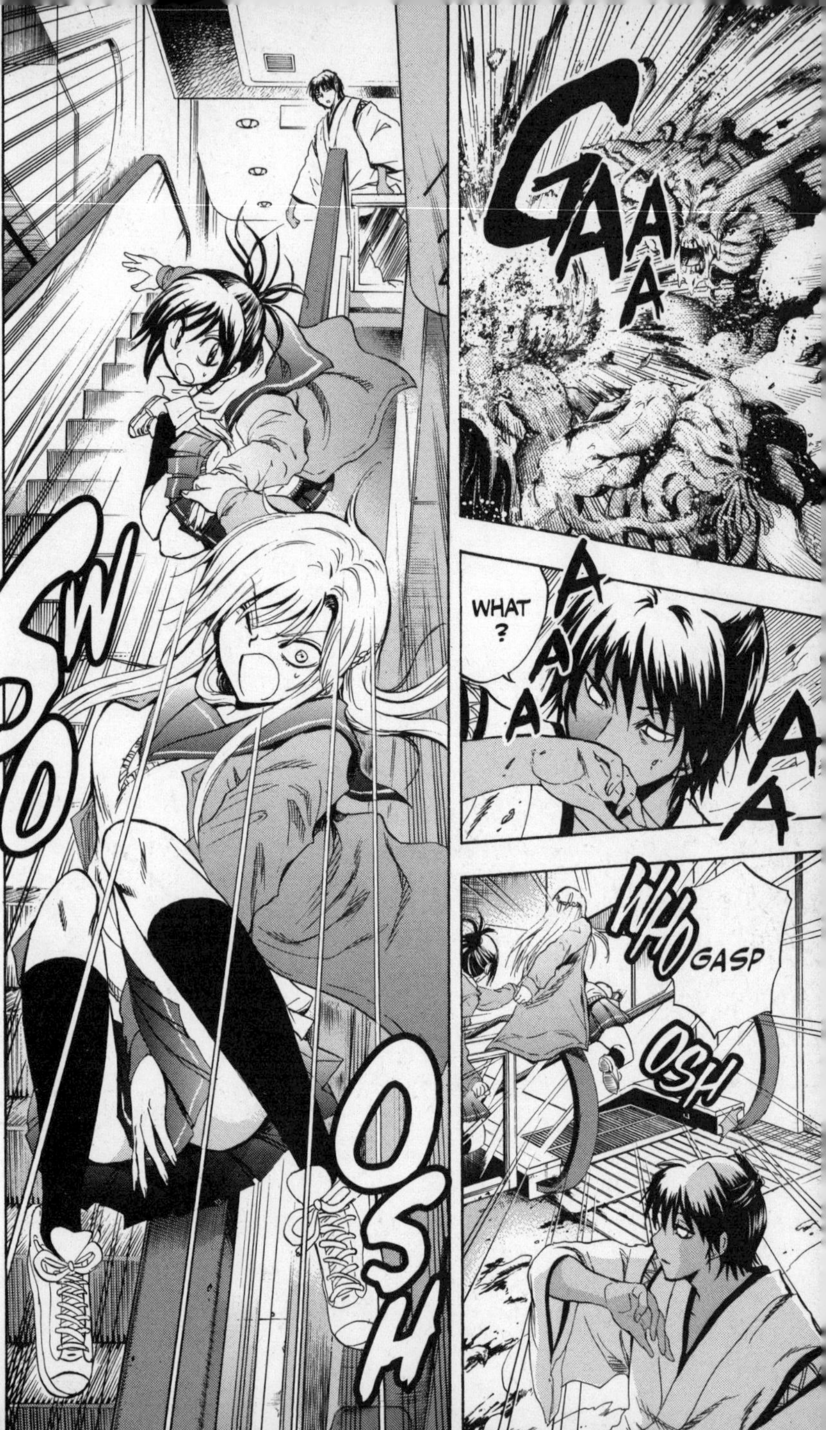
GAAAA
AAAA
WHAT?
AAA
WHOOSH
GASP
SWOOSH

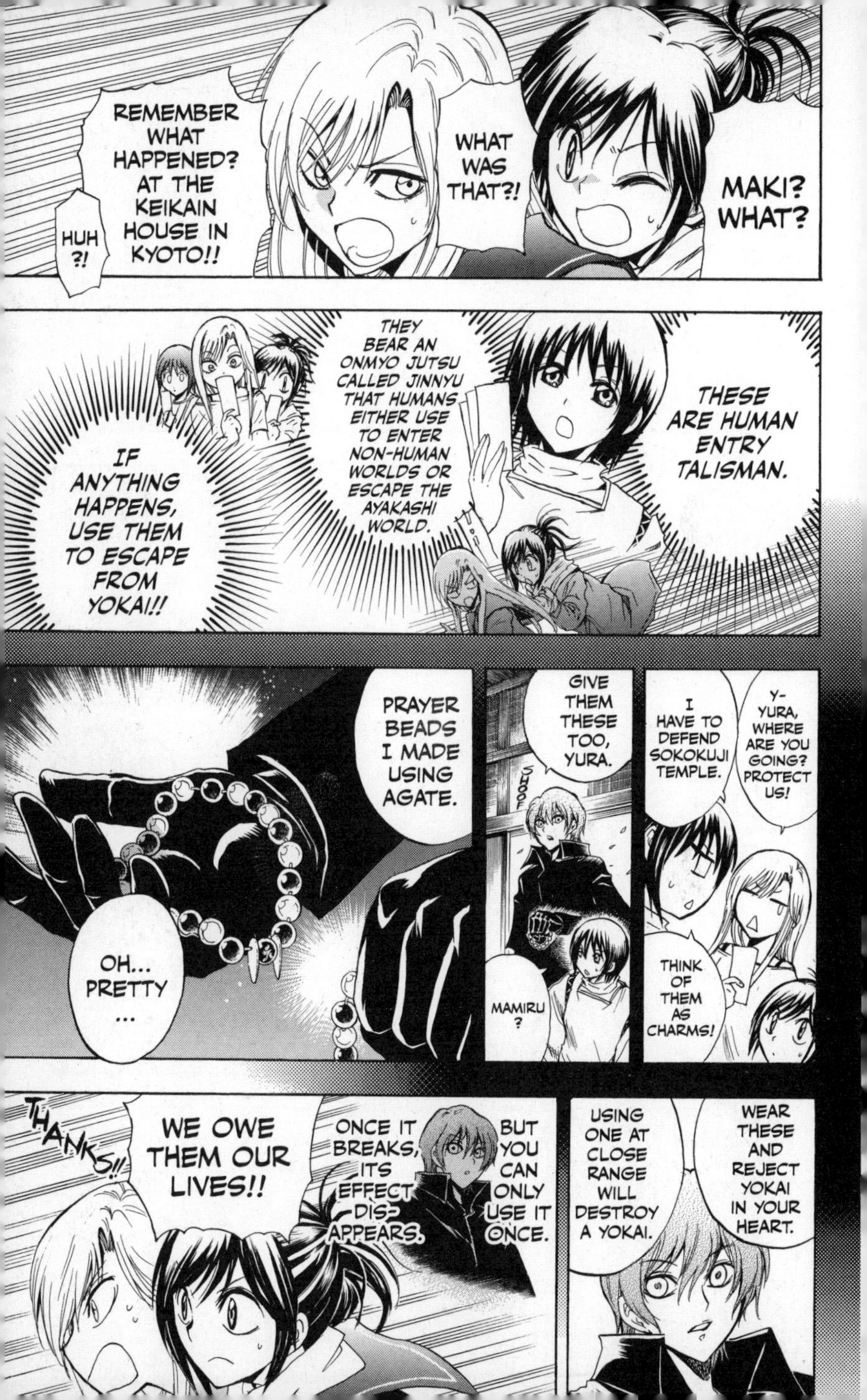
MAKI? WHAT?
WHAT WAS THAT?!
REMEMBER WHAT HAPPENED? AT THE KEIKAIN HOUSE IN KYOTO!!
HUH ?!
THESE ARE HUMAN ENTRY TALISMAN.
THEY BEAR AN ONMYO JUTSU CALLED JINNYU THAT HUMANS EITHER USE TO ENTER NON-HUMAN WORLDS OR ESCAPE THE AYAKASHI WORLD.
IF ANYTHING HAPPENS, USE THEM TO ESCAPE FROM YOKAI!!
Y-YURA, WHERE ARE YOU GOING? PROTECT US!
I HAVE TO DEFEND SOKOKUJI TEMPLE.
THINK OF THEM AS CHARMS!
GIVE THEM THESE TOO, YURA.
SHOOF
MAMIRU ?
PRAYER BEADS I MADE USING AGATE.
OH... PRETTY ...
WEAR THESE AND REJECT YOKAI IN YOUR HEART.
USING ONE AT CLOSE RANGE WILL DESTROY A YOKAI.
BUT YOU CAN ONLY USE IT ONCE.
ONCE IT BREAKS, ITS EFFECT DIS-APPEARS.
WE OWE THEM OUR LIVES!!
THANKS!!

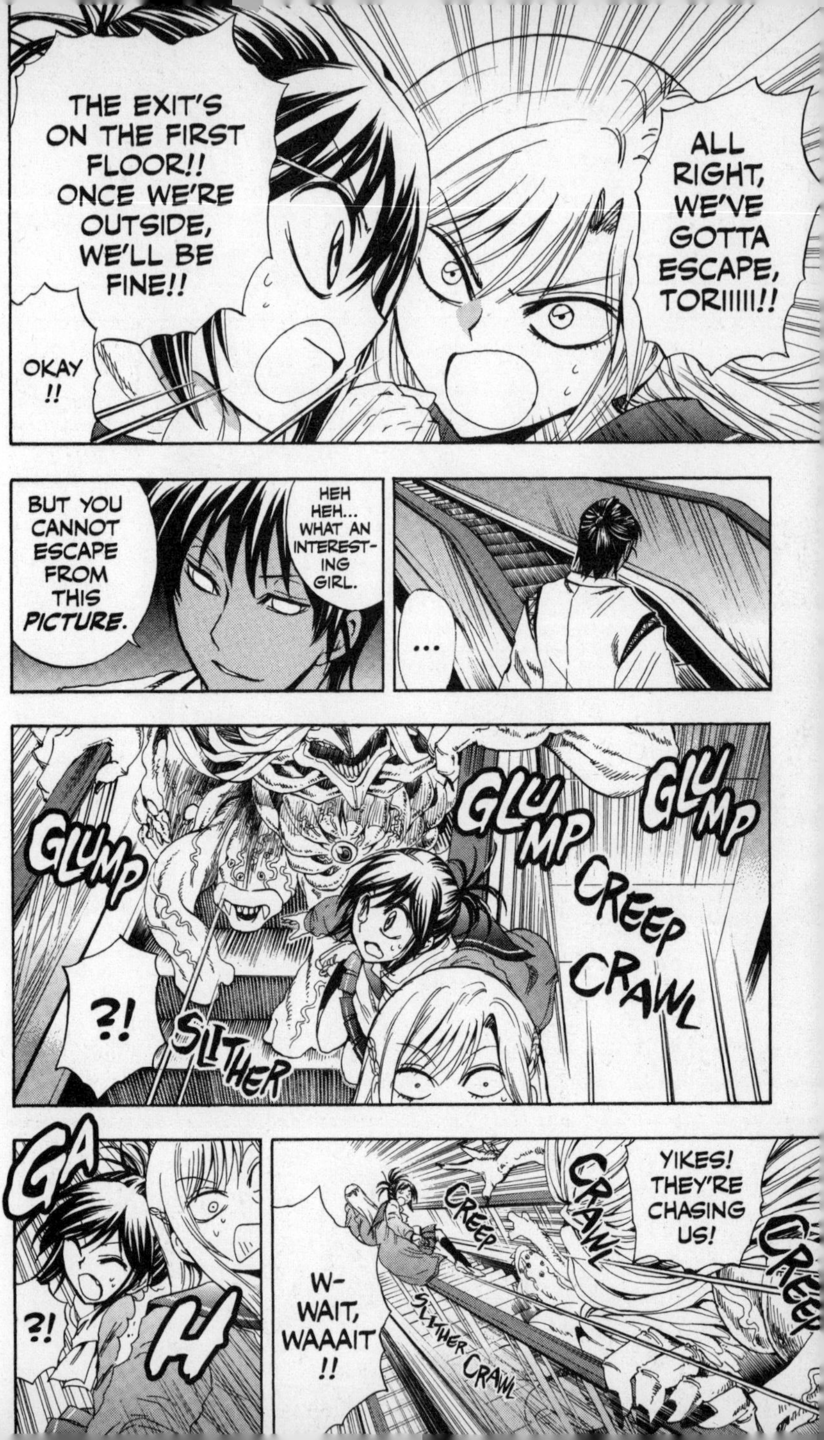
ALL RIGHT, WE'VE GOTTA ESCAPE, TORIIIIII!!
THE EXIT'S ON THE FIRST FLOOR!! ONCE WE'RE OUTSIDE, WE'LL BE FINE!!
OKAY !!
...
HEH HEH... WHAT AN INTEREST-ING GIRL.
BUT YOU CANNOT ESCAPE FROM THIS PICTURE.
GLUMP
GLUMP
GLUMP
CREEP
CRAWL
SLITHER
?!
YIKES! THEY'RE CHASING US!
CREEP
CRAWL
CREEP
W-WAIT, WAAAIT !!
SLITHER CRAWL
GAH
?!

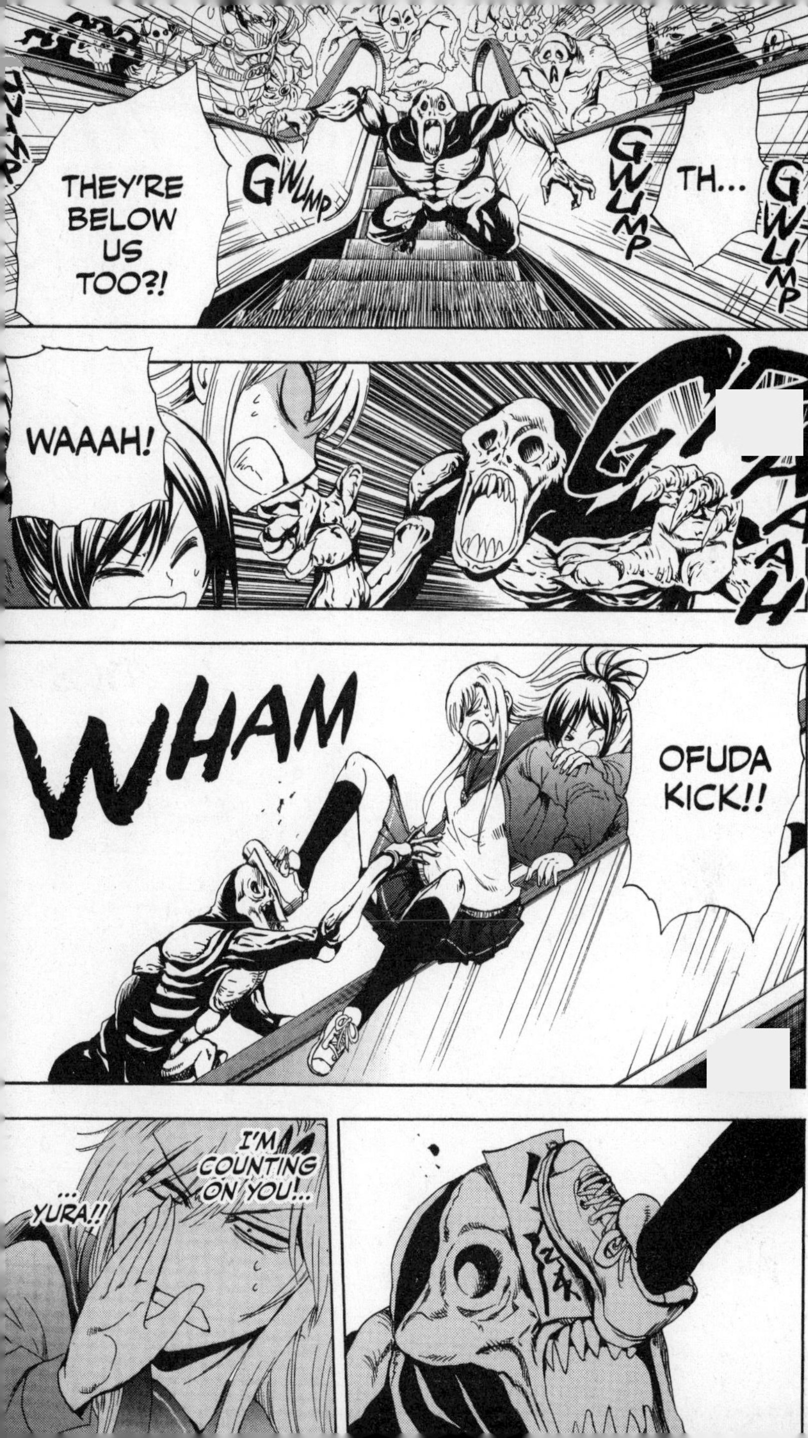
GWUMP
TH...
GWUMP
GWUMP
THEY'RE BELOW US TOO?!
WAAAH!
OFUDA KICK!!
WHAM
I'M COUNTING ON YOU!...
...YURA!!

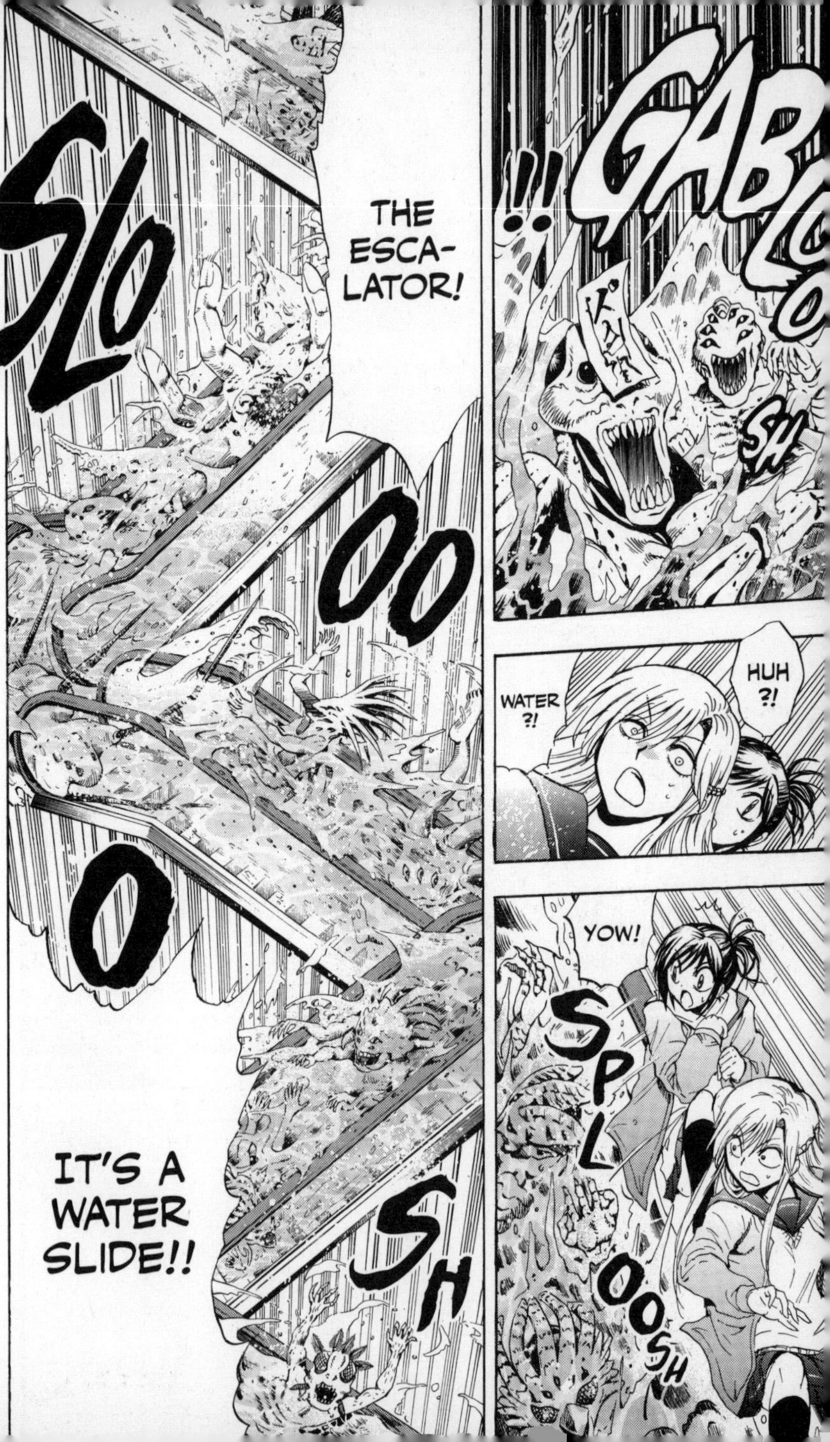
!!
GABLOO
SH
HUH ?!
WATER ?!
YOW!
SPLOOOSH
SLOOOOSH
THE ESCA-LATOR!
IT'S A WATER SLIDE!!

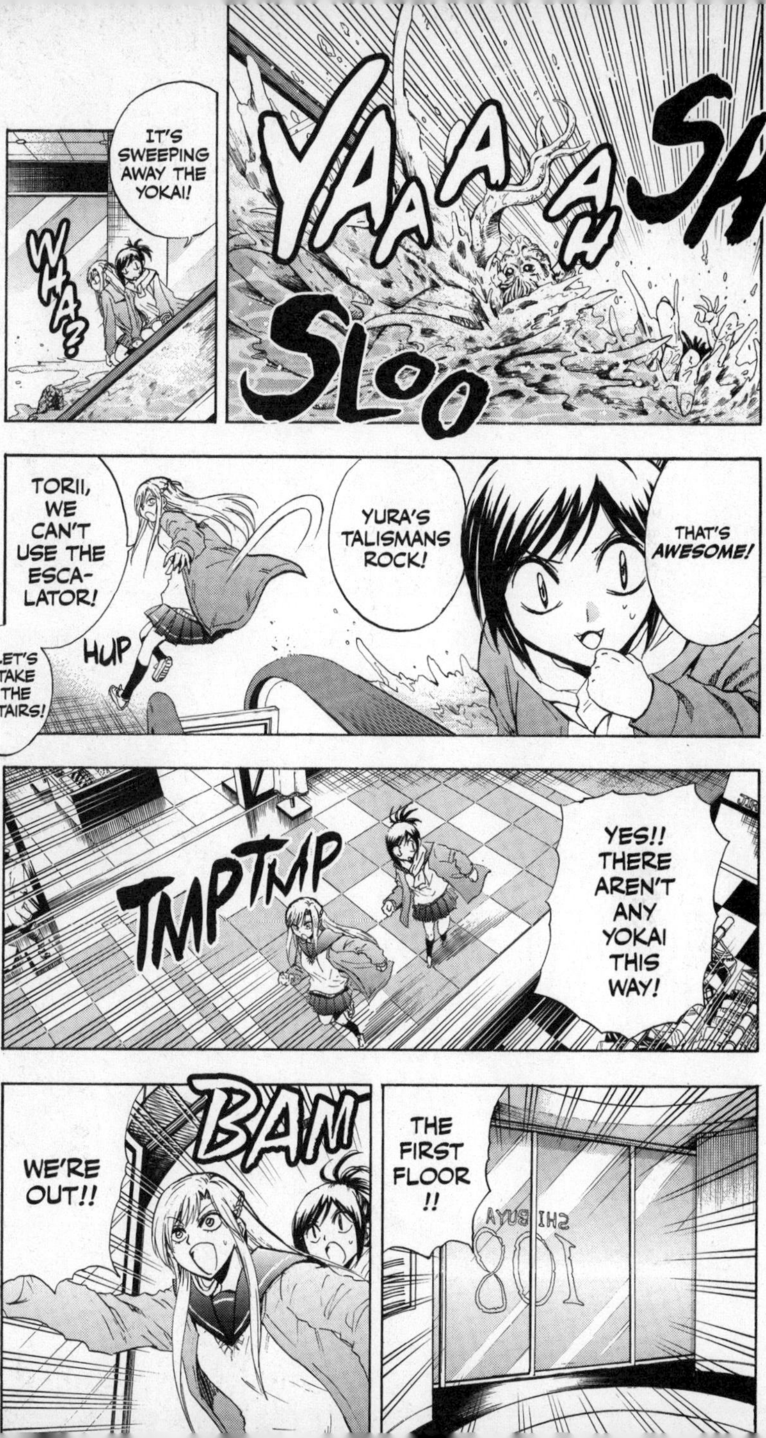
YAAAAASH
SLOO
IT'S SWEEPING AWAY THE YOKAI!
WHA?
THAT'S AWESOME!
YURA'S TALISMANS ROCK!
TORII, WE CAN'T USE THE ESCA-LATOR!
LET'S TAKE THE STAIRS!
HUP
YES!! THERE AREN'T ANY YOKAI THIS WAY!
TMPTMP
THE FIRST FLOOR !!
BAM
WE'RE OUT!!

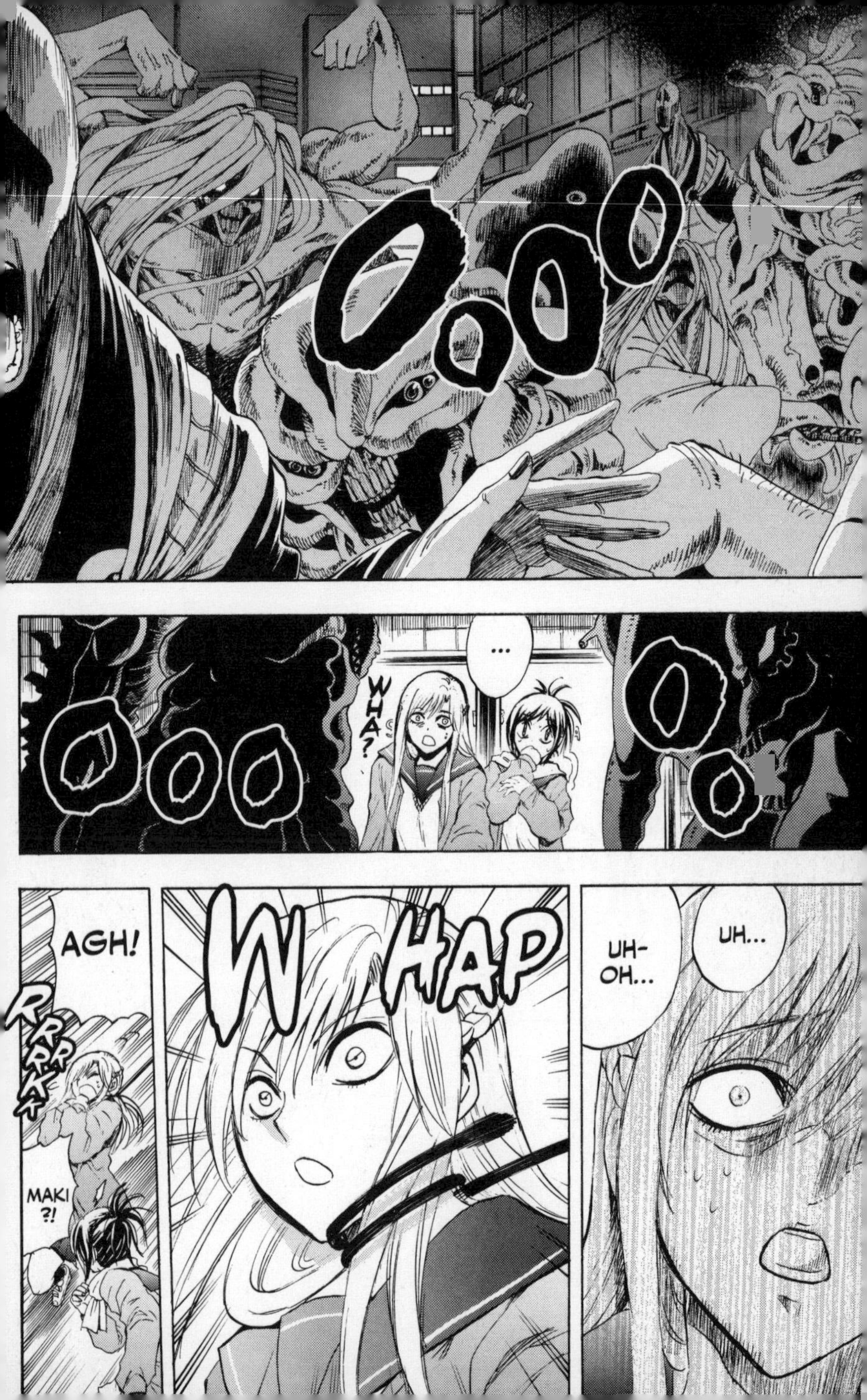
OOOO
OO
...
WHA?
OOO
UH...
UH-OH...
WHAP
AGH!
RRRRAK
MAKI?!

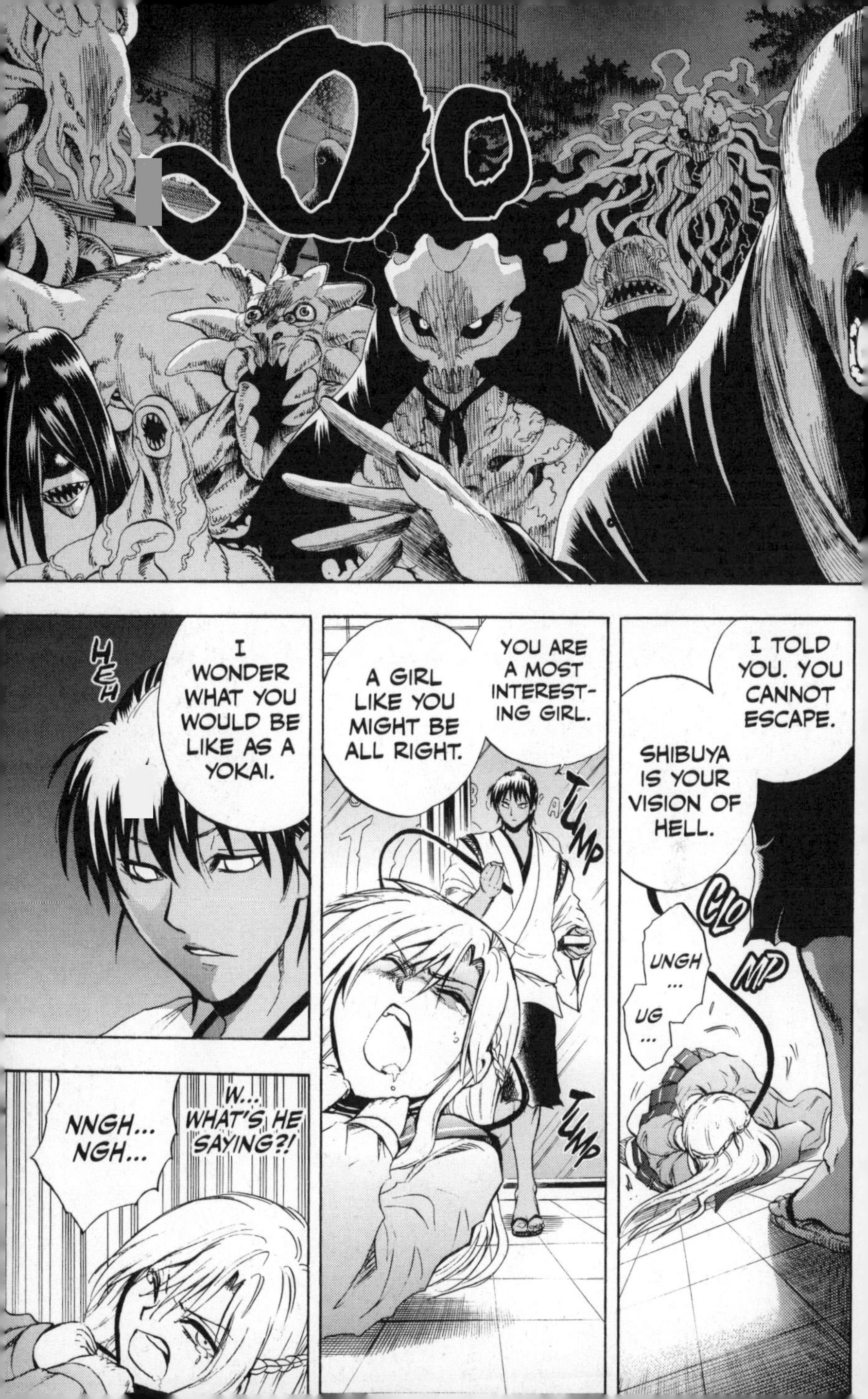
I TOLD YOU. YOU CANNOT ESCAPE.
SHIBUYA IS YOUR VISION OF HELL.
CLOMP
UNGH ...
UG ...
YOU ARE A MOST INTERESTING GIRL.
A GIRL LIKE YOU MIGHT BE ALL RIGHT.
TUMP
TUMP
HEH
I WONDER WHAT YOU WOULD BE LIKE AS A YOKAI.
W... WHAT'S HE SAYING?!
NNGH... NGH...

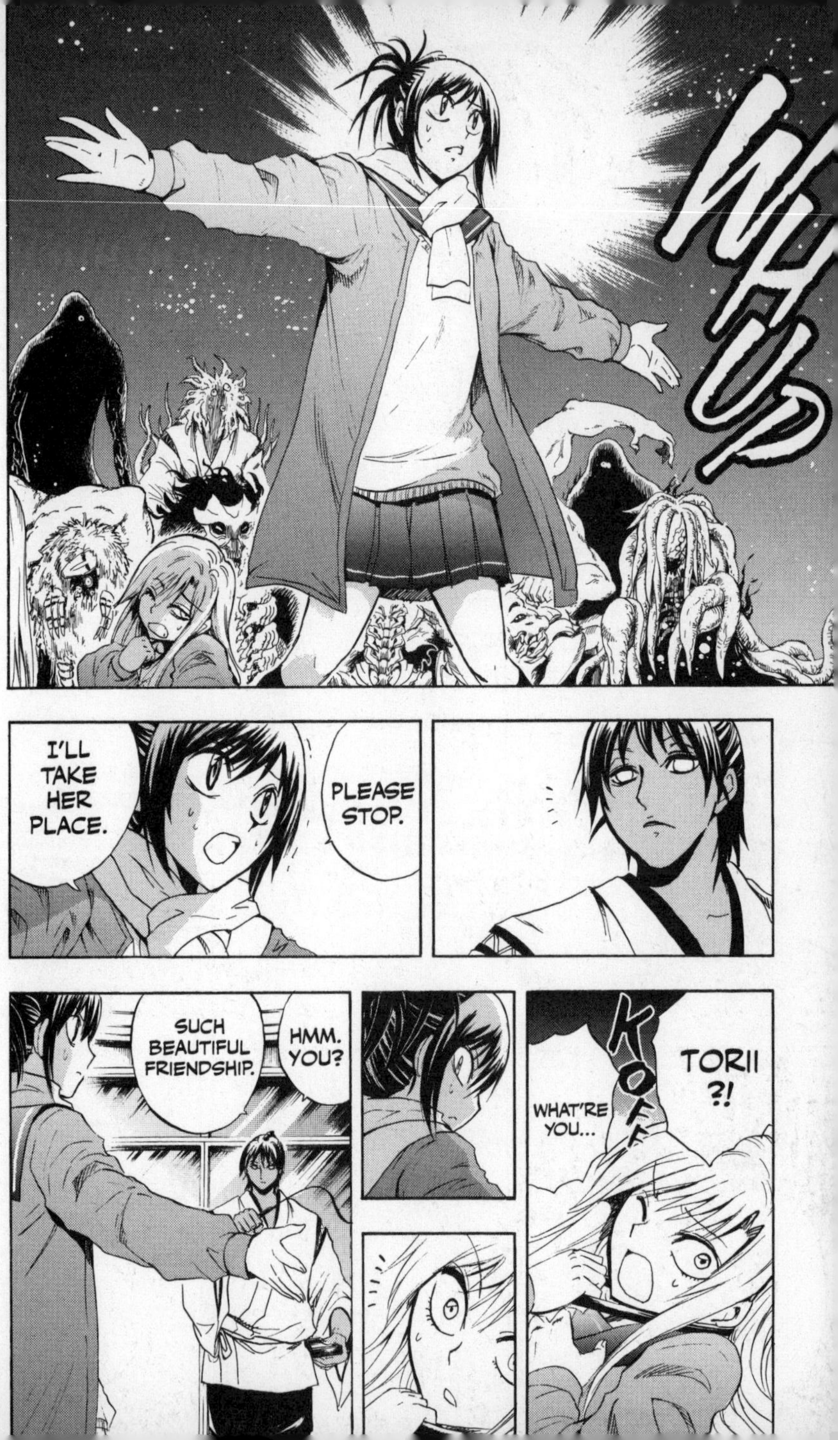
WHUP!
PLEASE STOP.
I'LL TAKE HER PLACE.
TORII ?!
KOFF
WHAT'RE YOU...
HMM. YOU?
SUCH BEAUTIFUL FRIENDSHIP.

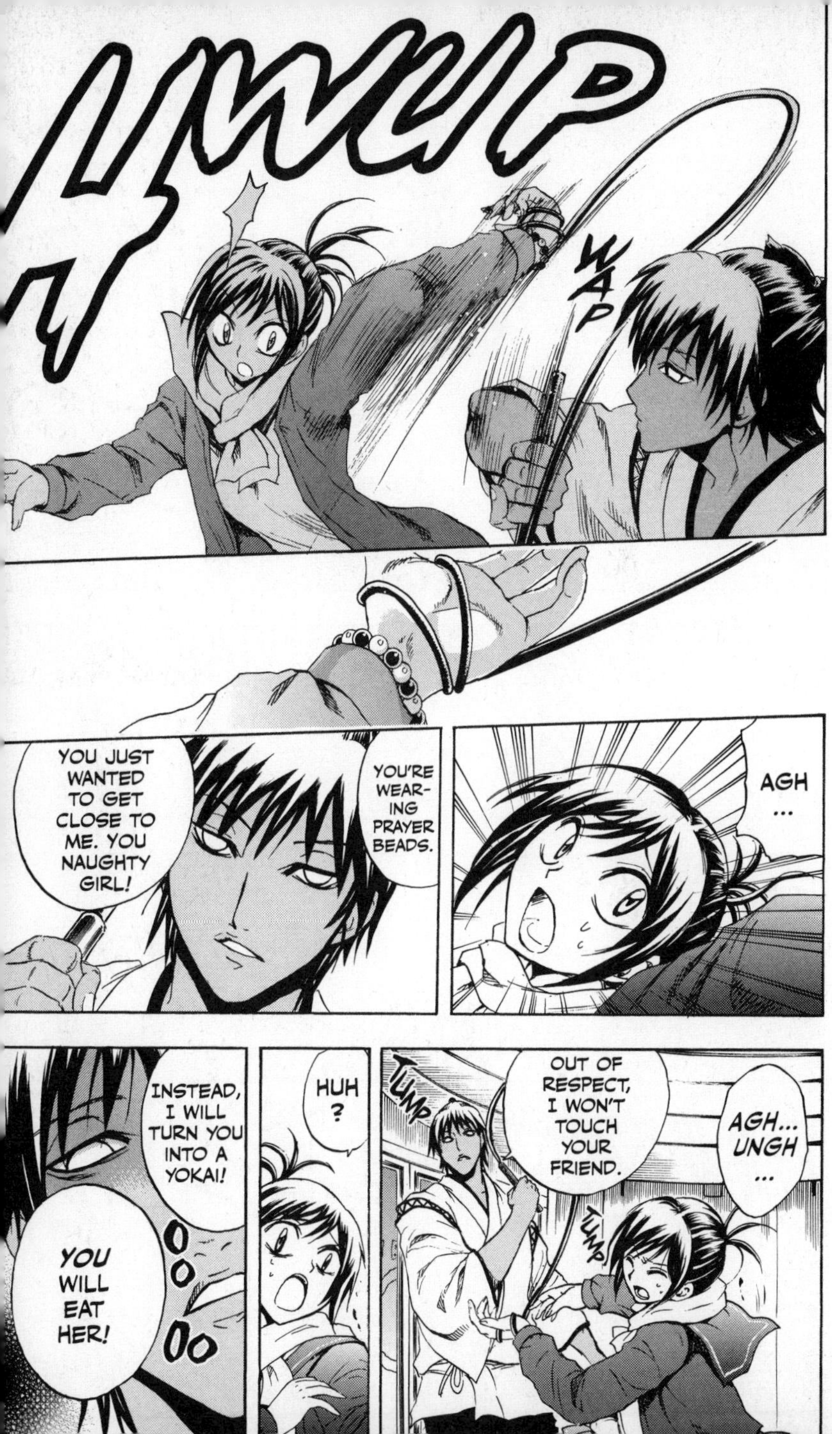
WHIP
WAP
AGH...
YOU'RE WEARING PRAYER BEADS.
YOU JUST WANTED TO GET CLOSE TO ME. YOU NAUGHTY GIRL!
AGH... UNGH...
OUT OF RESPECT, I WON'T TOUCH YOUR FRIEND.
TUMP
TUMP
HUH?
INSTEAD, I WILL TURN YOU INTO A YOKAI!
YOU WILL EAT HER!

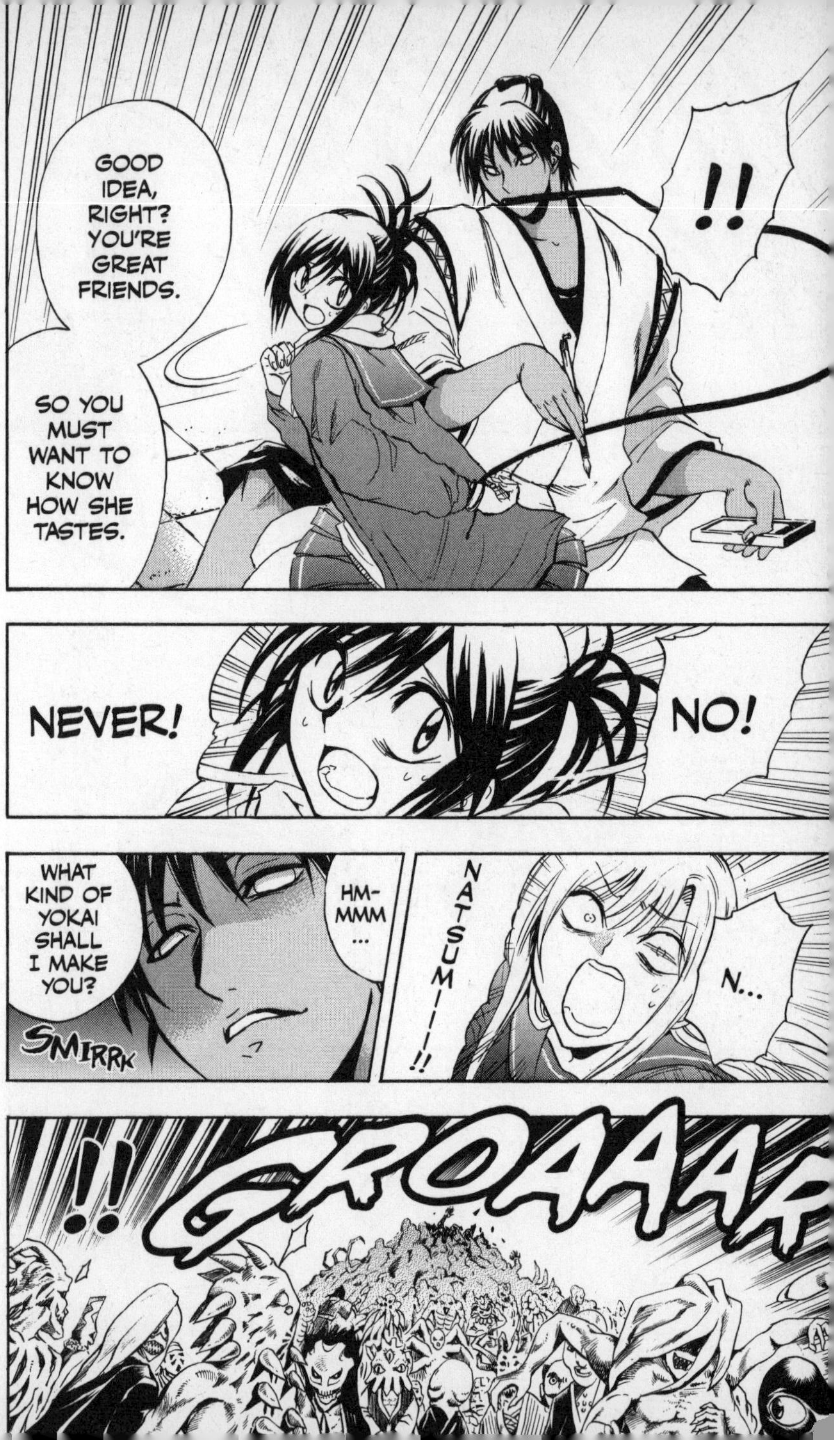
!!
GOOD IDEA, RIGHT? YOU'RE GREAT FRIENDS.
SO YOU MUST WANT TO KNOW HOW SHE TASTES.
NO!
NEVER!
N...
NATSUMI-I-I-I!!
HM-MMM...
WHAT KIND OF YOKAI SHALL I MAKE YOU?
SMIRRK
GROAAAR
!!

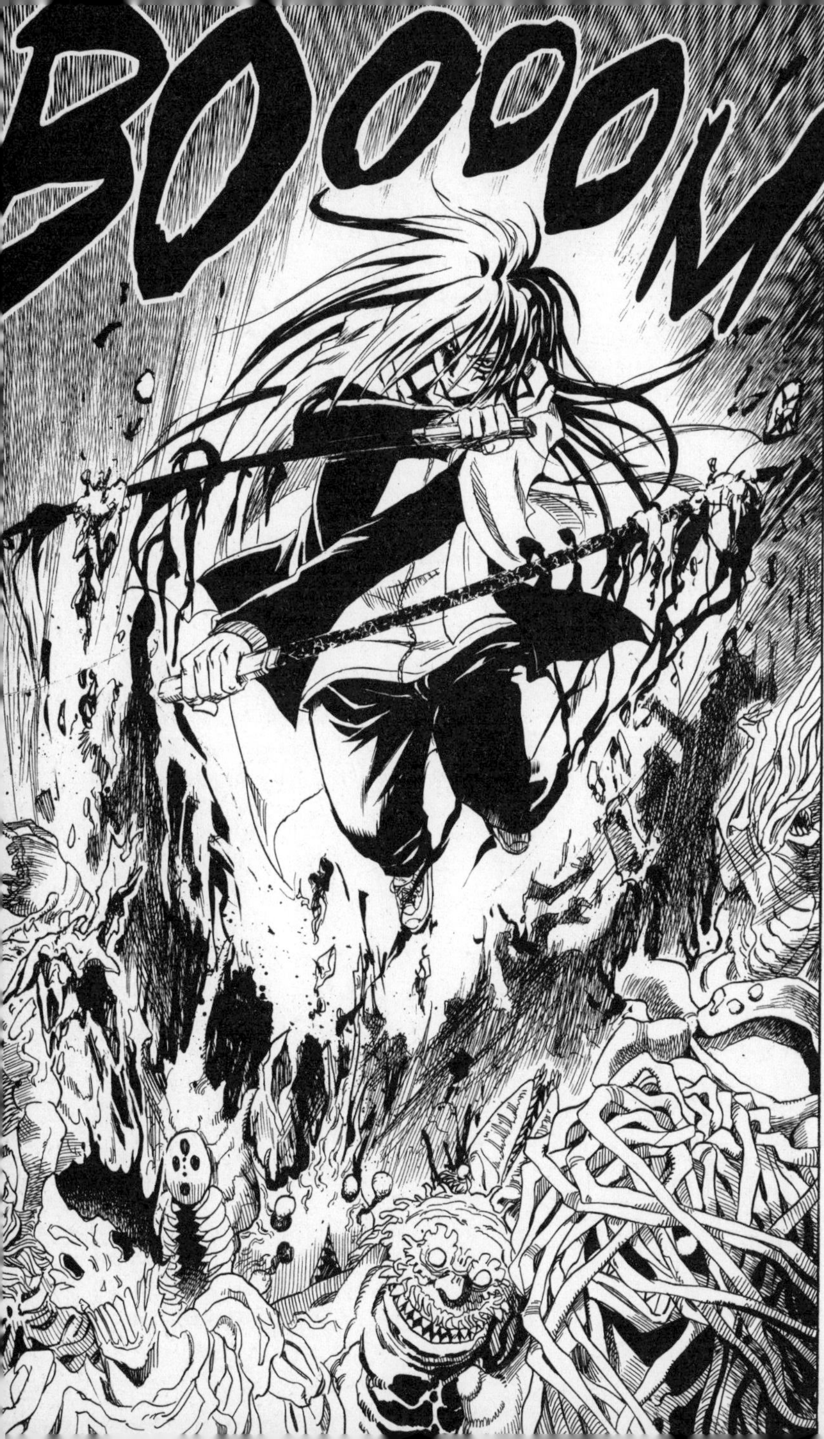
BOOOOM!

Tsurara's Fantasy Manga

We're in the Nura Fan Club! Part 3

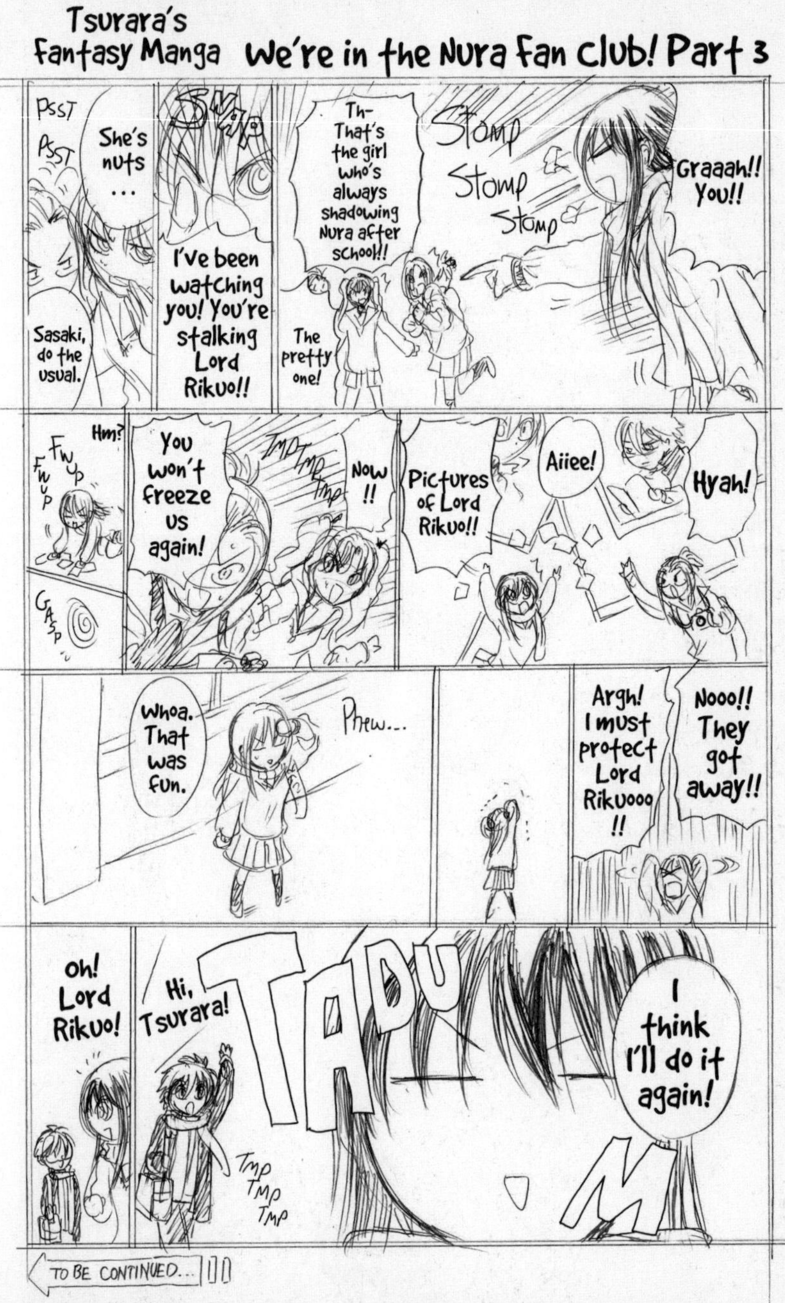
Graaah!! You!!
Stomp
Stomp
Stomp
Th- That's the girl who's always shadowing Nura after school!!
The pretty one!
I've been watching you! You're stalking Lord Rikuo!!
She's nuts...
PSST
PSST
Sasaki, do the usual.
Hyah!
Aiiee!
Pictures of Lord Rikuo!!
Now!!
TMP TMP TMP
You won't freeze us again!
Hm?
FWUP
FWUP
GASP
Nooo!! They got away!!
Argh! I must protect Lord Rikuooo!!
Phew...
Whoa. That was fun.
I think I'll do it again!
TADUM
Hi, Tsurara!
TMP
TMP
TMP
Oh! Lord Rikuo!
TO BE CONTINUED...

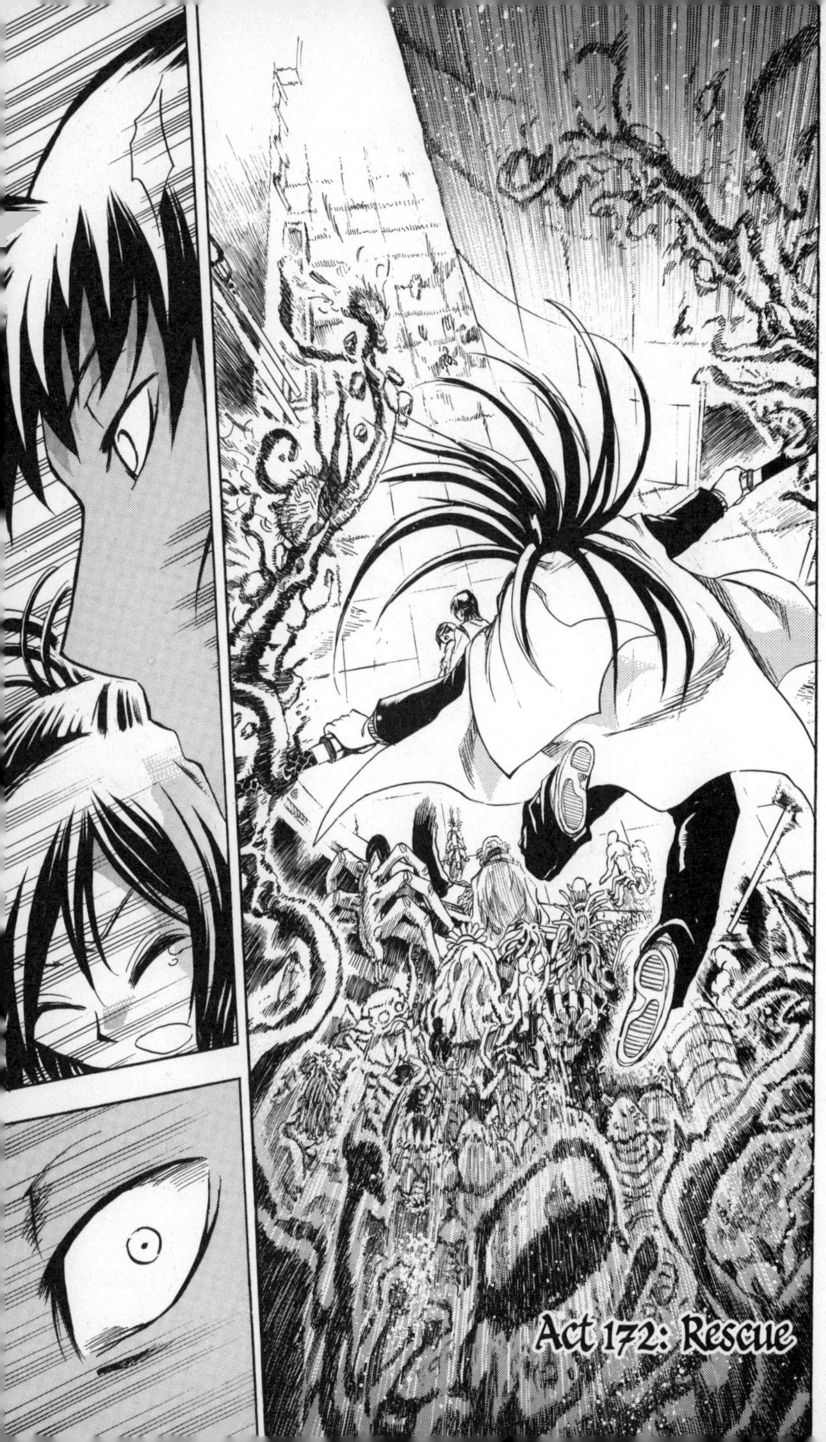
Act 172: Rescue

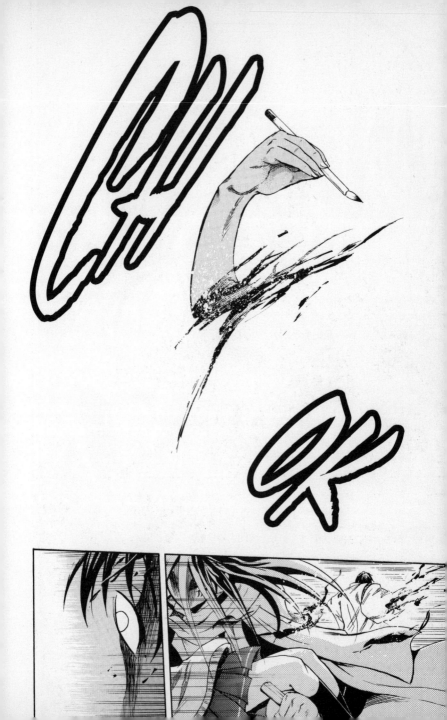

Act 172: Rescue

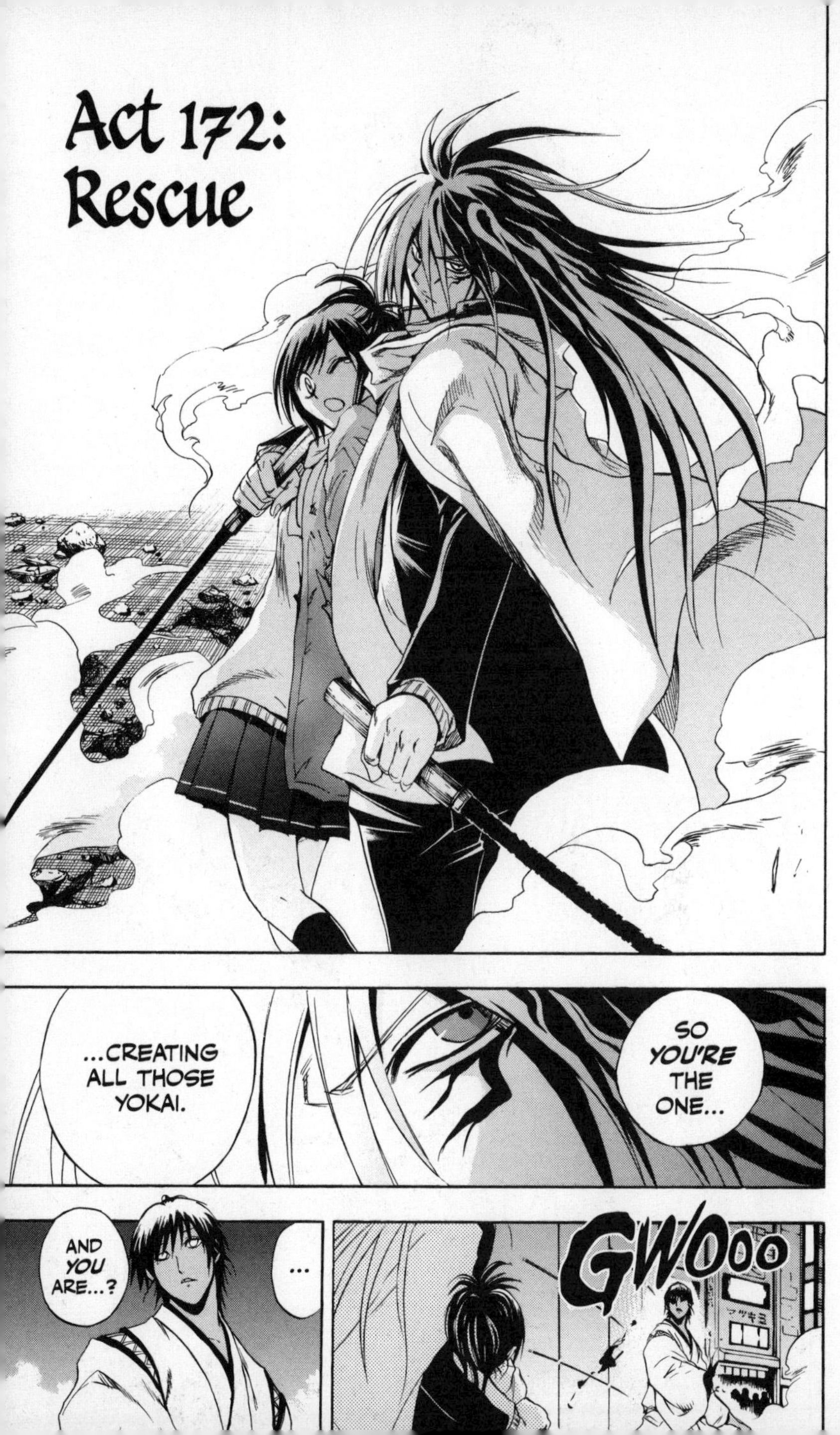
SO YOU'RE THE ONE...
...CREATING ALL THOSE YOKAI.
GWOOO
AND YOU ARE...?
...

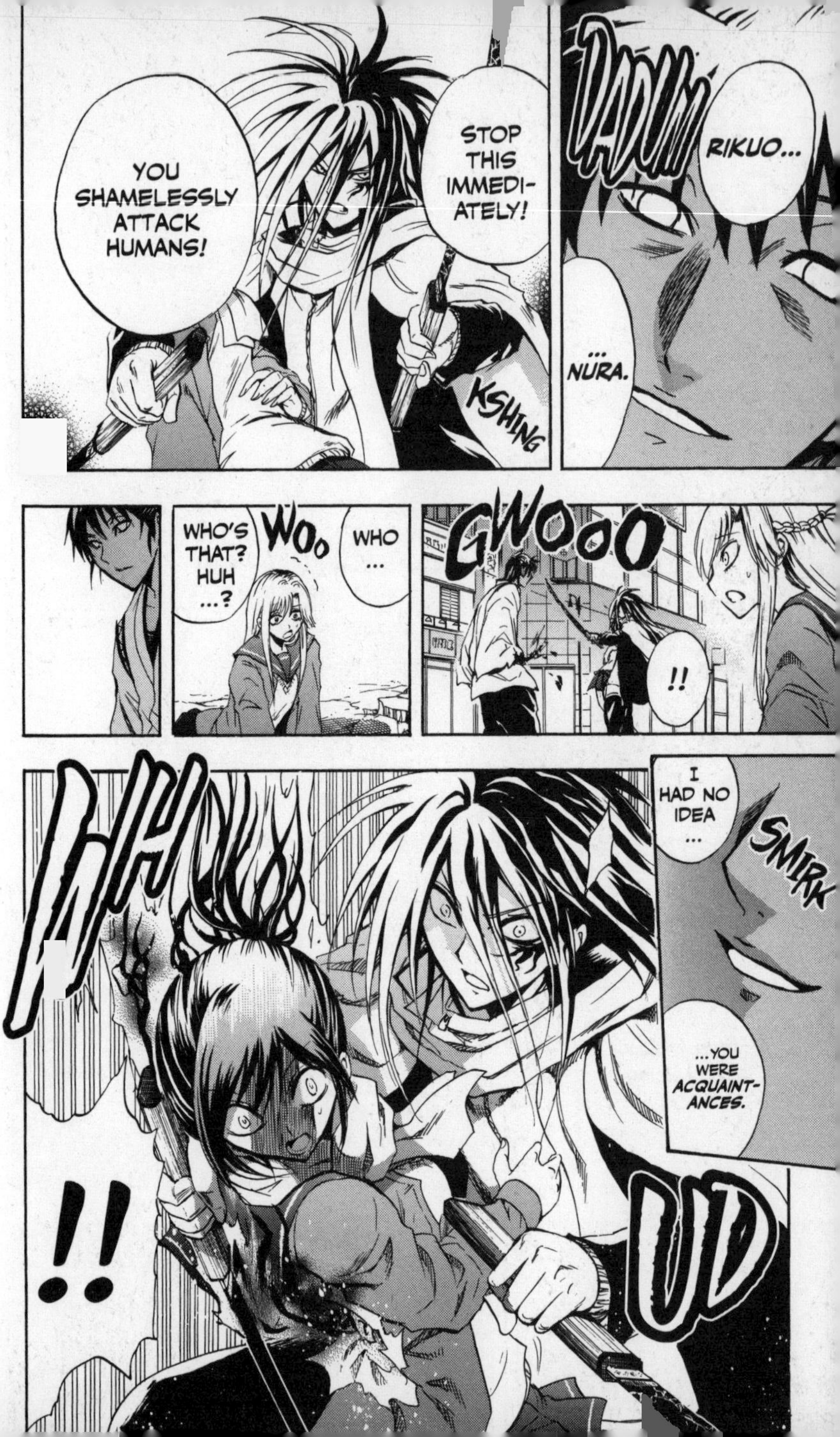

RIKUO...
...NÜRA.
STOP THIS IMMEDI-ATELY!
YOU SHAMELESSLY ATTACK HUMANS!
KSHING
GWOOO
!!
WHO ...
WOO
WHO'S THAT? HUH ...?
I HAD NO IDEA ...
SMIRK
...YOU WERE ACQUAINT-ANCES.
!!

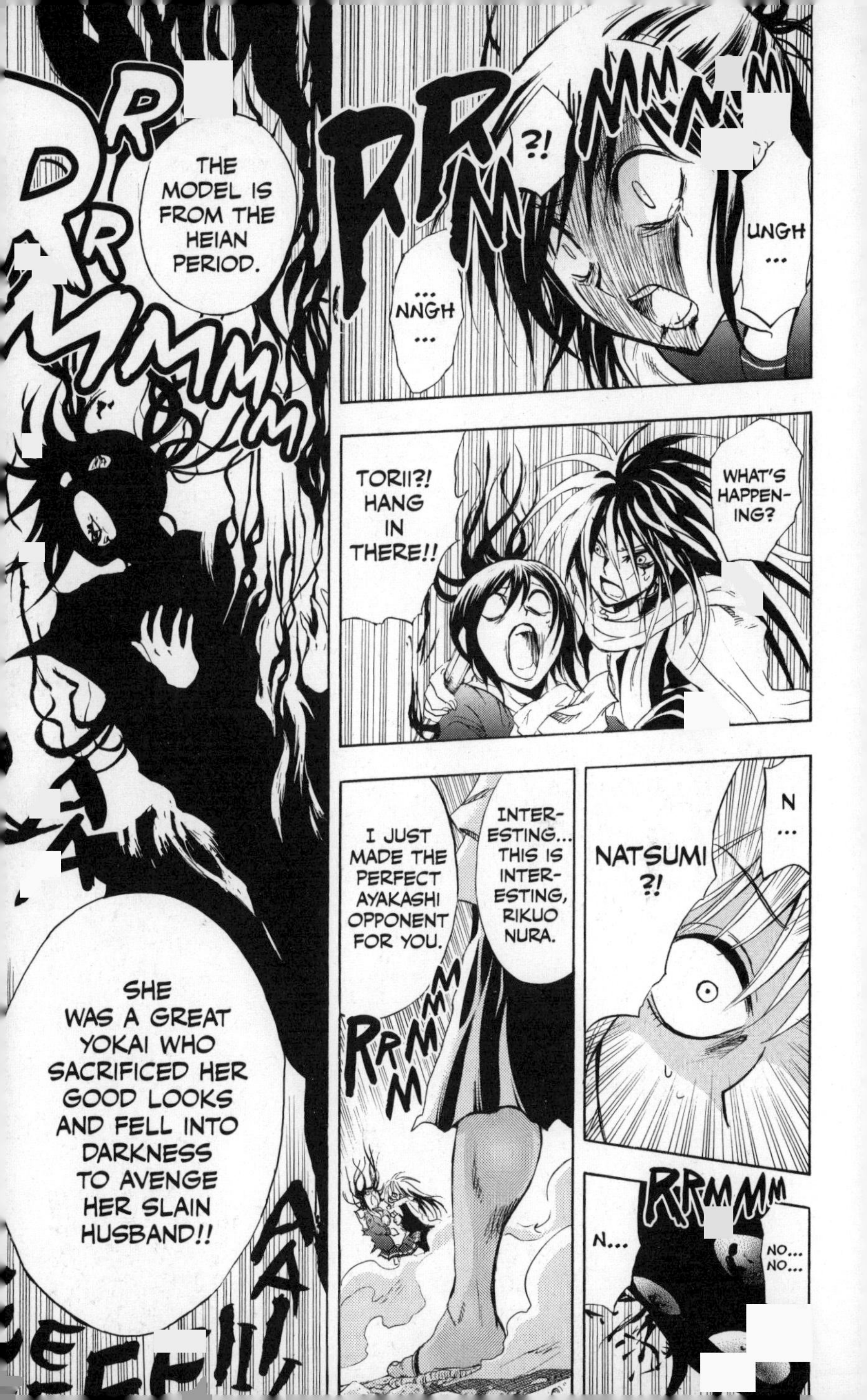
?!
UNGH...
...NNGH...
WHAT'S HAPPENING?
TORII?! HANG IN THERE!!
N...
NATSUMI?!
INTERESTING... THIS IS INTERESTING, RIKUO NURA.
I JUST MADE THE PERFECT AYAKASHI OPPONENT FOR YOU.
RRMMMM
RRMMM
NO... NO...
N...
THE MODEL IS FROM THE HEIAN PERIOD.
SHE WAS A GREAT YOKAI WHO SACRIFICED HER GOOD LOOKS AND FELL INTO DARKNESS TO AVENGE HER SLAIN HUSBAND!!

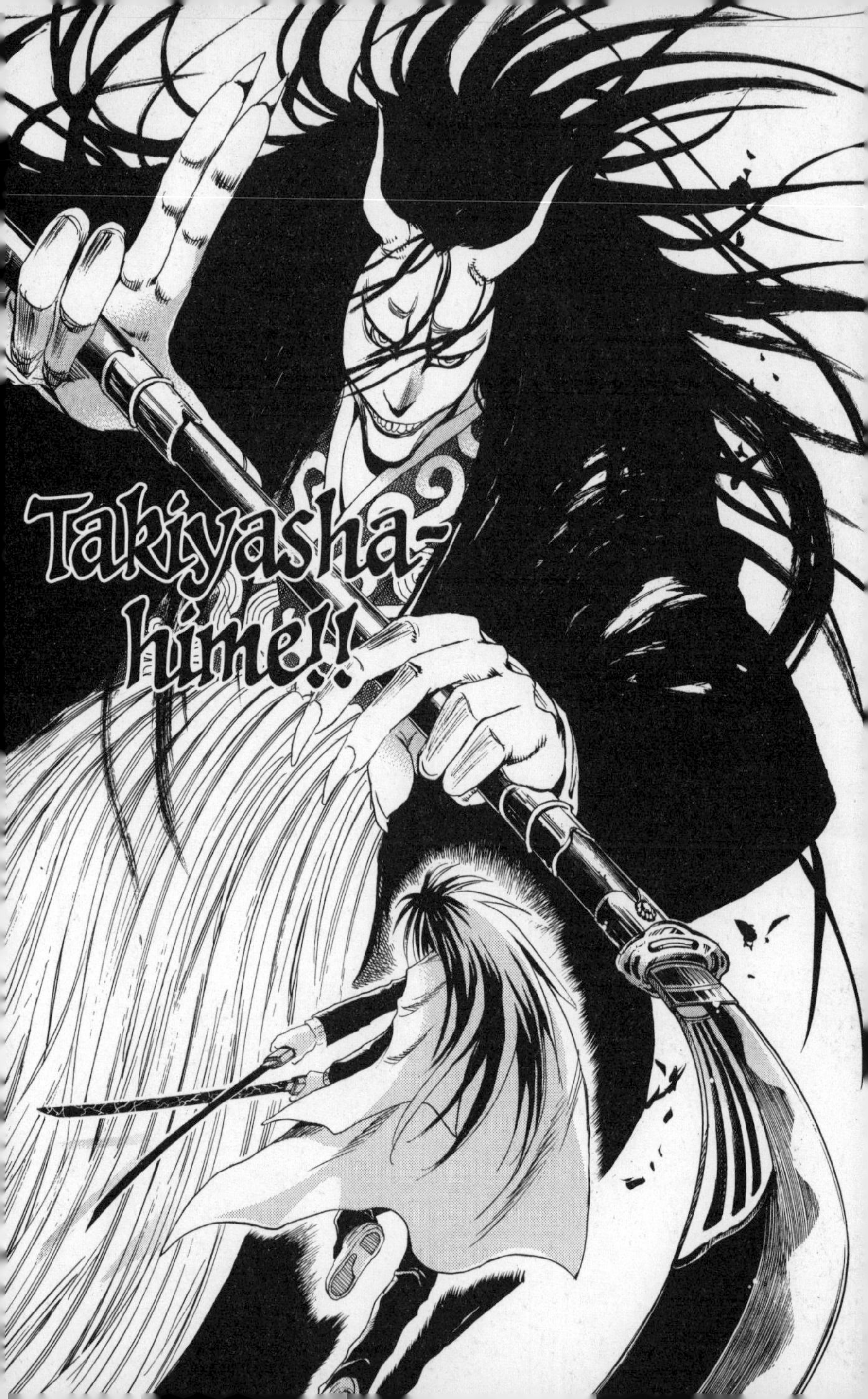
Takiyasha-hime!!

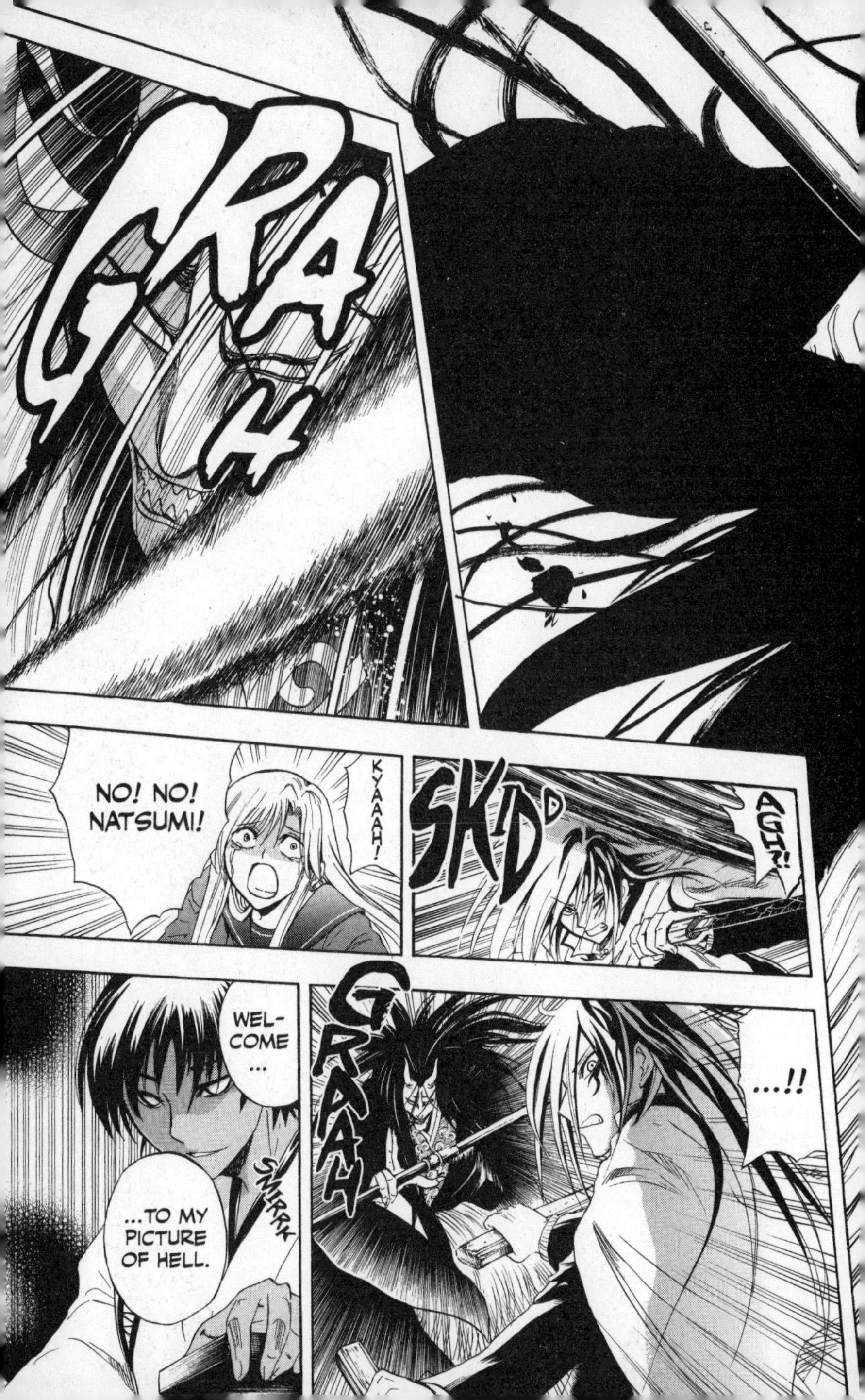
GRAH
AGHH?!
SKID
KYAAAH!
NO! NO! NATSUMI!
...!!
GRAAH
WEL-COME...
SMIRRK
...TO MY PICTURE OF HELL.

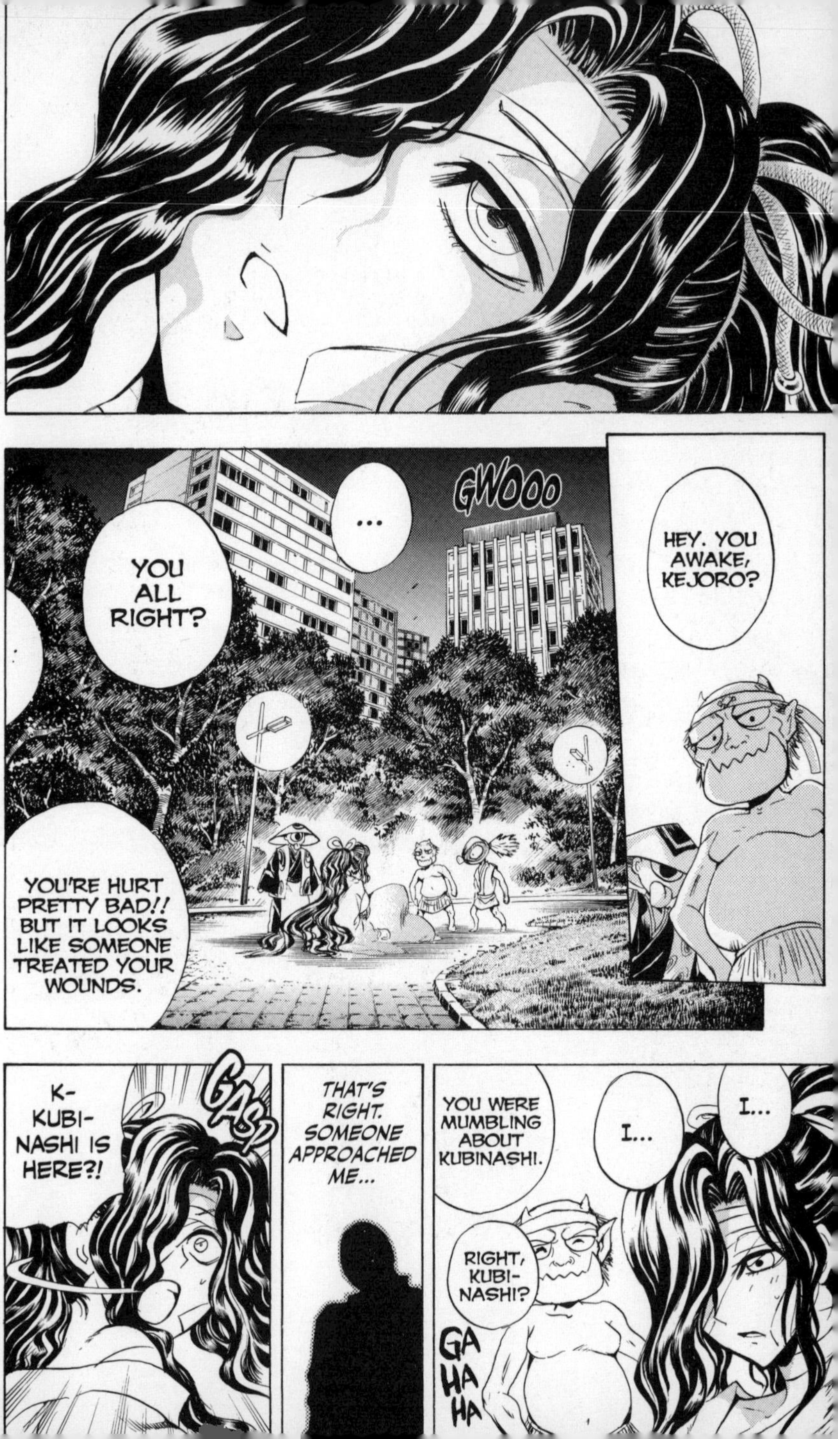
HEY. YOU AWAKE, KEJORO?
GWOOO
...
YOU ALL RIGHT?
YOU'RE HURT PRETTY BAD!! BUT IT LOOKS LIKE SOMEONE TREATED YOUR WOUNDS.
I...
I...
YOU WERE MUMBLING ABOUT KUBINASHI.
RIGHT, KUBINASHI?
GA HA HA
THAT'S RIGHT. SOMEONE APPROACHED ME...
GASP
K-KUBINASHI IS HERE?!

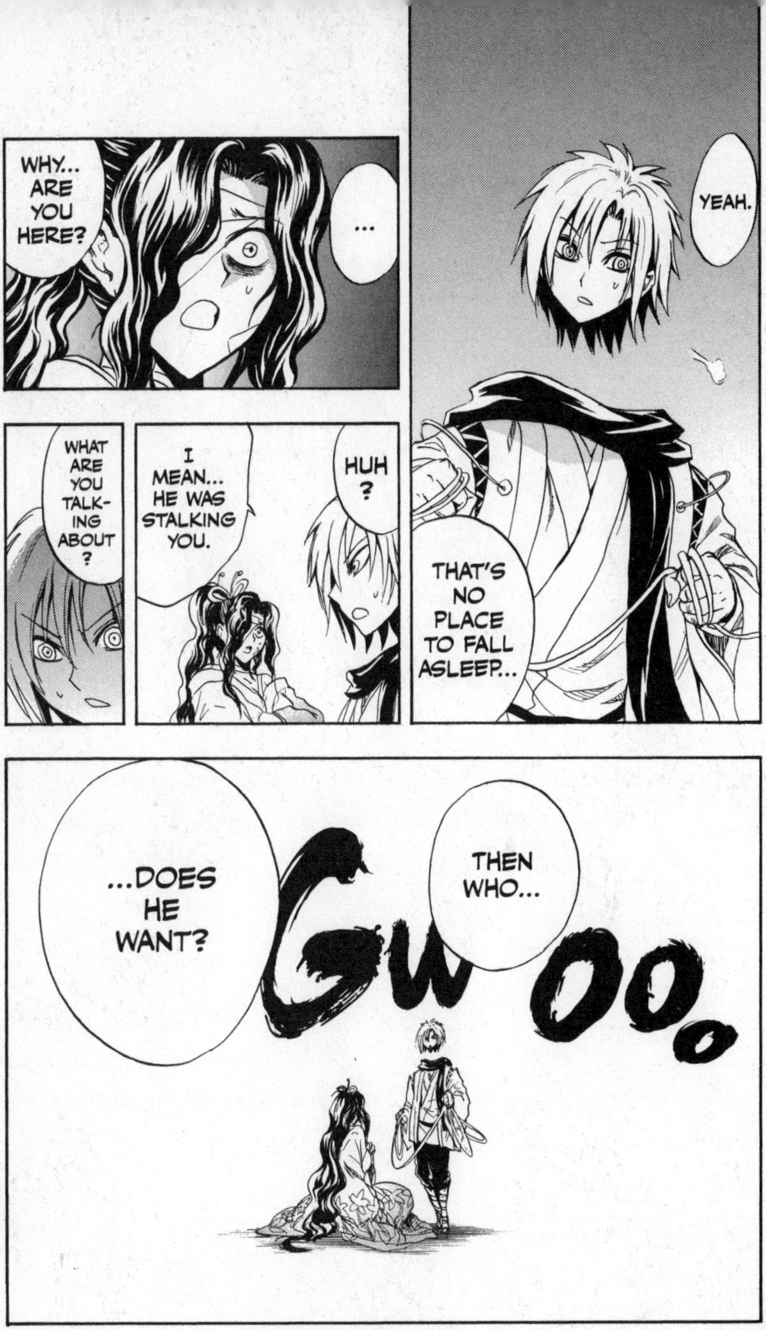
YEAH.
THAT'S NO PLACE TO FALL ASLEEP...
...
WHY... ARE YOU HERE?
HUH?
I MEAN... HE WAS STALKING YOU.
WHAT ARE YOU TALKING ABOUT?
THEN WHO...
...DOES HE WANT?
GWOOO

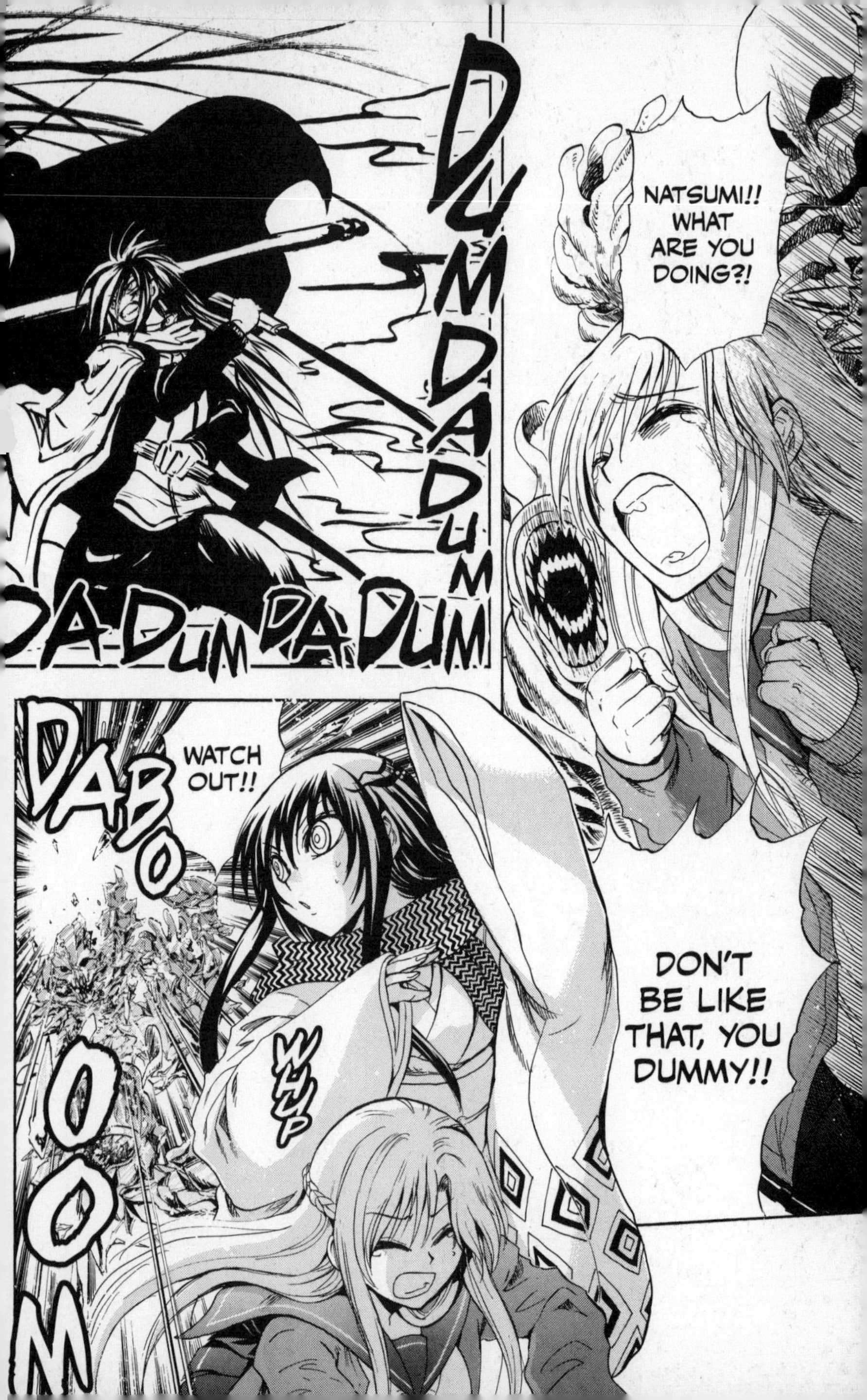

NATSUMI!! WHAT ARE YOU DOING?!
DUM DA DUM
DA DUM DA DUM
DON'T BE LIKE THAT, YOU DUMMY!!
WATCH OUT!!
DABOOOM
WHIP

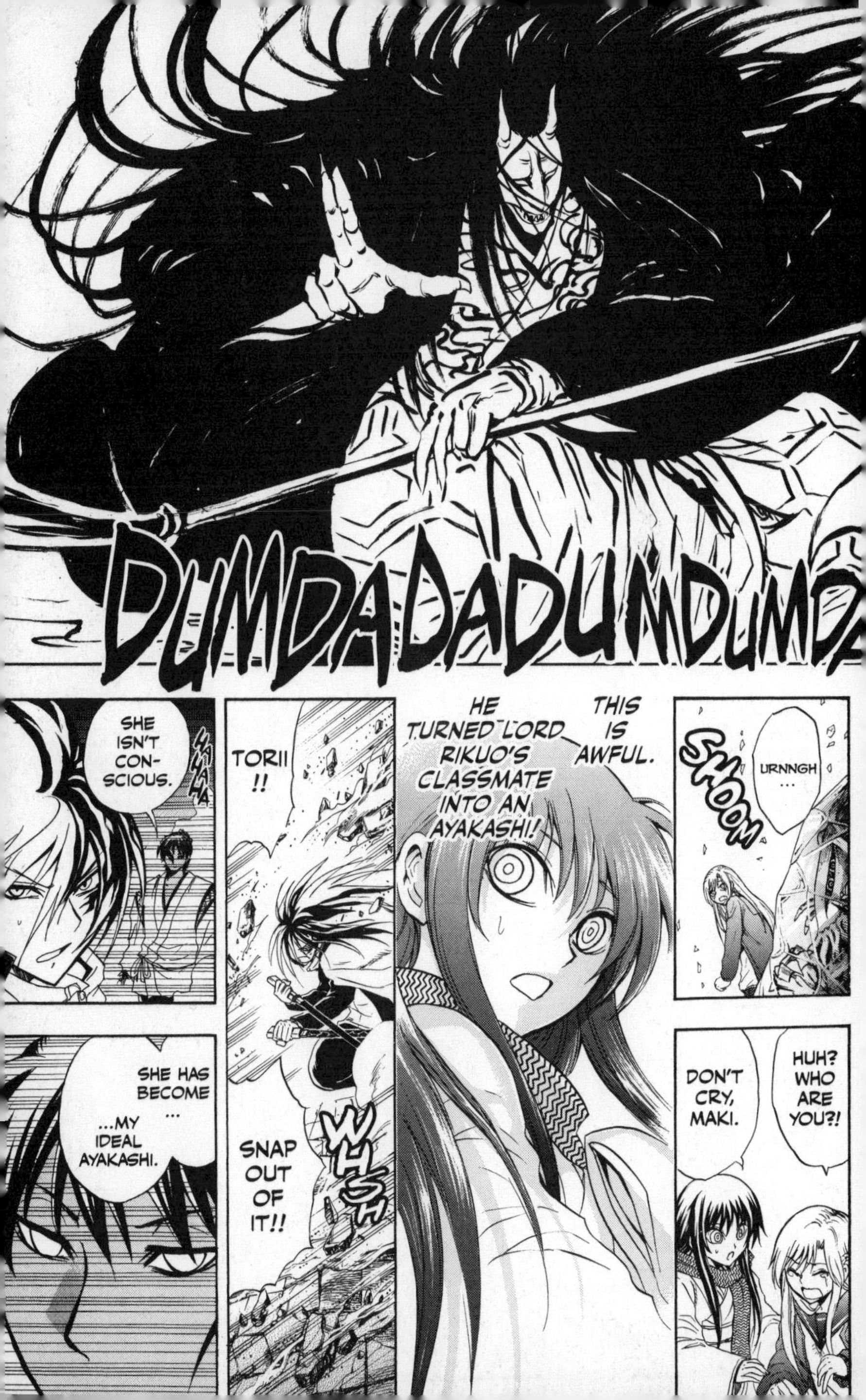
DUMDADADUMDUMDA
SHOOM
URNNGH ...
HUH? WHO ARE YOU?!
DON'T CRY, MAKI.
THIS IS AWFUL.
HE TURNED LORD RIKUO'S CLASSMATE INTO AN AYAKASHI!
TORII !!
SNAP OUT OF IT!!
WHSH
SHE ISN'T CON-SCIOUS.
HAHAHA
SHE HAS BECOME ...
...MY IDEAL AYAKASHI.

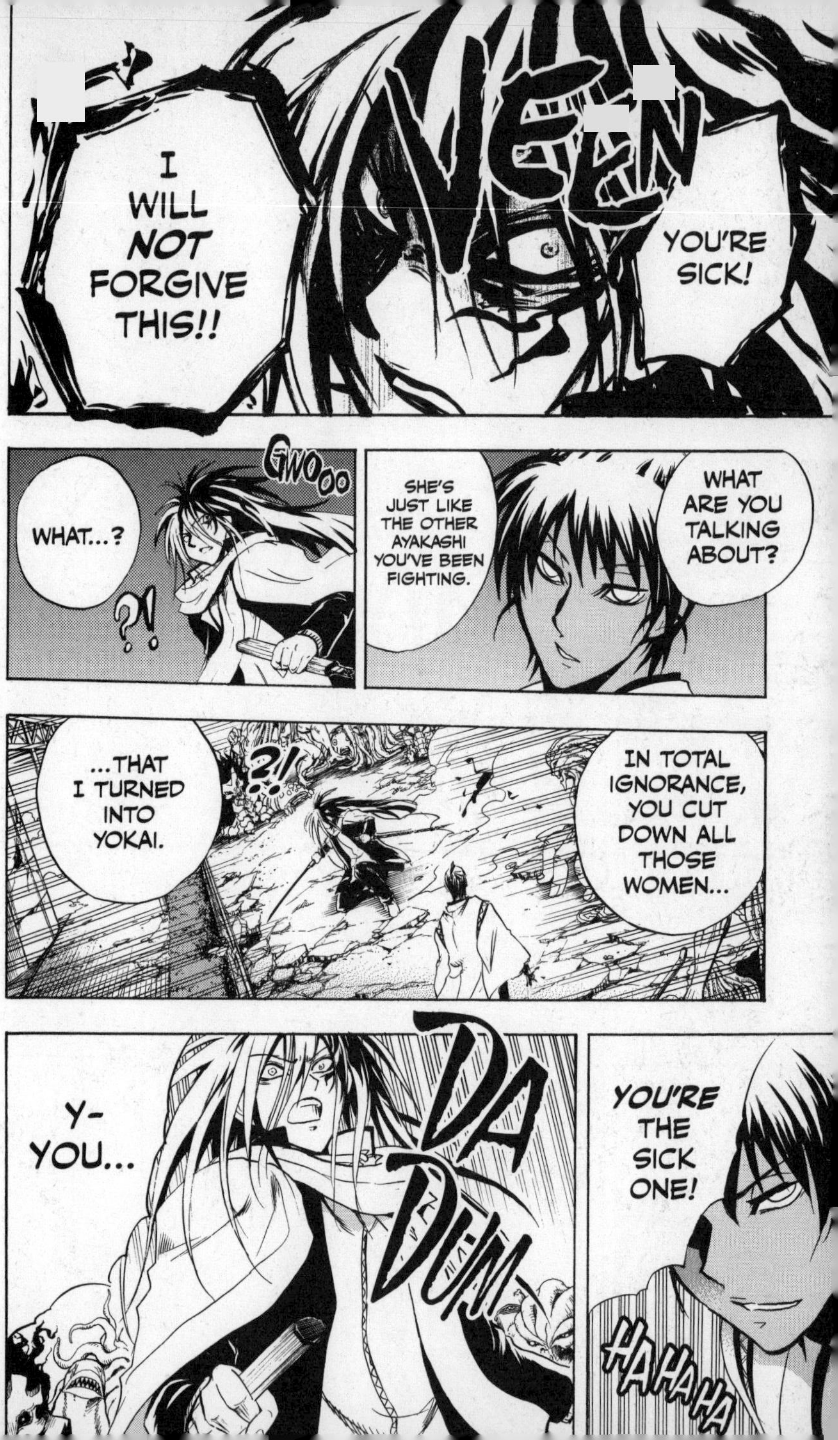
YOU'RE SICK!
I WILL NOT FORGIVE THIS!!
WHAT ARE YOU TALKING ABOUT?
SHE'S JUST LIKE THE OTHER AYAKASHI YOU'VE BEEN FIGHTING.
GWOOO
WHAT...?
?!
IN TOTAL IGNORANCE, YOU CUT DOWN ALL THOSE WOMEN...
...THAT I TURNED INTO YOKAI.
?!
YOU'RE THE SICK ONE!
HAHAHA
DA DUM
Y- YOU...

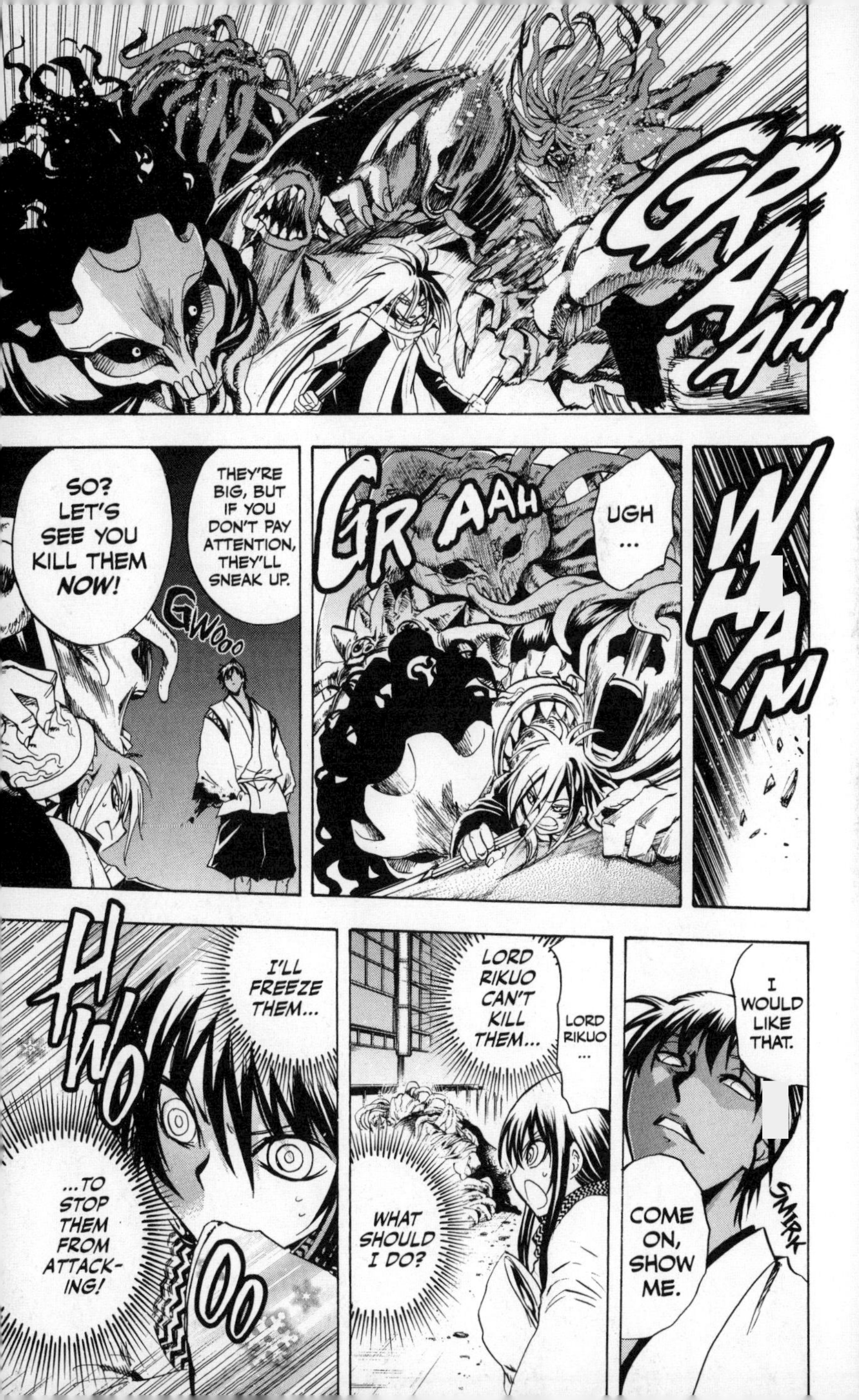
GRAAH
WHAM
UGH ...
GRAAH
THEY'RE BIG, BUT IF YOU DON'T PAY ATTENTION, THEY'LL SNEAK UP.
SO? LET'S SEE YOU KILL THEM NOW!
GWOOO
I WOULD LIKE THAT.
SMIRK
COME ON, SHOW ME.
LORD RIKUO ...
LORD RIKUO CAN'T KILL THEM...
WHAT SHOULD I DO?
I'LL FREEZE THEM...
HWOOO
...TO STOP THEM FROM ATTACK-ING!

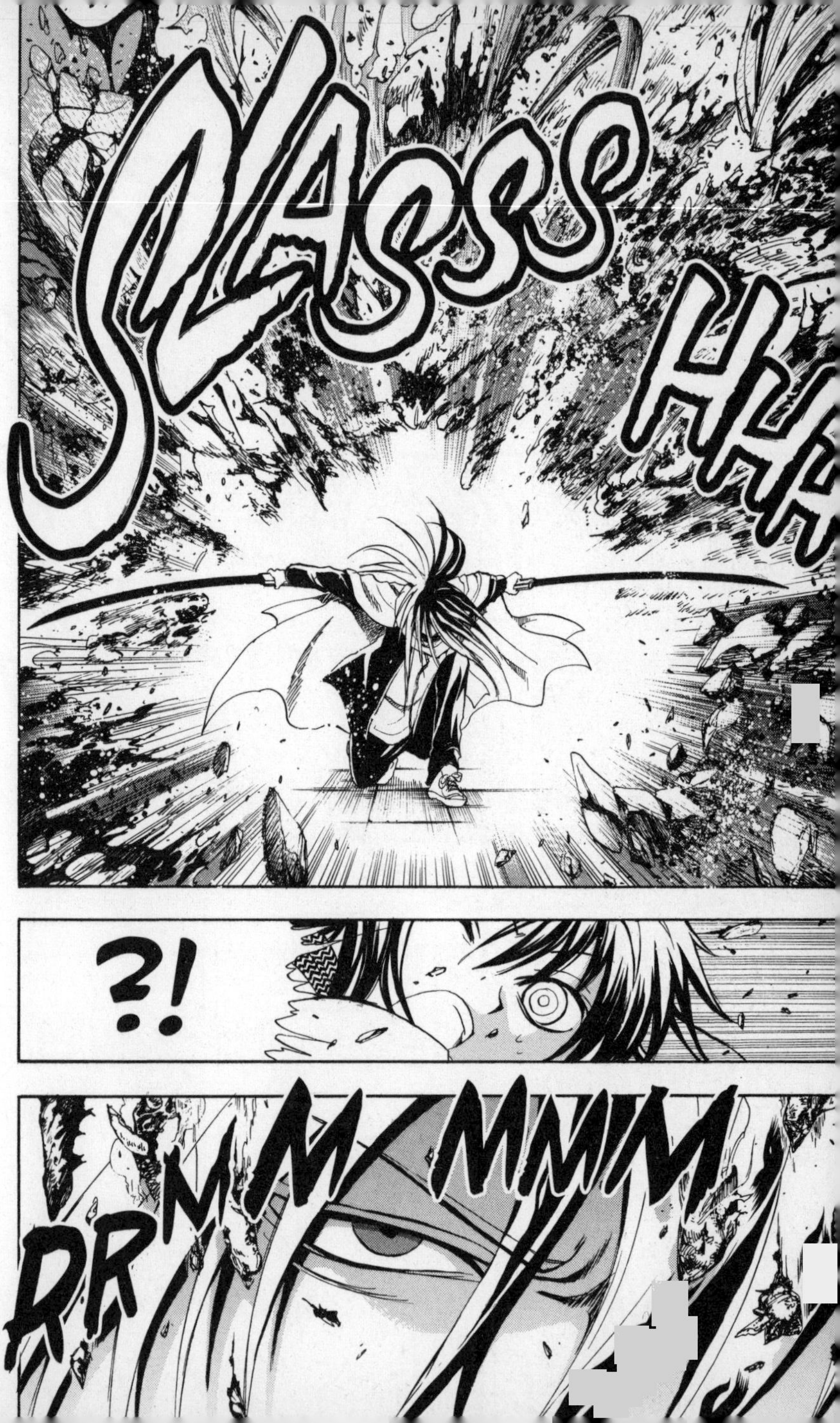
SLASSSHH
?!
RRMMMMMM

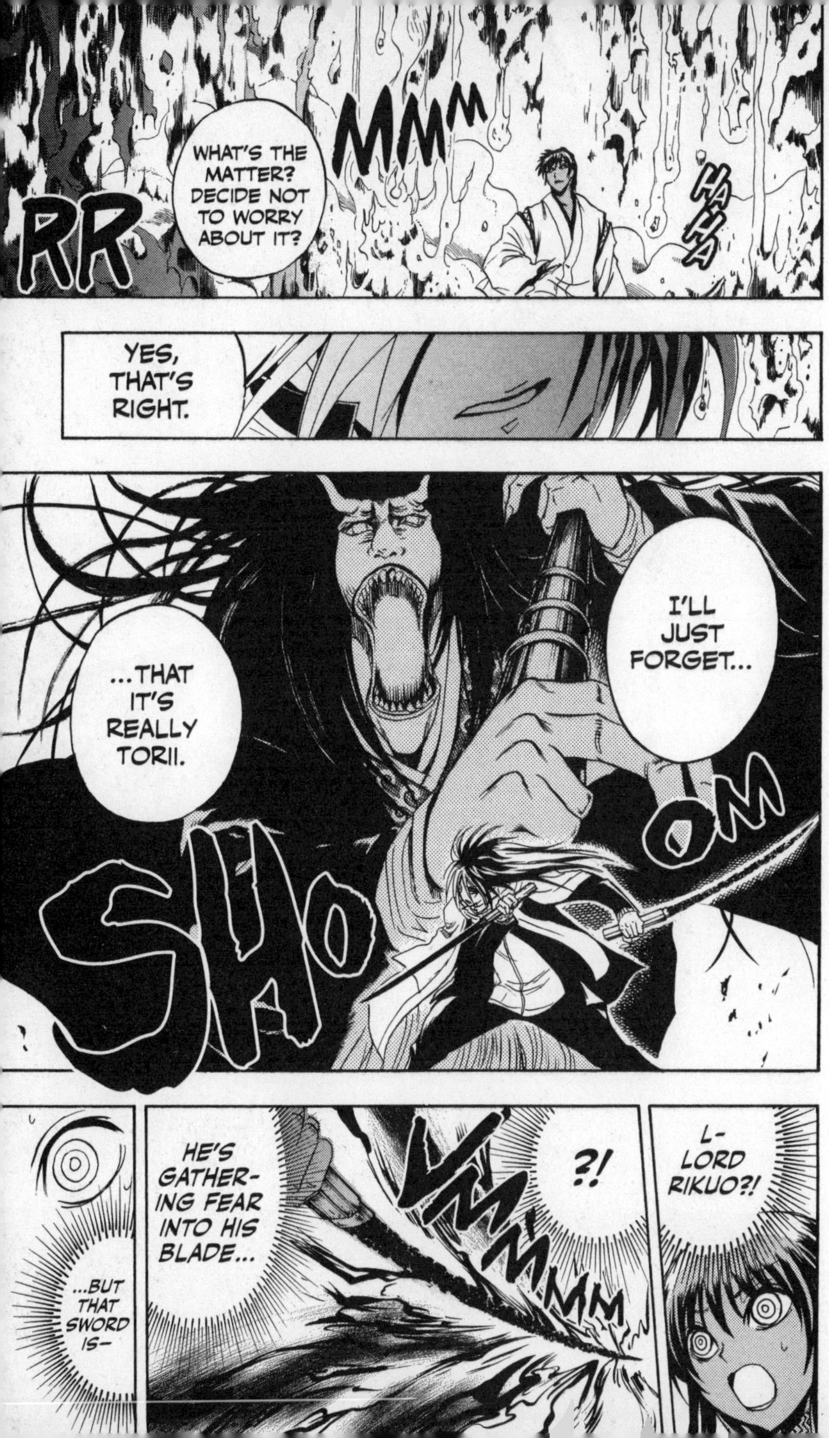
HAHA
MMM
WHAT'S THE MATTER? DECIDE NOT TO WORRY ABOUT IT?
RR
YES, THAT'S RIGHT.
I'LL JUST FORGET...
...THAT IT'S REALLY TORII.
SHOOM
L- LORD RIKUO?!
?!
VMMMMM
HE'S GATHER-ING FEAR INTO HIS BLADE...
...BUT THAT SWORD IS—

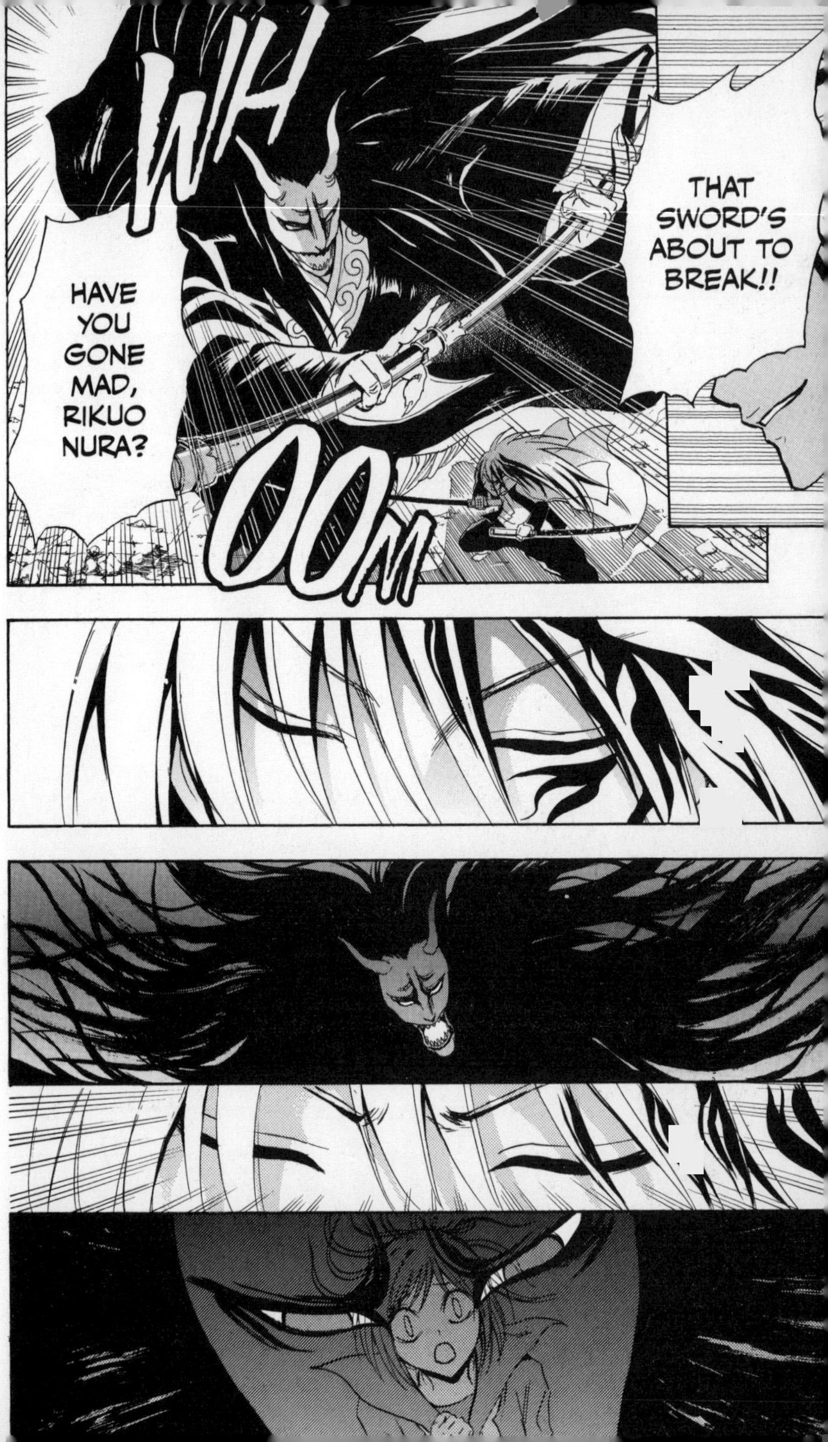
THAT SWORD'S ABOUT TO BREAK!!
WHOOM
HAVE YOU GONE MAD, RIKUO NURA?

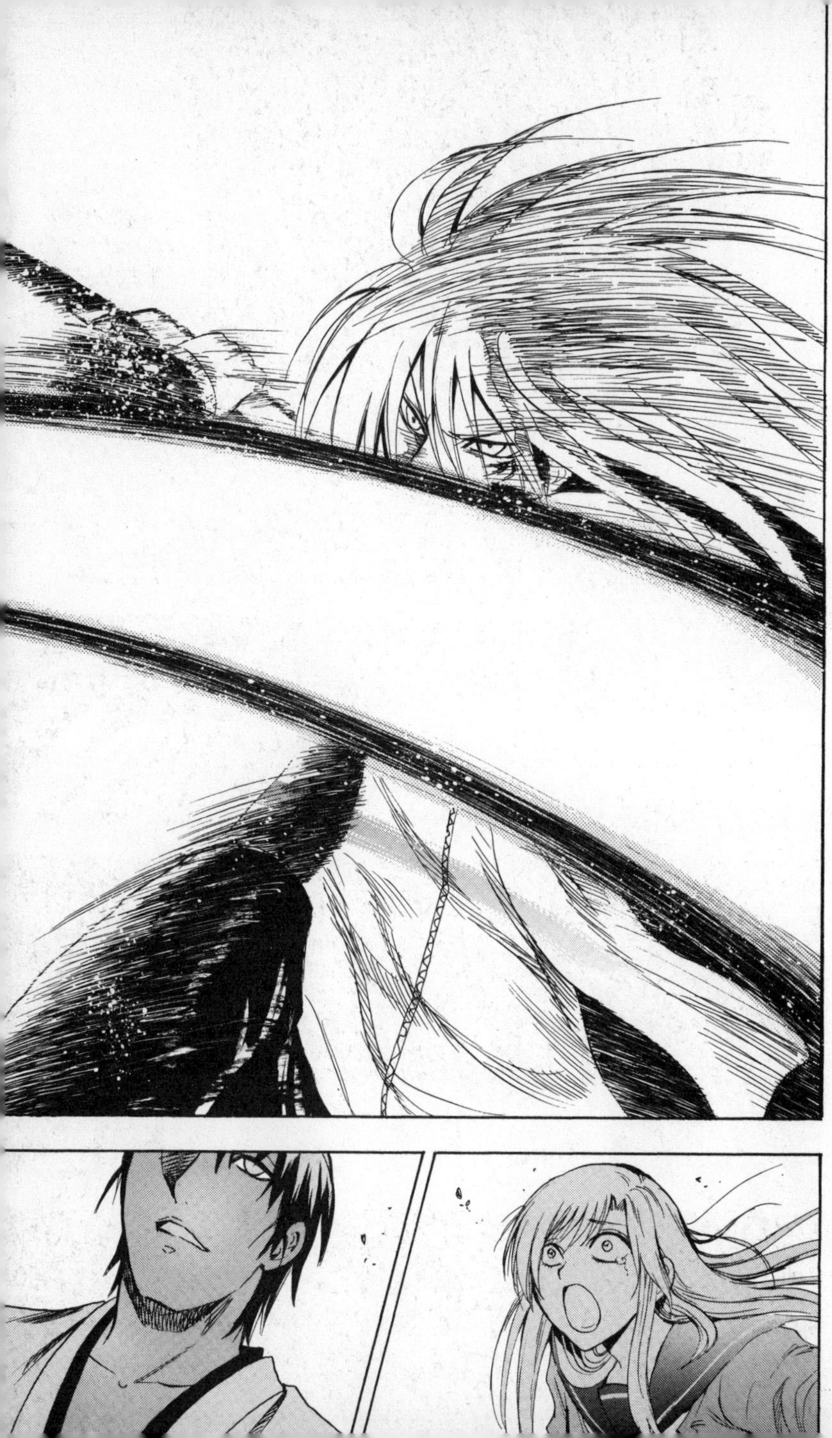

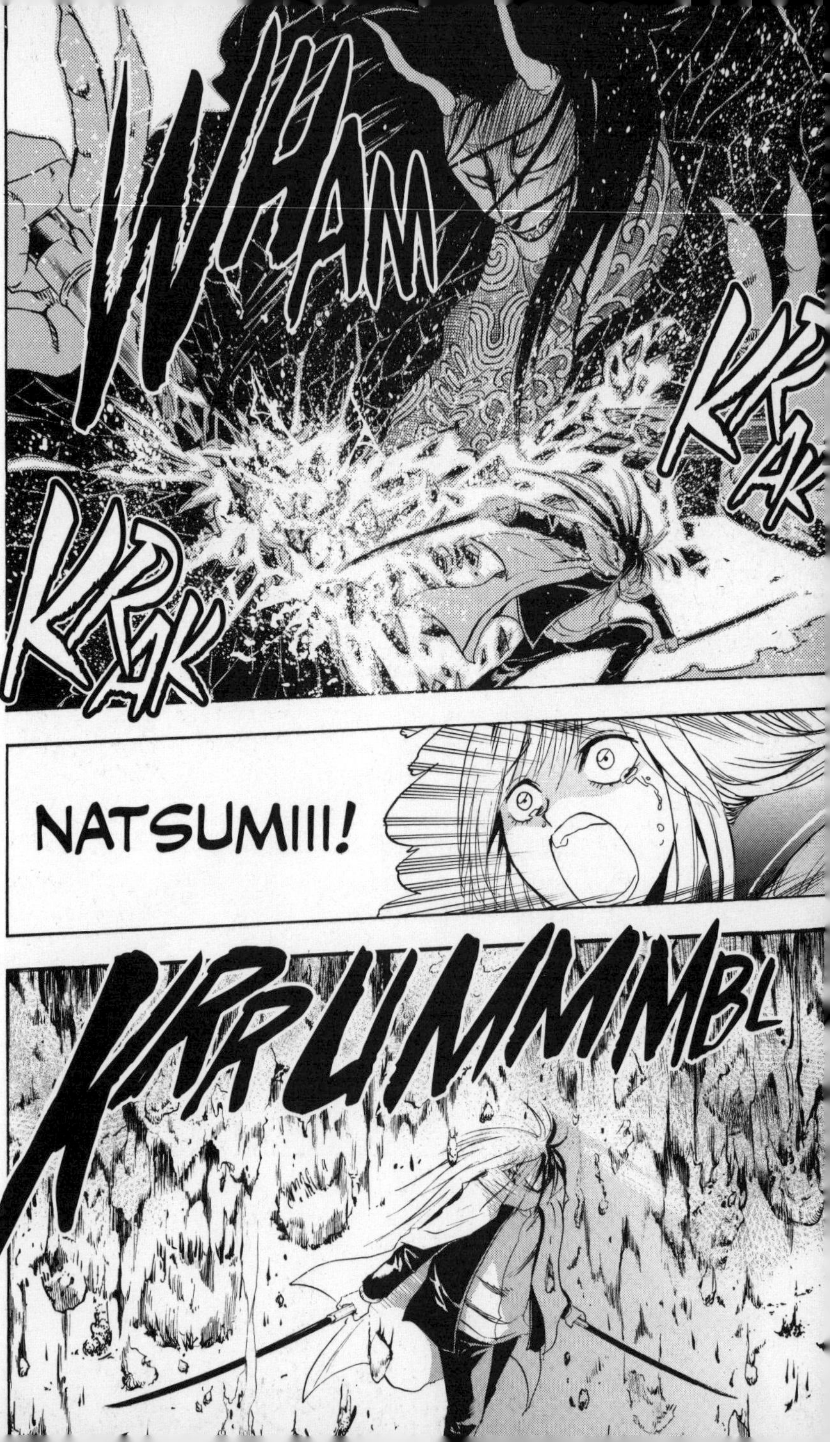
WHAM
KRAK
KRAK
NATSUMIII!
KRUMMMBL

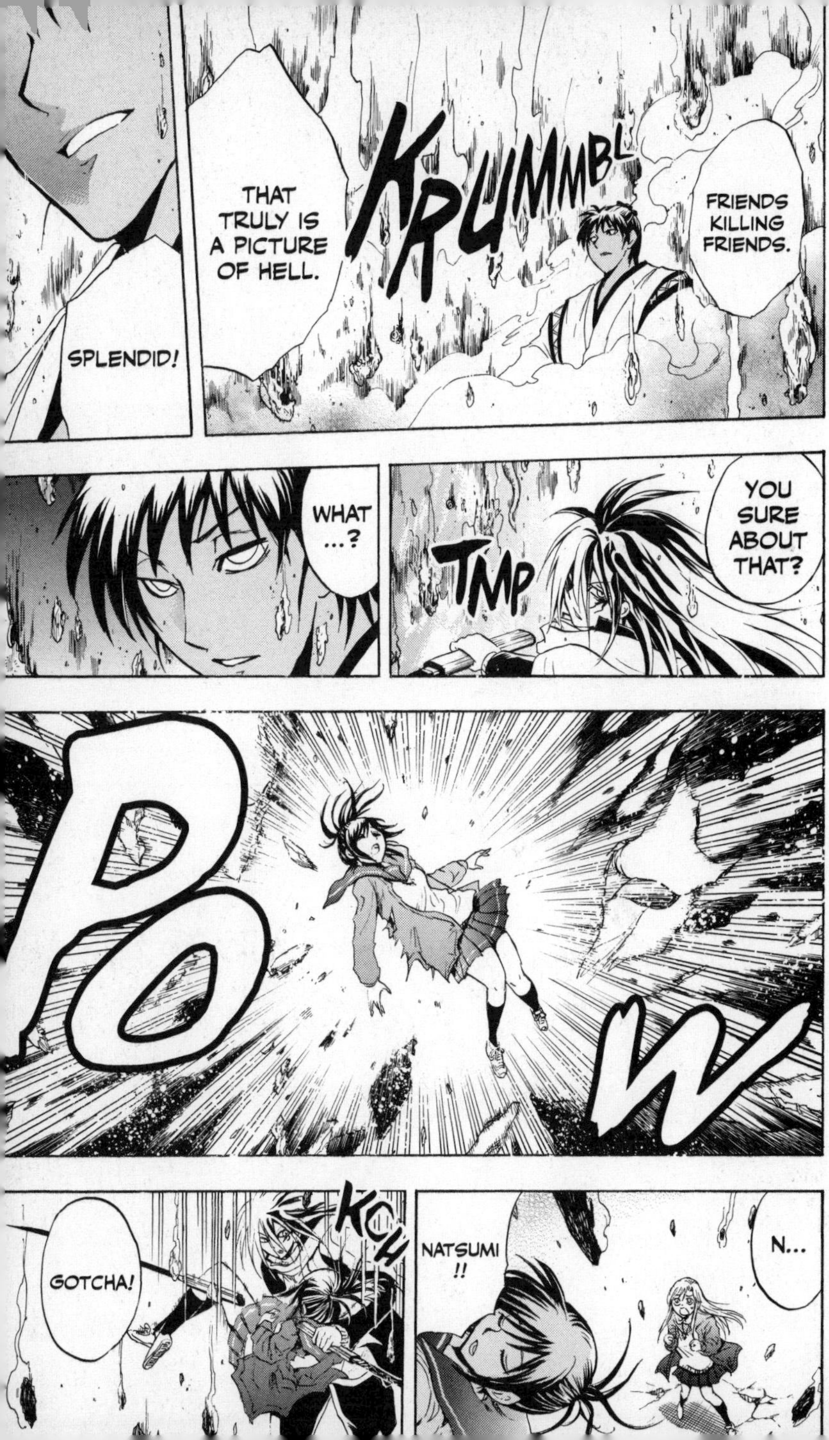
FRIENDS KILLING FRIENDS.
KRUMMBL
THAT TRULY IS A PICTURE OF HELL.
SPLENDID!
YOU SURE ABOUT THAT?
TMP
WHAT ...?
POW
N...
NATSUMI !!
KCH
GOTCHA!

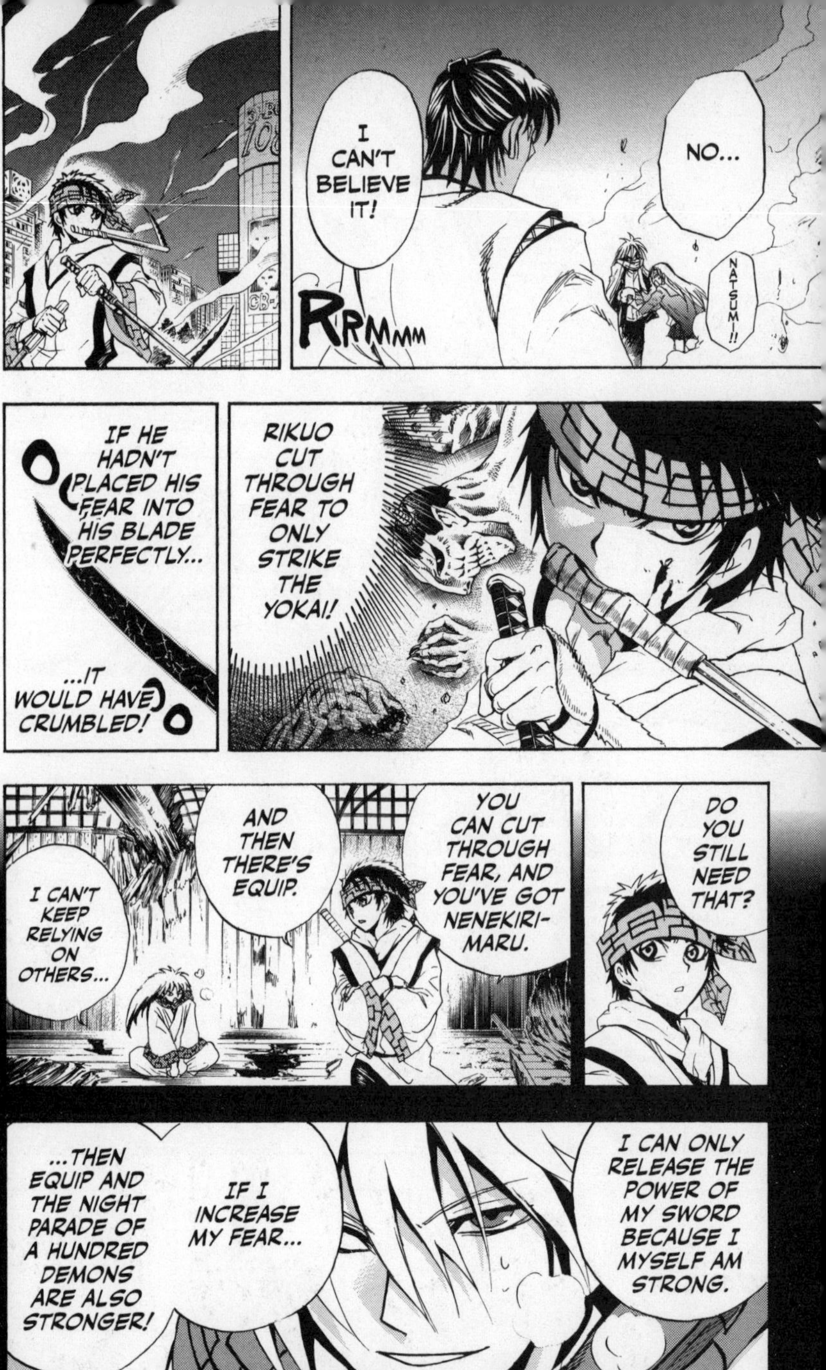
NO...
NATSUMI!!
I CAN'T BELIEVE IT!
RRMMM
RIKUO CUT THROUGH FEAR TO ONLY STRIKE THE YOKAI!
IF HE HADN'T PLACED HIS FEAR INTO HIS BLADE PERFECTLY...
...IT WOULD HAVE CRUMBLED!
DO YOU STILL NEED THAT?
YOU CAN CUT THROUGH FEAR, AND YOU'VE GOT NENEKIRI-MARU.
AND THEN THERE'S EQUIP.
I CAN'T KEEP RELYING ON OTHERS...
I CAN ONLY RELEASE THE POWER OF MY SWORD BECAUSE I MYSELF AM STRONG.
IF I INCREASE MY FEAR...
...THEN EQUIP AND THE NIGHT PARADE OF A HUNDRED DEMONS ARE ALSO STRONGER!

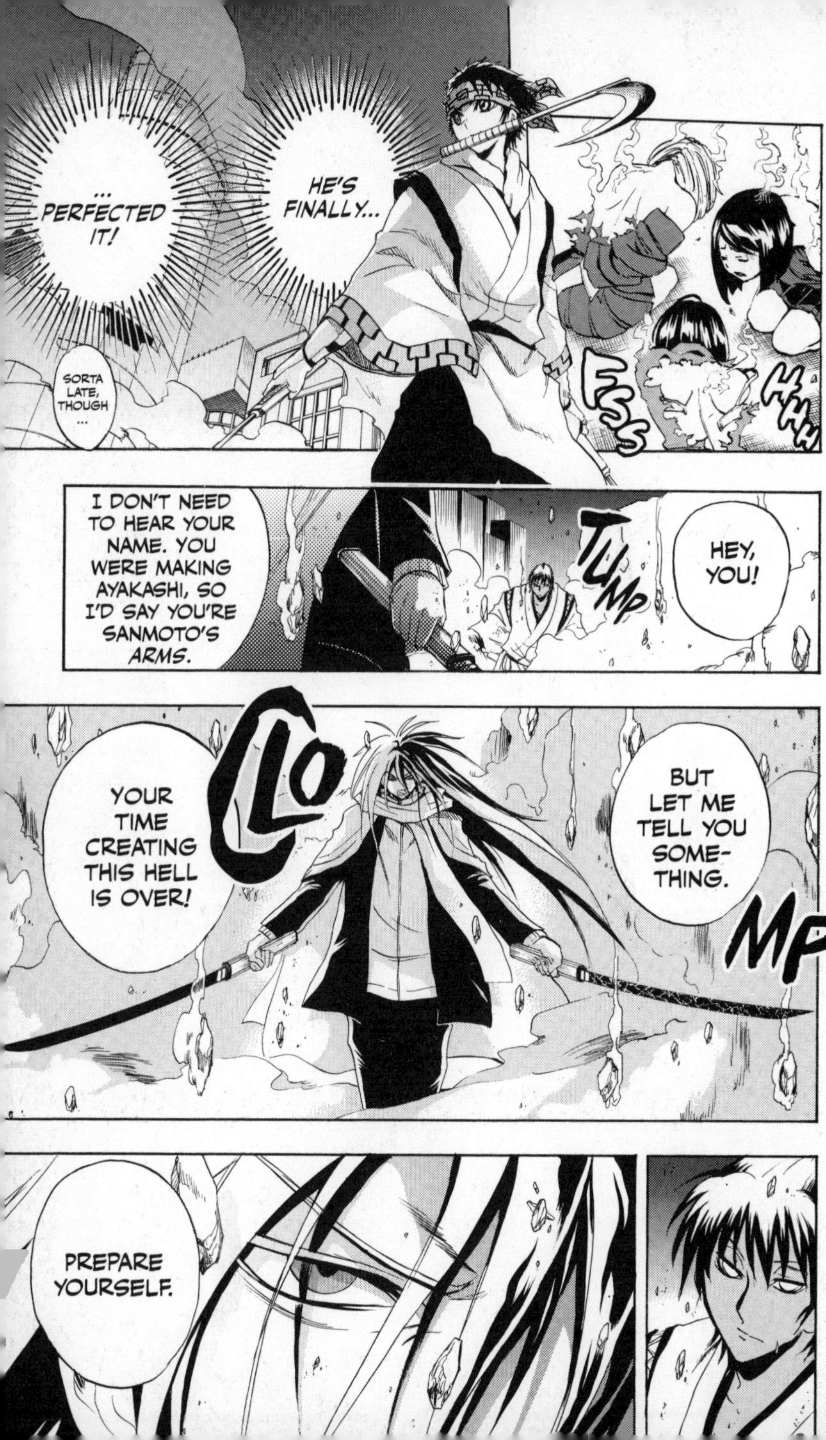
HE'S FINALLY...
... PERFECTED IT!
FSS
HHH
SORTA LATE, THOUGH ...
HEY, YOU!
TUMP
I DON'T NEED TO HEAR YOUR NAME. YOU WERE MAKING AYAKASHI, SO I'D SAY YOU'RE SANMOTO'S ARMS.
BUT LET ME TELL YOU SOME-THING.
CLO
MP
YOUR TIME CREATING THIS HELL IS OVER!
PREPARE YOURSELF.

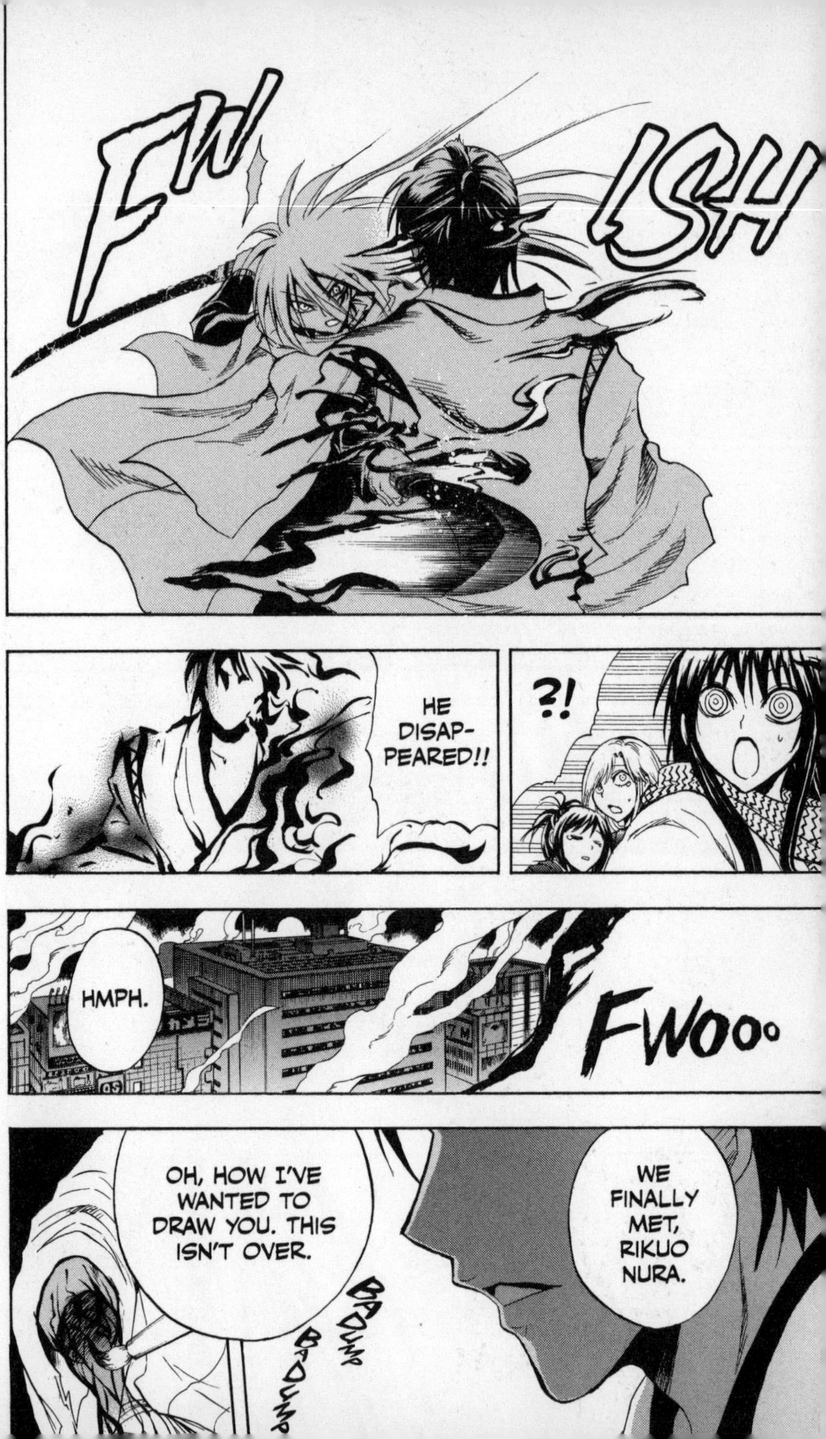
FWISH
?!
HE DISAPPEARED!!
FWOOO
HMPH.
WE FINALLY MET, RIKUO NURA.
OH, HOW I'VE WANTED TO DRAW YOU. THIS ISN'T OVER.
BA-DUMP
BA-DUMP

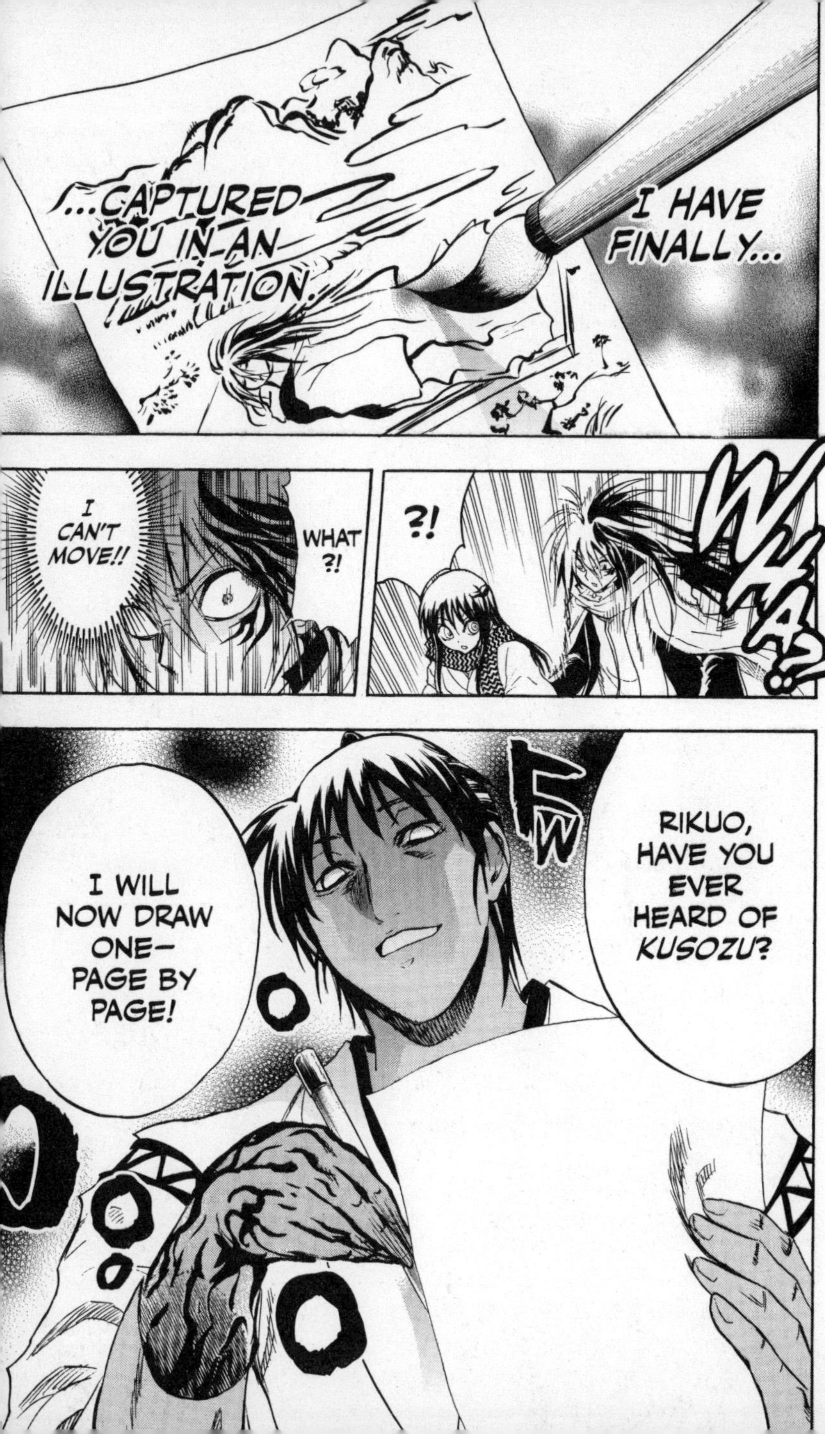
I HAVE FINALLY...
...CAPTURED YOU IN AN ILLUSTRATION.
WHA?!
?!
WHAT?!
I CAN'T MOVE!!
FW
RIKUO, HAVE YOU EVER HEARD OF KUSOZU?
I WILL NOW DRAW ONE—PAGE BY PAGE!

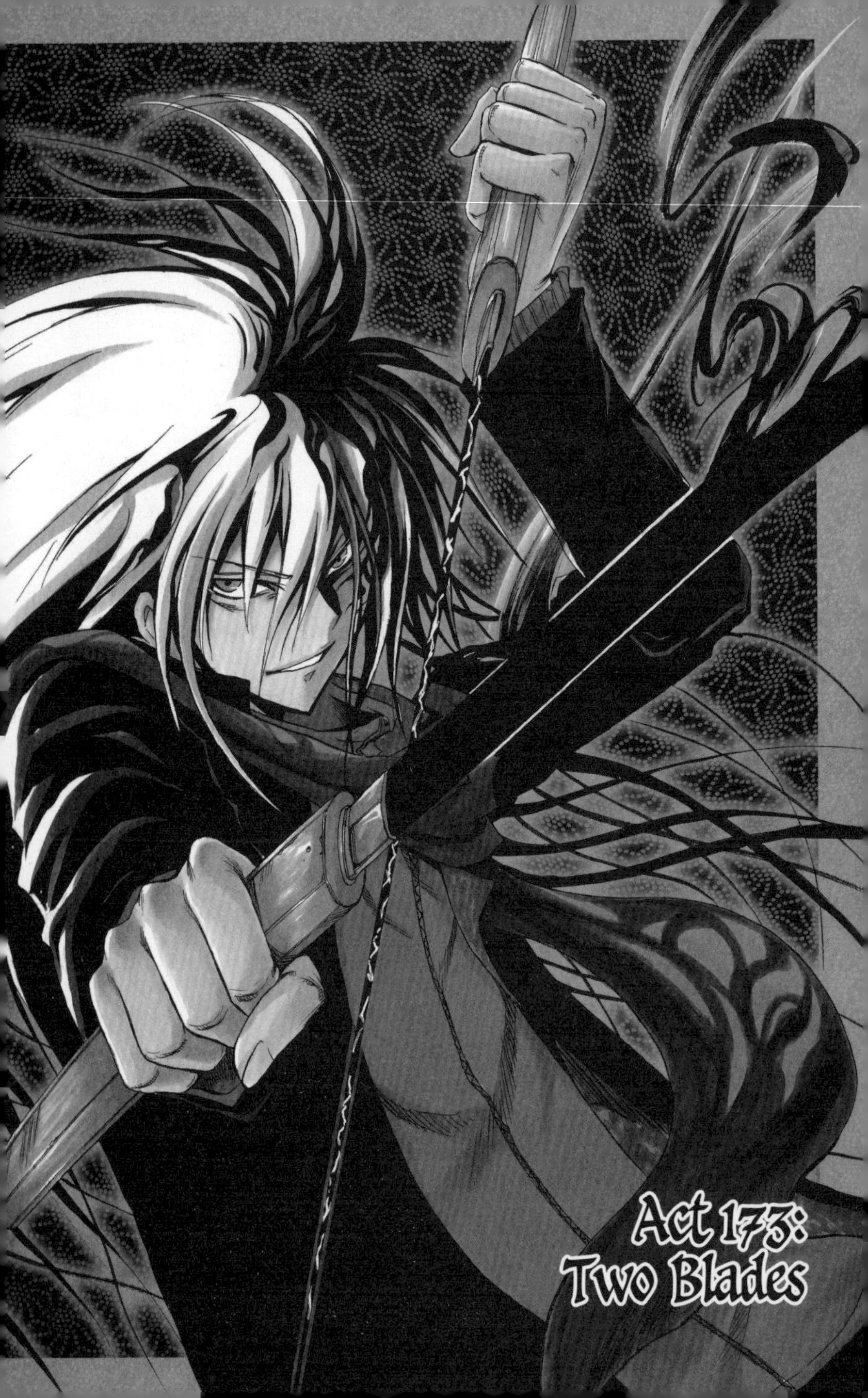
Act 173:
Two Blades

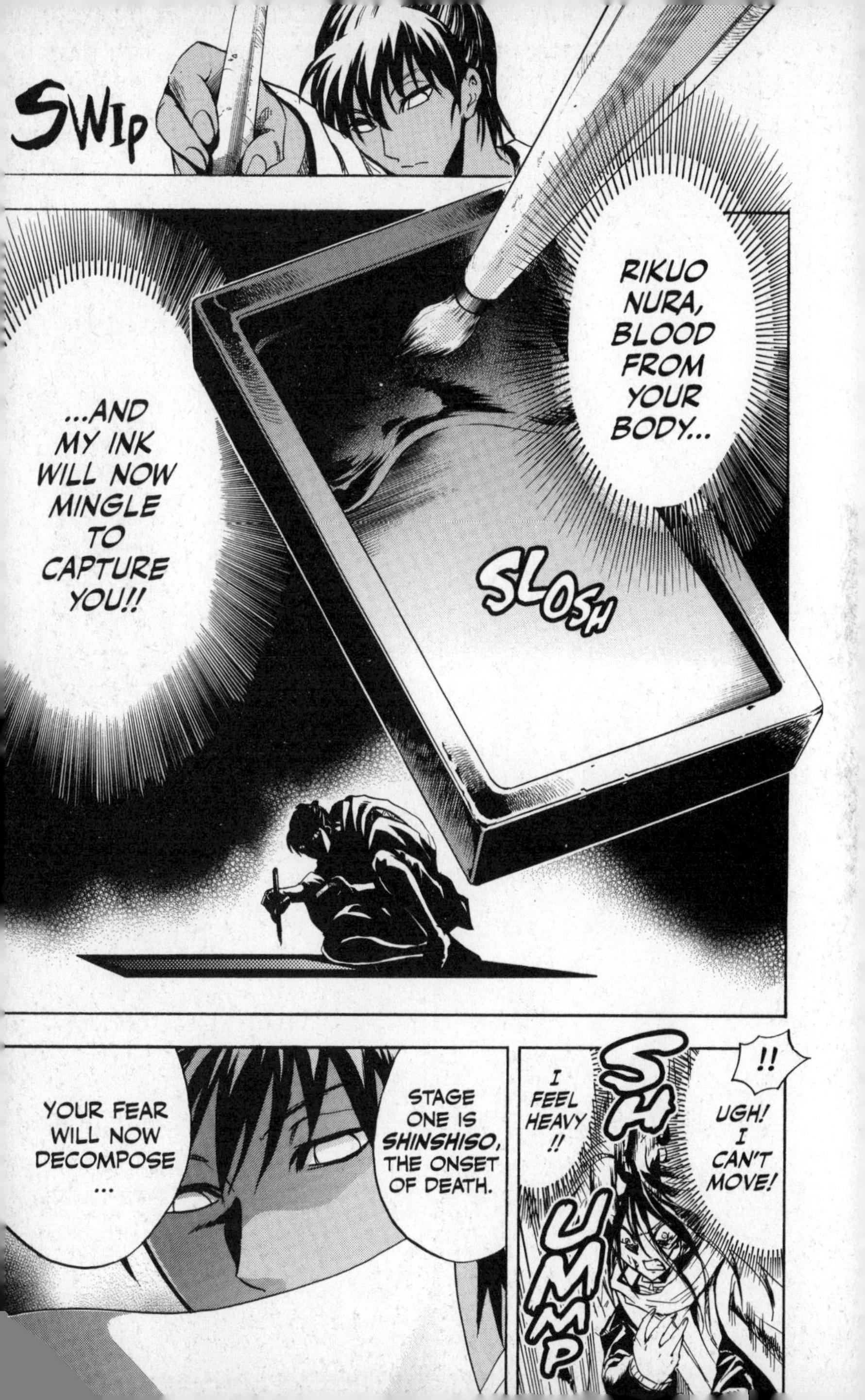
SWIP
RIKUO NURA, BLOOD FROM YOUR BODY...
...AND MY INK WILL NOW MINGLE TO CAPTURE YOU!!
SLOSH
!!
UGH! I CAN'T MOVE!
SHUMMP
I FEEL HEAVY!!
STAGE ONE IS SHINSHISO, THE ONSET OF DEATH.
YOUR FEAR WILL NOW DECOMPOSE...

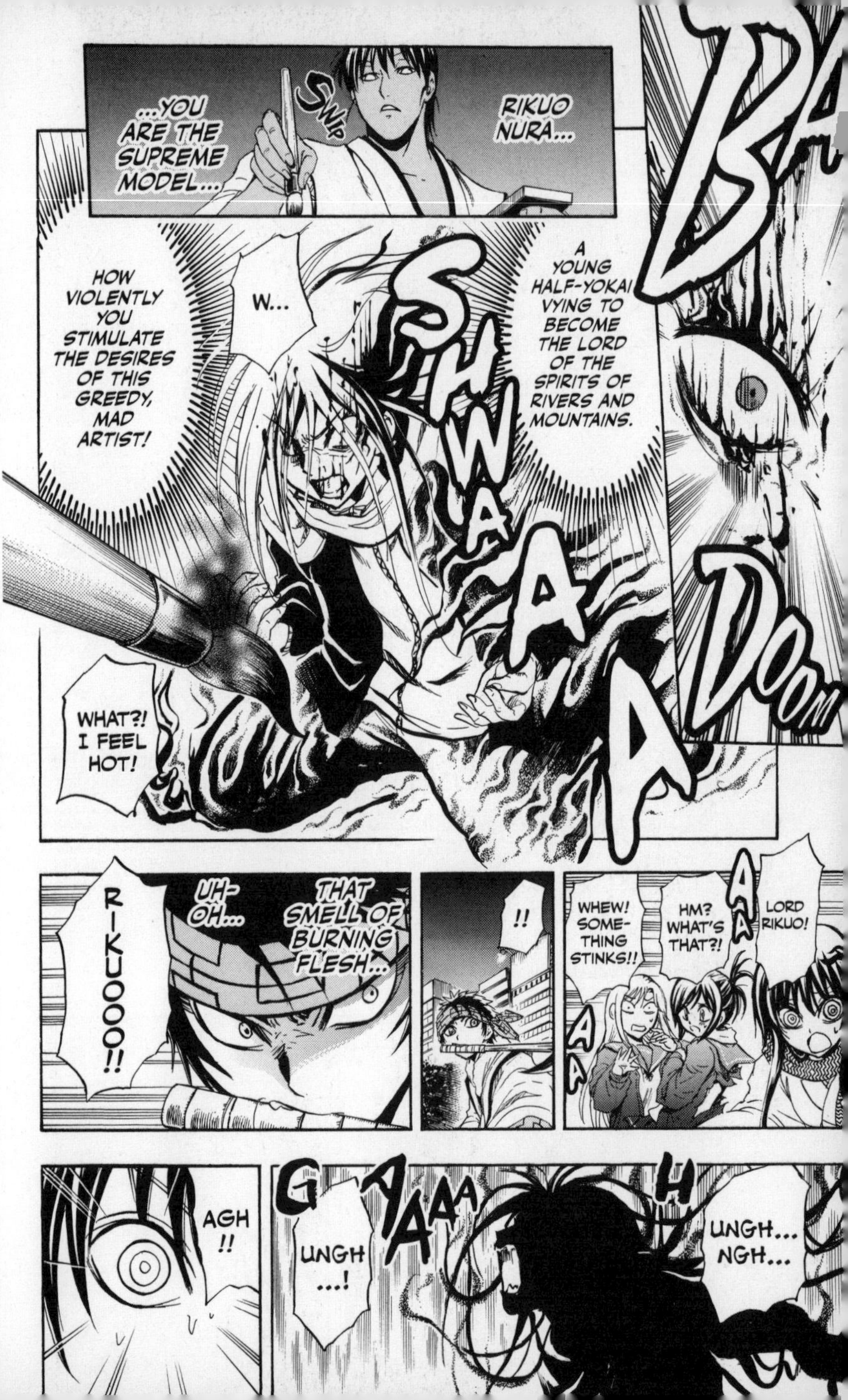
BA
DOOO
RIKUO NURA...
SWIP
...YOU ARE THE SUPREME MODEL...
A YOUNG HALF-YOKAI VYING TO BECOME THE LORD OF THE SPIRITS OF RIVERS AND MOUNTAINS.
SHWAAAA
W...
HOW VIOLENTLY YOU STIMULATE THE DESIRES OF THIS GREEDY, MAD ARTIST!
WHAT?! I FEEL HOT!
AAA
LORD RIKUO!
HM? WHAT'S THAT?!
WHEW! SOMETHING STINKS!!
AAA
!!
THAT SMELL OF BURNING FLESH...
UH-OH...
RIKUOOOO!!
GAAAAAAH
UNGH... NGH...
UNGH ...!
AGH !!

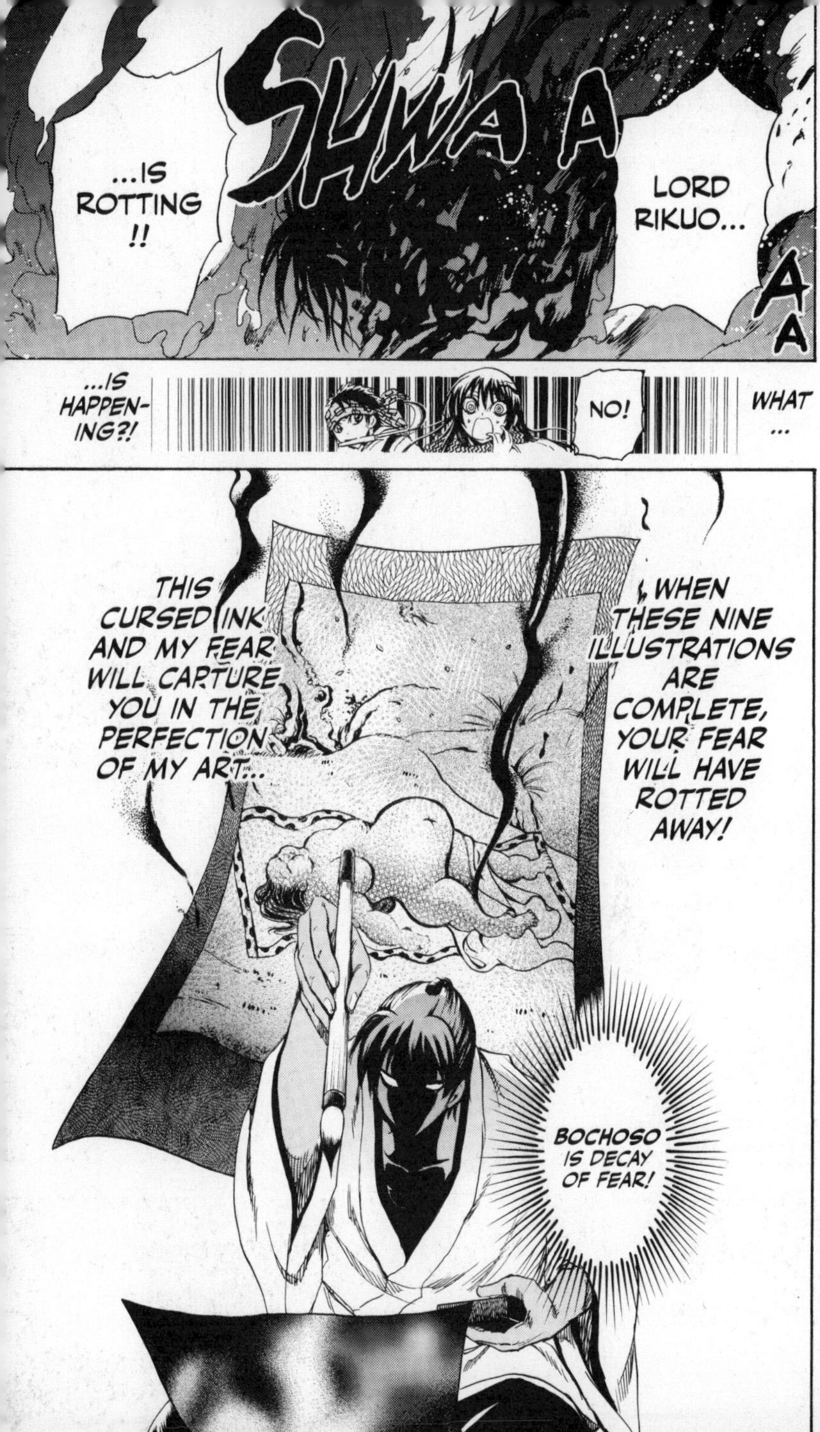
A A A
LORD RIKUO...
SUWA A
...IS ROTTING !!
WHAT ...
NO!
...IS HAPPENING?!
WHEN THESE NINE ILLUSTRATIONS ARE COMPLETE, YOUR FEAR WILL HAVE ROTTED AWAY!
THIS CURSED INK AND MY FEAR WILL CAPTURE YOU IN THE PERFECTION OF MY ART...
BOCHOSO IS DECAY OF FEAR!

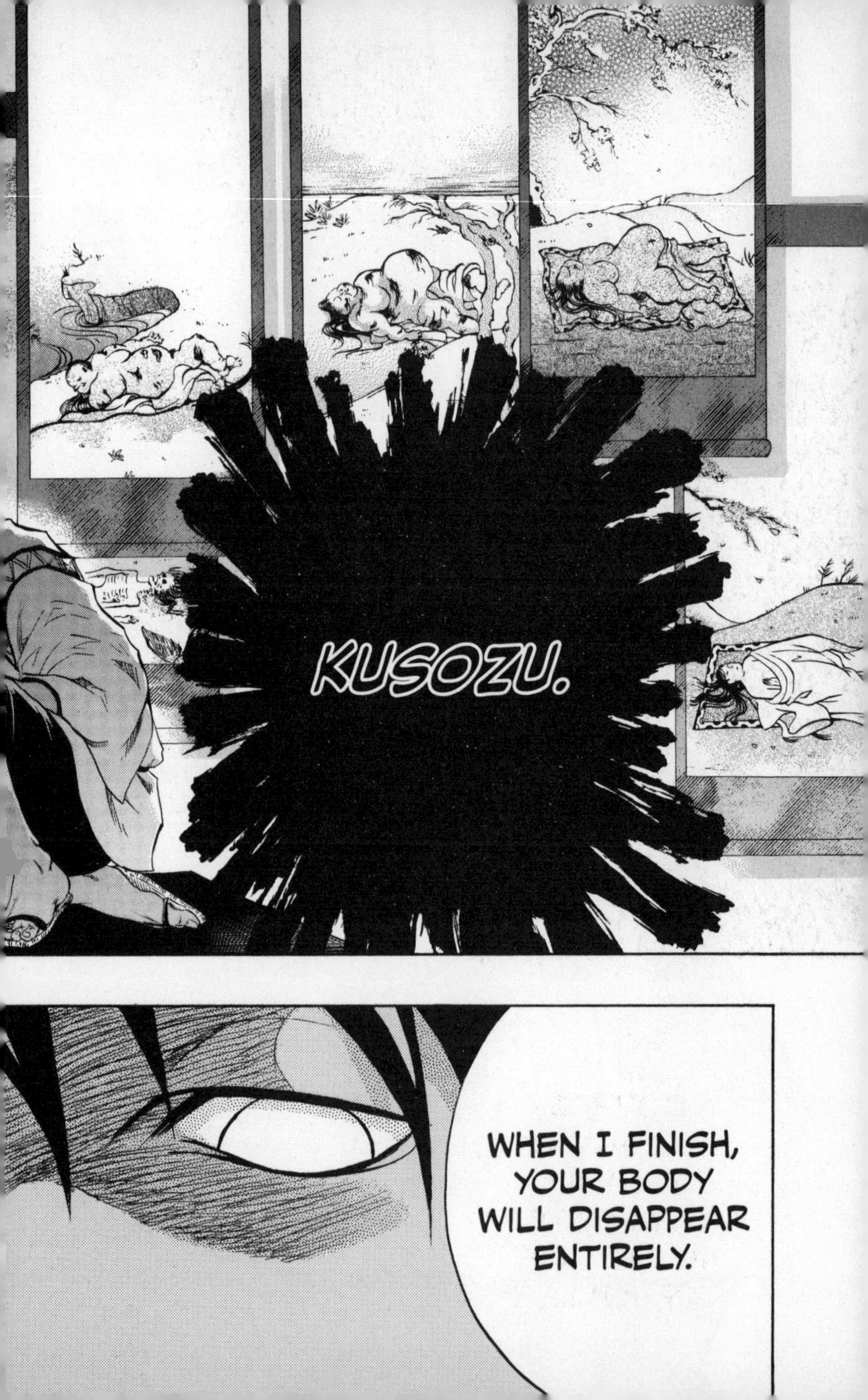
KUSOZU.
WHEN I FINISH, YOUR BODY WILL DISAPPEAR ENTIRELY.

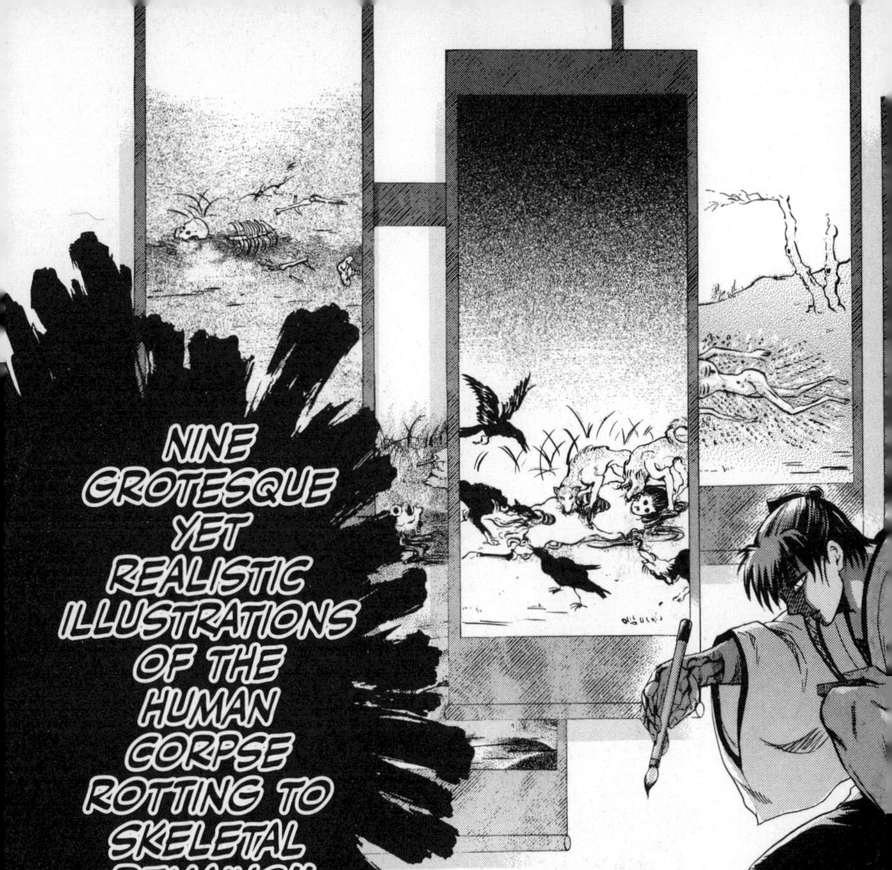
NINE GROTESQUE YET REALISTIC ILLUSTRATIONS OF THE HUMAN CORPSE ROTTING TO SKELETAL REMAINS!!
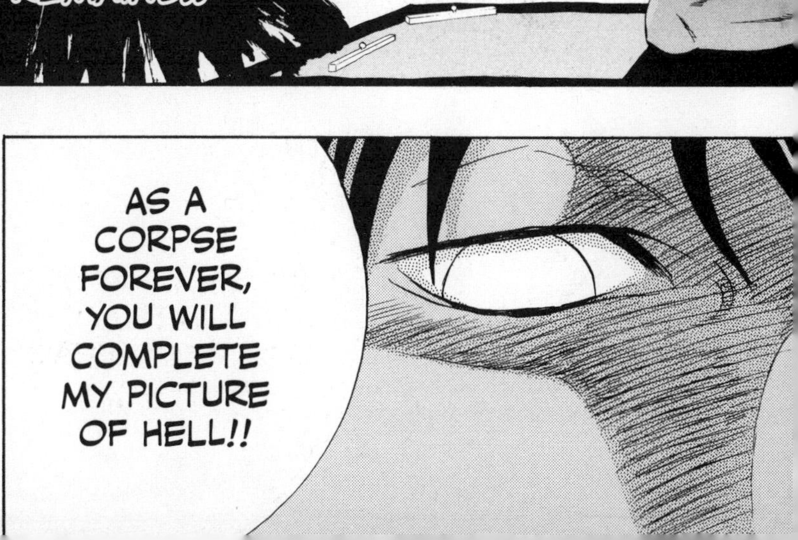
AS A CORPSE FOREVER, YOU WILL COMPLETE MY PICTURE OF HELL!!

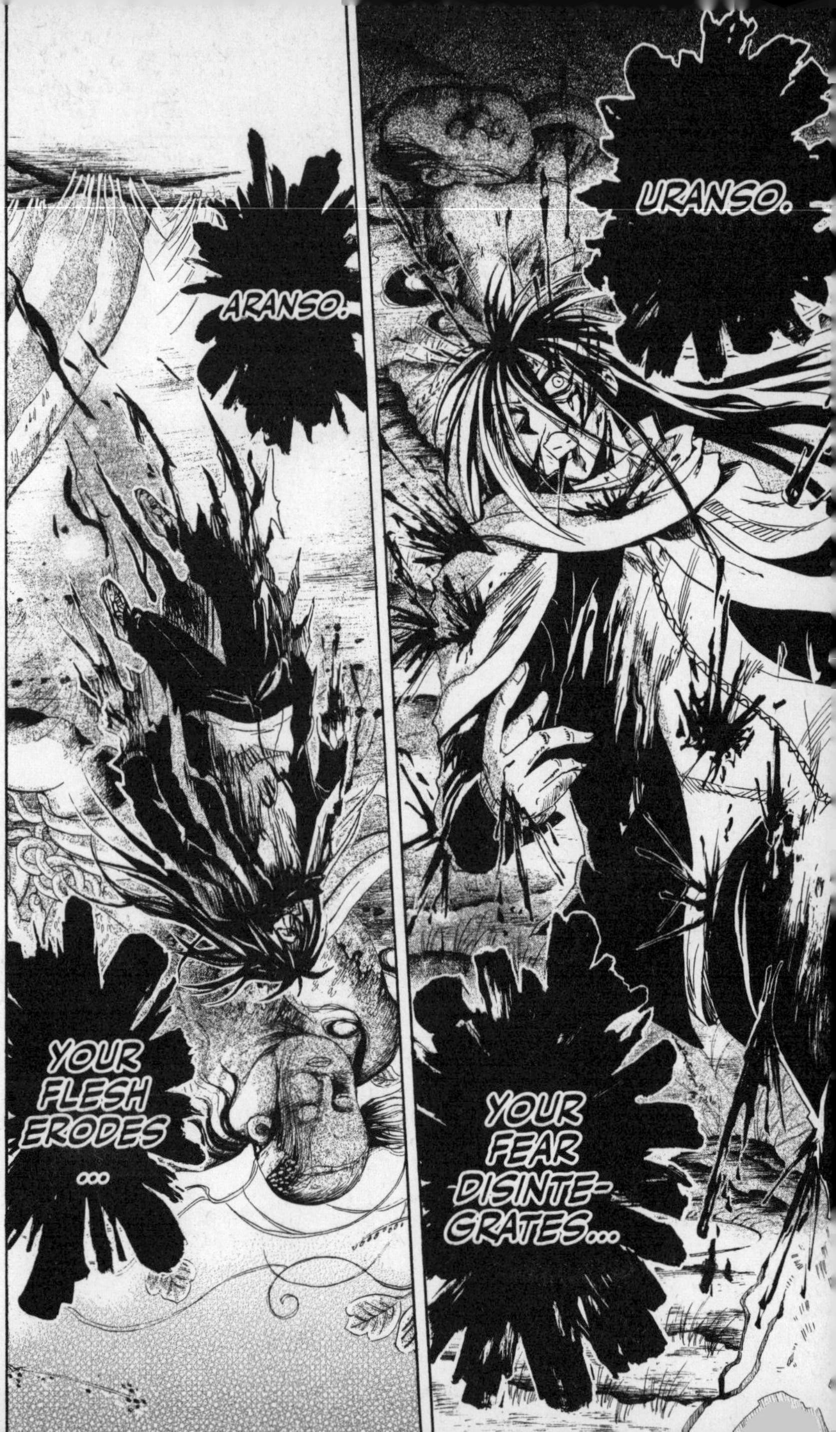
URANSO.
YOUR FEAR DISINTE-
GRATES...
ARANSO.
YOUR FLESH ERODES ...

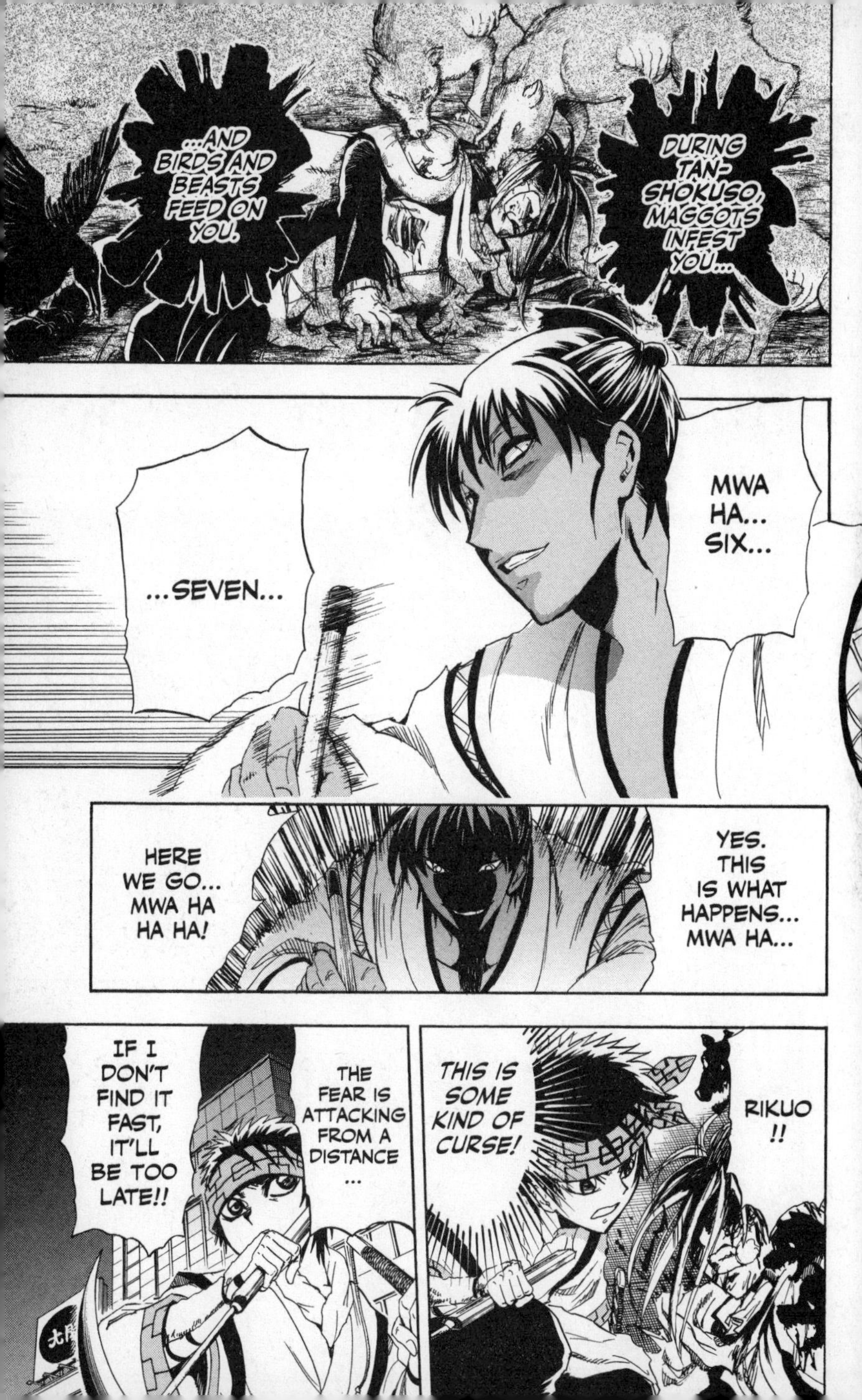
DURING TAN-SHOKUSO, MAGGOTS INFEST YOU...
...AND BIRDS AND BEASTS FEED ON YOU.
MWA HA... SIX...
...SEVEN...
YES. THIS IS WHAT HAPPENS... MWA HA...
HERE WE GO... MWA HA HA HA!
RIKUO !!
THIS IS SOME KIND OF CURSE!
THE FEAR IS ATTACKING FROM A DISTANCE ...
IF I DON'T FIND IT FAST, IT'LL BE TOO LATE!!

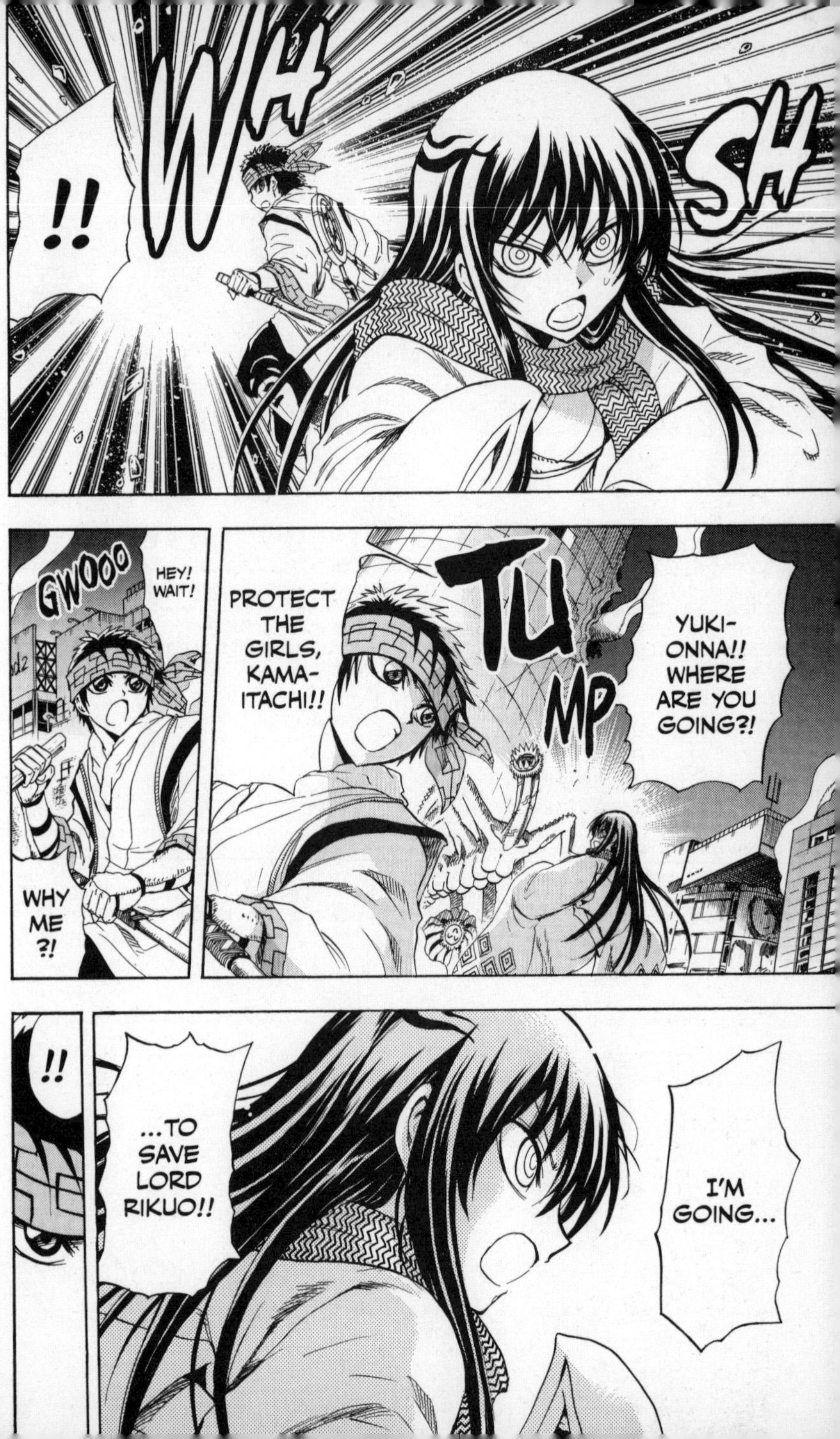
WHSH
!!
YUKI-ONNA!! WHERE ARE YOU GOING?!
TUMP
PROTECT THE GIRLS, KAMA-ITACHI!!
HEY! WAIT!
GWOOO
WHY ME?!
I'M GOING...
...TO SAVE LORD RIKUO!!
!!

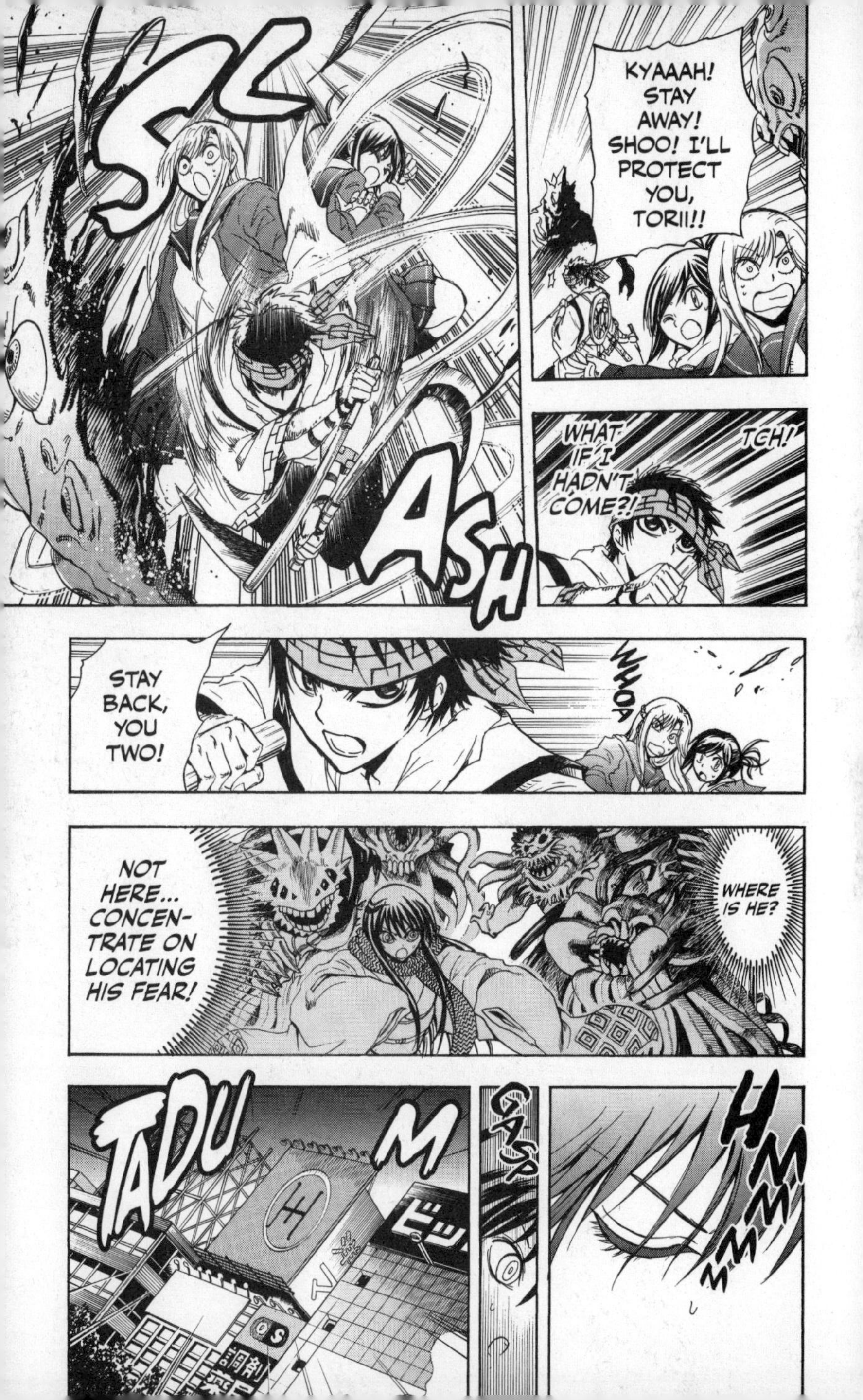
KYAAAH! STAY AWAY! SHOO! I'LL PROTECT YOU, TORII!!
TCH!
WHAT IF I HADN'T COME?!
SL
ASH
WHOA
STAY BACK, YOU TWO!
WHERE IS HE?
NOT HERE... CONCENTRATE ON LOCATING HIS FEAR!
HMMMMMM
GASP
TADU
M

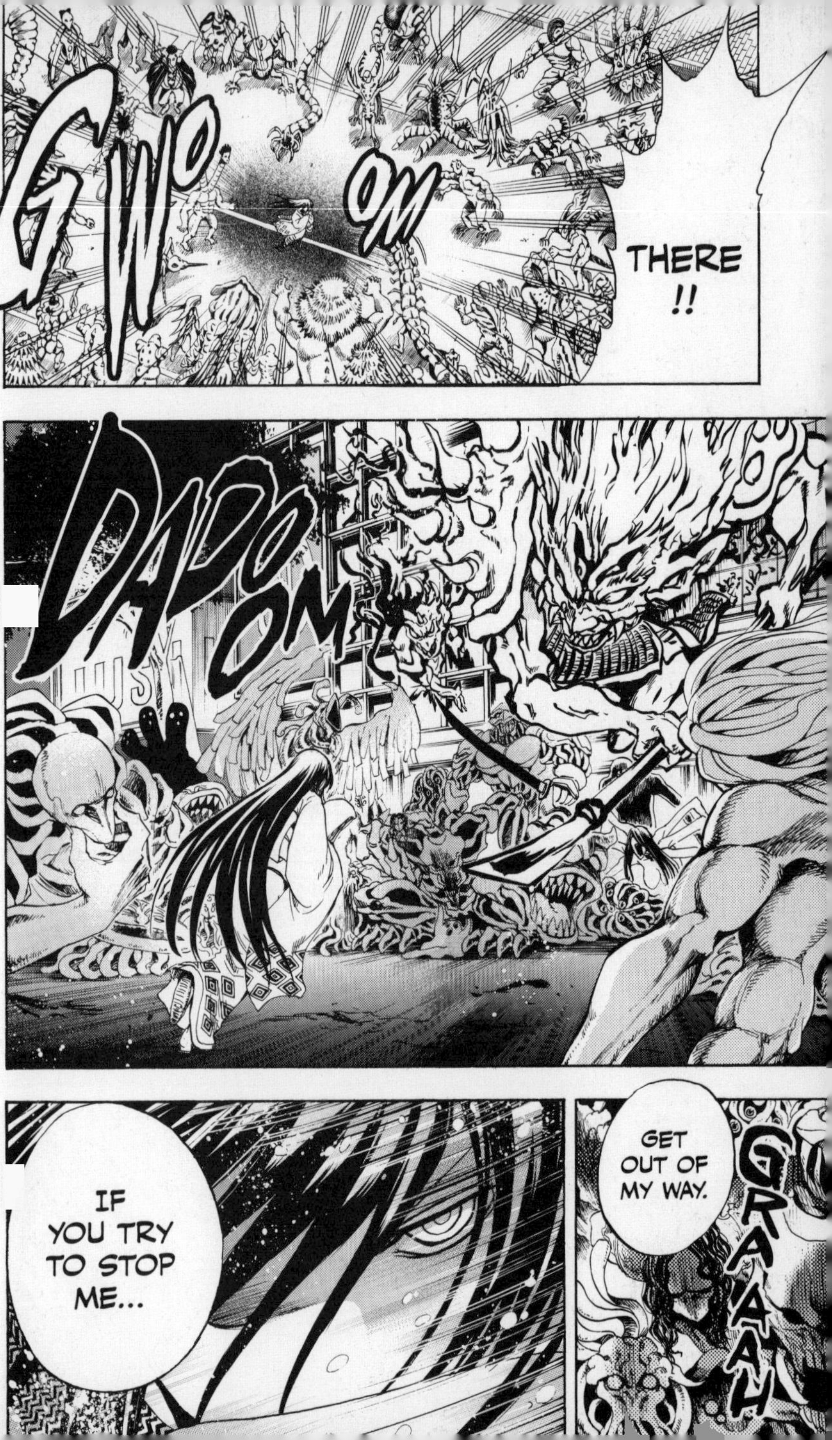
GWOOM
THERE!!
DADOOM
GET OUT OF MY WAY.
GRAAAH
IF YOU TRY TO STOP ME...

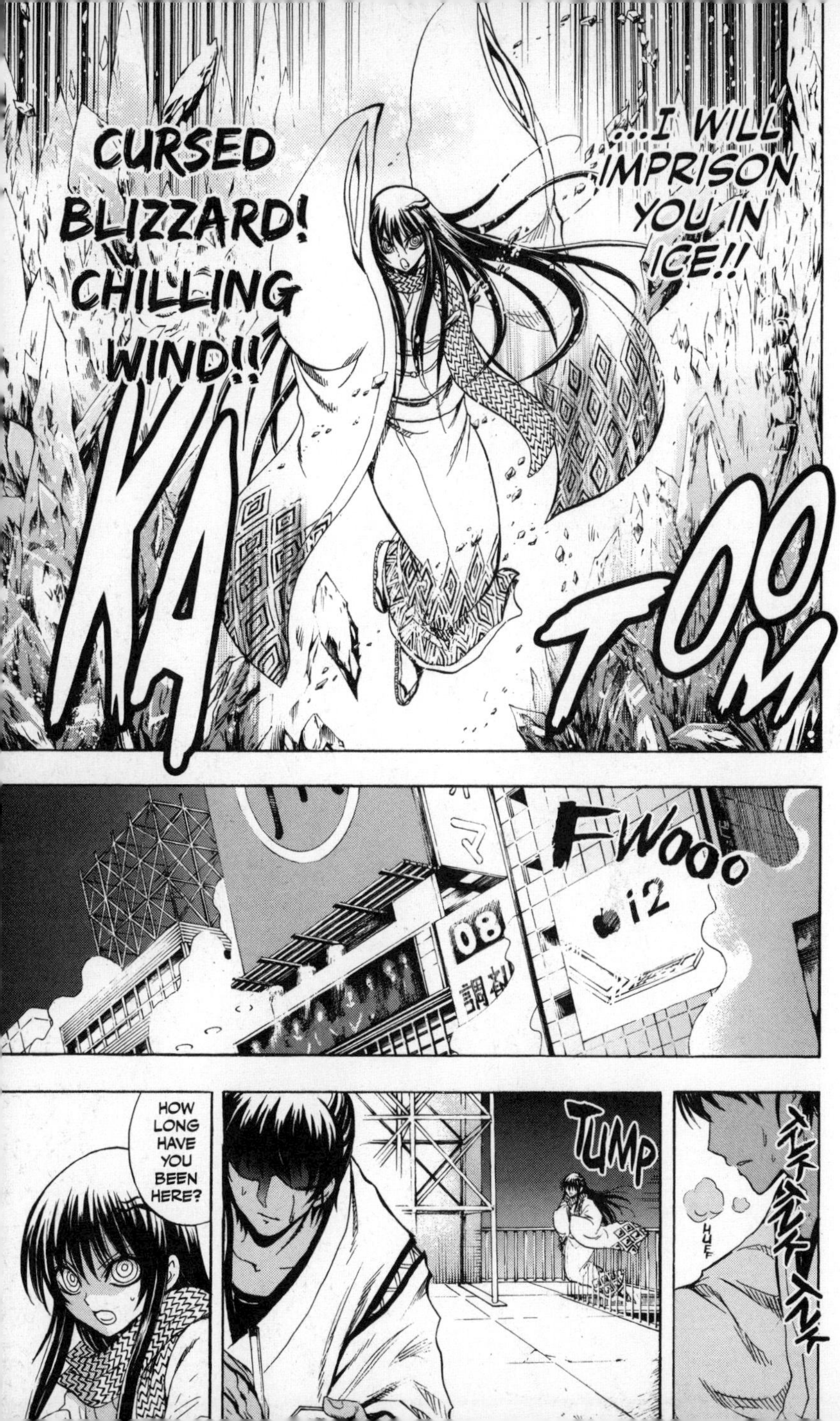

...I WILL IMPRISON YOU IN ICE!!
CURSED BLIZZARD! CHILLING WIND!!
KA
TOOOM
FWOOO
i2
08
HUFF
TUMP
HOW LONG HAVE YOU BEEN HERE?

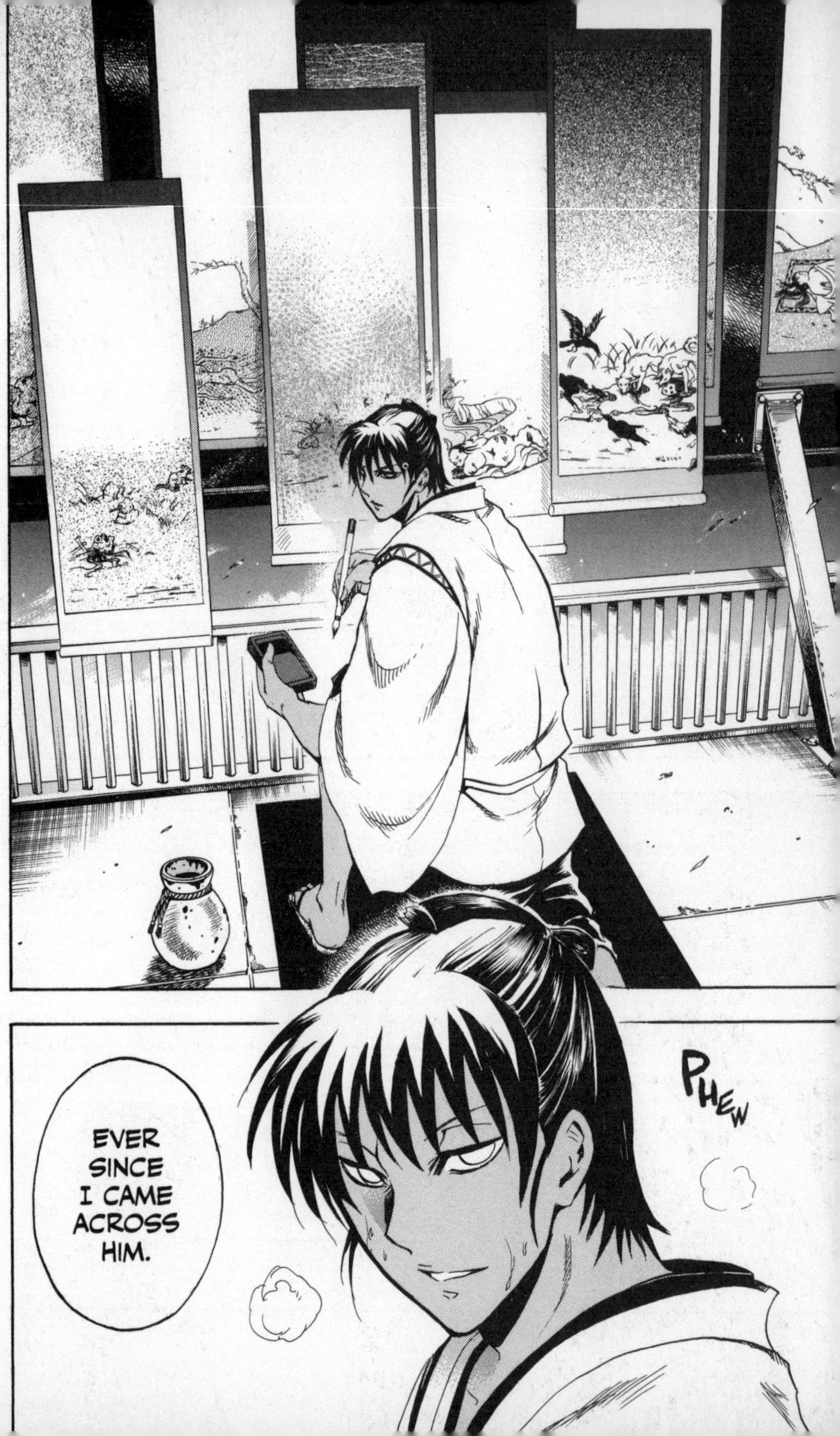
PHEW
EVER SINCE I CAME ACROSS HIM.

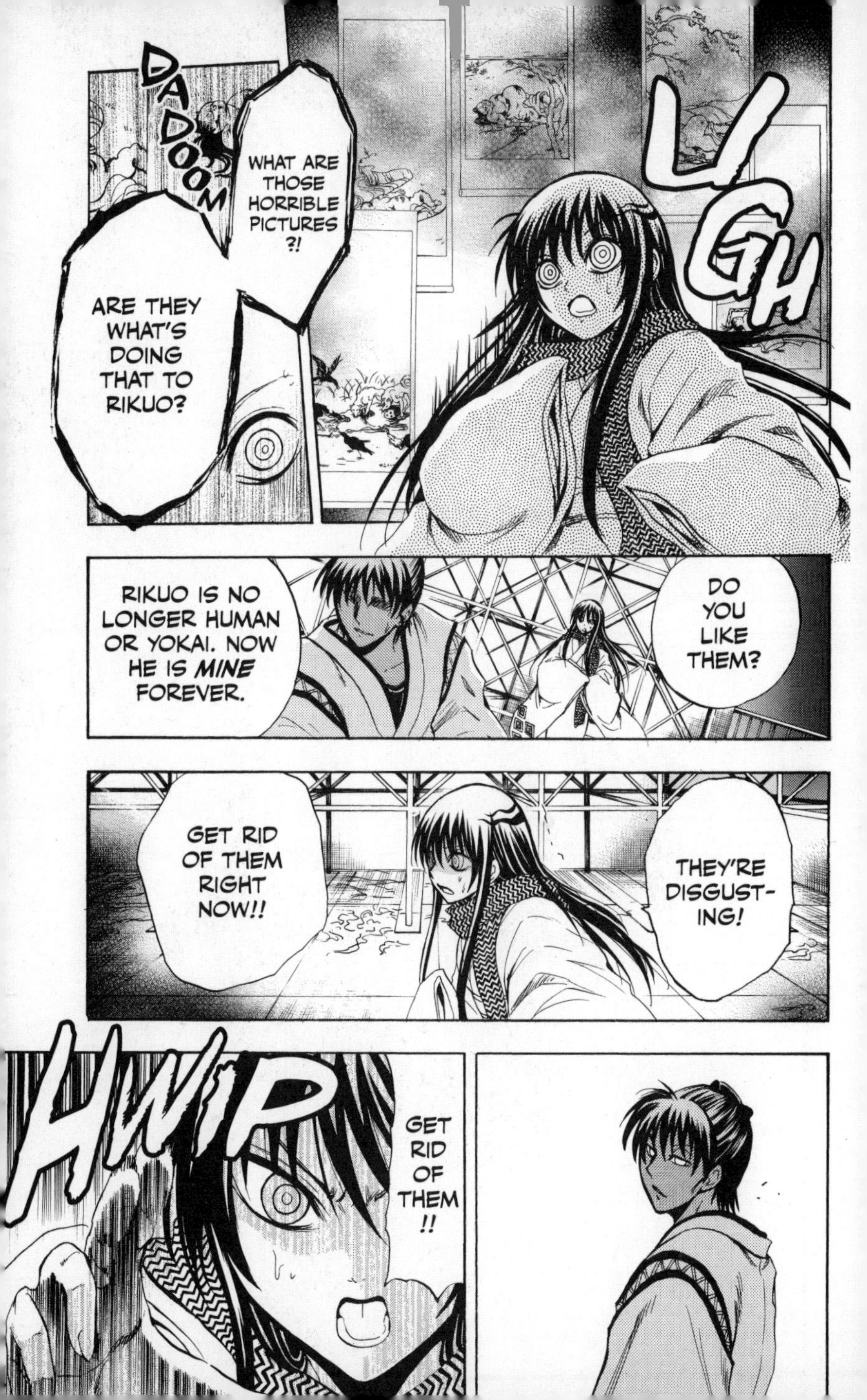
UGH
WHAT ARE THOSE HORRIBLE PICTURES?!
DADOOM
ARE THEY WHAT'S DOING THAT TO RIKUO?
DO YOU LIKE THEM?
RIKUO IS NO LONGER HUMAN OR YOKAI. NOW HE IS *MINE* FOREVER.
THEY'RE DISGUST-ING!
GET RID OF THEM RIGHT NOW!!
GET RID OF THEM!!
HWIP

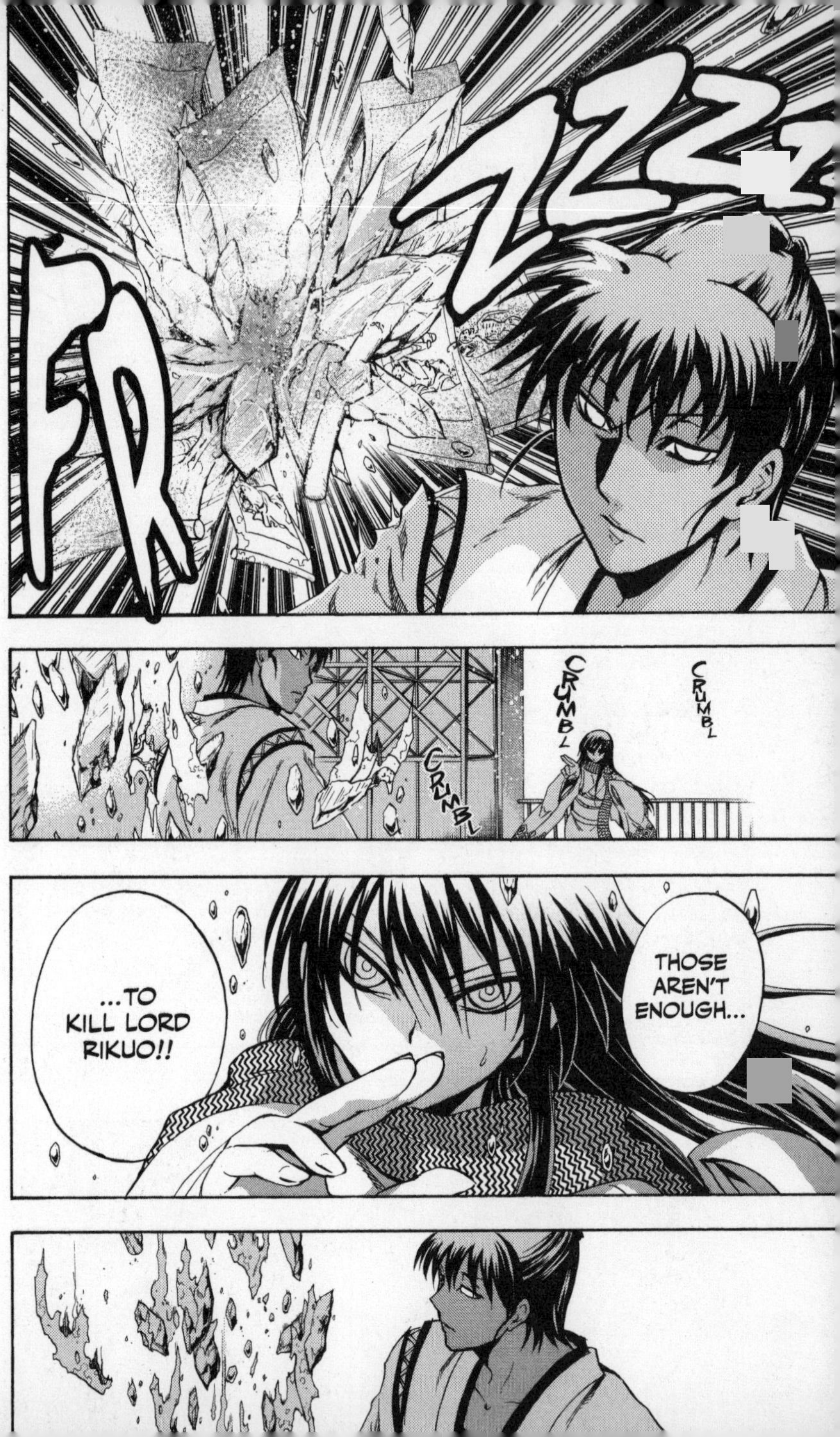
FR
ZZZ
CRUMBL
CRUMBL
CRUMBL
THOSE AREN'T ENOUGH...
...TO KILL LORD RIKUO!!

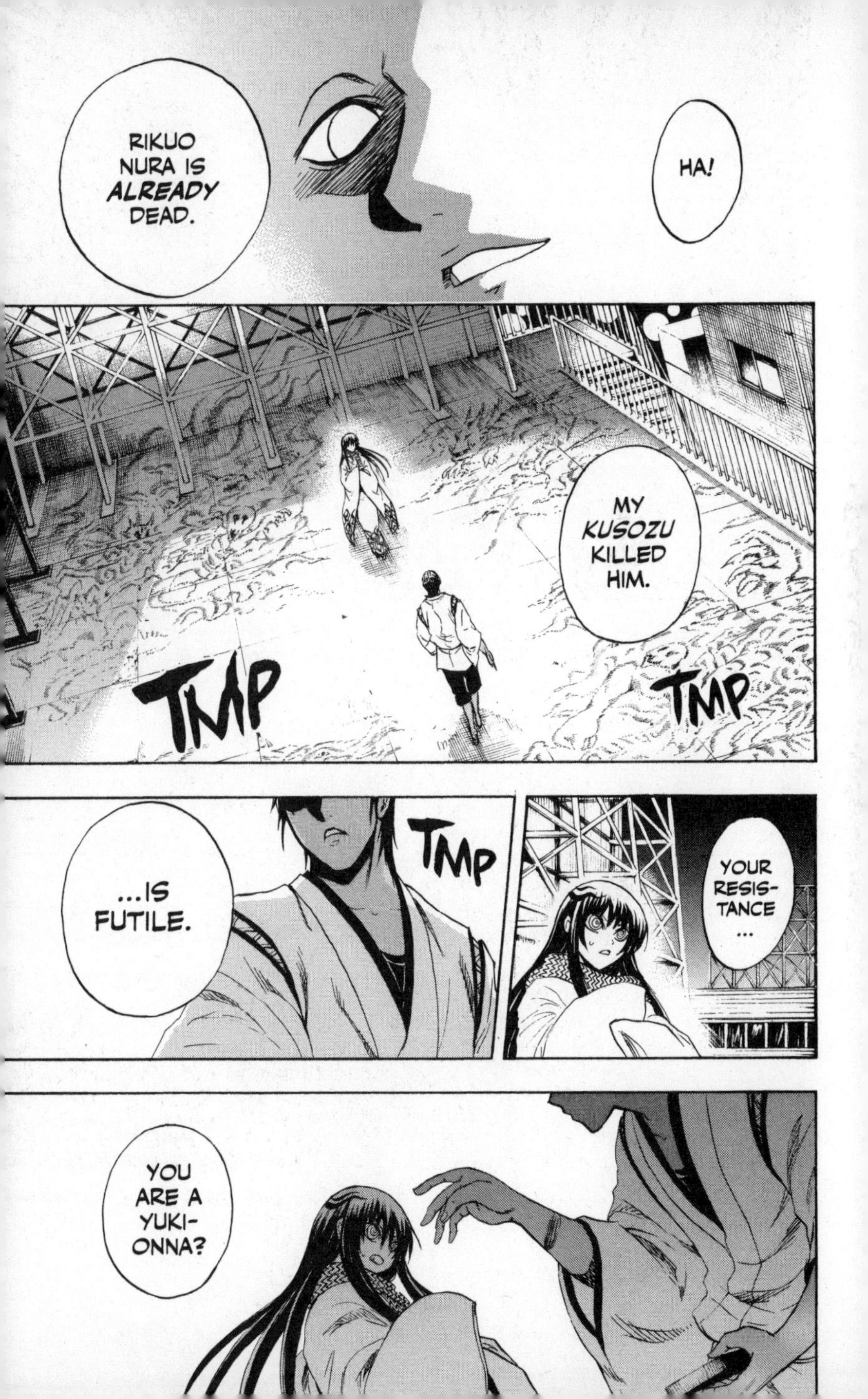
HA!
RIKUO NURA IS ALREADY DEAD.
MY KUSOZU KILLED HIM.
TMP
TMP
YOUR RESIS-TANCE...
TMP
...IS FUTILE.
YOU ARE A YUKI-ONNA?

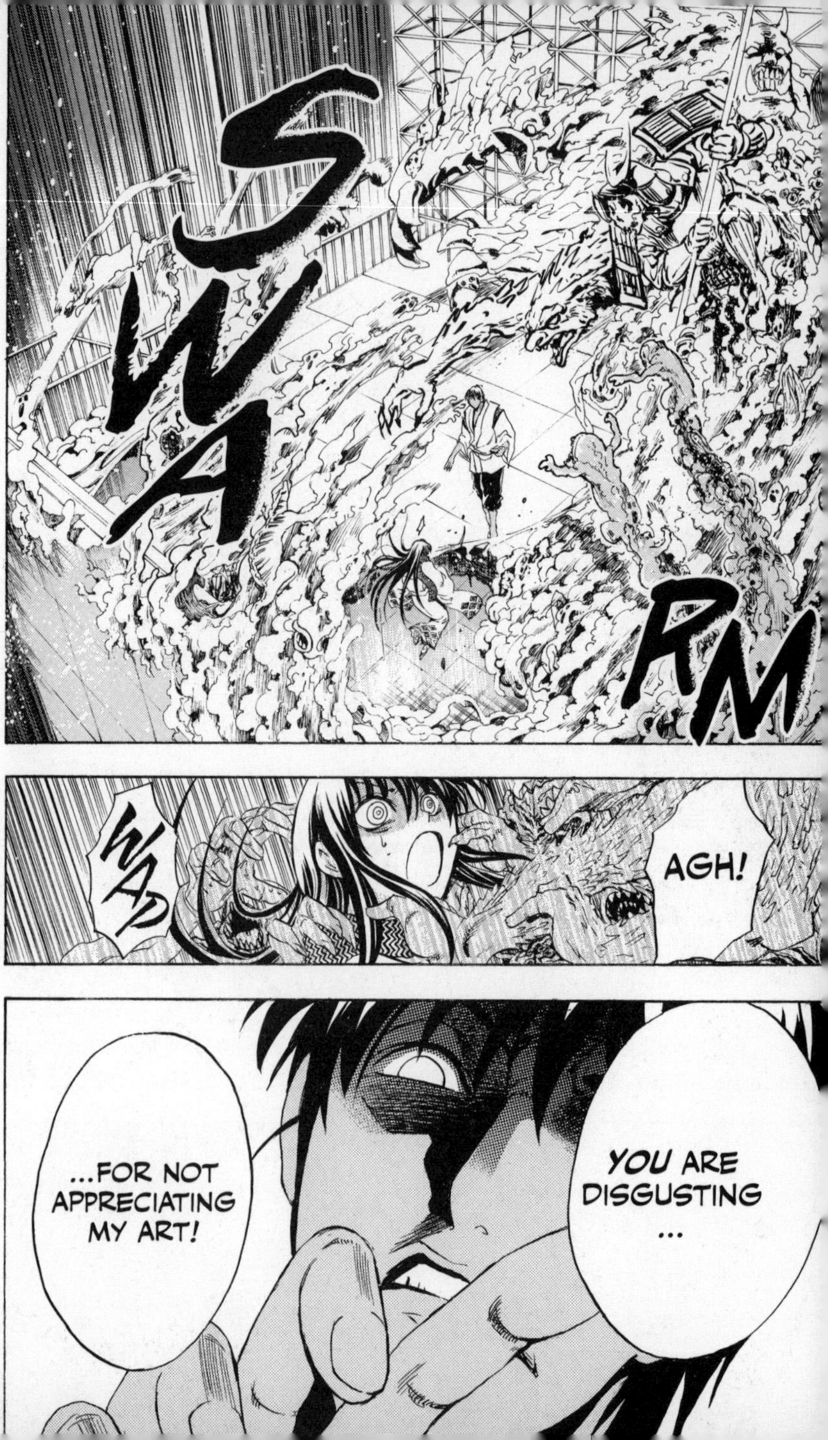
SWA
RM
AGH!
WAP
YOU ARE DISGUSTING ...
...FOR NOT APPRECIATING MY ART!

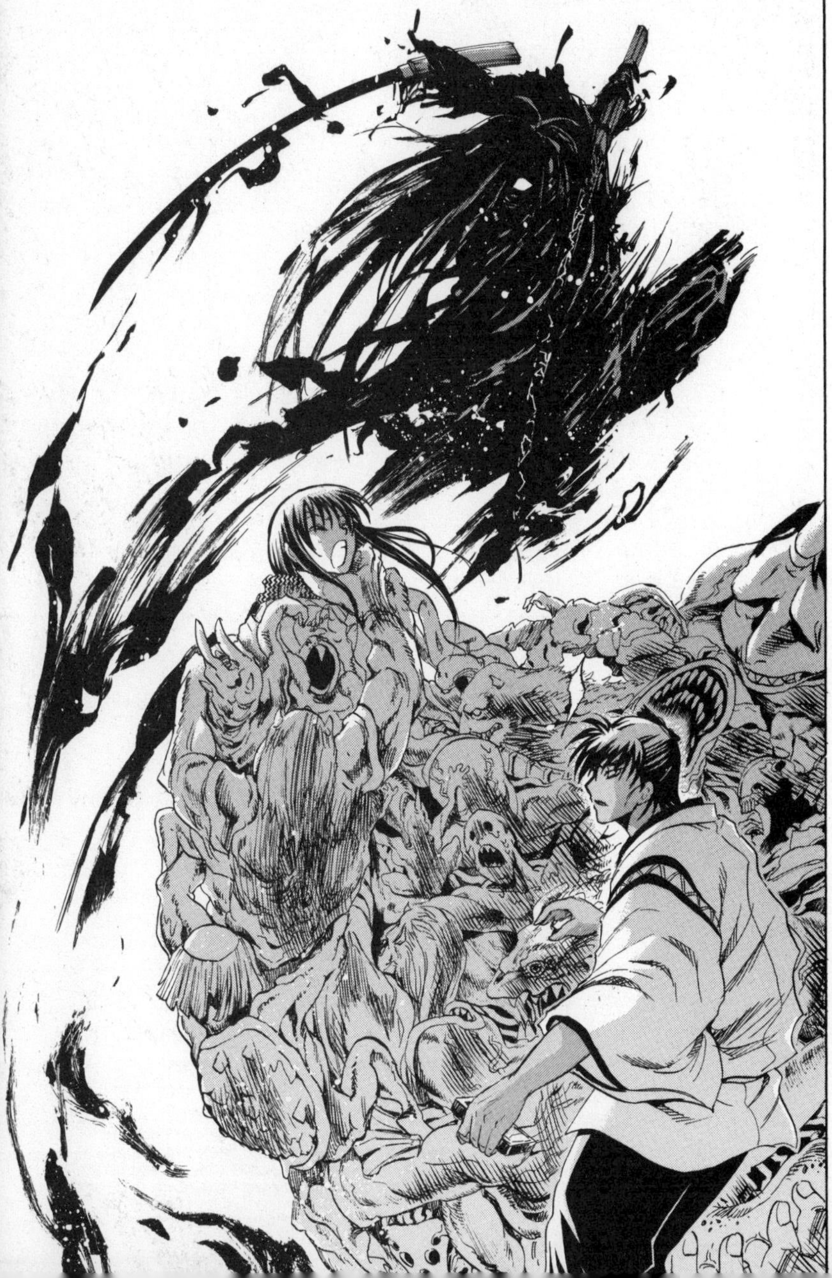

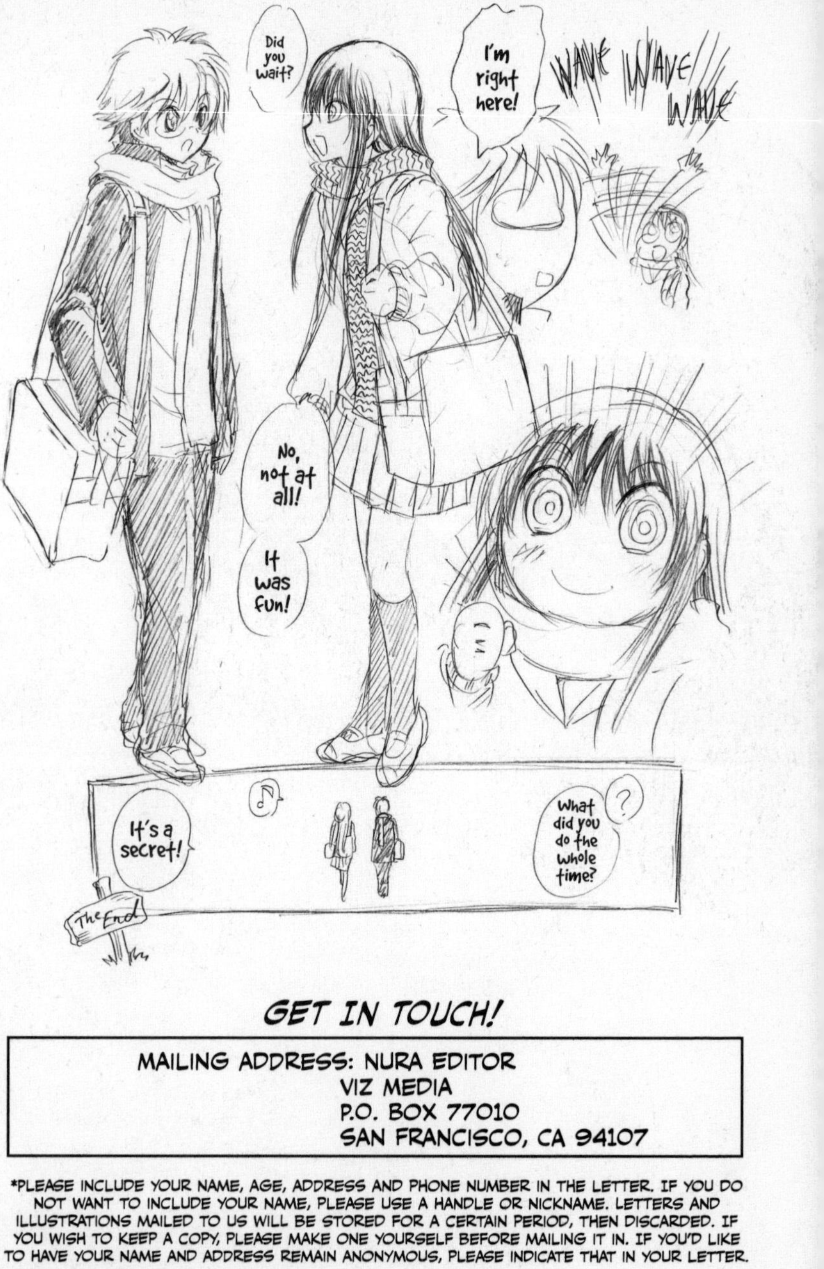
WAVE WAVE
WAVE
I'm right here!
Did you wait?
No, not at all!
It was fun!
What did you do the whole time?
?
It's a secret!
The End

GET IN TOUCH!

MAILING ADDRESS: NURA EDITOR
VIZ MEDIA
P.O. BOX 77010
SAN FRANCISCO, CA 94107

*PLEASE INCLUDE YOUR NAME, AGE, ADDRESS AND PHONE NUMBER IN THE LETTER. IF YOU DO NOT WANT TO INCLUDE YOUR NAME, PLEASE USE A HANDLE OR NICKNAME. LETTERS AND ILLUSTRATIONS MAILED TO US WILL BE STORED FOR A CERTAIN PERIOD, THEN DISCARDED. IF YOU WISH TO KEEP A COPY, PLEASE MAKE ONE YOURSELF BEFORE MAILING IT IN. IF YOU'D LIKE TO HAVE YOUR NAME AND ADDRESS REMAIN ANONYMOUS, PLEASE INDICATE THAT IN YOUR LETTER.

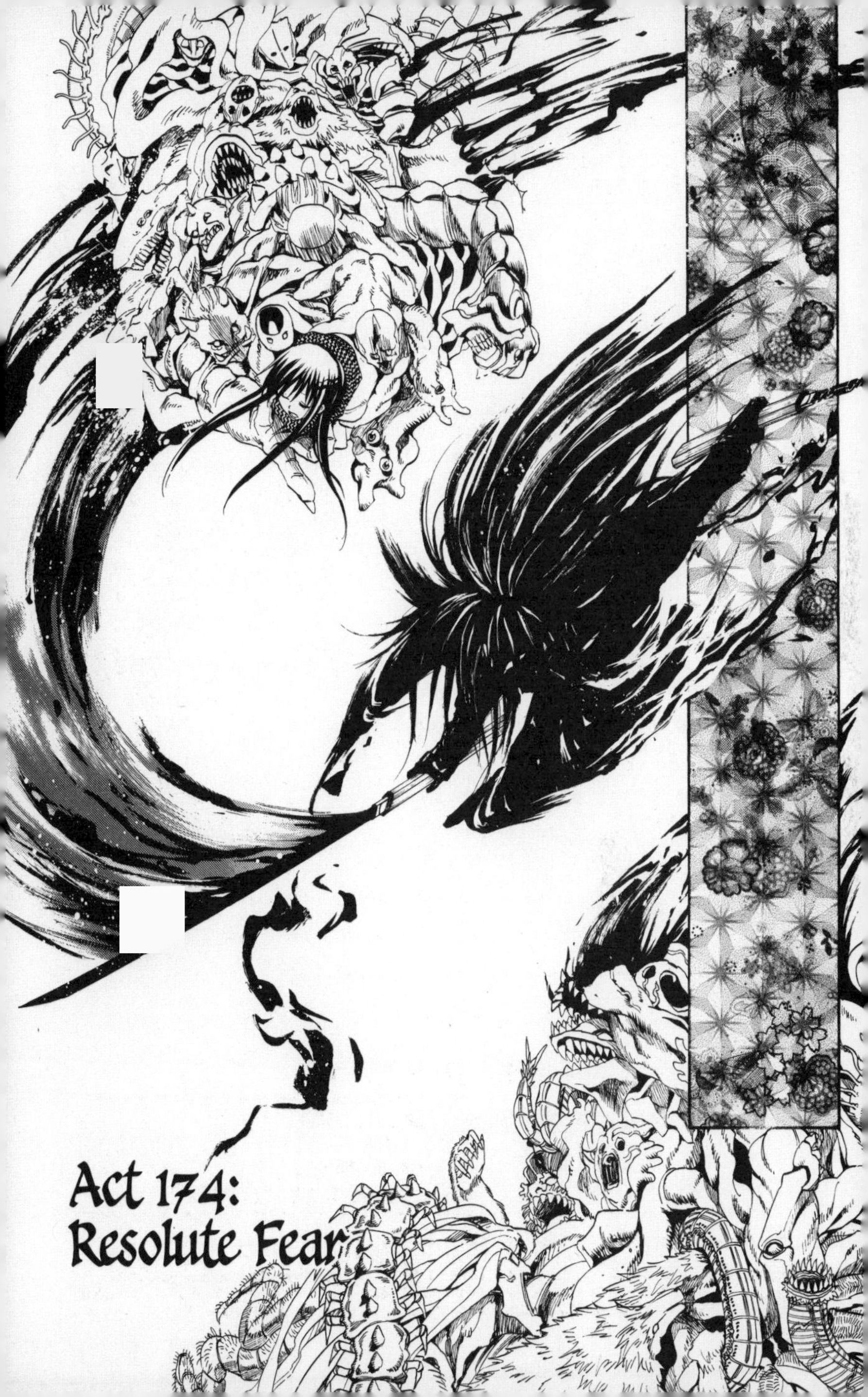
Act 174:
Resolute Fear

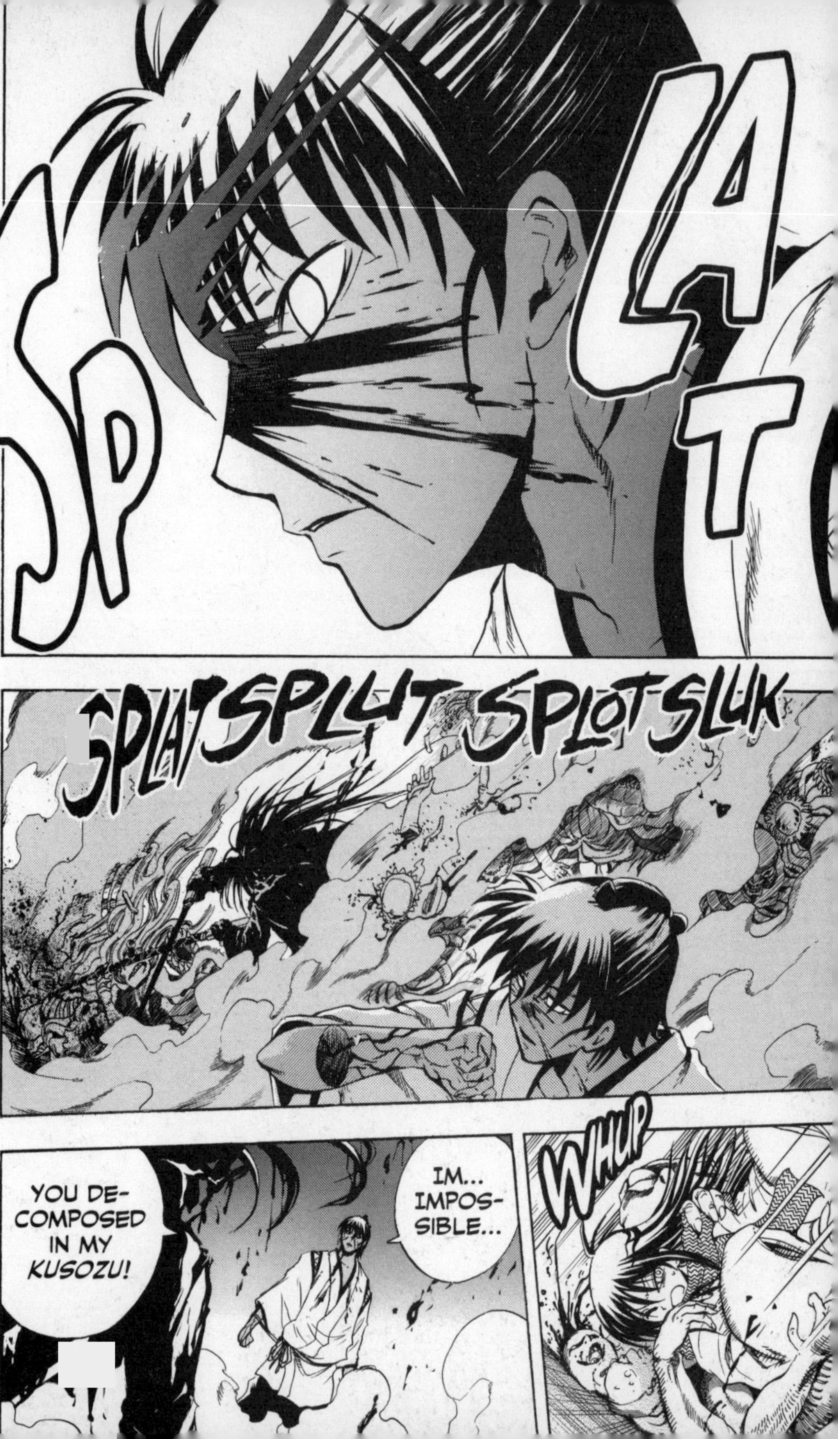
SPLAT
SPLAT SPLUT SPLOT SLUK
WHUP
IM... IMPOSSIBLE...
YOU DECOMPOSED IN MY KUSOZU!

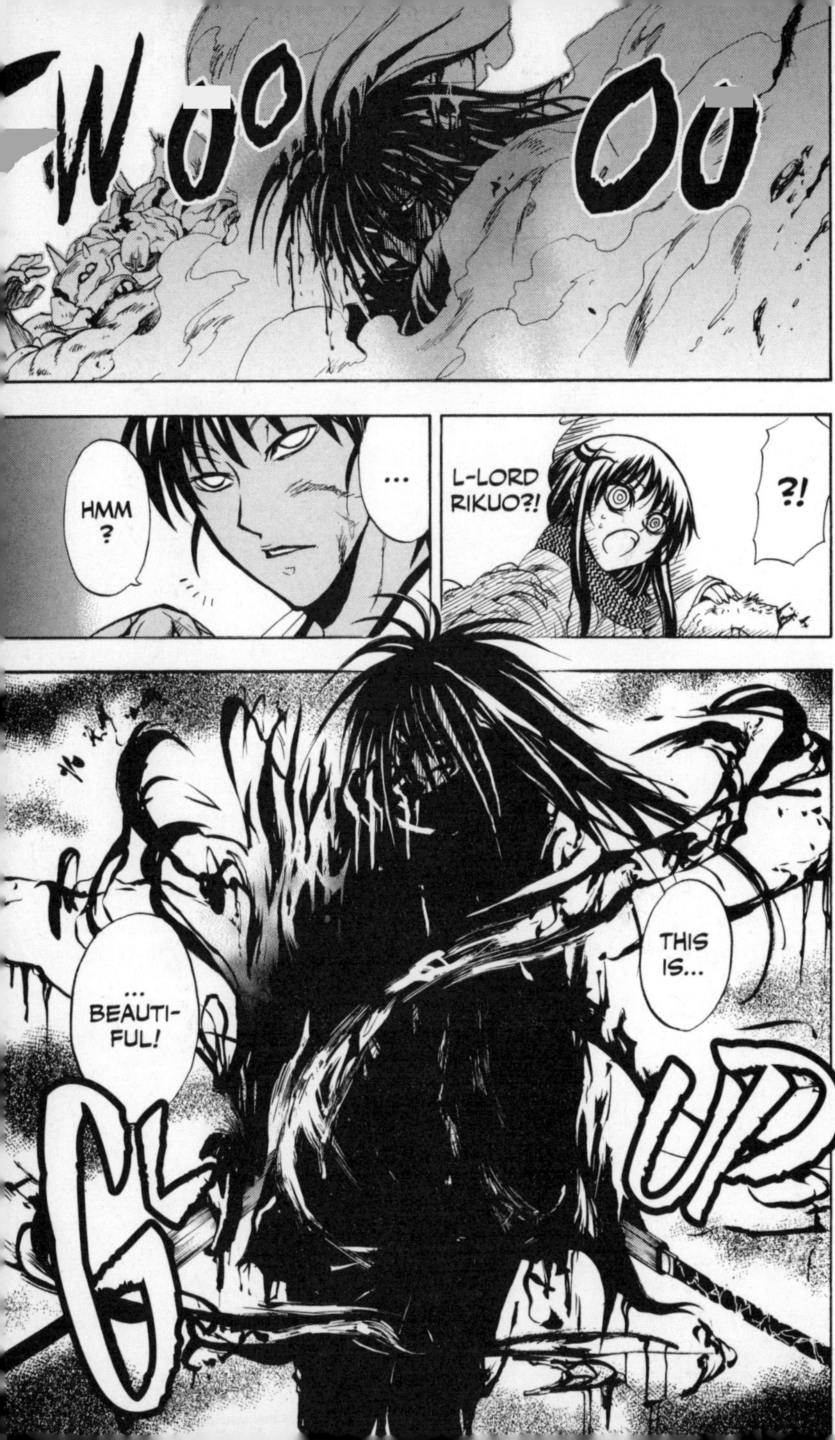

WOO OOO
?!
L-LORD RIKUO?!
...
HMM ?
THIS IS...
... BEAUTI-FUL!
GLUP

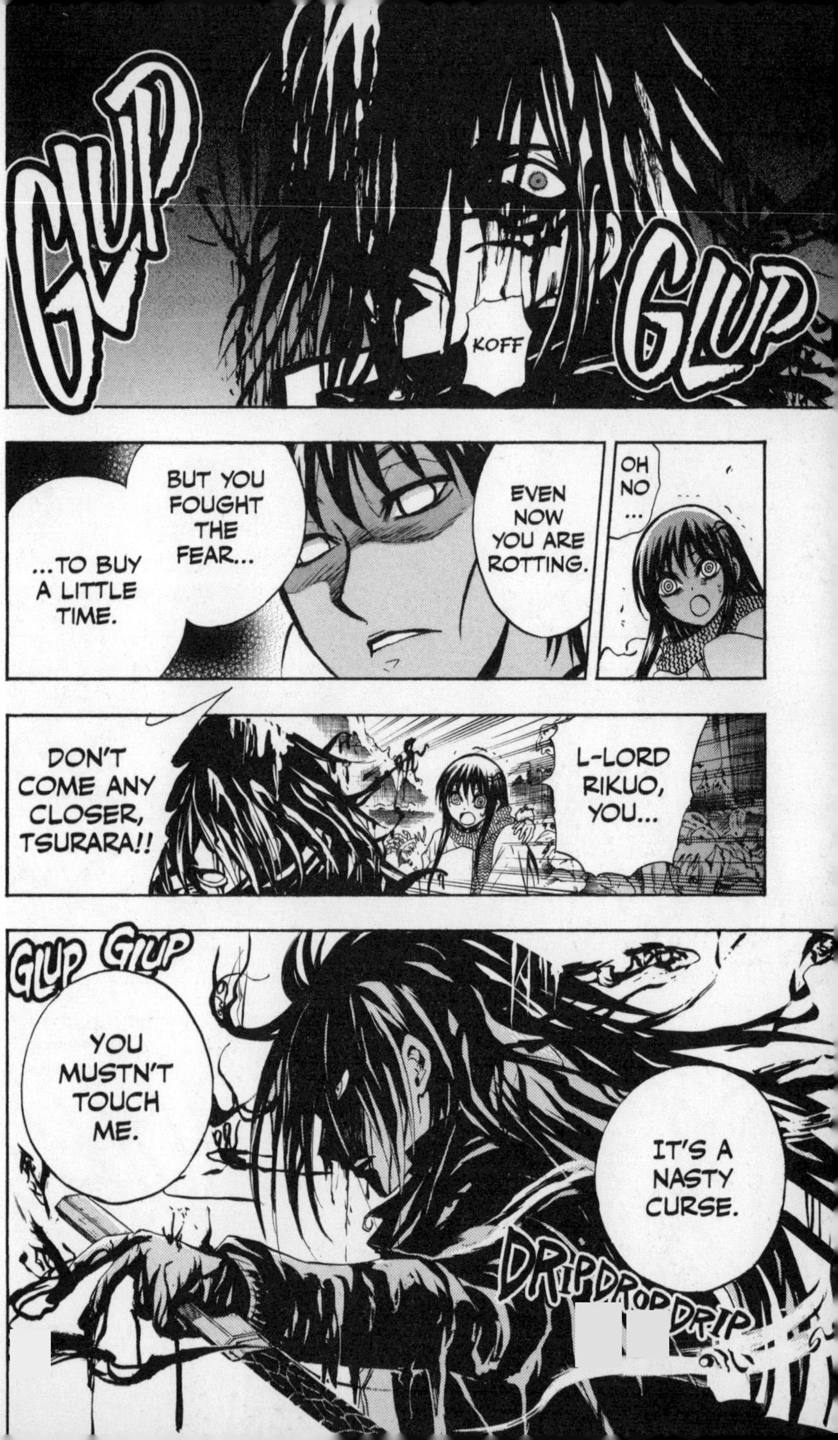
GLUP
KOFF
GLUP
OH NO ...
EVEN NOW YOU ARE ROTTING.
BUT YOU FOUGHT THE FEAR...
...TO BUY A LITTLE TIME.
L-LORD RIKUO, YOU...
DON'T COME ANY CLOSER, TSURARA!!
GLUP GLUP
YOU MUSTN'T TOUCH ME.
IT'S A NASTY CURSE.
DRIPDROPDRIP

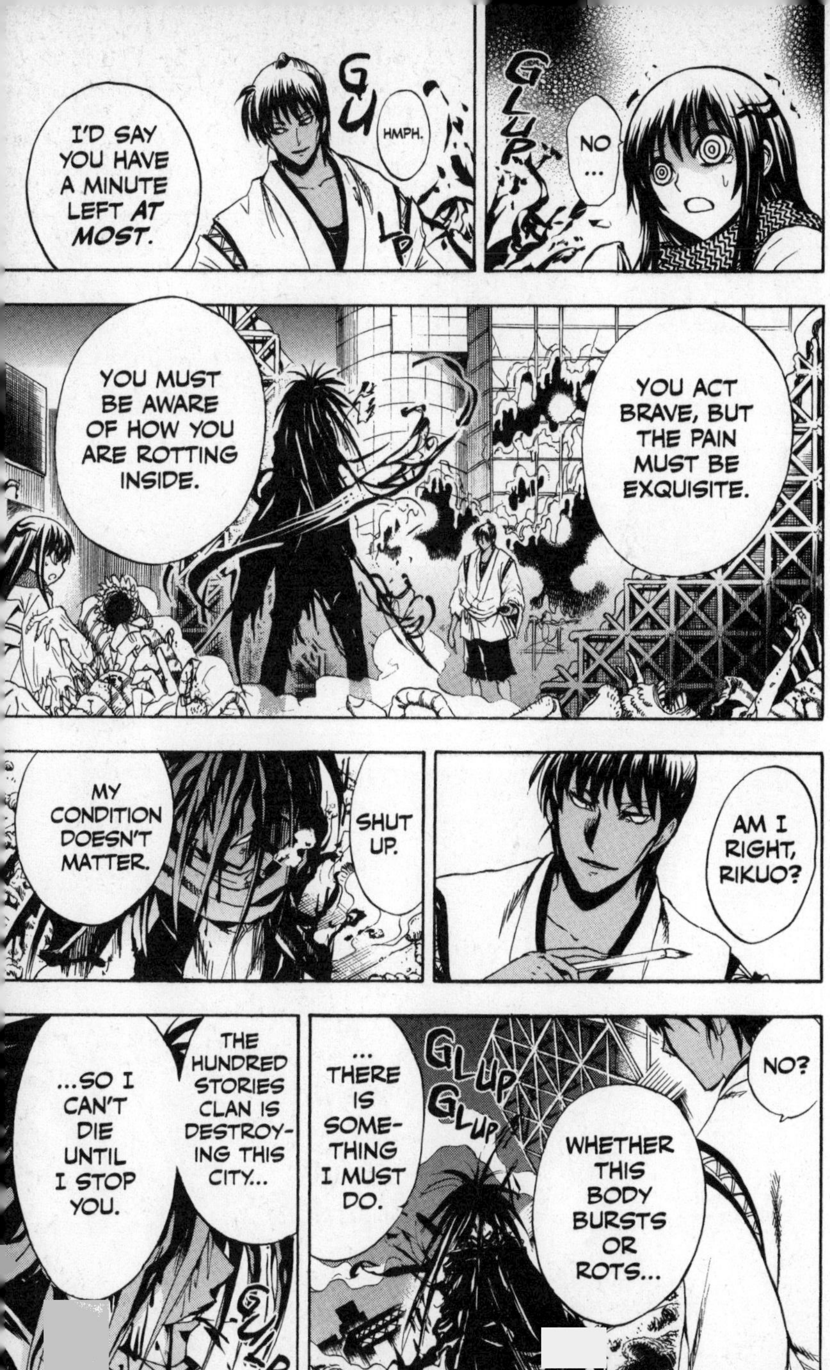
GLURP
NO ...
HMPH.
GULP
I'D SAY YOU HAVE A MINUTE LEFT AT MOST.
YOU ACT BRAVE, BUT THE PAIN MUST BE EXQUISITE.
YOU MUST BE AWARE OF HOW YOU ARE ROTTING INSIDE.
AM I RIGHT, RIKUO?
SHUT UP.
MY CONDITION DOESN'T MATTER.
NO?
GLUP GLUP
WHETHER THIS BODY BURSTS OR ROTS...
...THERE IS SOME-THING I MUST DO.
THE HUNDRED STORIES CLAN IS DESTROY-ING THIS CITY...
...SO I CAN'T DIE UNTIL I STOP YOU.
GULP

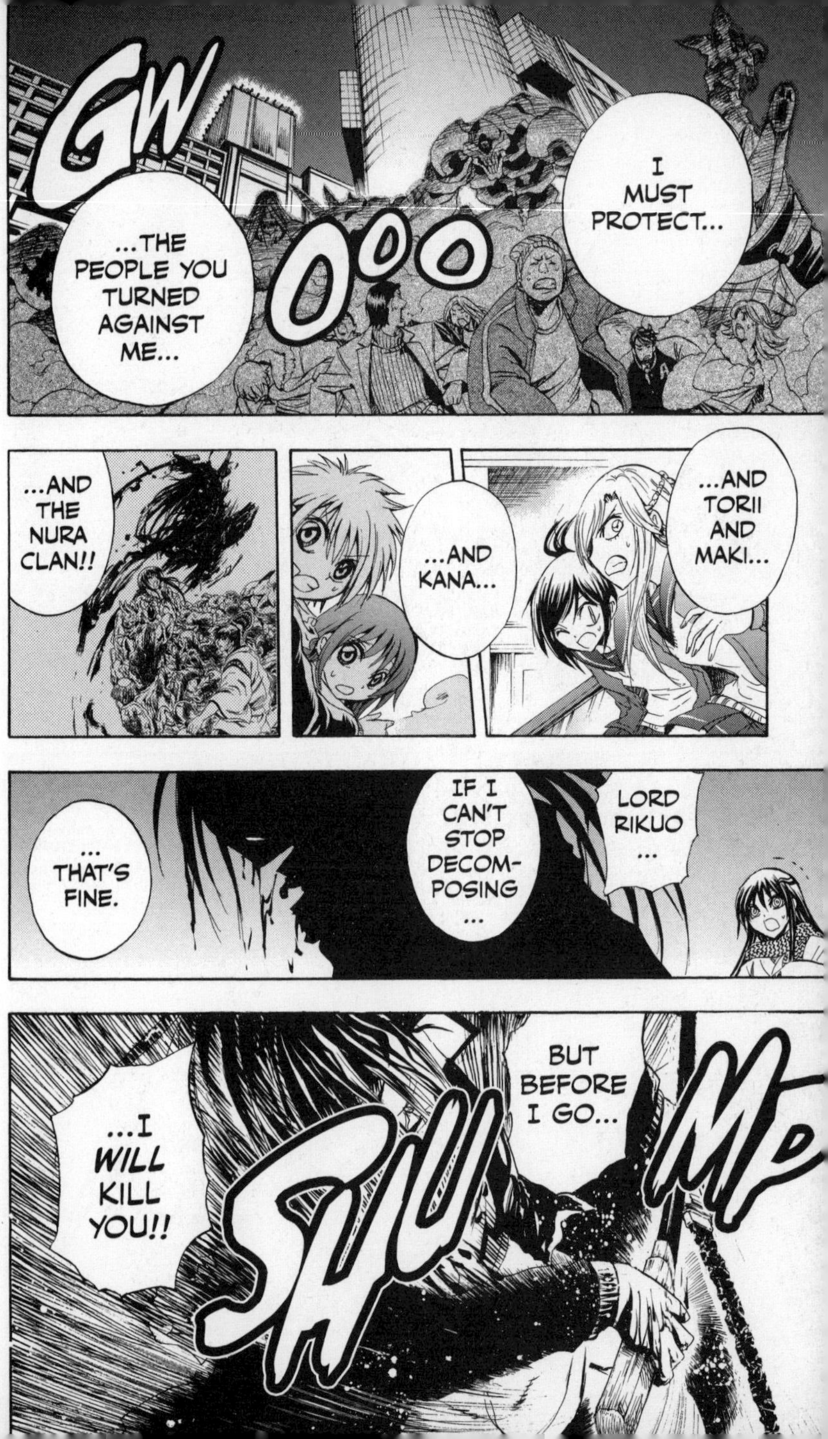
I MUST PROTECT...
GWOOO
...THE PEOPLE YOU TURNED AGAINST ME...
...AND TORII AND MAKI...
...AND KANA...
...AND THE NURA CLAN!!
LORD RIKUO ...
IF I CAN'T STOP DECOMPOSING ...
... THAT'S FINE.
BUT BEFORE I GO...
SHUM
...I *WILL* KILL YOU!!

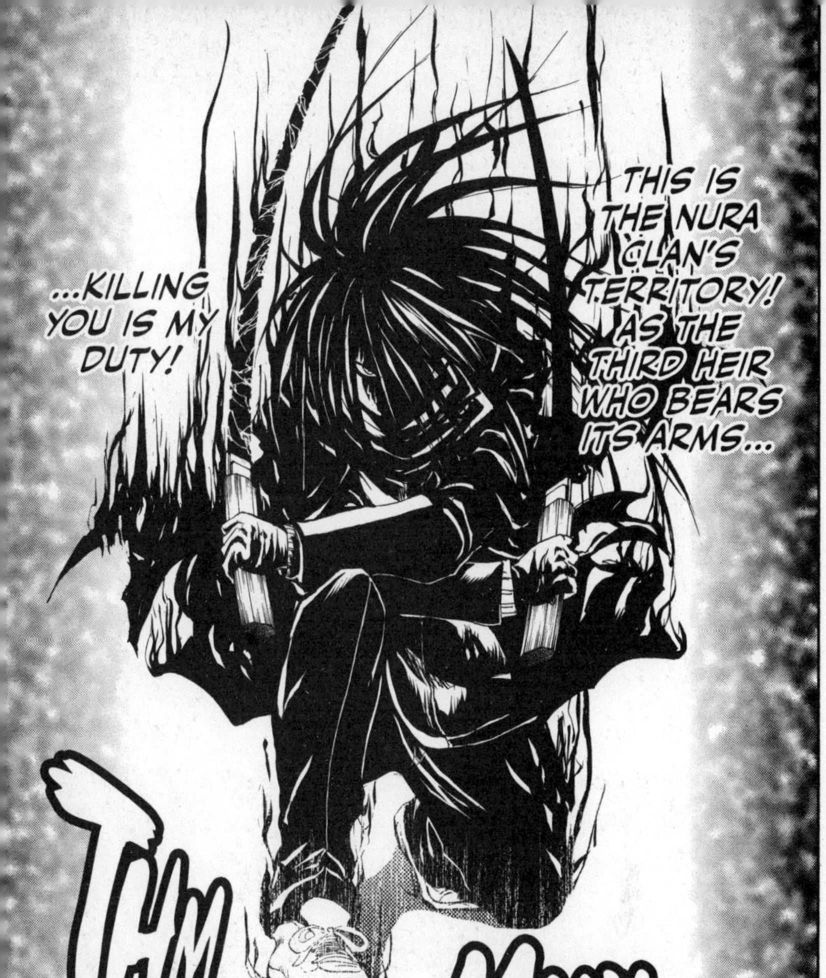
THIS IS THE NURA CLAN'S TERRITORY! AS THE THIRD HEIR WHO BEARS ITS ARMS...
...KILLING YOU IS MY DUTY!
THM
MMM
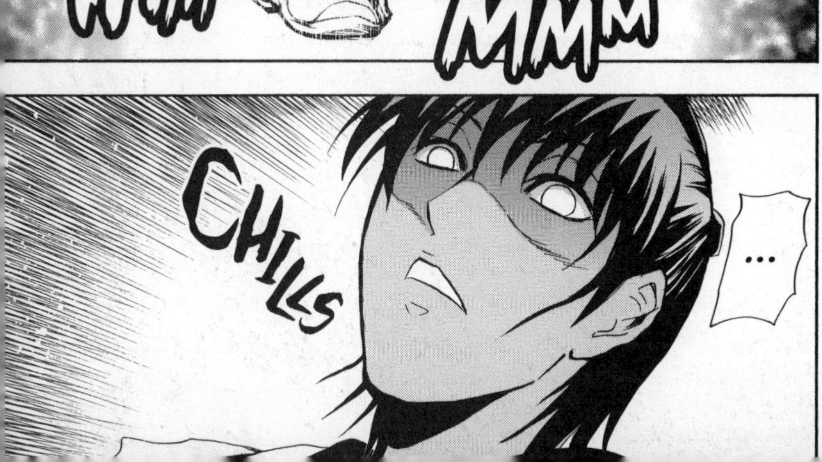
...
CHILLS

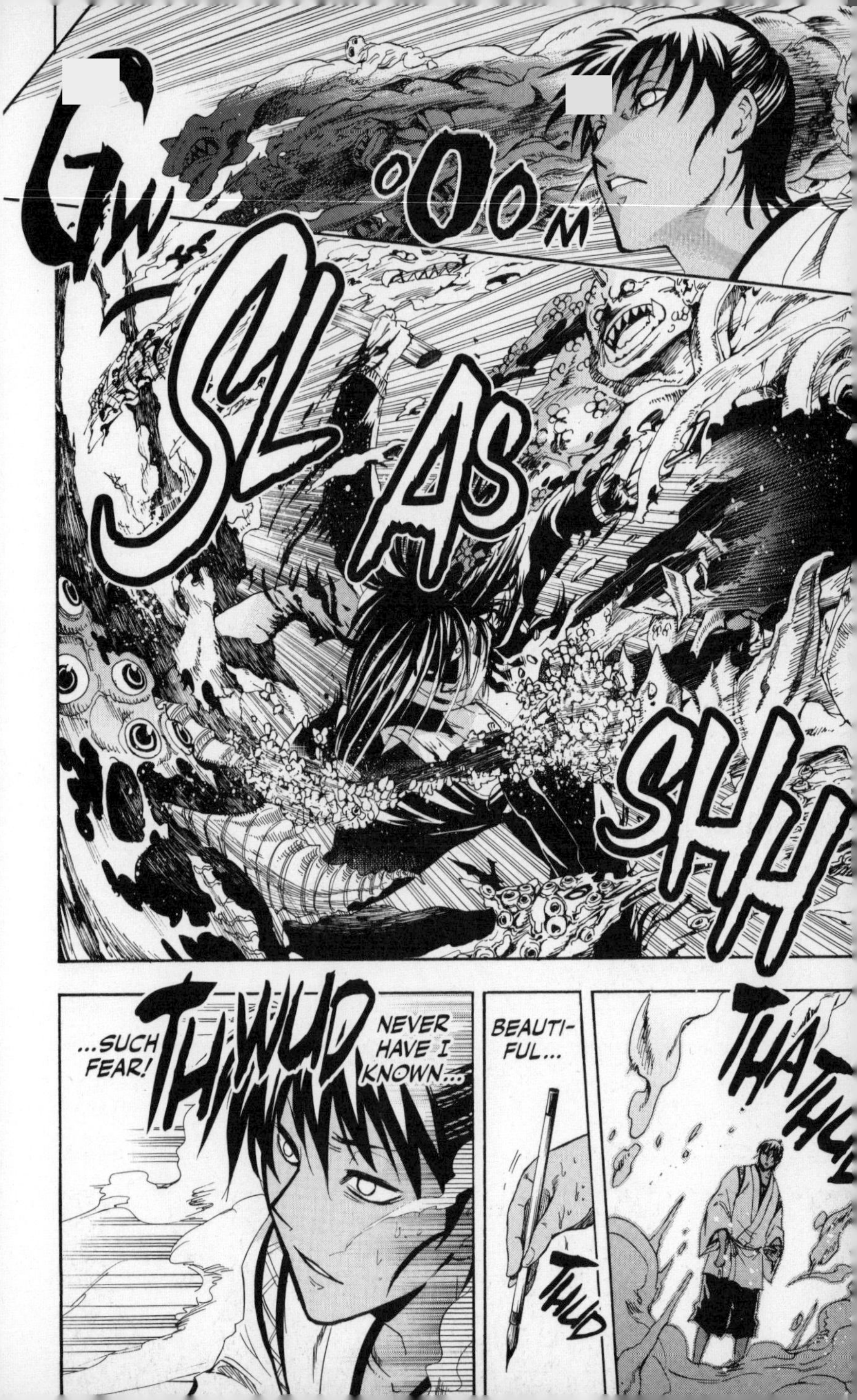
GWOOOM
SLASH
SHH
THATHUD
BEAUTI-FUL...
THUD
NEVER HAVE I KNOWN...
THWUD
...SUCH FEAR!

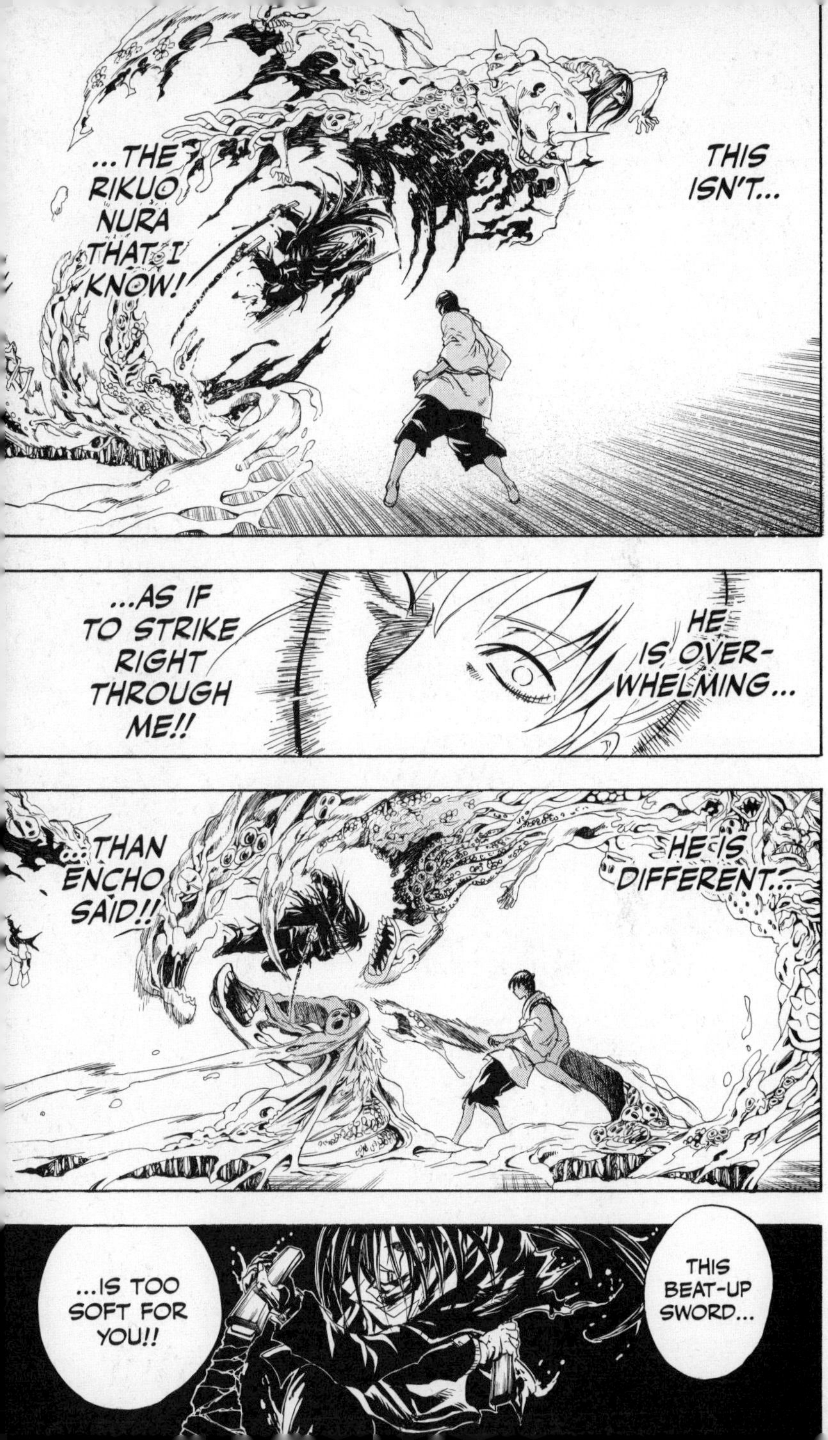
THIS ISN'T...
...THE RIKUO NURA THAT I KNOW!
HE IS OVER-WHELMING...
...AS IF TO STRIKE RIGHT THROUGH ME!!
HE IS DIFFERENT...
...THAN ENCHO SAID!!
THIS BEAT-UP SWORD...
...IS TOO SOFT FOR YOU!!

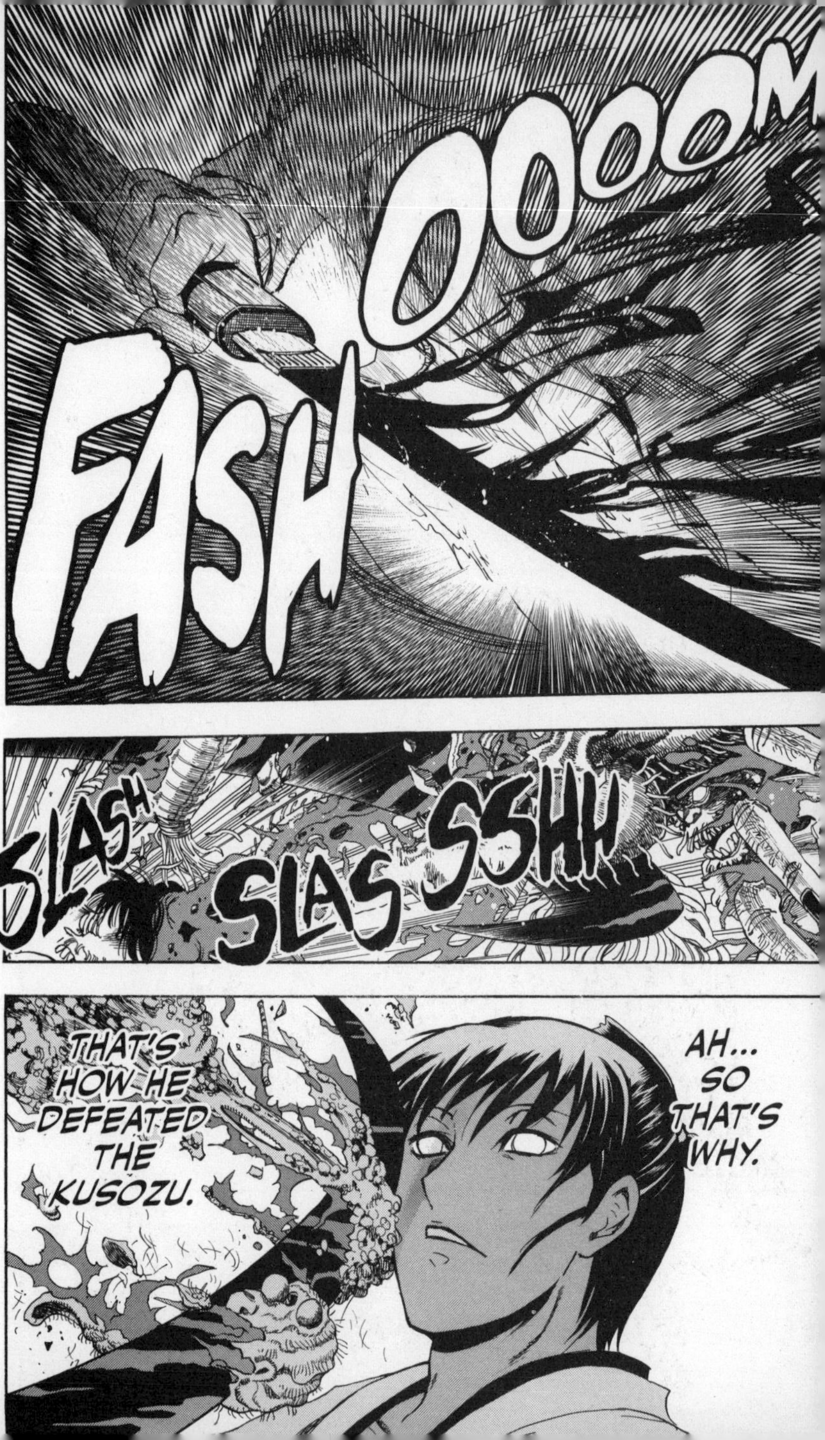
FASH
OOOOOM
SLASH
SLAS
SSHH
AH... SO THAT'S WHY.
THAT'S HOW HE DEFEATED THE KUSOZU.

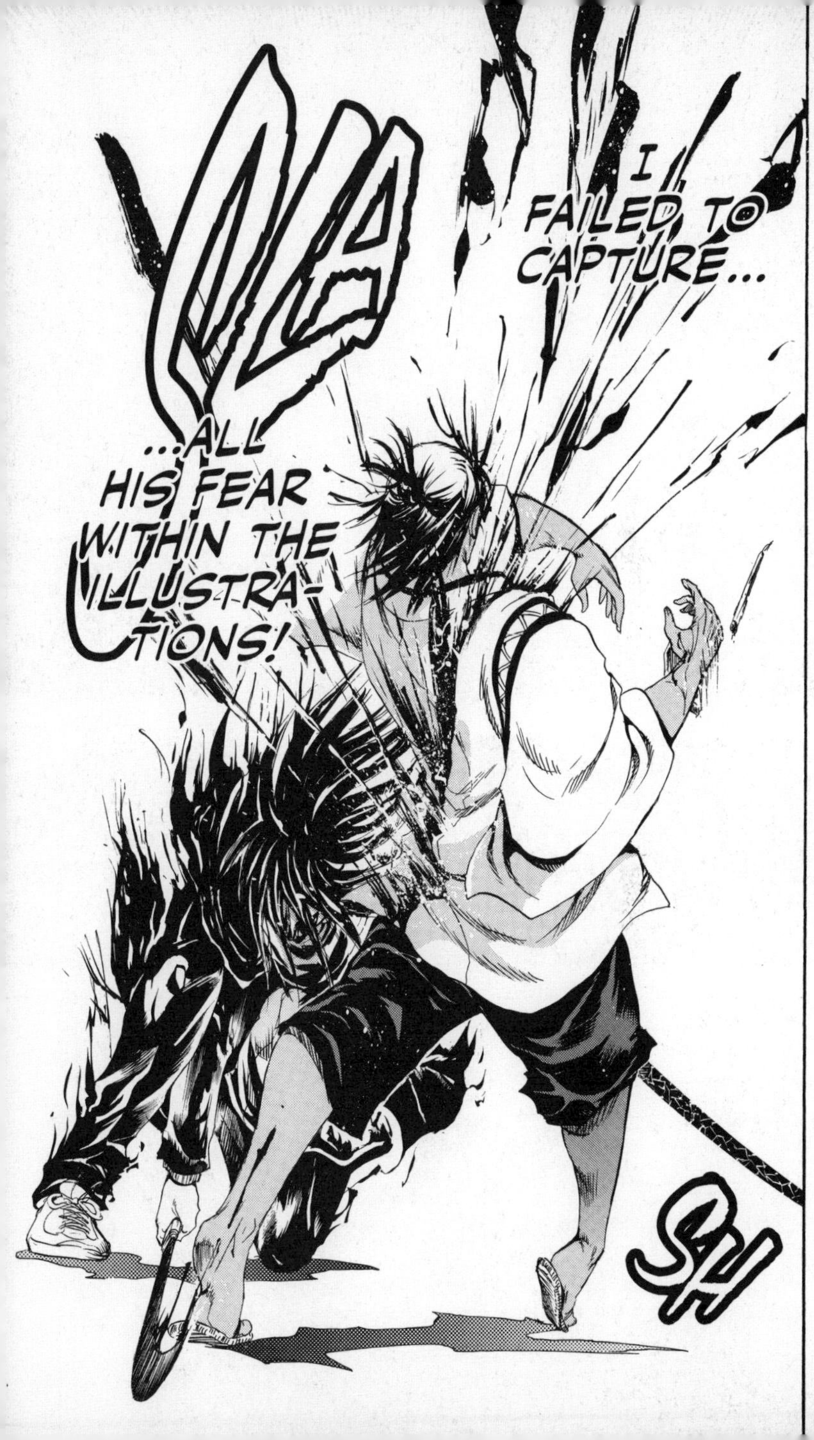
I FAILED TO CAPTURE...
...ALL HIS FEAR WITHIN THE ILLUSTRA-TIONS!

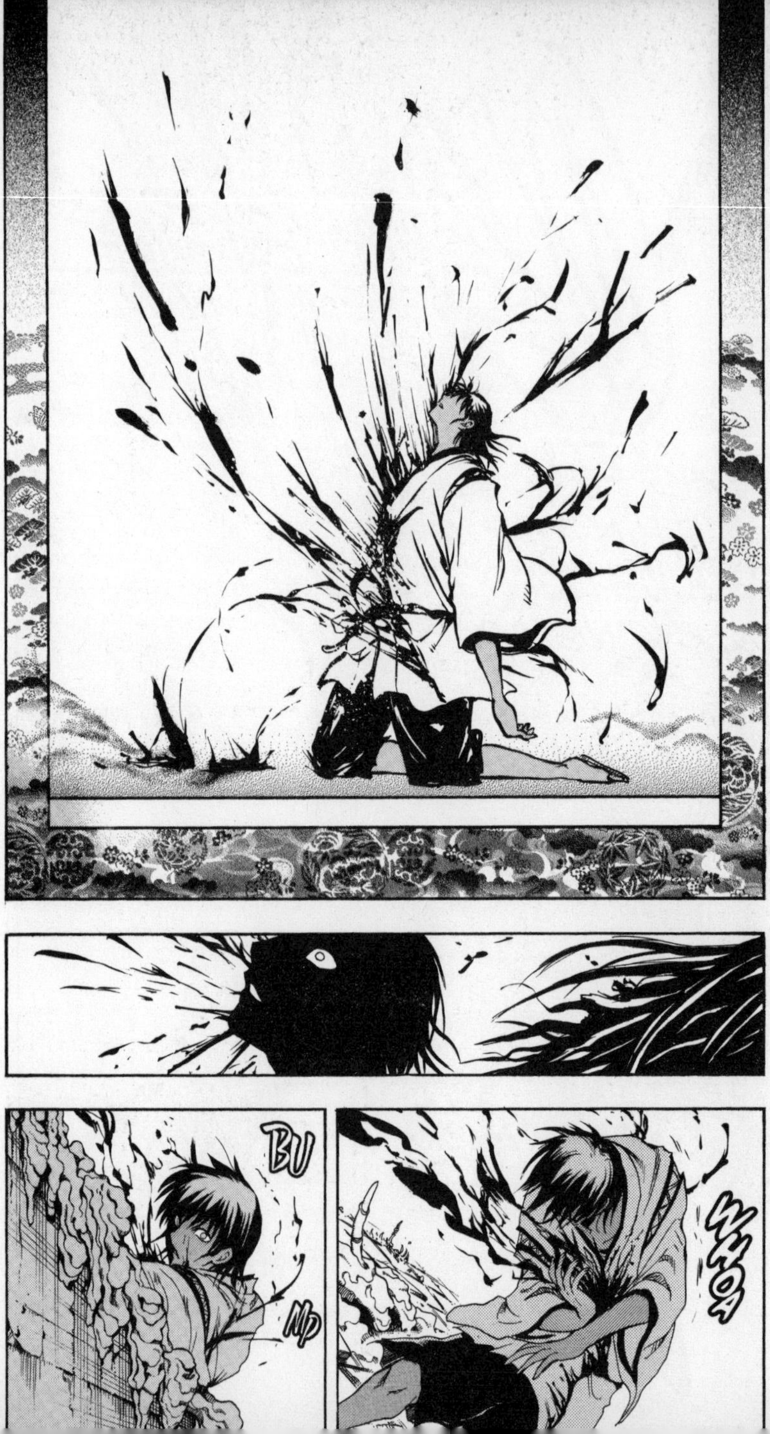
WHOA
BU
Mp

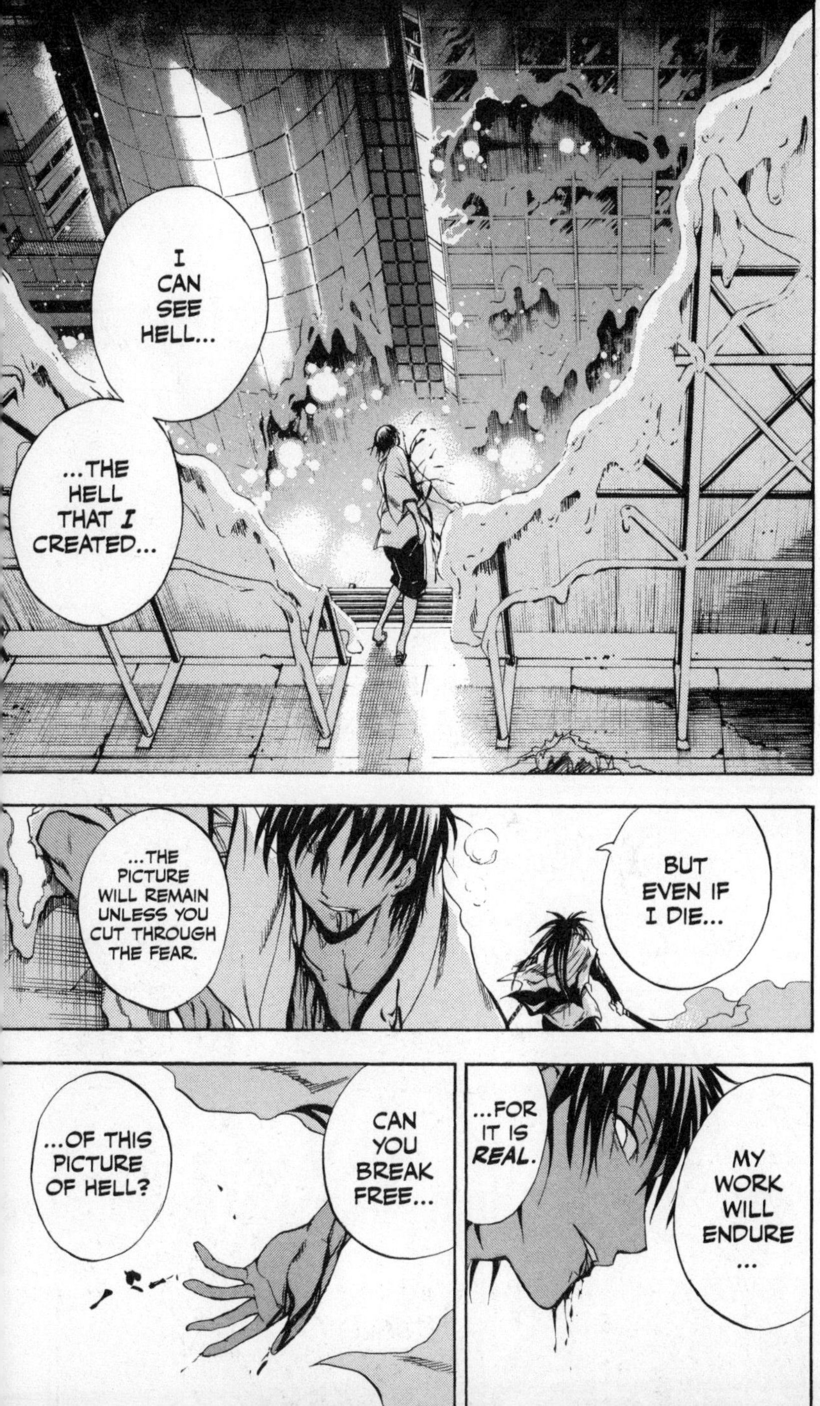
I CAN SEE HELL...
...THE HELL THAT *I* CREATED...
BUT EVEN IF I DIE...
...THE PICTURE WILL REMAIN UNLESS YOU CUT THROUGH THE FEAR.
MY WORK WILL ENDURE ...
...FOR IT IS *REAL*.
CAN YOU BREAK FREE...
...OF THIS PICTURE OF HELL?

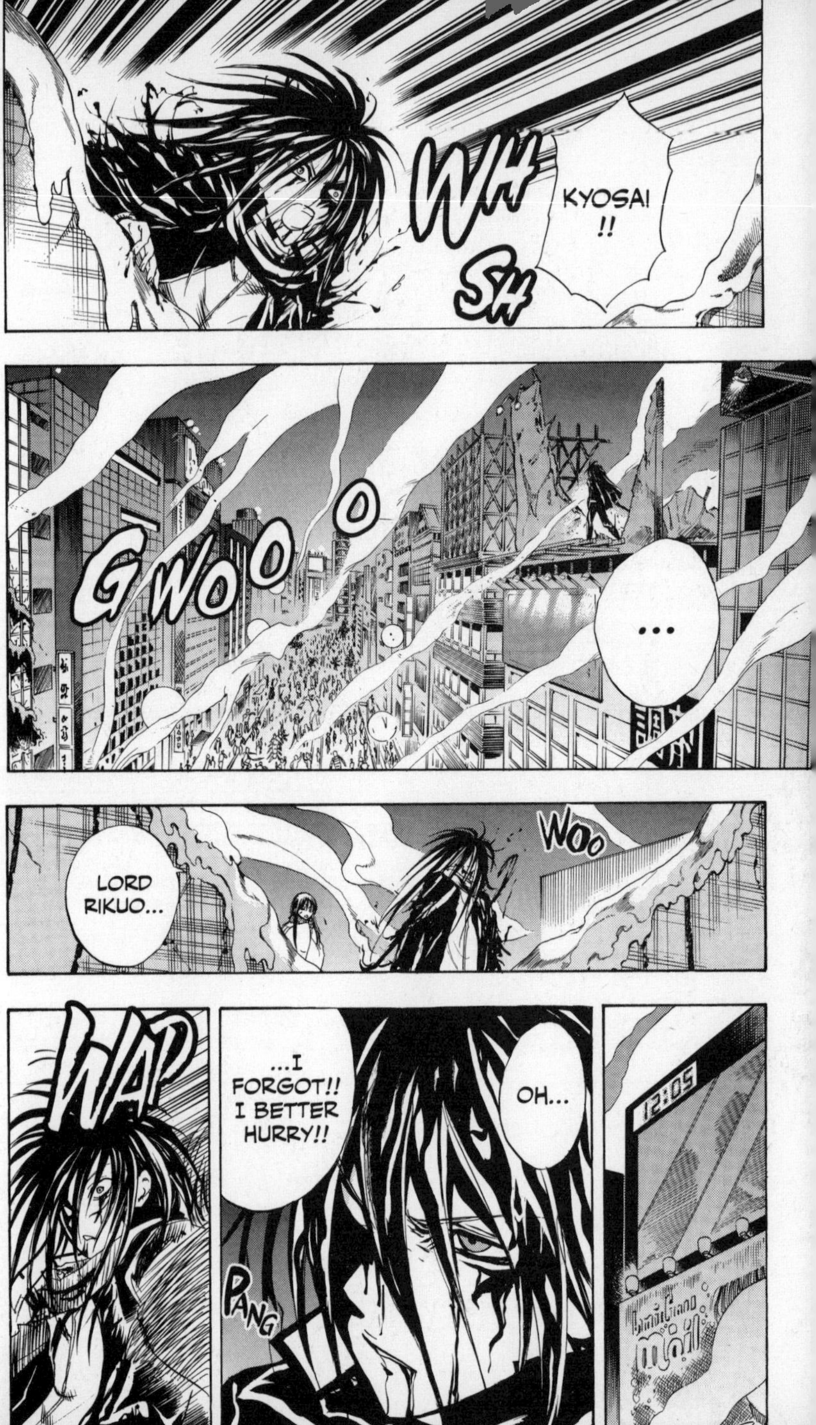
KYOSAI !!
WHASH
...
GWOOO
WOO
LORD RIKUO...
12:05
OH...
...I FORGOT!! I BETTER HURRY!!
PANG
WAP

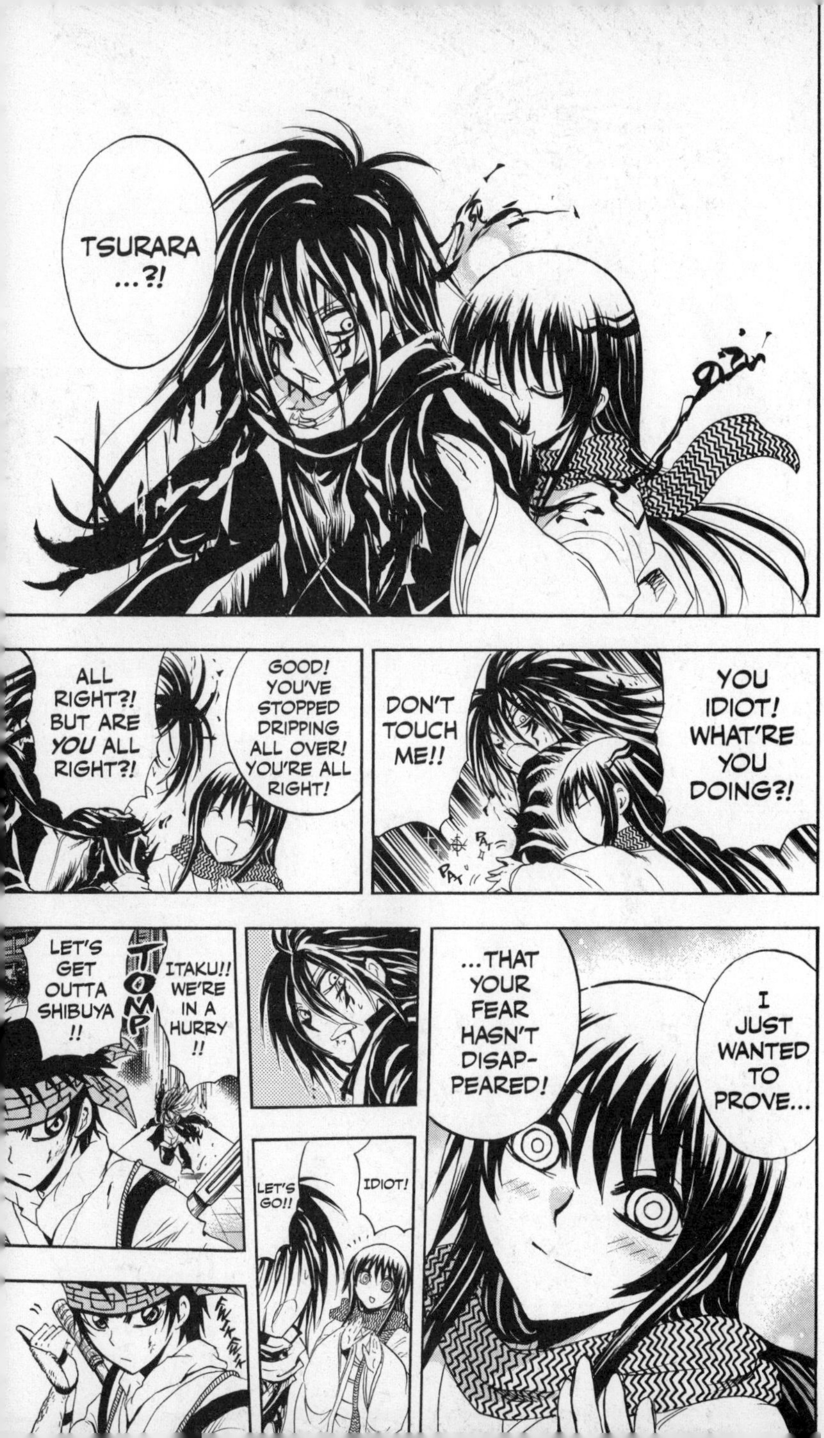
TSURARA ...?!
YOU IDIOT! WHAT'RE YOU DOING?!
DON'T TOUCH ME!!
PAT
PAT
GOOD! YOU'VE STOPPED DRIPPING ALL OVER! YOU'RE ALL RIGHT!
ALL RIGHT?! BUT ARE YOU ALL RIGHT?!
I JUST WANTED TO PROVE...
...THAT YOUR FEAR HASN'T DISAP-PEARED!
IDIOT!
LET'S GO!!
ITAKU!! WE'RE IN A HURRY!!
TOMP
LET'S GET OUTTA SHIBUYA!!
FWIK FWIK

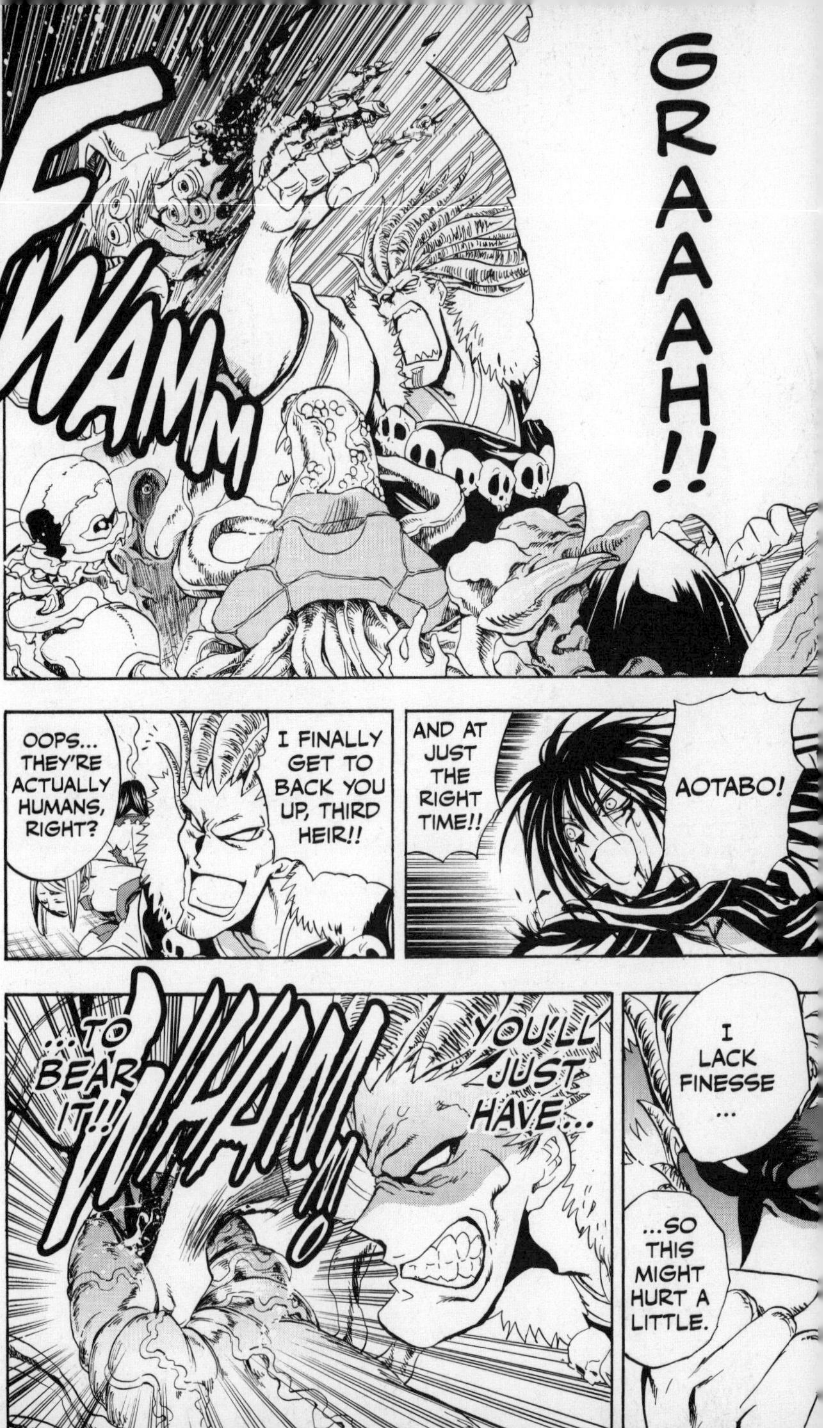
GRAAAH!!
WAMM
AOTABO!
AND AT JUST THE RIGHT TIME!!
I FINALLY GET TO BACK YOU UP, THIRD HEIR!!
OOPS... THEY'RE ACTUALLY HUMANS, RIGHT?
I LACK FINESSE ...
...SO THIS MIGHT HURT A LITTLE.
YOU'LL JUST HAVE...
WHAM
...TO BEAR IT!!

The brain controls the various parts...
...
HUFF
...and shares the thoughts of Sanmoto in Hell.
UNGH ...
FOLLOWING BONES...
... EVERYONE DESCENDS INTO HELL...
HUFF

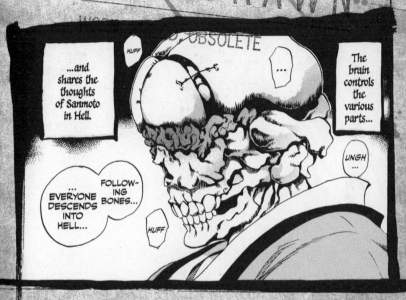

IN THE NEXT VOLUME...

GHOST STORY: AOANDON

Rikuo and the Nura clan fight off the devious body parts of a dissected Sanmoto Gorozaemon, while Rikuo's allies fight back against his reputation as the harbinger of the apocalypse. But battle still looms against the members of the Hundred Stories clan... And it's possible that Sanmoto himself could be reborn in the form of yet another ghost story!

AVAILABLE JUNE 2014!

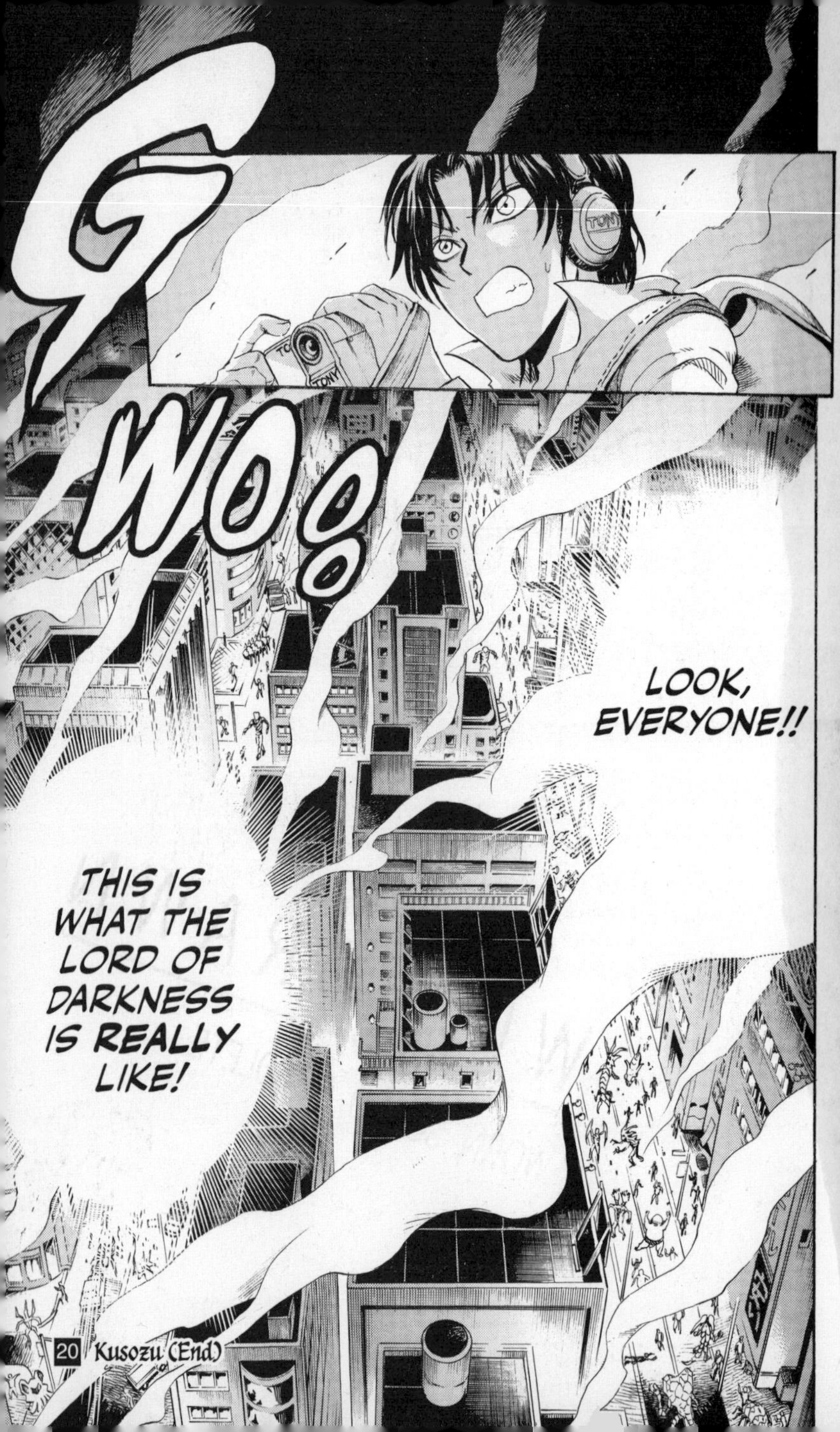
GWOO
TONY
LOOK, EVERYONE!!
THIS IS WHAT THE LORD OF DARKNESS IS REALLY LIKE!

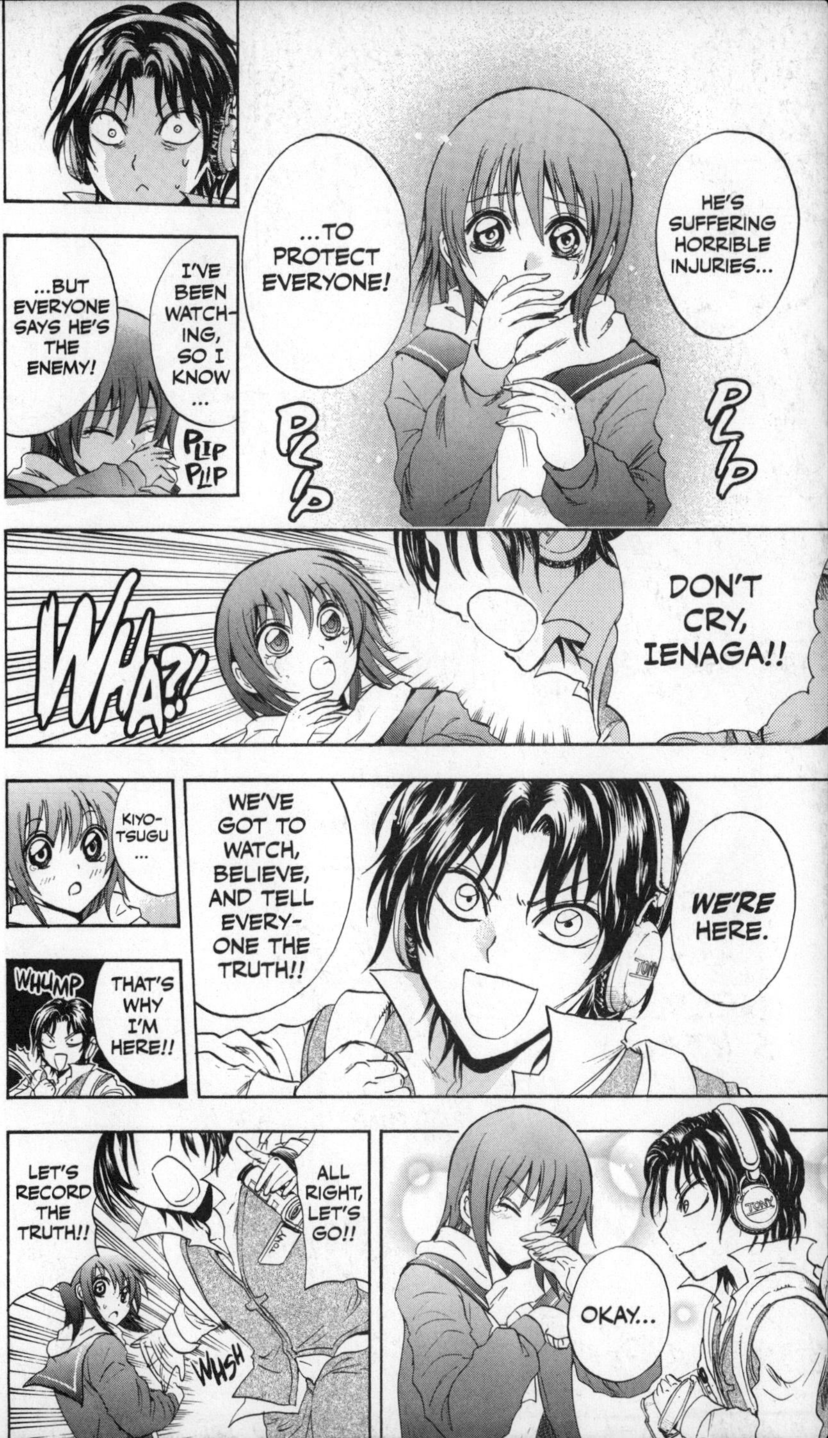
HE'S SUFFERING HORRIBLE INJURIES...
PLIP
...TO PROTECT EVERYONE!
PLIP
I'VE BEEN WATCHING, SO I KNOW...
...BUT EVERYONE SAYS HE'S THE ENEMY!
PLIP PLIP
DON'T CRY, IENAGA!!
WHA?!
WE'RE HERE.
WE'VE GOT TO WATCH, BELIEVE, AND TELL EVERYONE THE TRUTH!!
KIYOTSUGU...
WHUMP
THAT'S WHY I'M HERE!!
OKAY...
ALL RIGHT, LET'S GO!!
LET'S RECORD THE TRUTH!!
WHSH

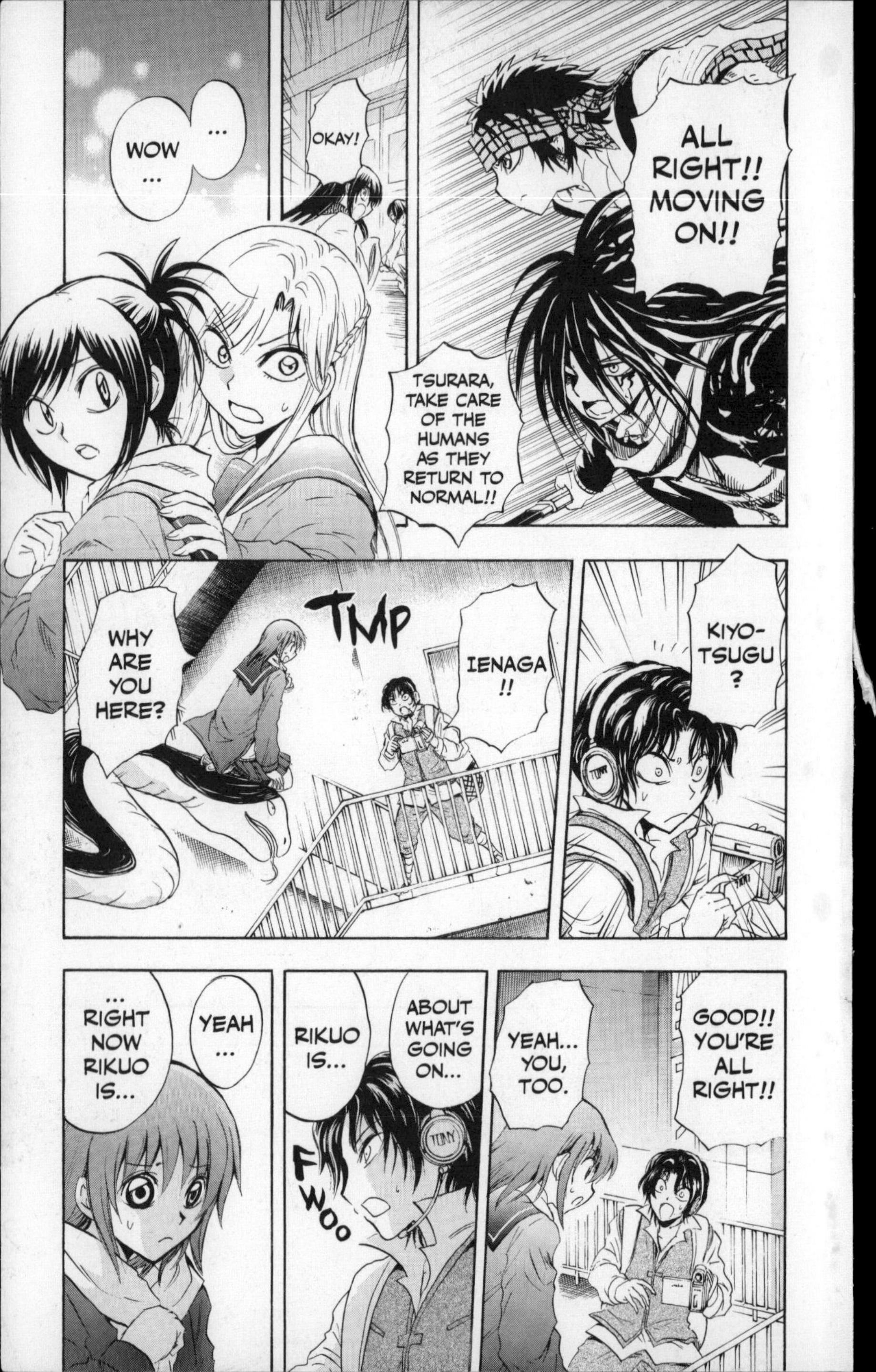
ALL RIGHT!! MOVING ON!!
TSURARA, TAKE CARE OF THE HUMANS AS THEY RETURN TO NORMAL!!
OKAY!
...
WOW ...
KIYO-TSUGU?
TMP
IENAGA!!
WHY ARE YOU HERE?
GOOD!! YOU'RE ALL RIGHT!!
YEAH... YOU, TOO.
ABOUT WHAT'S GOING ON...
RIKUO IS...
FWOO
YEAH ...
... RIGHT NOW RIKUO IS...